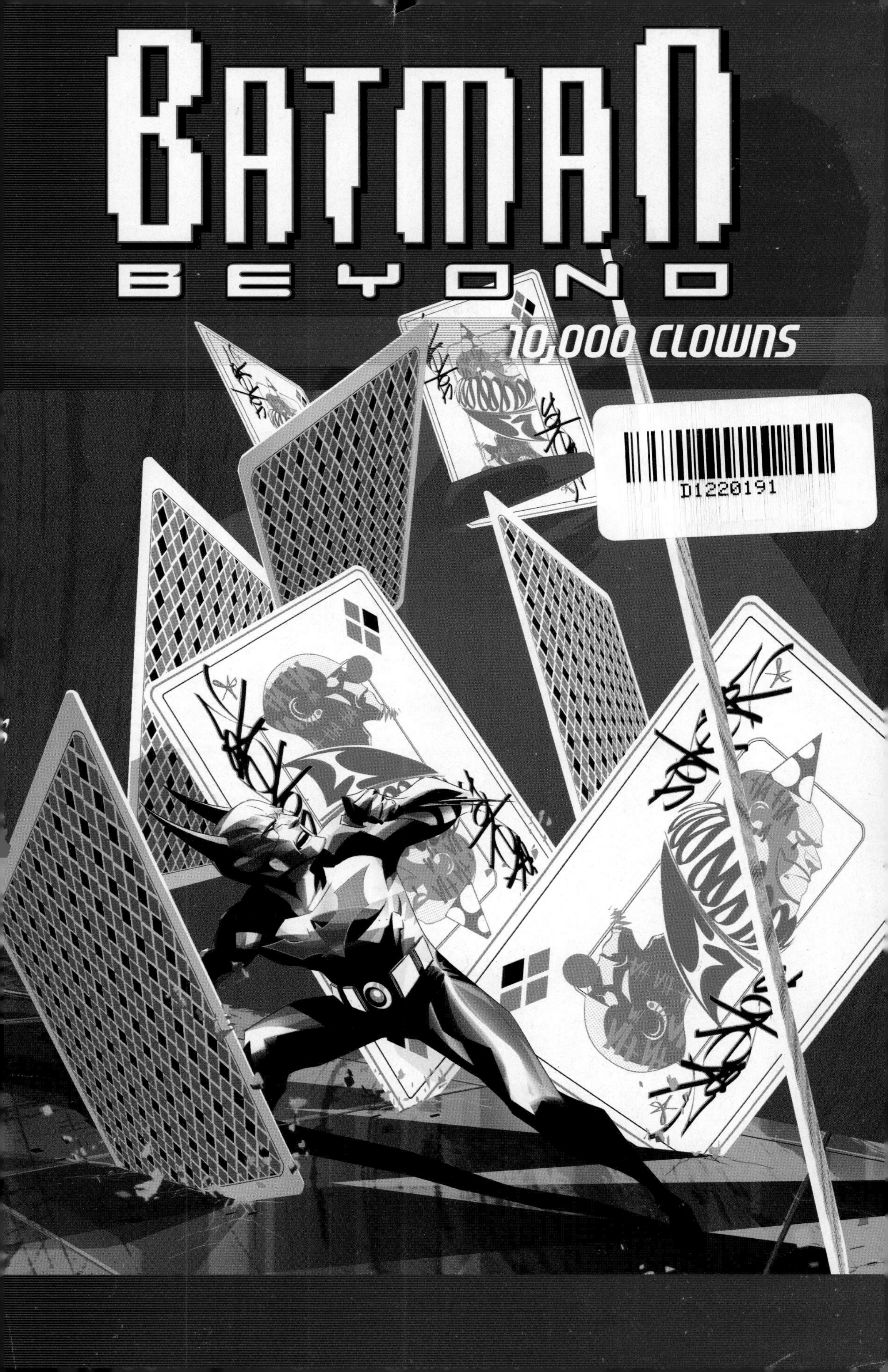
BATMAN
BEYOND
10,000 CLOWNS

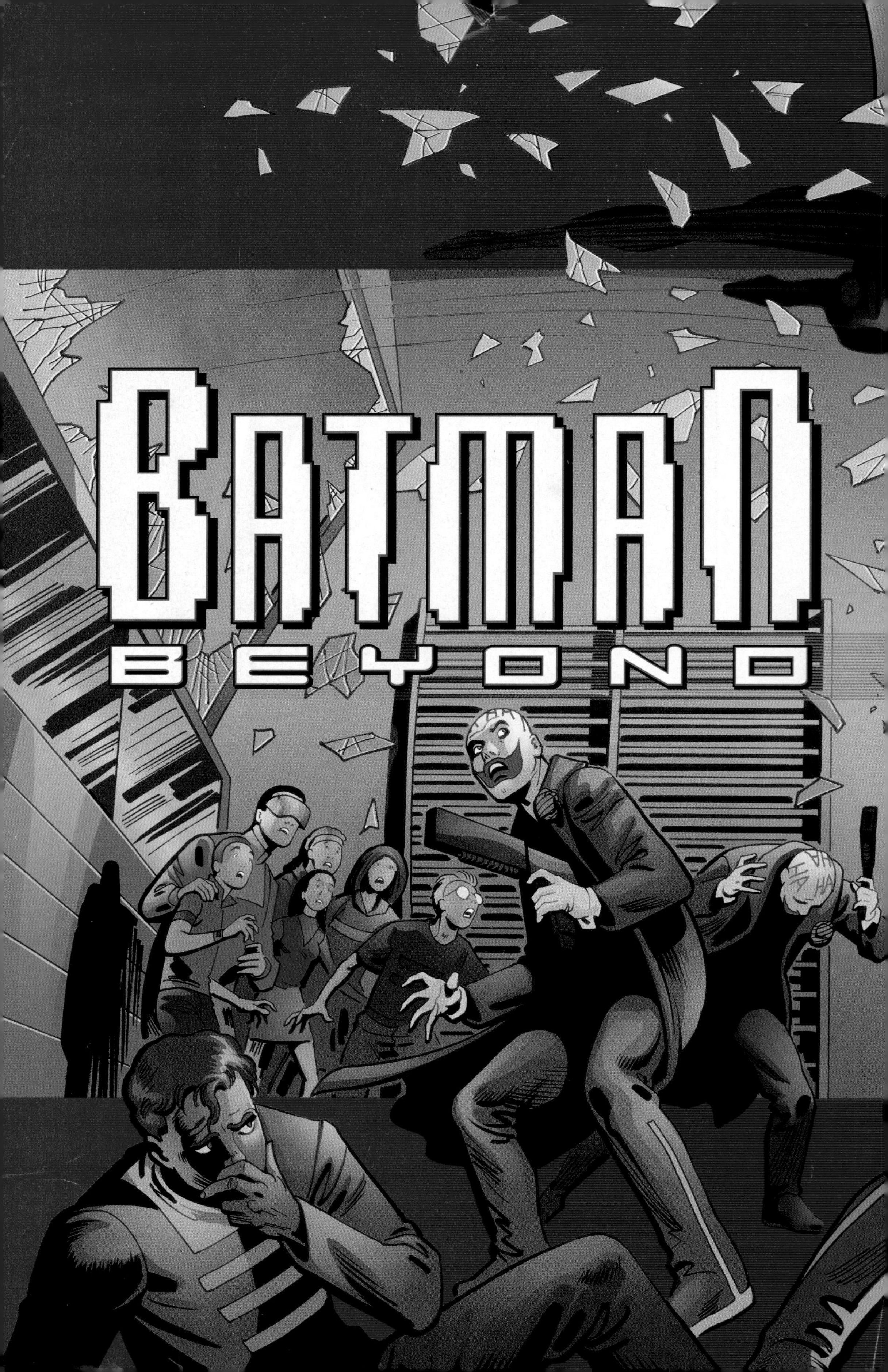
BATMAN
BEYOND

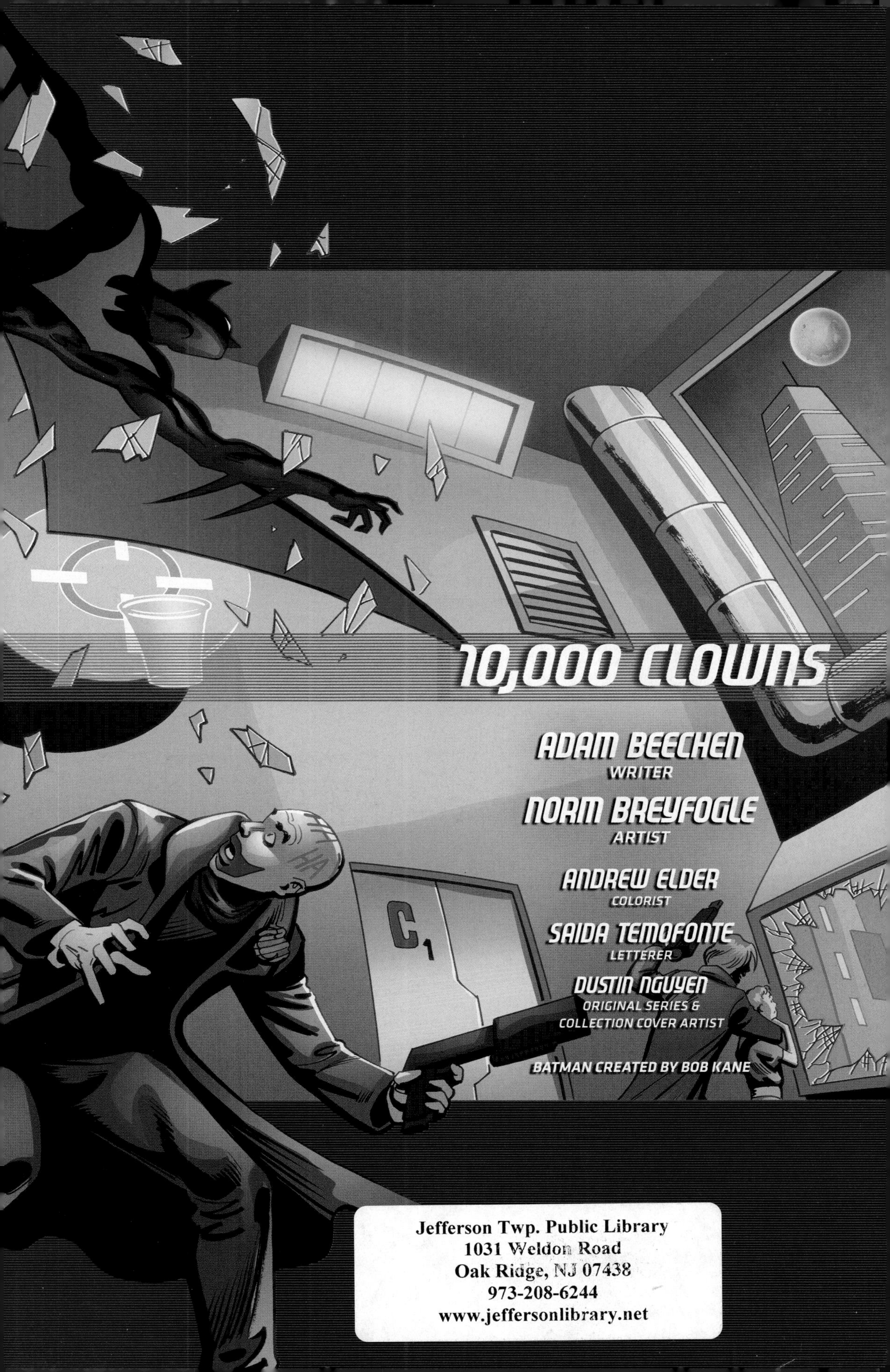

10,000 CLOWNS

ADAM BEECHEN
WRITER

NORM BREYFOGLE
ARTIST

ANDREW ELDER
COLORIST

SAIDA TEMOFONTE
LETTERER

DUSTIN NGUYEN
ORIGINAL SERIES &
COLLECTION COVER ARTIST

BATMAN CREATED BY BOB KANE

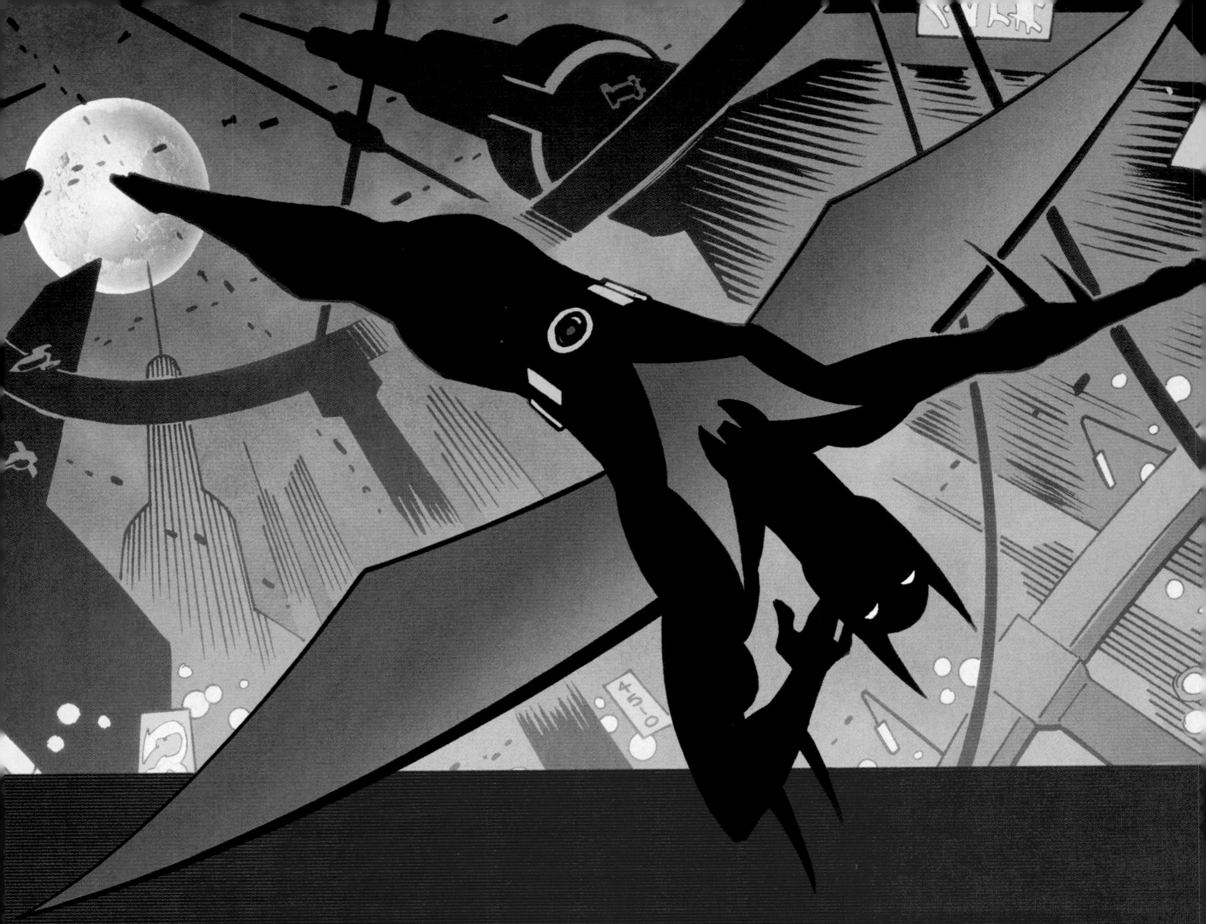

Jim Chadwick
Ben Abernathy
Alex Antone Editors – Original Series
Kristy Quinn Associate Editor – Original Series
Sarah Gaydos Assistant Editor – Original Series
Rachel Pinnelas Editor
Robbin Brosterman Design Director – Books
Curtis King Jr. Publication Design

Bob Harras VP – Editor-in-Chief

Diane Nelson President
Dan DiDio and **Jim Lee** Co-Publishers
Geoff Johns Chief Creative Officer
John Rood Executive VP – Sales, Marketing and Business Development
Amy Genkins Senior VP – Business and Legal Affairs
Nairi Gardiner Senior VP – Finance
Jeff Boison VP – Publishing Operations
Mark Chiarello VP – Art Direction and Design
John Cunningham VP – Marketing
Terri Cunningham VP – Talent Relations and Services
Alison Gill Senior VP – Manufacturing and Operations
Hank Kanalz Senior VP – Digital
Jay Kogan VP – Business and Legal Affairs, Publishing
Jack Mahan VP – Business Affairs, Talent
Nick Napolitano VP – Manufacturing Administration
Sue Pohja VP – Book Sales
Courtney Simmons Senior VP – Publicity
Bob Wayne Senior VP – Sales

BATMAN BEYOND: 10,000 CLOWNS

DC Comics, 1700 Broadway, New York, NY 10019
A Warner Bros. Entertainment Company.
Printed by RR Donnelley, Salem, VA, USA. 4/12/13. First Printing.
ISBN: 978-1-4012-4034-9

Library of Congress Cataloging-in-Publication Data

Beechen, Adam.
Batman Beyond : 10,000 Clowns / Adam Beechen, Norm Breyfogle.
pages cm
"Originally published in single magazine form in Batman Beyond digital chapters 1-16."
ISBN 978-1-4012-4034-9
1. Graphic novels. I. Breyfogle, Norm, illustrator. II. Title.
PN6728.B36B57 2013
741.5'973—dc23
2012050770

SUSTAINABLE FORESTRY INITIATIVE
Certified Chain of Custody
At Least 20% Certified Forest Content
www.sfiprogram.org
SFI-01042
APPLIES TO TEXT STOCK ONLY

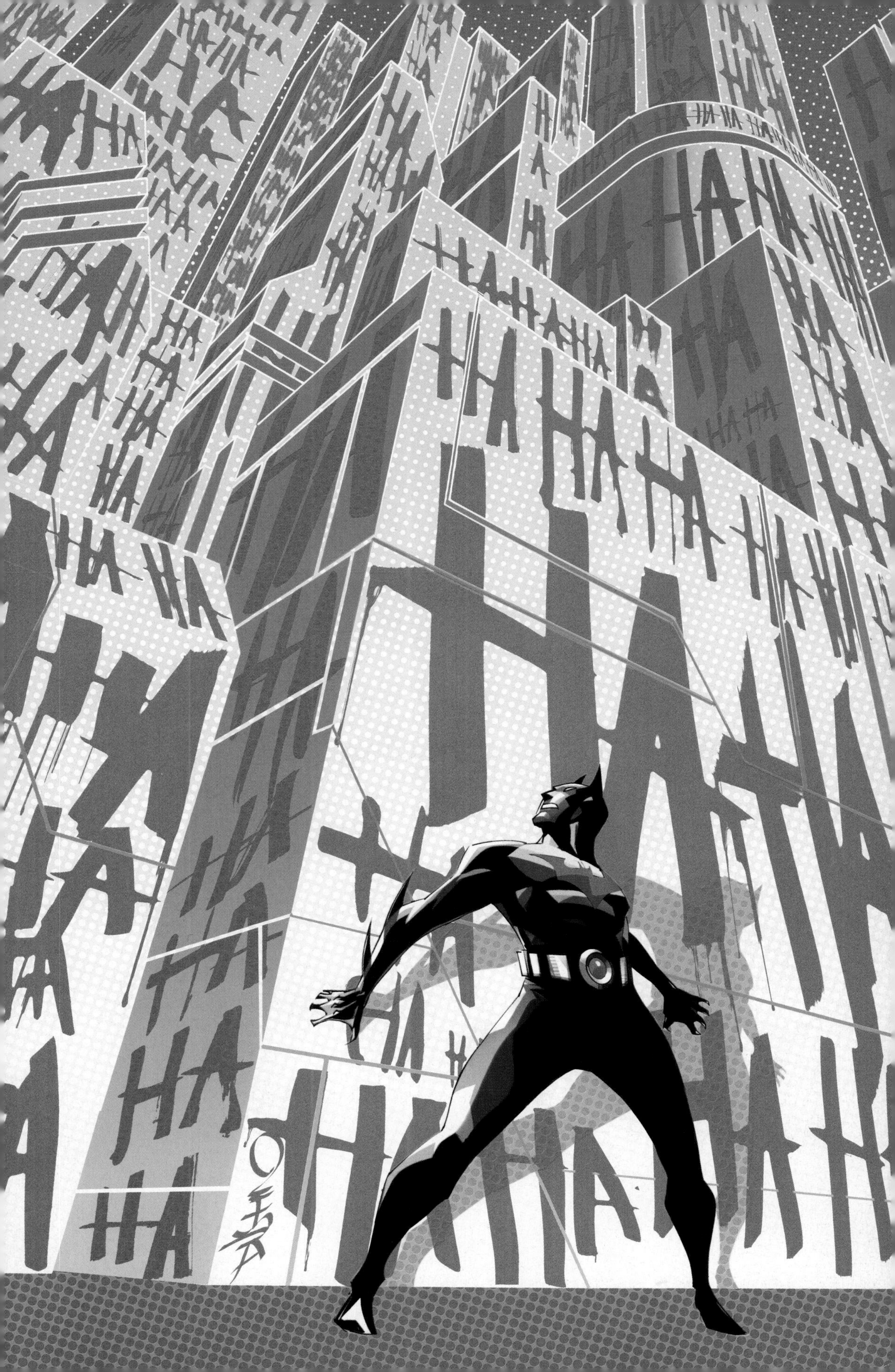
HA HA HA HA

10,000 CLOWNS
PRELUDE

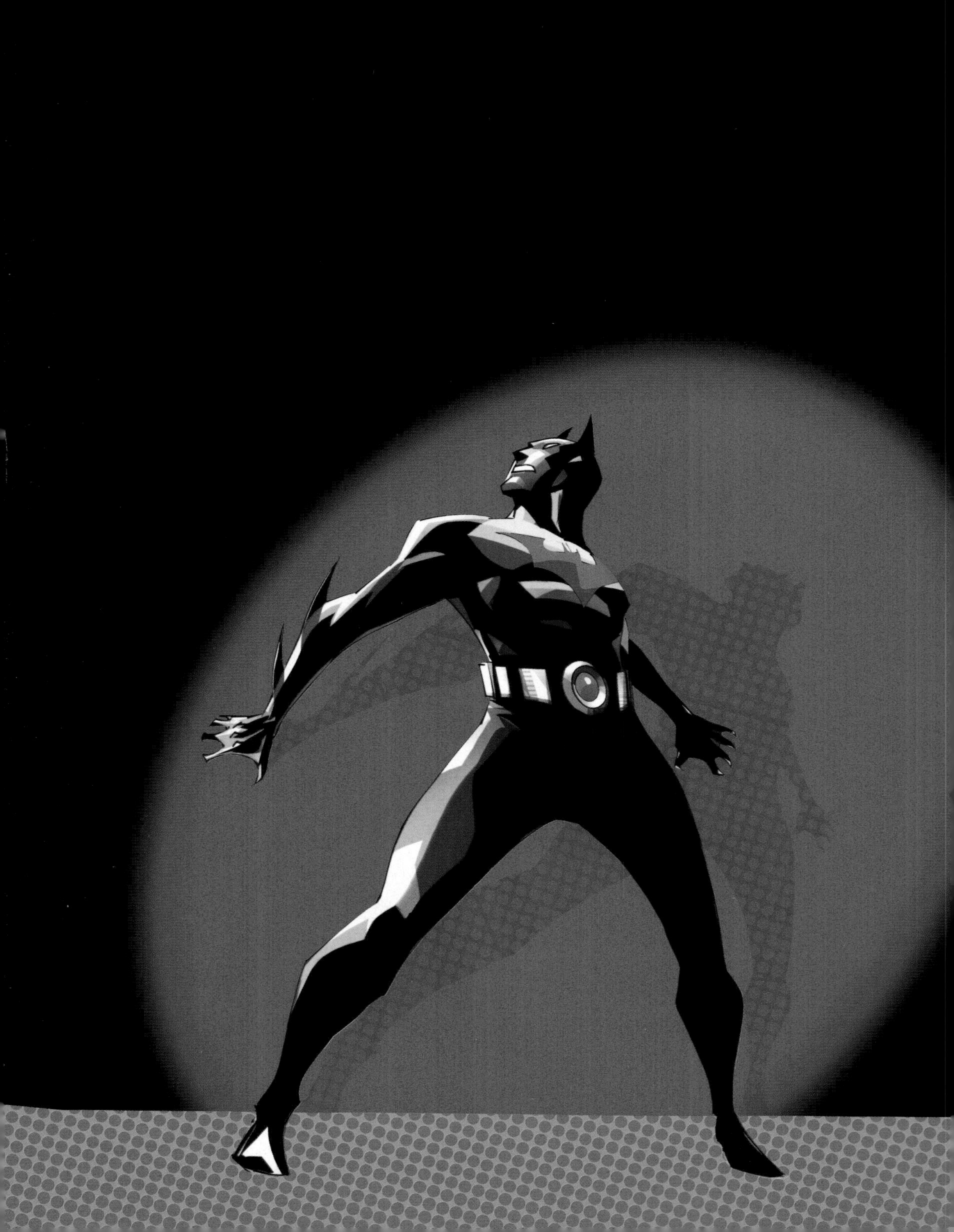

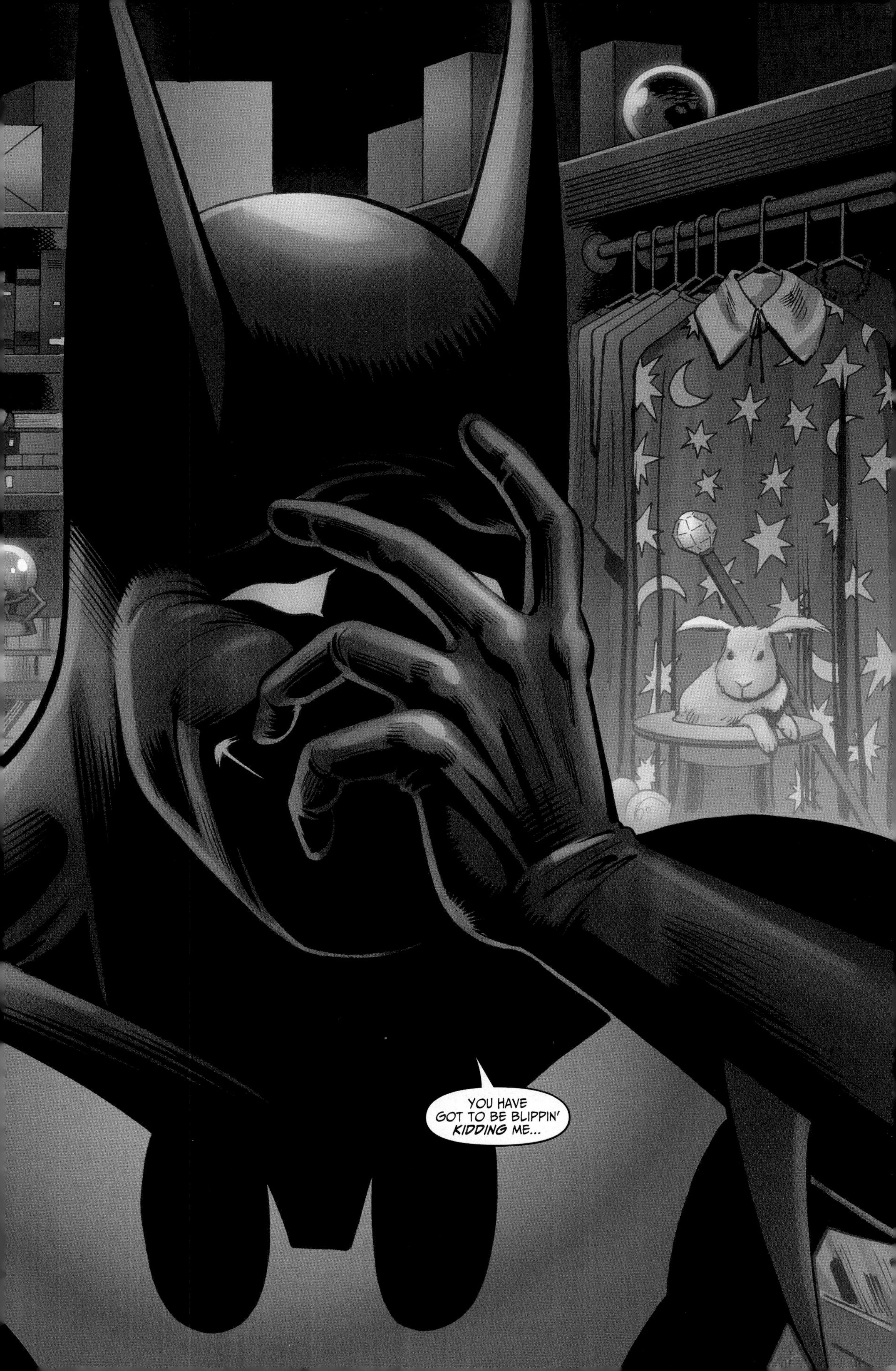
YOU HAVE GOT TO BE BLIPPIN' *KIDDING* ME...

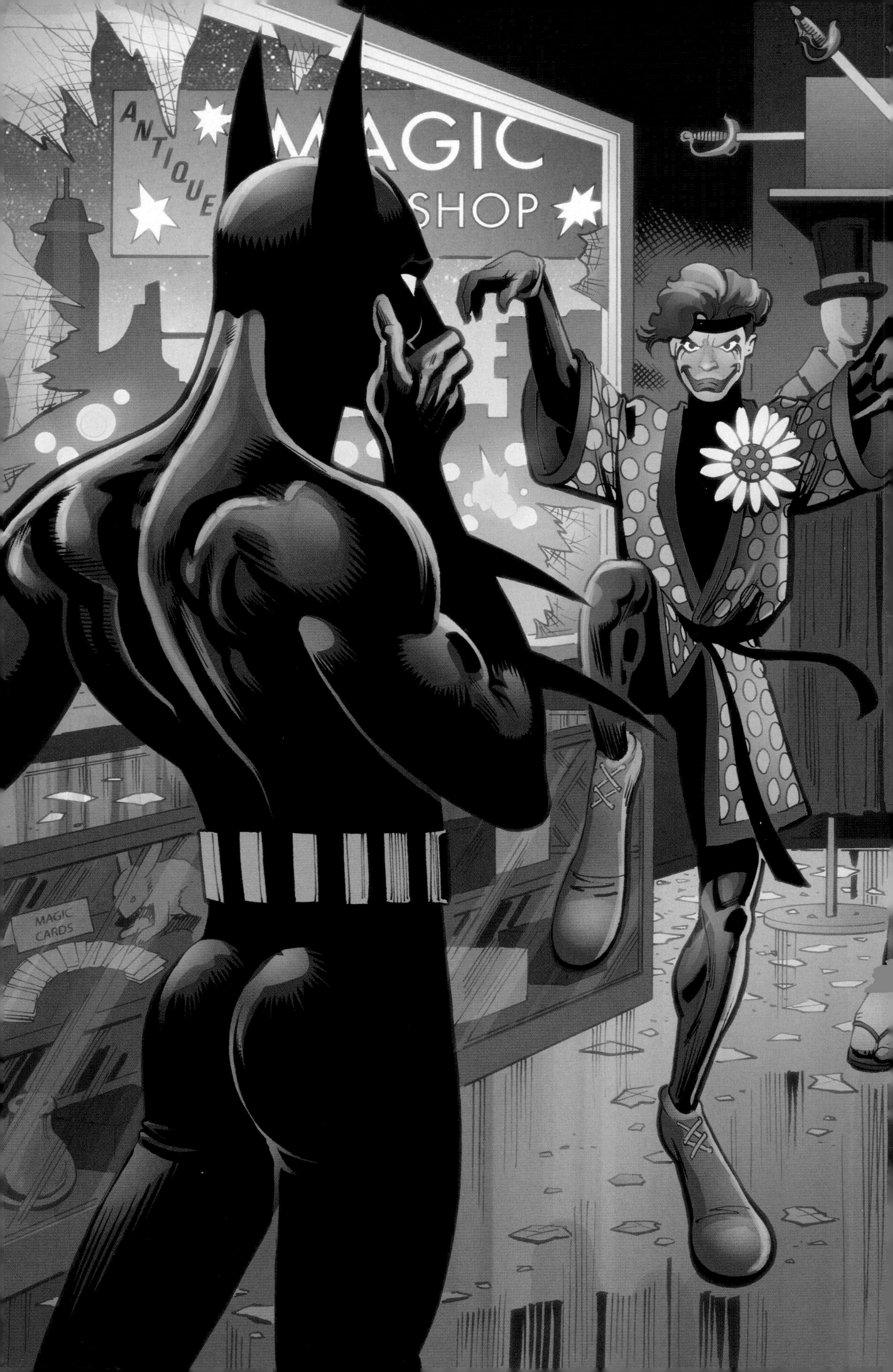
ANTIQUE MAGIC SHOP
MAGIC CARDS

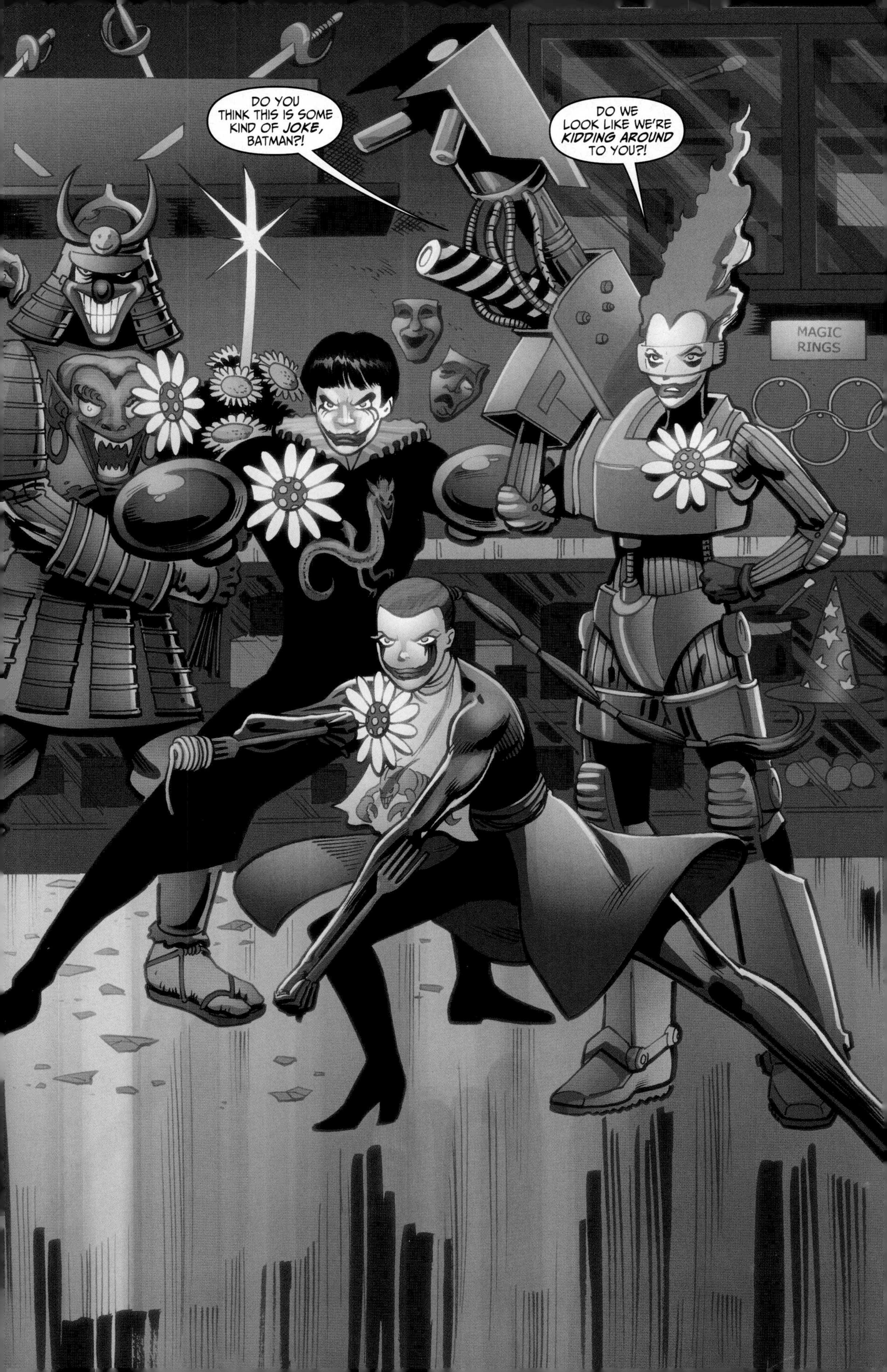
DO YOU THINK THIS IS SOME KIND OF *JOKE,* BATMAN?!
DO WE LOOK LIKE WE'RE *KIDDING AROUND* TO YOU?!
MAGIC RINGS

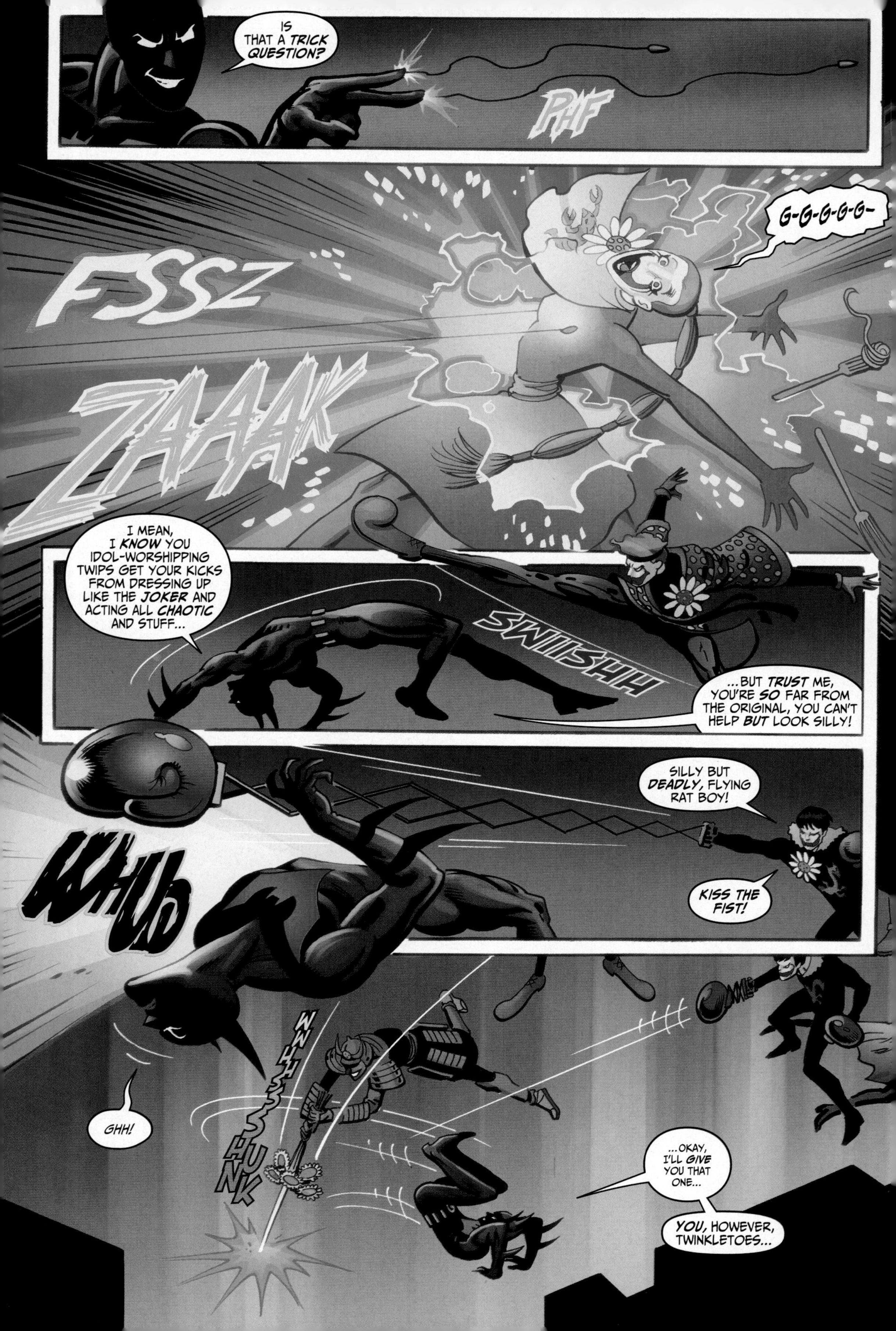

IS THAT A TRICK QUESTION?
PHF
FSSZ
ZAAAK
G-G-G-G-G-
I MEAN, I KNOW YOU IDOL-WORSHIPPING TWIPS GET YOUR KICKS FROM DRESSING UP LIKE THE JOKER AND ACTING ALL CHAOTIC AND STUFF...
SWIISHH
...BUT TRUST ME, YOU'RE SO FAR FROM THE ORIGINAL, YOU CAN'T HELP BUT LOOK SILLY!
SILLY BUT DEADLY, FLYING RAT BOY!
KISS THE FIST!
GHH!
SHUNK
...OKAY, I'LL GIVE YOU THAT ONE...
YOU, HOWEVER, TWINKLETOES...

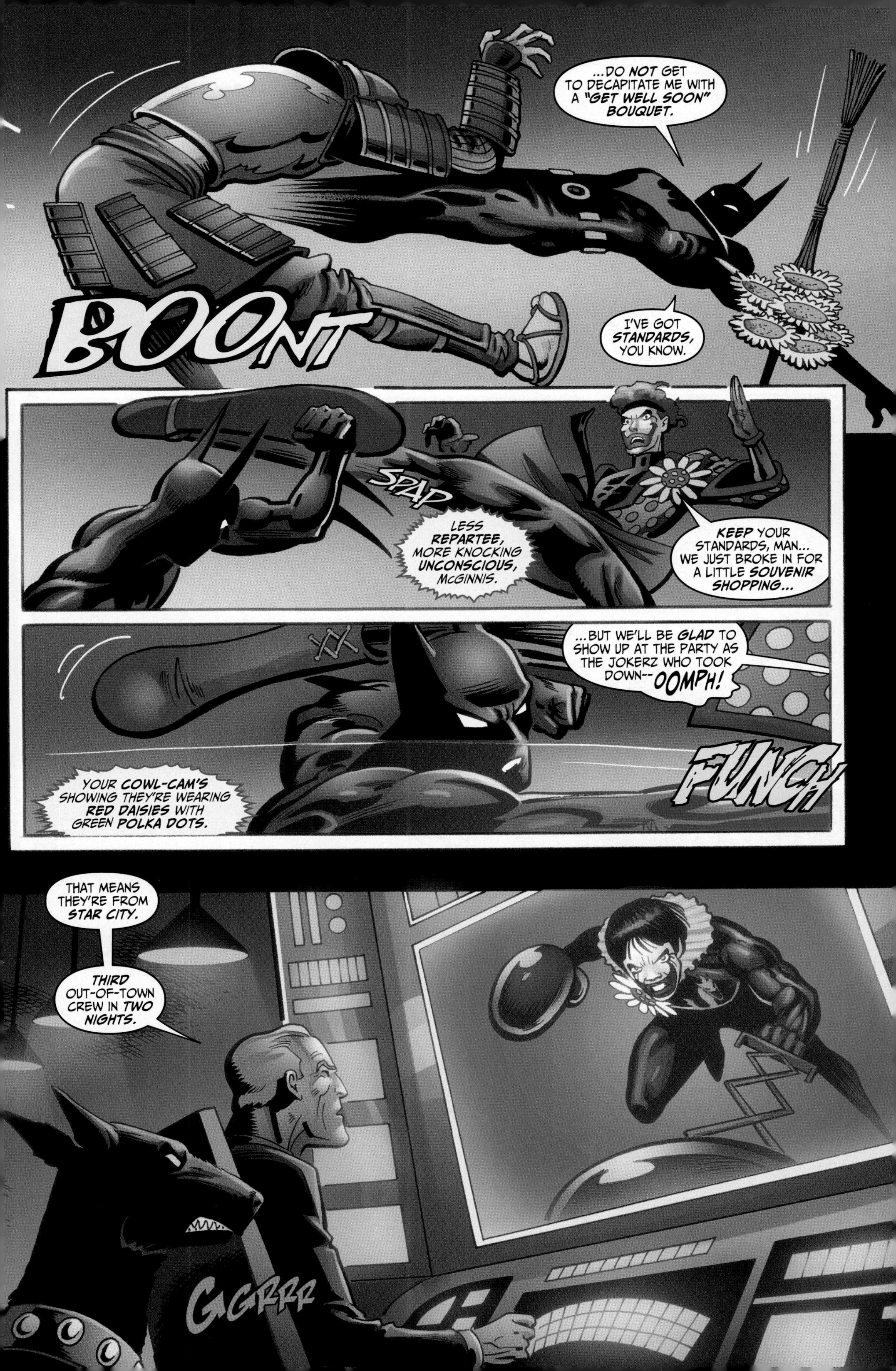
...DO NOT GET TO DECAPITATE ME WITH A "GET WELL SOON" BOUQUET.
BOONT
I'VE GOT STANDARDS, YOU KNOW.
SPAP
LESS REPARTEE, MORE KNOCKING UNCONSCIOUS, McGINNIS.
KEEP YOUR STANDARDS, MAN... WE JUST BROKE IN FOR A LITTLE SOUVENIR SHOPPING...
...BUT WE'LL BE GLAD TO SHOW UP AT THE PARTY AS THE JOKERZ WHO TOOK DOWN--OOMPH!
FUNCH
YOUR COWL-CAM'S SHOWING THEY'RE WEARING RED DAISIES WITH GREEN POLKA DOTS.
THAT MEANS THEY'RE FROM STAR CITY.
THIRD OUT-OF-TOWN CREW IN TWO NIGHTS.
GGRRR

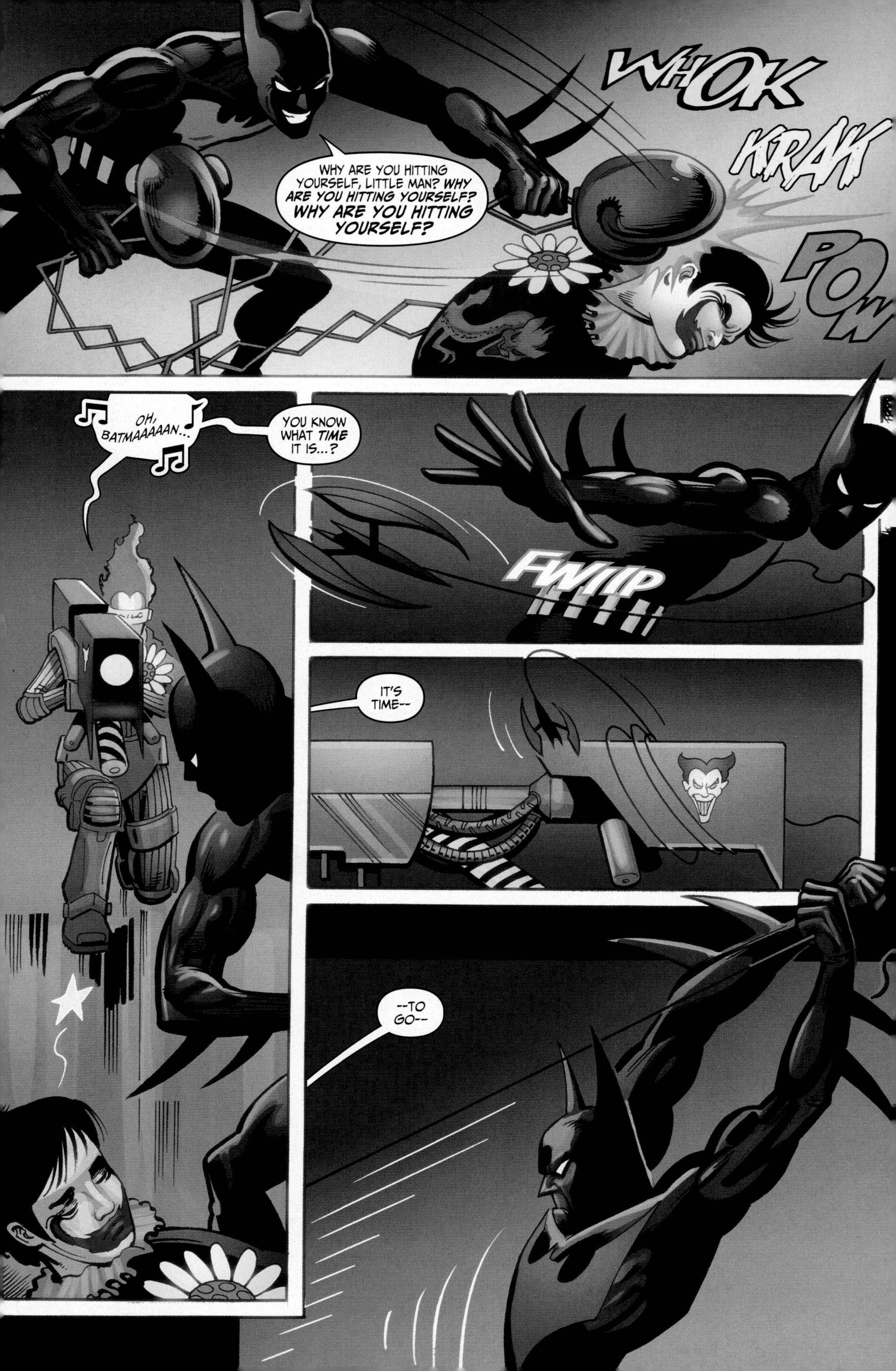
WHOK
KRAK
WHY ARE YOU HITTING YOURSELF, LITTLE MAN? WHY ARE YOU HITTING YOURSELF? WHY ARE YOU HITTING YOURSELF?
POW
OH, BATMAAAAAN...
YOU KNOW WHAT TIME IT IS...?
FWIP
IT'S TIME--
--TO GO--

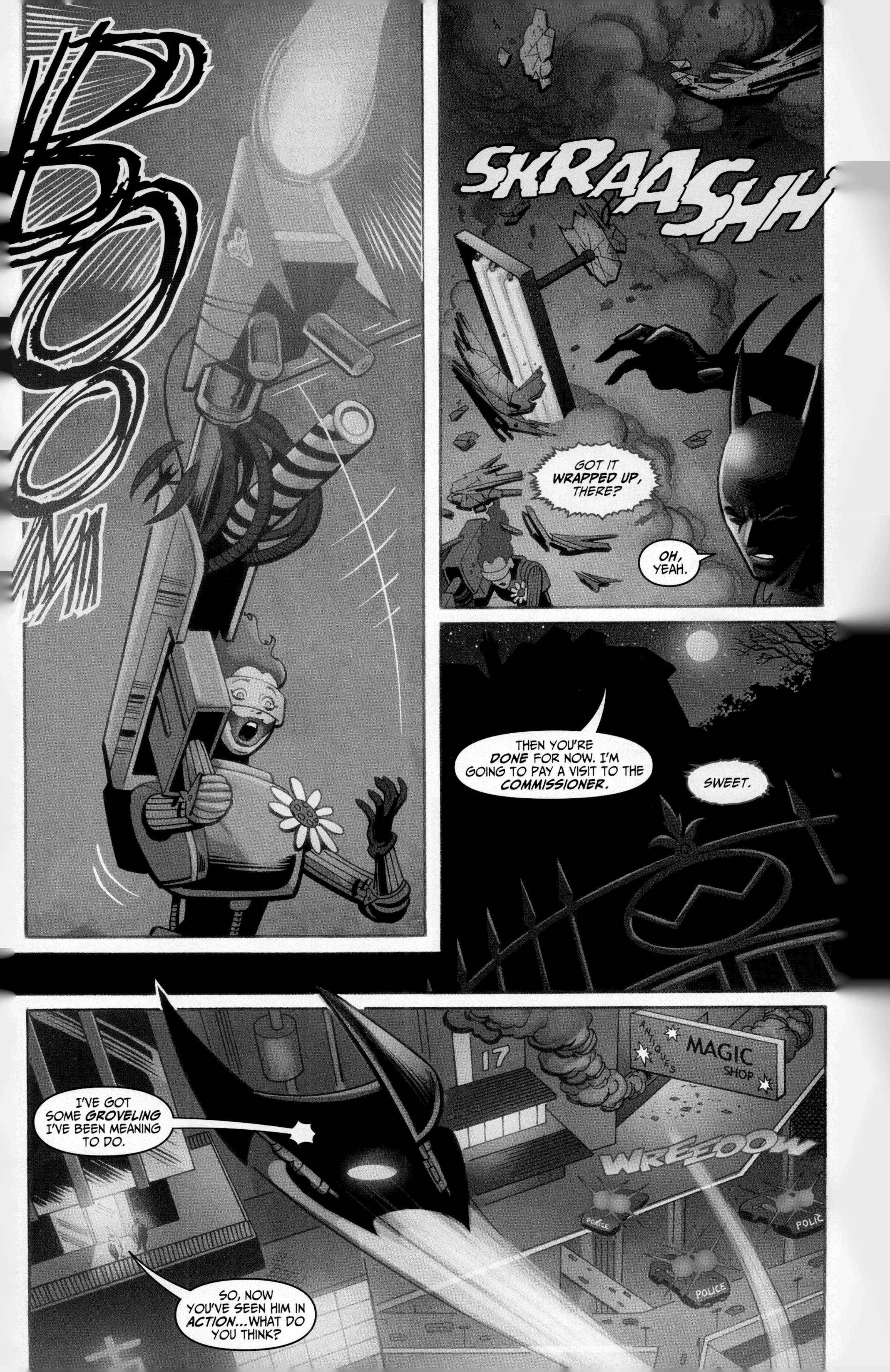
BOOOM
SKRAASHH
GOT IT WRAPPED UP, THERE?
OH, YEAH.
THEN YOU'RE DONE FOR NOW. I'M GOING TO PAY A VISIT TO THE COMMISSIONER.
SWEET.
17
ANTIQUES
MAGIC SHOP
I'VE GOT SOME GROVELING I'VE BEEN MEANING TO DO.
WREEOOW
POLICE
POLIC
POLICE
SO, NOW YOU'VE SEEN HIM IN ACTION...WHAT DO YOU THINK?

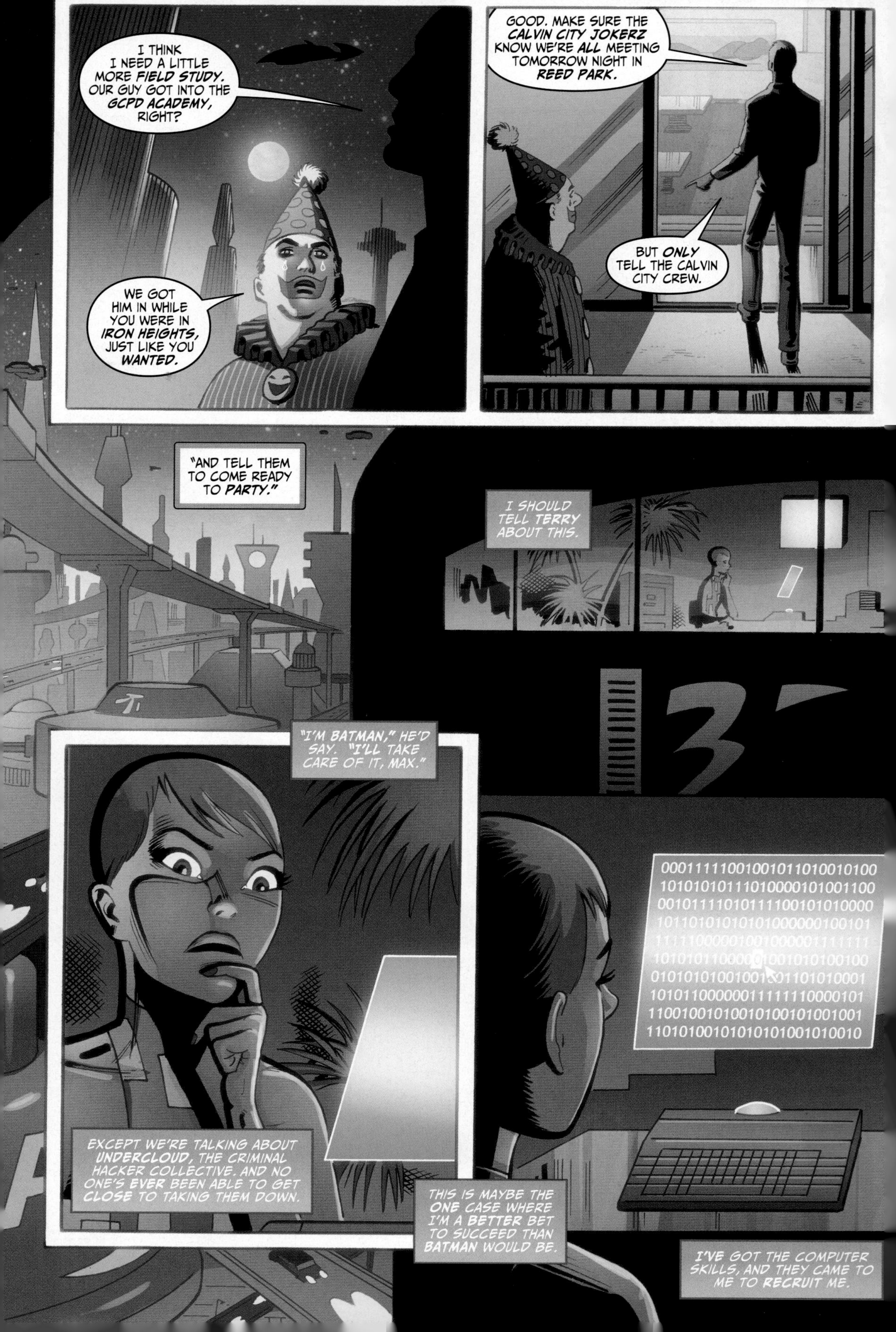
I THINK I NEED A LITTLE MORE FIELD STUDY. OUR GUY GOT INTO THE GCPD ACADEMY, RIGHT?
WE GOT HIM IN WHILE YOU WERE IN IRON HEIGHTS, JUST LIKE YOU WANTED.
GOOD. MAKE SURE THE CALVIN CITY JOKERZ KNOW WE'RE ALL MEETING TOMORROW NIGHT IN REED PARK.
BUT ONLY TELL THE CALVIN CITY CREW.
"AND TELL THEM TO COME READY TO PARTY."
I SHOULD TELL TERRY ABOUT THIS.
"I'M BATMAN," HE'D SAY. "I'LL TAKE CARE OF IT, MAX."
EXCEPT WE'RE TALKING ABOUT UNDERCLOUD, THE CRIMINAL HACKER COLLECTIVE. AND NO ONE'S EVER BEEN ABLE TO GET CLOSE TO TAKING THEM DOWN.
THIS IS MAYBE THE ONE CASE WHERE I'M A BETTER BET TO SUCCEED THAN BATMAN WOULD BE.
I'VE GOT THE COMPUTER SKILLS, AND THEY CAME TO ME TO RECRUIT ME.

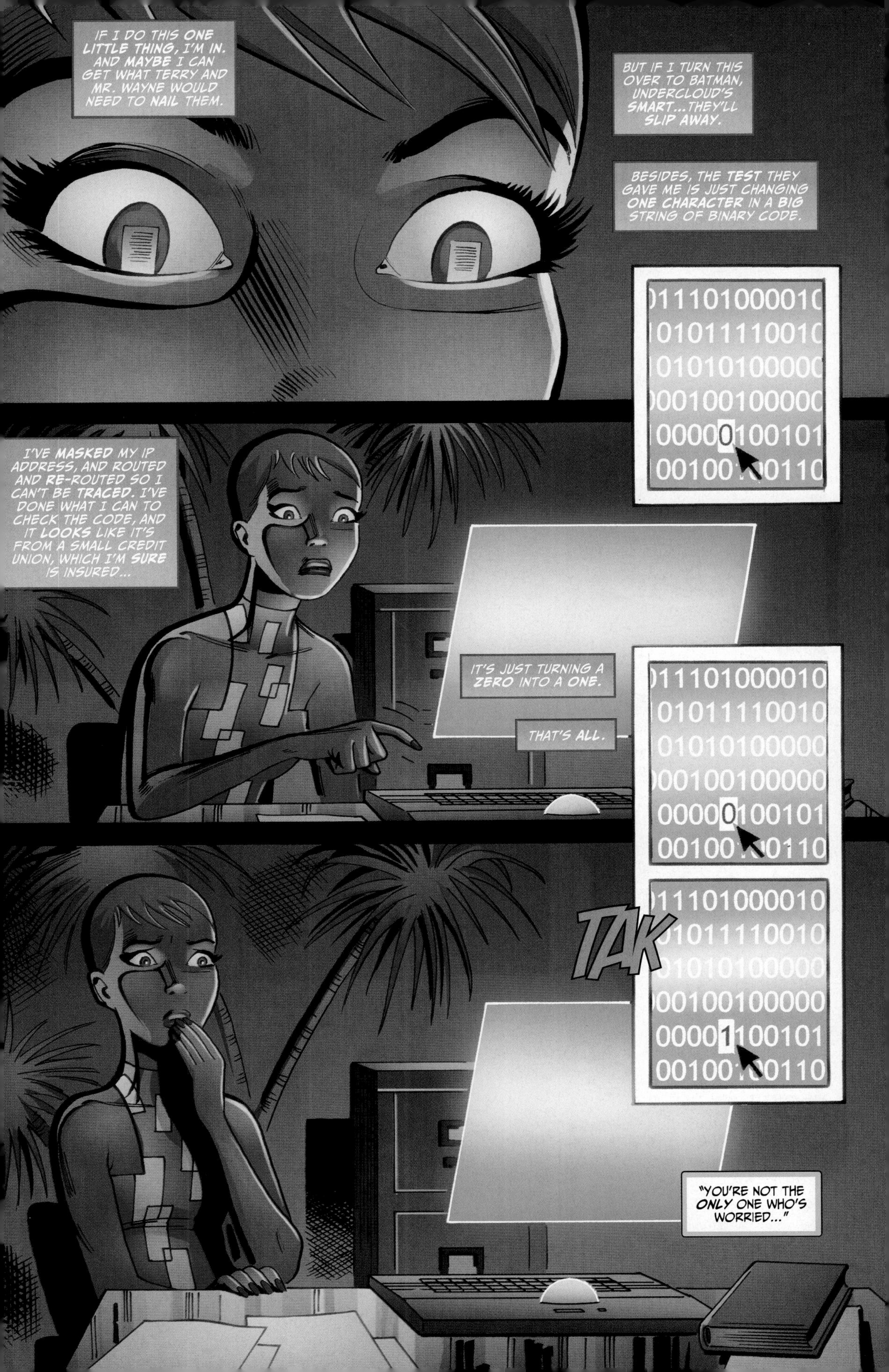
IF I DO THIS ONE LITTLE THING, I'M IN. AND MAYBE I CAN GET WHAT TERRY AND MR. WAYNE WOULD NEED TO NAIL THEM.
BUT IF I TURN THIS OVER TO BATMAN, UNDERCLOUD'S SMART...THEY'LL SLIP AWAY.
BESIDES, THE TEST THEY GAVE ME IS JUST CHANGING ONE CHARACTER IN A BIG STRING OF BINARY CODE.
I'VE MASKED MY IP ADDRESS, AND ROUTED AND RE-ROUTED SO I CAN'T BE TRACED. I'VE DONE WHAT I CAN TO CHECK THE CODE, AND IT LOOKS LIKE IT'S FROM A SMALL CREDIT UNION, WHICH I'M SURE IS INSURED...
IT'S JUST TURNING A ZERO INTO A ONE.
THAT'S ALL.
TAK
"YOU'RE NOT THE ONLY ONE WHO'S WORRIED..."

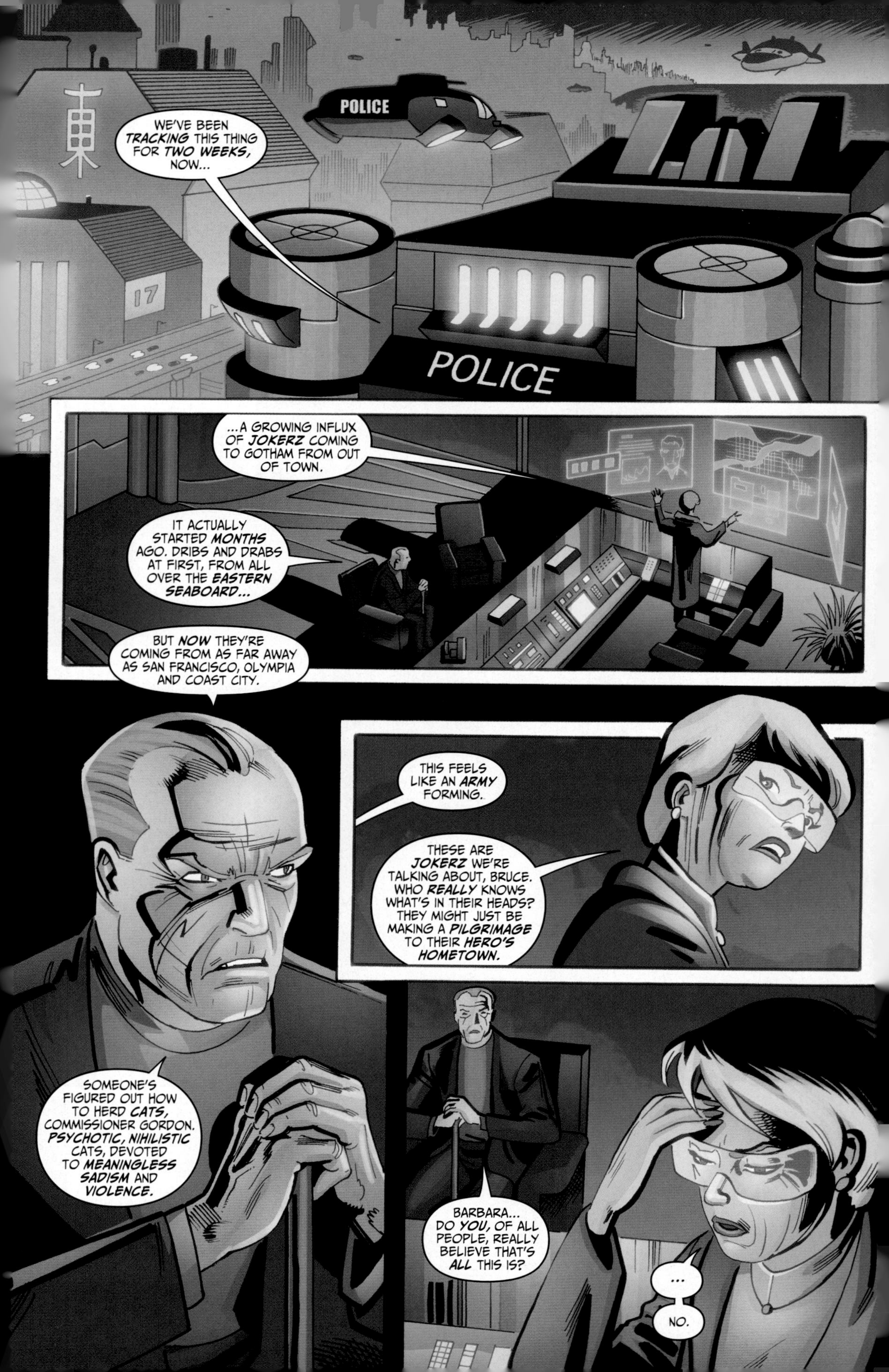

東
POLICE
WE'VE BEEN TRACKING THIS THING FOR TWO WEEKS, NOW...
17
POLICE
...A GROWING INFLUX OF JOKERZ COMING TO GOTHAM FROM OUT OF TOWN.
IT ACTUALLY STARTED MONTHS AGO. DRIBS AND DRABS AT FIRST, FROM ALL OVER THE EASTERN SEABOARD...
BUT NOW THEY'RE COMING FROM AS FAR AWAY AS SAN FRANCISCO, OLYMPIA AND COAST CITY.
THIS FEELS LIKE AN ARMY FORMING.
THESE ARE JOKERZ WE'RE TALKING ABOUT, BRUCE. WHO REALLY KNOWS WHAT'S IN THEIR HEADS? THEY MIGHT JUST BE MAKING A PILGRIMAGE TO THEIR HERO'S HOMETOWN.
SOMEONE'S FIGURED OUT HOW TO HERD CATS, COMMISSIONER GORDON. PSYCHOTIC, NIHILISTIC CATS, DEVOTED TO MEANINGLESS SADISM AND VIOLENCE.
BARBARA... DO YOU, OF ALL PEOPLE, REALLY BELIEVE THAT'S ALL THIS IS?
...
NO.

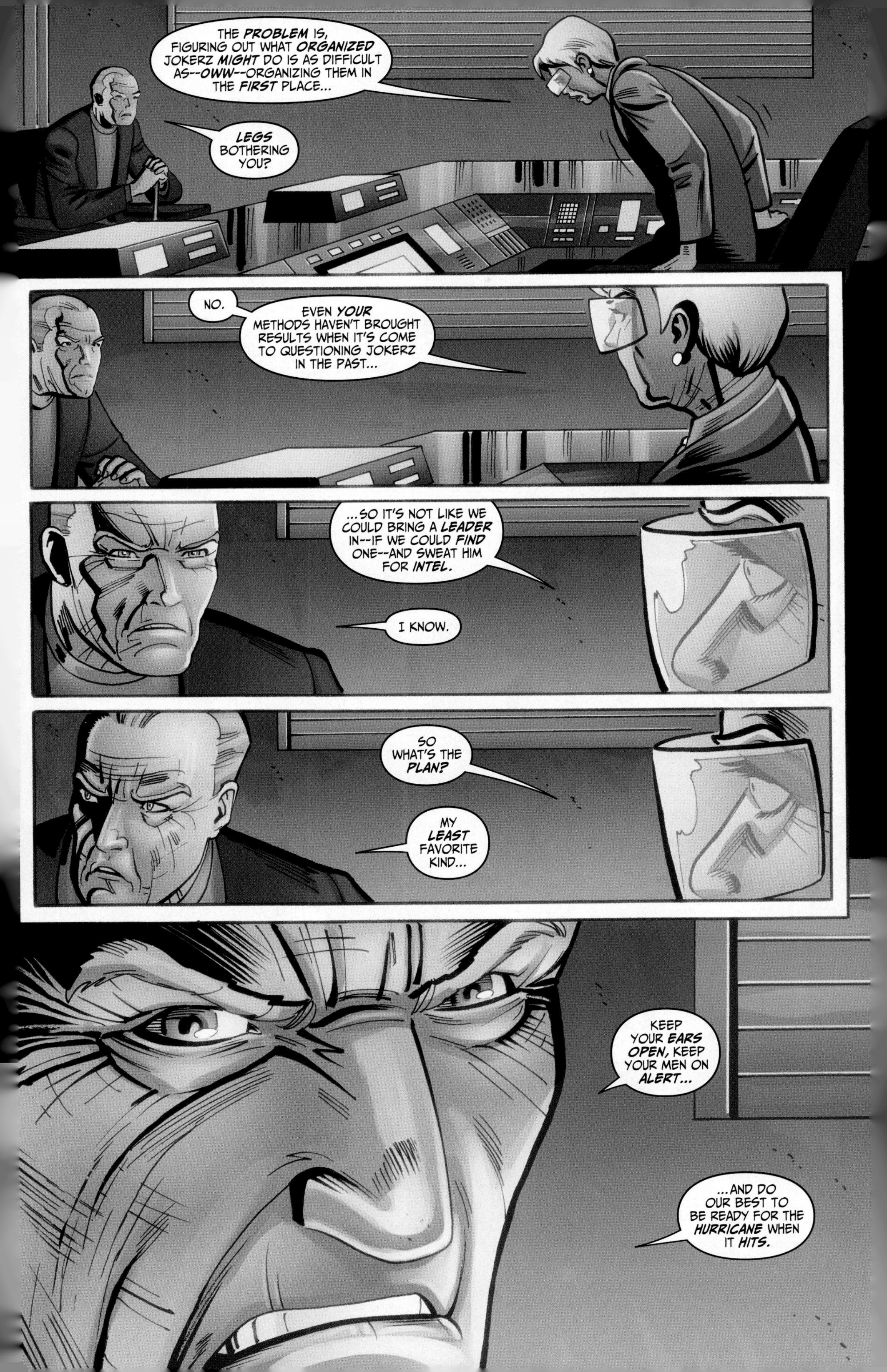
THE PROBLEM IS, FIGURING OUT WHAT ORGANIZED JOKERZ MIGHT DO IS AS DIFFICULT AS--OWW--ORGANIZING THEM IN THE FIRST PLACE...
LEGS BOTHERING YOU?
NO.
EVEN YOUR METHODS HAVEN'T BROUGHT RESULTS WHEN IT'S COME TO QUESTIONING JOKERZ IN THE PAST...
...SO IT'S NOT LIKE WE COULD BRING A LEADER IN--IF WE COULD FIND ONE--AND SWEAT HIM FOR INTEL.
I KNOW.
SO WHAT'S THE PLAN?
MY LEAST FAVORITE KIND...
KEEP YOUR EARS OPEN, KEEP YOUR MEN ON ALERT...
...AND DO OUR BEST TO BE READY FOR THE HURRICANE WHEN IT HITS.

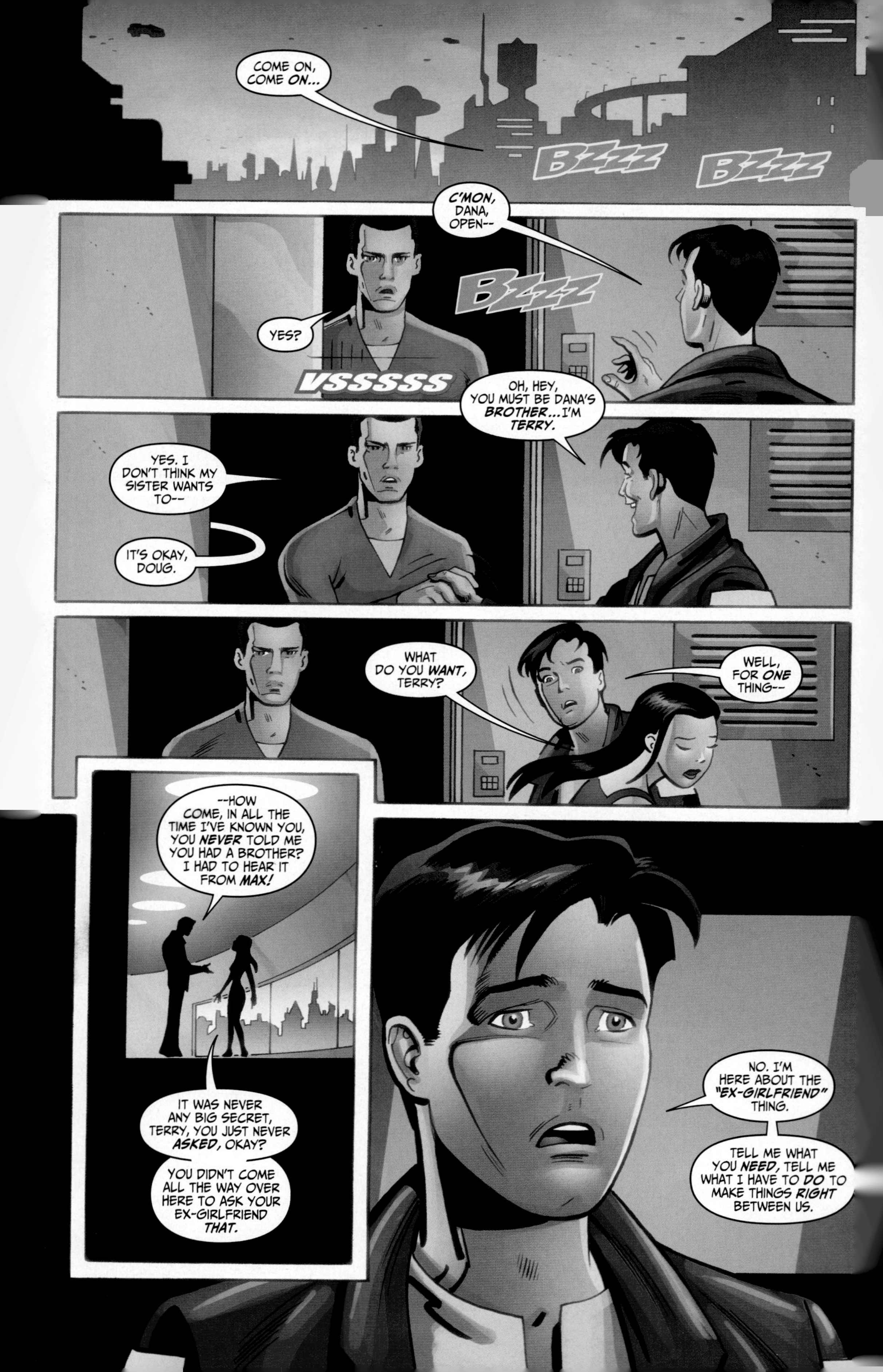
COME ON, COME ON...
BZZZ
BZZZ
C'MON, DANA, OPEN--
BZZZ
YES?
VSSSSS
OH, HEY, YOU MUST BE DANA'S BROTHER...I'M TERRY.
YES. I DON'T THINK MY SISTER WANTS TO--
IT'S OKAY, DOUG.
WHAT DO YOU WANT, TERRY?
WELL, FOR ONE THING--
--HOW COME, IN ALL THE TIME I'VE KNOWN YOU, YOU NEVER TOLD ME YOU HAD A BROTHER? I HAD TO HEAR IT FROM MAX!
IT WAS NEVER ANY BIG SECRET, TERRY, YOU JUST NEVER ASKED, OKAY?
YOU DIDN'T COME ALL THE WAY OVER HERE TO ASK YOUR EX-GIRLFRIEND THAT.
NO. I'M HERE ABOUT THE "EX-GIRLFRIEND" THING.
TELL ME WHAT YOU NEED, TELL ME WHAT I HAVE TO DO TO MAKE THINGS RIGHT BETWEEN US.

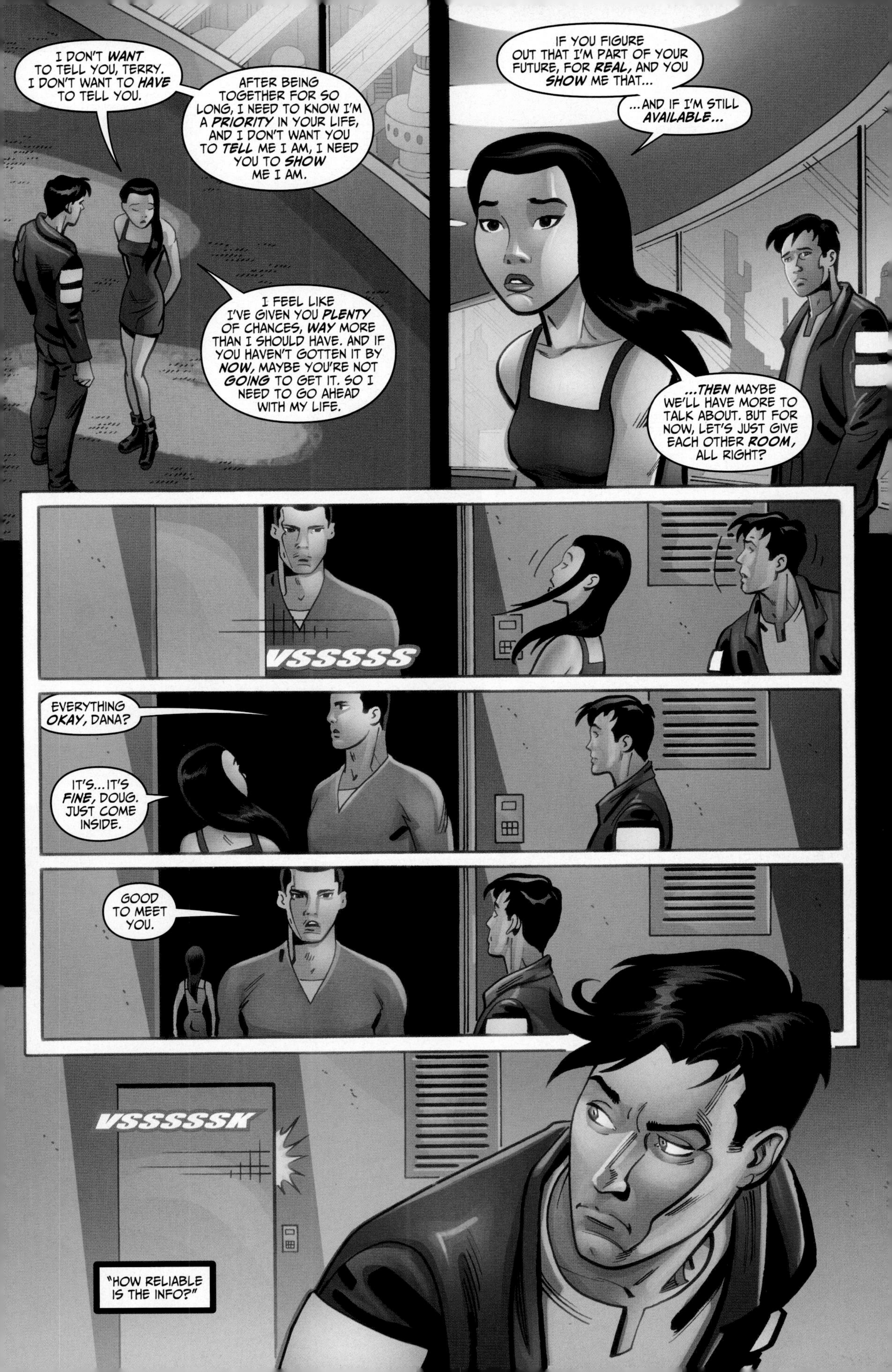
I DON'T WANT TO TELL YOU, TERRY. I DON'T WANT TO HAVE TO TELL YOU.
AFTER BEING TOGETHER FOR SO LONG, I NEED TO KNOW I'M A PRIORITY IN YOUR LIFE, AND I DON'T WANT YOU TO TELL ME I AM, I NEED YOU TO SHOW ME I AM.
I FEEL LIKE I'VE GIVEN YOU PLENTY OF CHANCES, WAY MORE THAN I SHOULD HAVE. AND IF YOU HAVEN'T GOTTEN IT BY NOW, MAYBE YOU'RE NOT GOING TO GET IT. SO I NEED TO GO AHEAD WITH MY LIFE.
IF YOU FIGURE OUT THAT I'M PART OF YOUR FUTURE, FOR REAL, AND YOU SHOW ME THAT...
...AND IF I'M STILL AVAILABLE...
...THEN MAYBE WE'LL HAVE MORE TO TALK ABOUT. BUT FOR NOW, LET'S JUST GIVE EACH OTHER ROOM, ALL RIGHT?
VSSSSS
EVERYTHING OKAY, DANA?
IT'S...IT'S FINE, DOUG. JUST COME INSIDE.
GOOD TO MEET YOU.
VSSSSSK
"HOW RELIABLE IS THE INFO?"

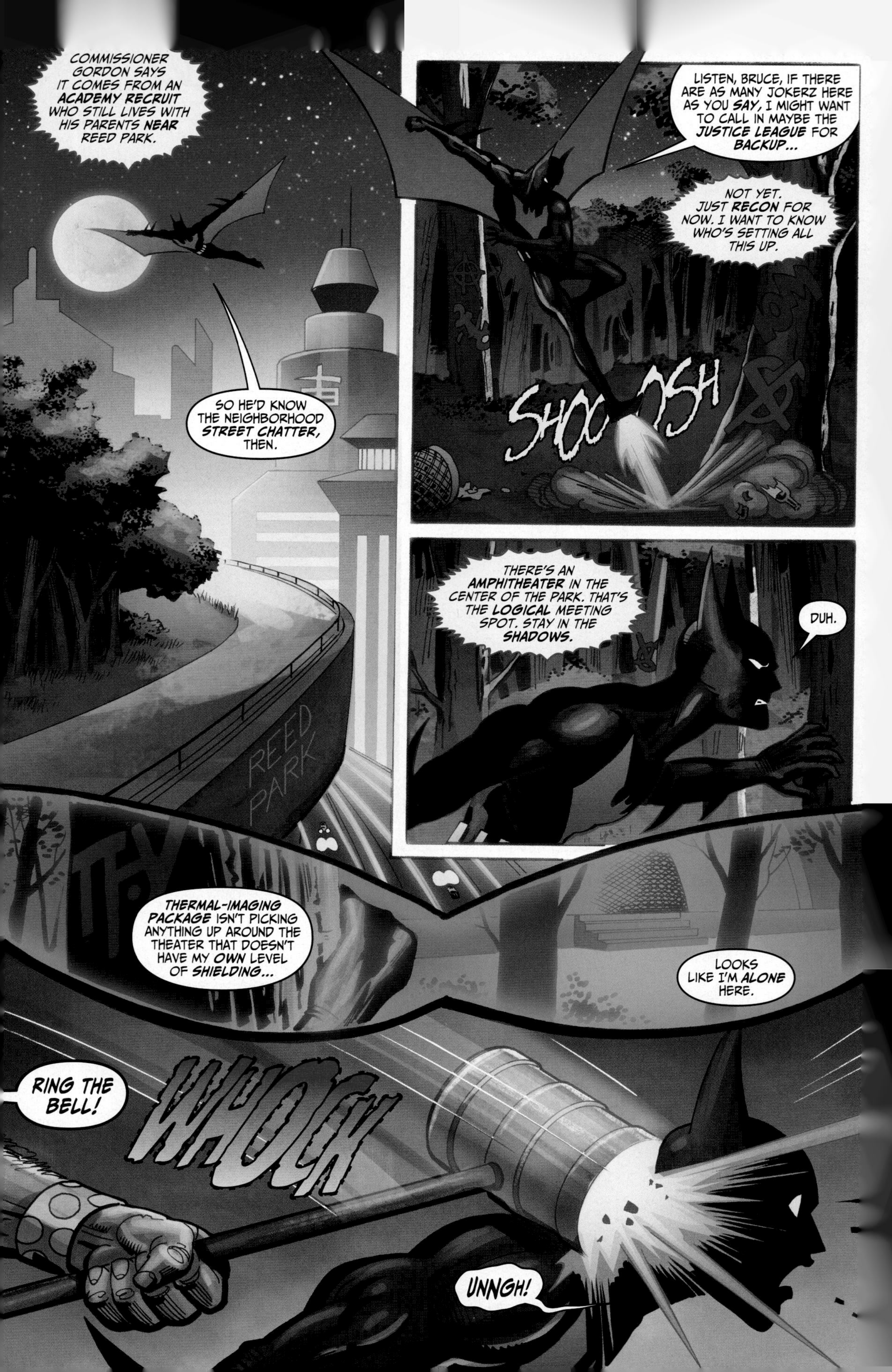
COMMISSIONER GORDON SAYS IT COMES FROM AN ACADEMY RECRUIT WHO STILL LIVES WITH HIS PARENTS NEAR REED PARK.
SO HE'D KNOW THE NEIGHBORHOOD STREET CHATTER, THEN.
REED PARK
LISTEN, BRUCE, IF THERE ARE AS MANY JOKERZ HERE AS YOU SAY, I MIGHT WANT TO CALL IN MAYBE THE JUSTICE LEAGUE FOR BACKUP...
NOT YET. JUST RECON FOR NOW. I WANT TO KNOW WHO'S SETTING ALL THIS UP.
THERE'S AN AMPHITHEATER IN THE CENTER OF THE PARK. THAT'S THE LOGICAL MEETING SPOT. STAY IN THE SHADOWS.
DUH.
THERMAL-IMAGING PACKAGE ISN'T PICKING ANYTHING UP AROUND THE THEATER THAT DOESN'T HAVE MY OWN LEVEL OF SHIELDING...
LOOKS LIKE I'M ALONE HERE.
RING THE BELL!
WHOCK
UNNGH!

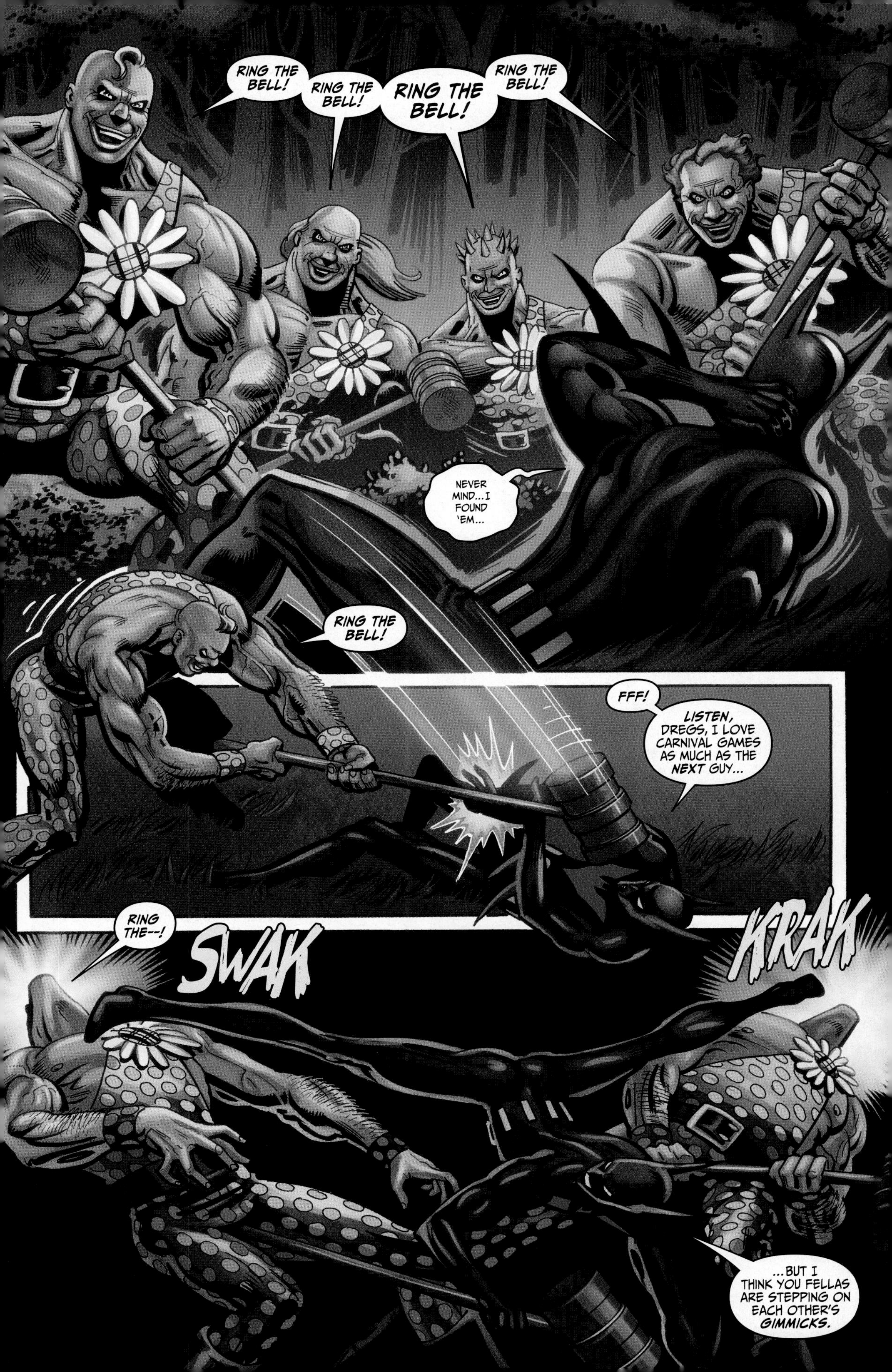
RING THE BELL!
RING THE BELL!
RING THE BELL!
RING THE BELL!
NEVER MIND...I FOUND 'EM...
RING THE BELL!
FFF!
LISTEN, DREGS, I LOVE CARNIVAL GAMES AS MUCH AS THE NEXT GUY...
RING THE--!
SWAK
KRAK
...BUT I THINK YOU FELLAS ARE STEPPING ON EACH OTHER'S GIMMICKS.

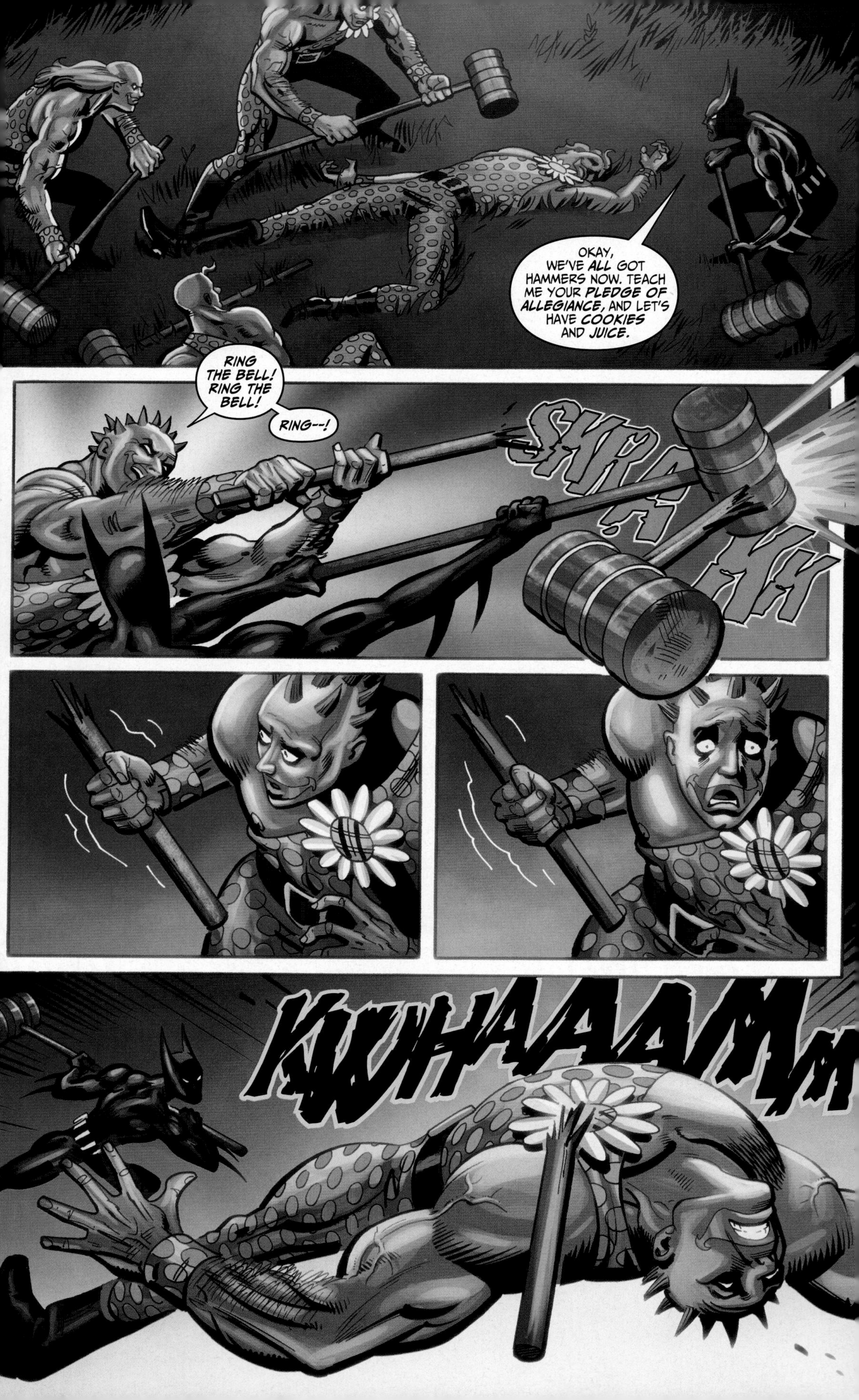
OKAY, WE'VE ALL GOT HAMMERS NOW. TEACH ME YOUR PLEDGE OF ALLEGIANCE, AND LET'S HAVE COOKIES AND JUICE.
RING THE BELL! RING THE BELL!
RING--!
SKRAAKK
KUHAAAMM

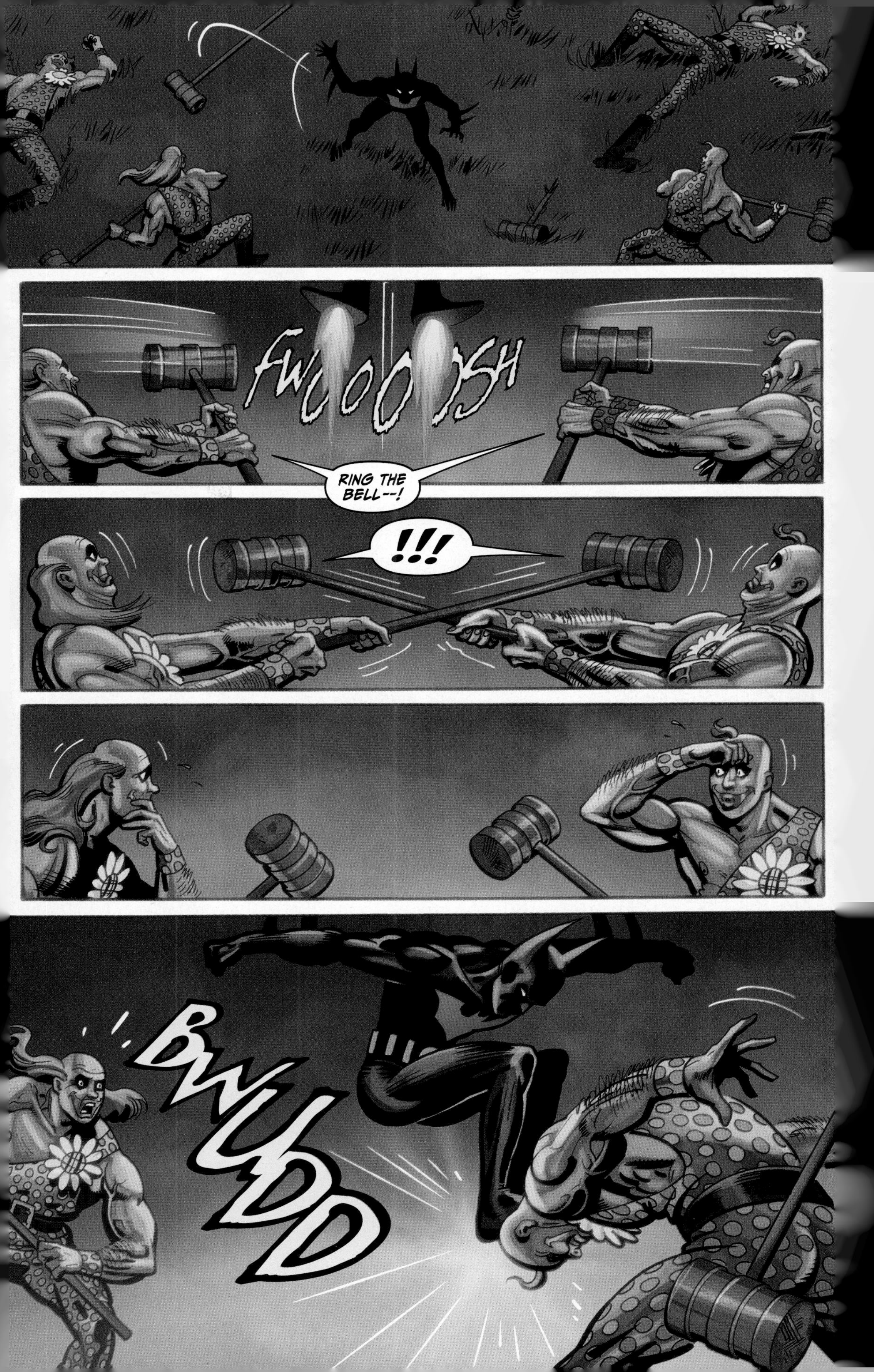
FWOOOOSH
RING THE BELL--!
!!!
BWUDD

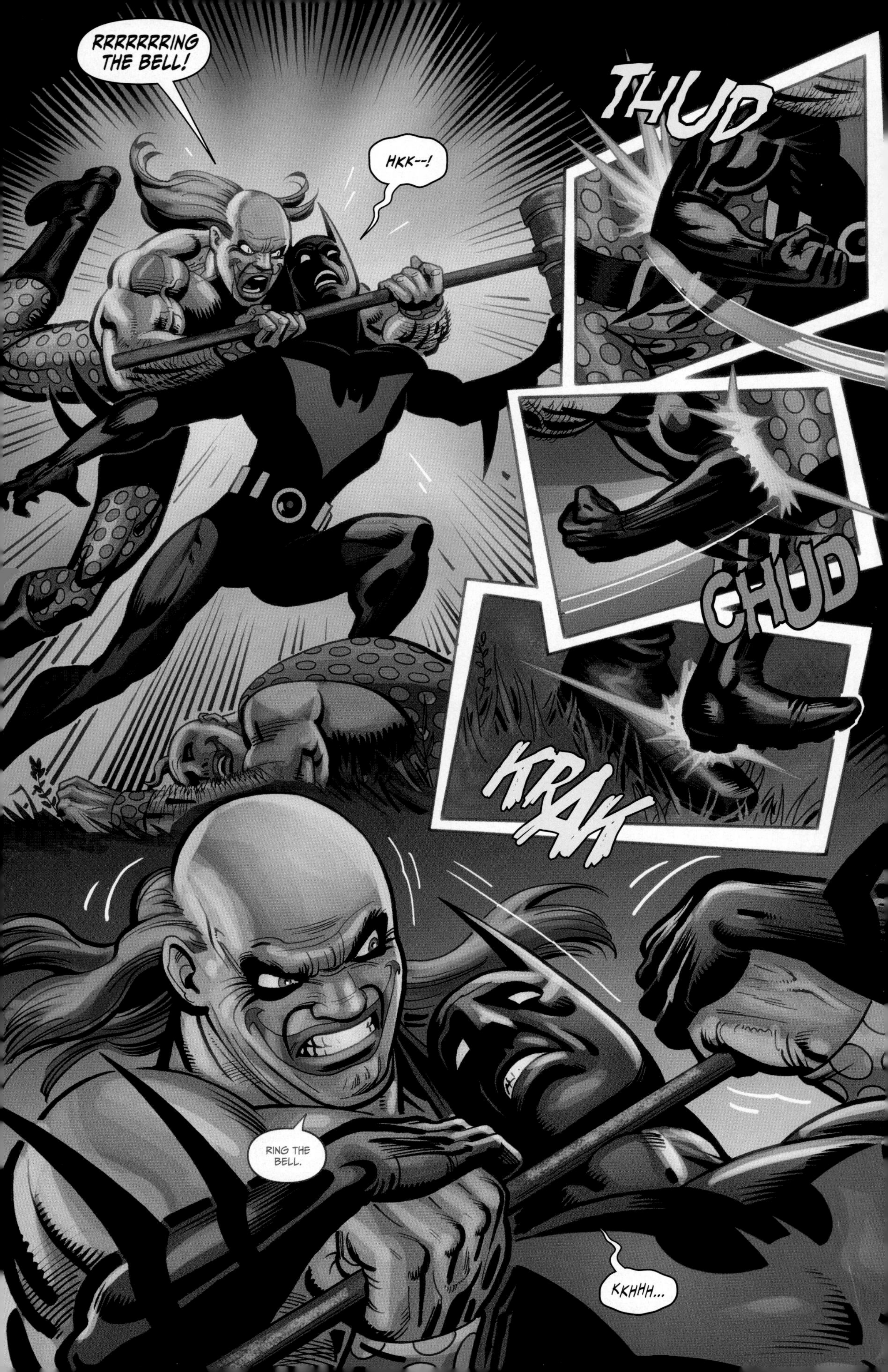
RRRRRRRING THE BELL!
HKK--!
THUD
CHUD
KRAK
RING THE BELL.
KKHHH...

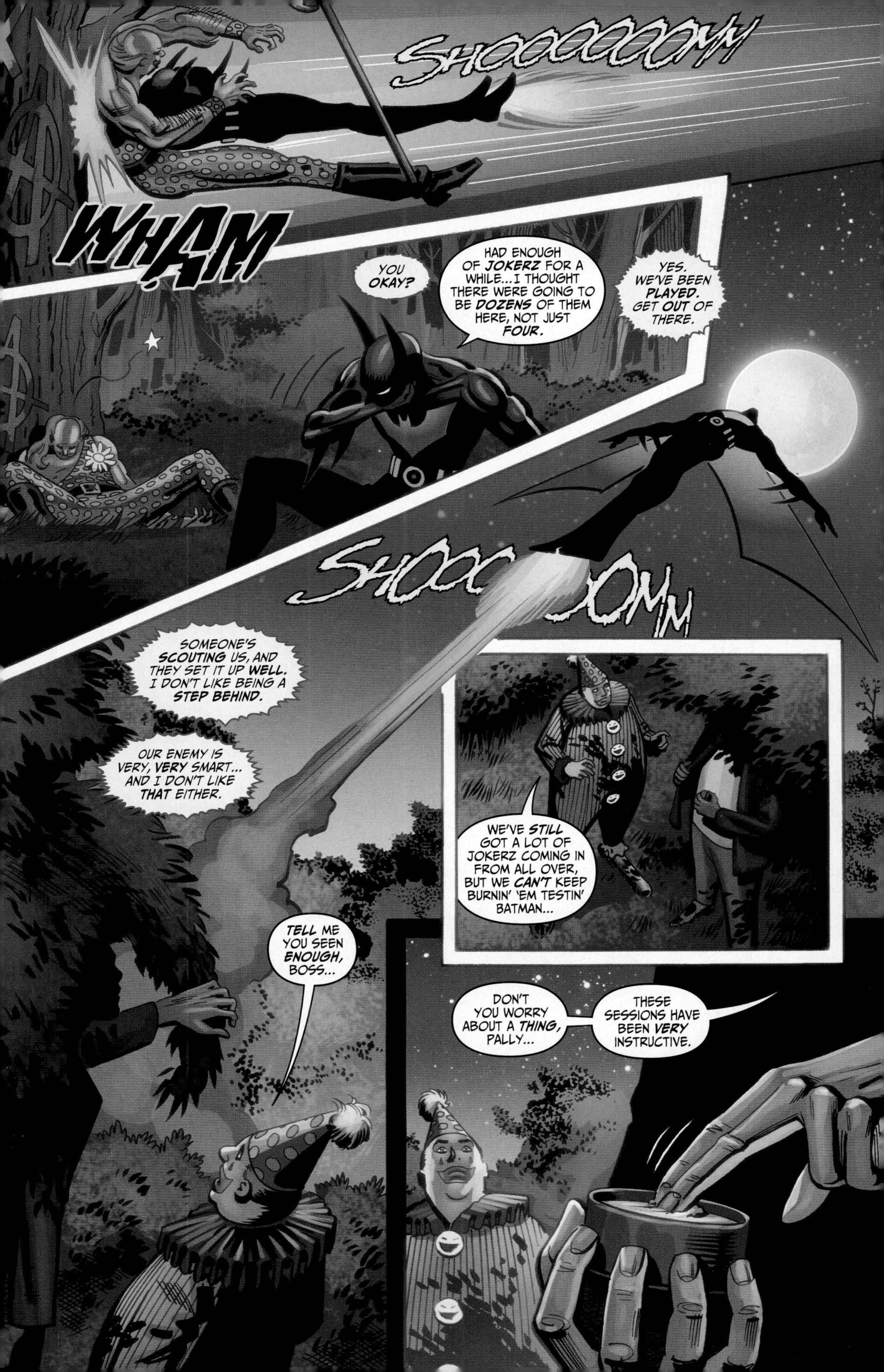
SHOOOOOOOMM
WHAM
YOU OKAY?
HAD ENOUGH OF JOKERZ FOR A WHILE... I THOUGHT THERE WERE GOING TO BE DOZENS OF THEM HERE, NOT JUST FOUR.
YES. WE'VE BEEN PLAYED. GET OUT OF THERE.
SHOOOOOOMM
SOMEONE'S SCOUTING US, AND THEY SET IT UP WELL. I DON'T LIKE BEING A STEP BEHIND.
OUR ENEMY IS VERY, VERY SMART... AND I DON'T LIKE THAT EITHER.
WE'VE STILL GOT A LOT OF JOKERZ COMING IN FROM ALL OVER, BUT WE CAN'T KEEP BURNIN' 'EM TESTIN' BATMAN...
TELL ME YOU SEEN ENOUGH, BOSS...
DON'T YOU WORRY ABOUT A THING, PALLY...
THESE SESSIONS HAVE BEEN VERY INSTRUCTIVE.

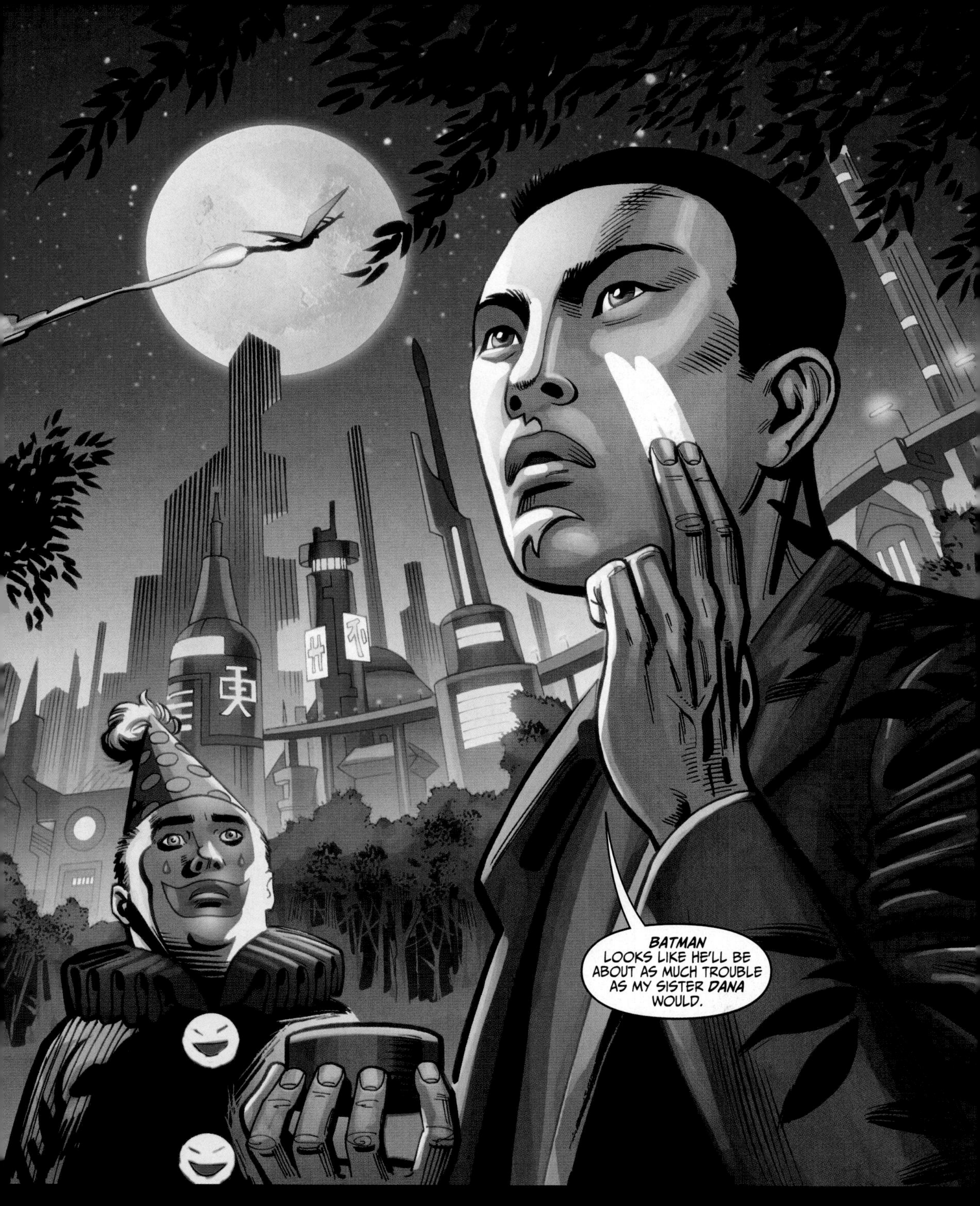
BATMAN LOOKS LIKE HE'LL BE ABOUT AS MUCH TROUBLE AS MY SISTER DANA WOULD.

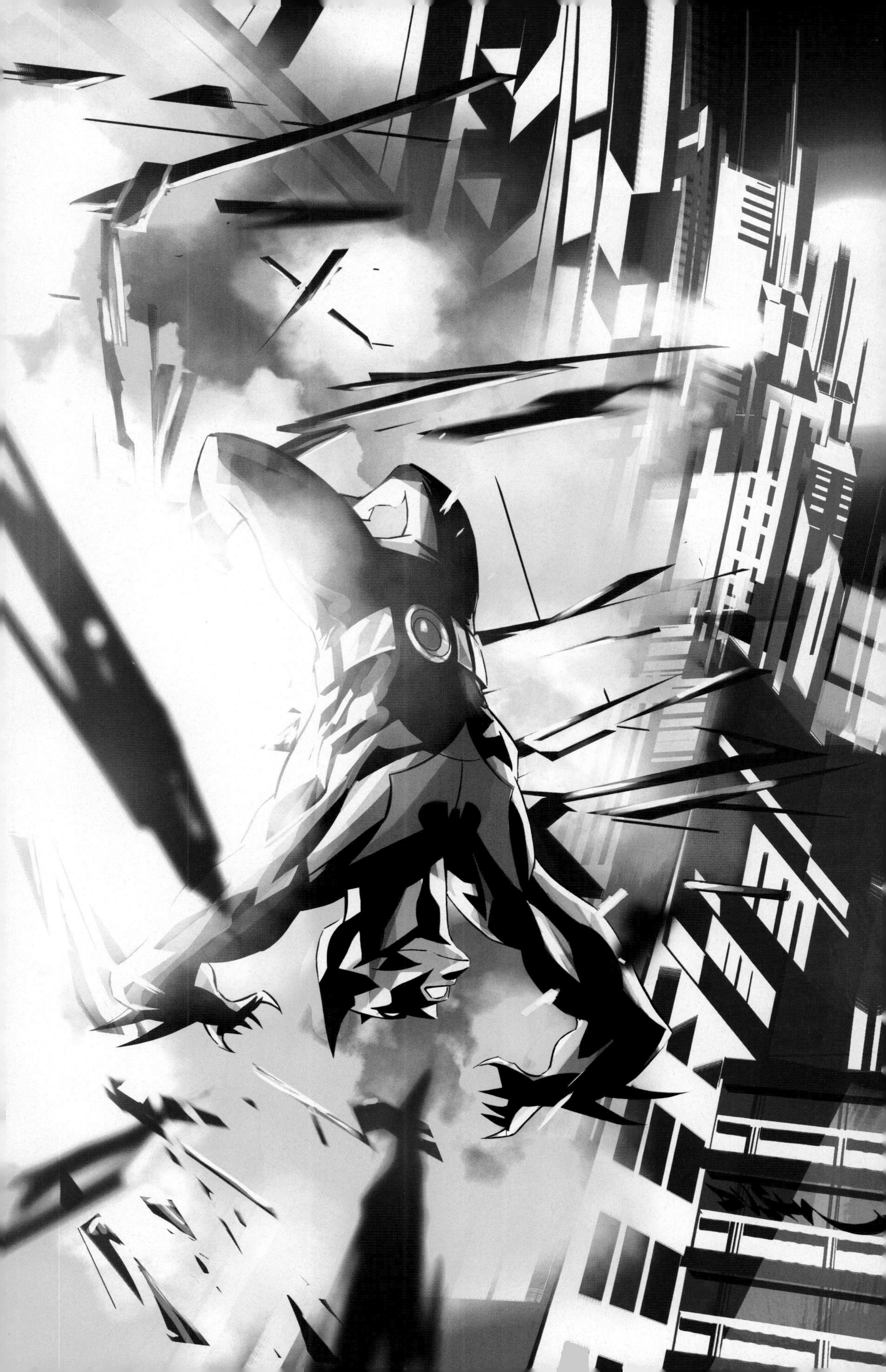

THE TRIGGER MAN

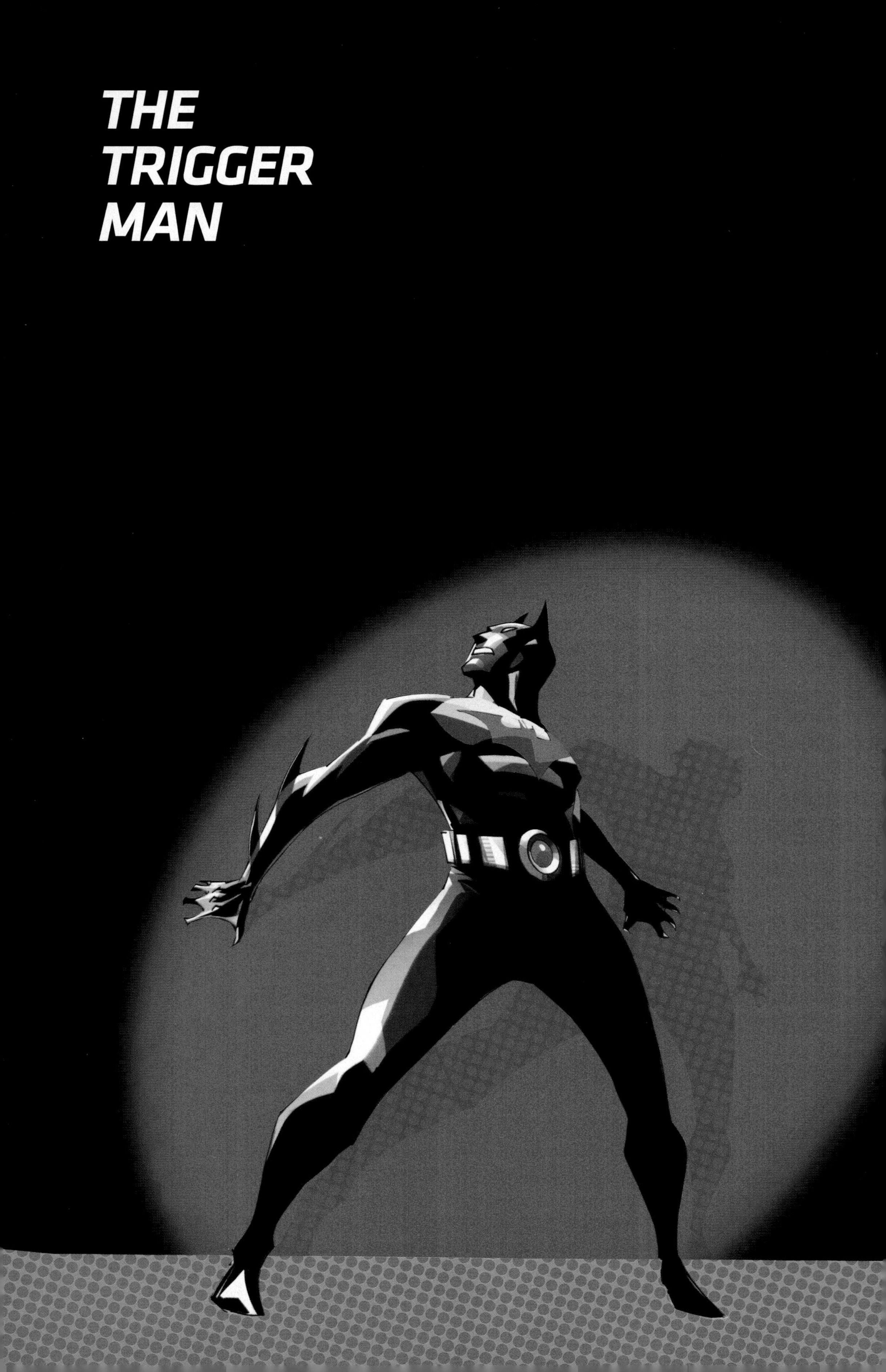

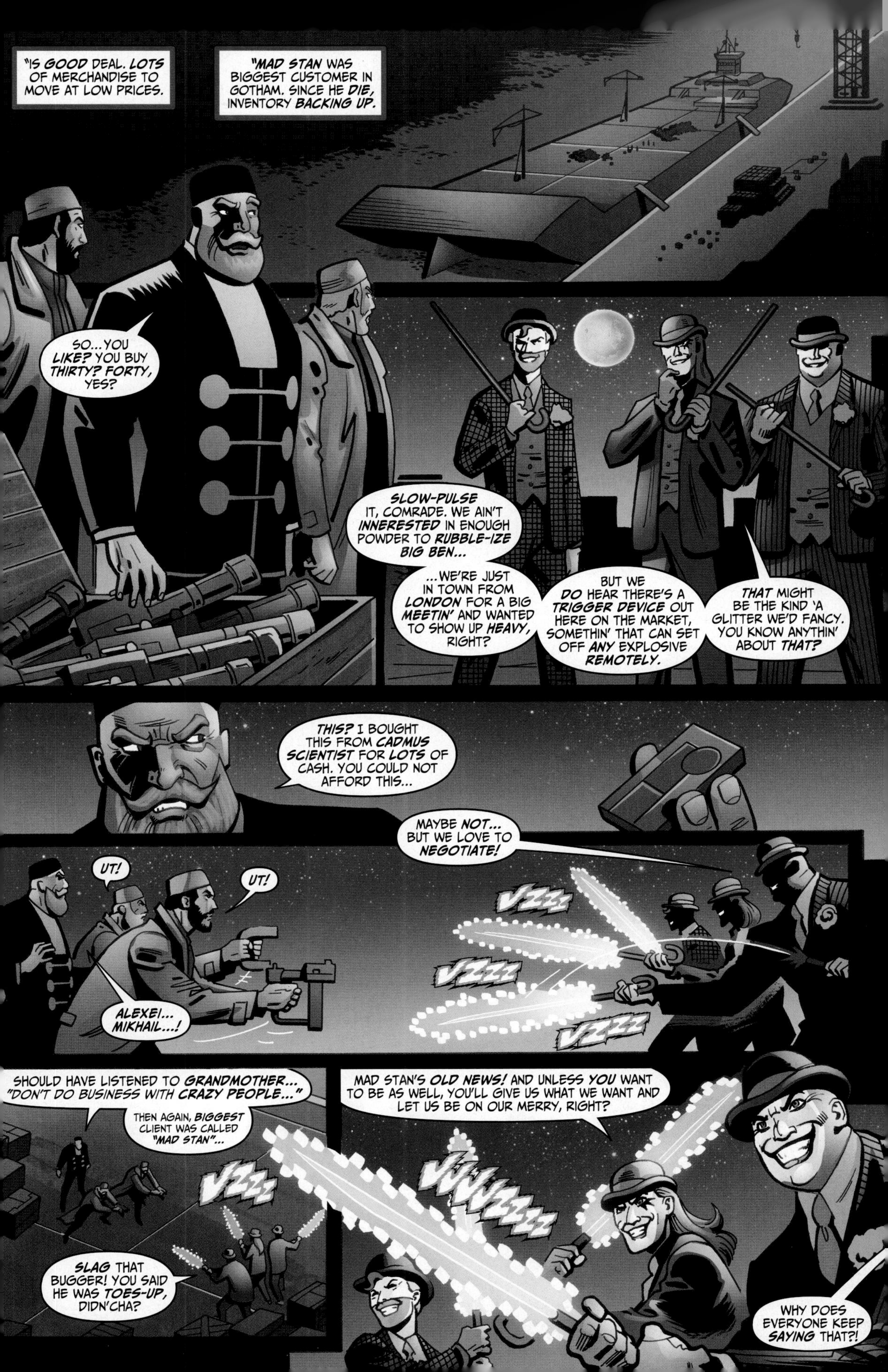

"IS GOOD DEAL. LOTS OF MERCHANDISE TO MOVE AT LOW PRICES.
"MAD STAN WAS BIGGEST CUSTOMER IN GOTHAM. SINCE HE DIE, INVENTORY BACKING UP.
SO...YOU LIKE? YOU BUY THIRTY? FORTY, YES?
SLOW-PULSE IT, COMRADE. WE AIN'T INNERESTED IN ENOUGH POWDER TO RUBBLE-IZE BIG BEN...
...WE'RE JUST IN TOWN FROM LONDON FOR A BIG MEETIN' AND WANTED TO SHOW UP HEAVY, RIGHT?
BUT WE DO HEAR THERE'S A TRIGGER DEVICE OUT HERE ON THE MARKET, SOMETHIN' THAT CAN SET OFF ANY EXPLOSIVE REMOTELY.
THAT MIGHT BE THE KIND 'A GLITTER WE'D FANCY. YOU KNOW ANYTHIN' ABOUT THAT?
THIS? I BOUGHT THIS FROM CADMUS SCIENTIST FOR LOTS OF CASH. YOU COULD NOT AFFORD THIS...
MAYBE NOT... BUT WE LOVE TO NEGOTIATE!
UT!
UT!
VZZZ
VZZZ
VZZZ
ALEXEI... MIKHAIL...!
SHOULD HAVE LISTENED TO GRANDMOTHER... "DON'T DO BUSINESS WITH CRAZY PEOPLE..."
THEN AGAIN, BIGGEST CLIENT WAS CALLED "MAD STAN"...
VZZZ
SLAG THAT BUGGER! YOU SAID HE WAS TOES-UP, DIDN'CHA?
MAD STAN'S OLD NEWS! AND UNLESS YOU WANT TO BE AS WELL, YOU'LL GIVE US WHAT WE WANT AND LET US BE ON OUR MERRY, RIGHT?
VVVVZZZZ
WHY DOES EVERYONE KEEP SAYING THAT?!

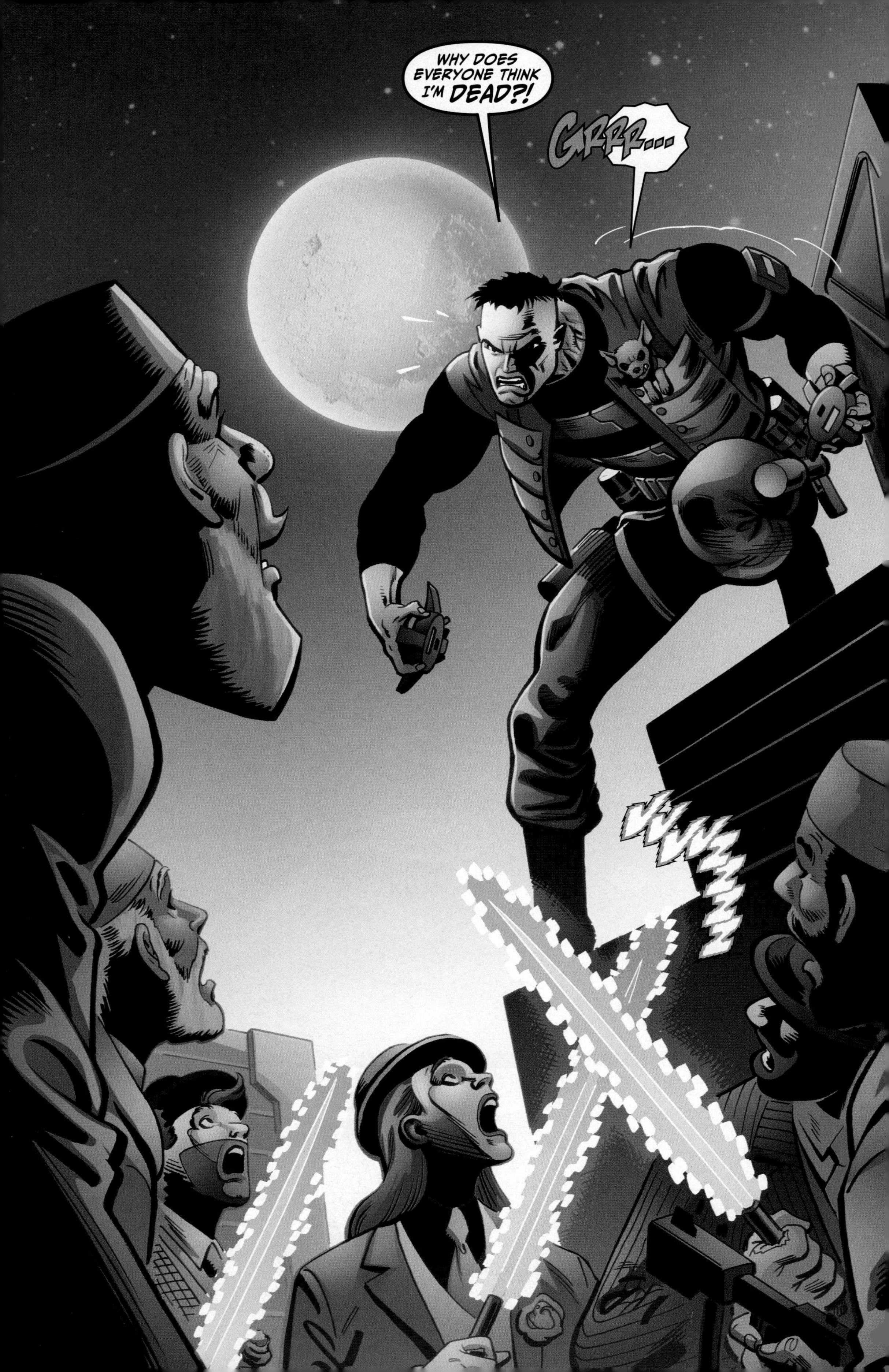
WHY DOES EVERYONE THINK I'M DEAD?!
GRRR...
VVVVMMMM

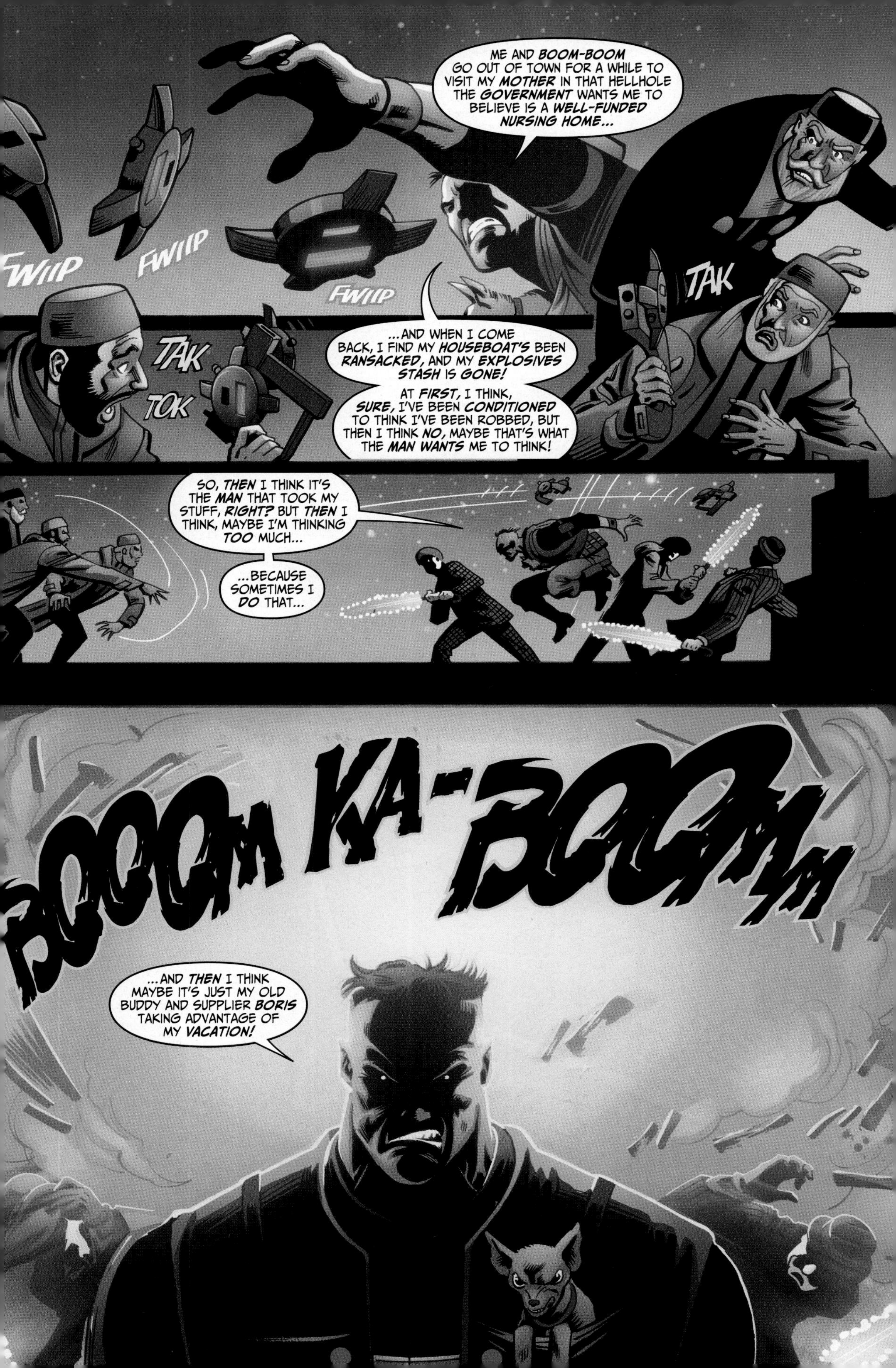
FWIIP
FWIIP
FWIIP
ME AND BOOM-BOOM GO OUT OF TOWN FOR A WHILE TO VISIT MY MOTHER IN THAT HELLHOLE THE GOVERNMENT WANTS ME TO BELIEVE IS A WELL-FUNDED NURSING HOME...
TAK
TAK
TOK
...AND WHEN I COME BACK, I FIND MY HOUSEBOAT'S BEEN RANSACKED, AND MY EXPLOSIVES STASH IS GONE!
AT FIRST, I THINK, SURE, I'VE BEEN CONDITIONED TO THINK I'VE BEEN ROBBED, BUT THEN I THINK NO, MAYBE THAT'S WHAT THE MAN WANTS ME TO THINK!
SO, THEN I THINK IT'S THE MAN THAT TOOK MY STUFF, RIGHT? BUT THEN I THINK, MAYBE I'M THINKING TOO MUCH...
...BECAUSE SOMETIMES I DO THAT...
BOOM KA-BOOM
...AND THEN I THINK MAYBE IT'S JUST MY OLD BUDDY AND SUPPLIER BORIS TAKING ADVANTAGE OF MY VACATION!

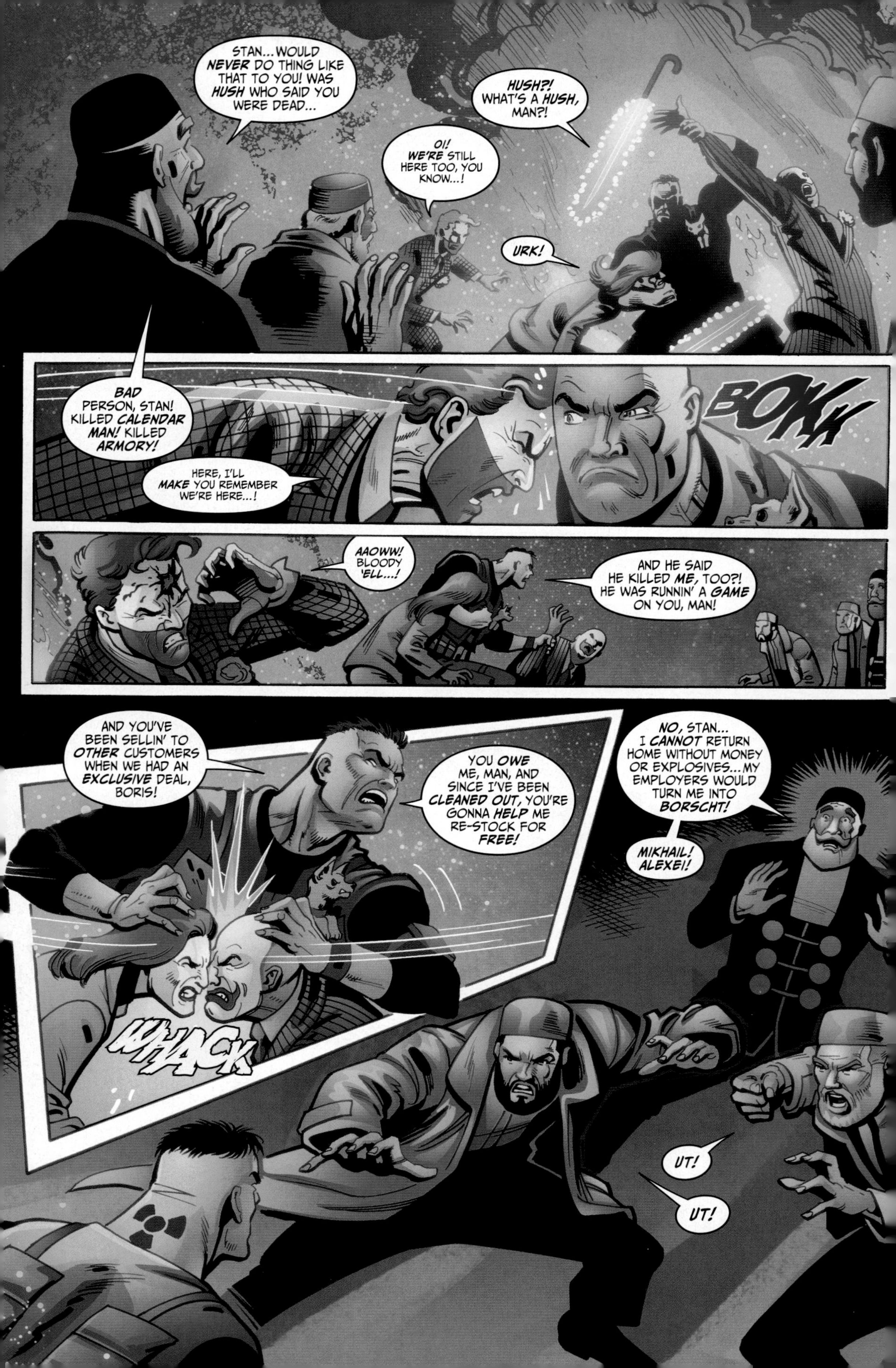
STAN... WOULD NEVER DO THING LIKE THAT TO YOU! WAS HUSH WHO SAID YOU WERE DEAD...
HUSH?! WHAT'S A HUSH, MAN?!
OI! WE'RE STILL HERE TOO, YOU KNOW...!
URK!
BAD PERSON, STAN! KILLED CALENDAR MAN! KILLED ARMORY!
HERE, I'LL MAKE YOU REMEMBER WE'RE HERE...!
BOKK
AAOWW! BLOODY 'ELL...!
AND HE SAID HE KILLED ME, TOO?! HE WAS RUNNIN' A GAME ON YOU, MAN!
AND YOU'VE BEEN SELLIN' TO OTHER CUSTOMERS WHEN WE HAD AN EXCLUSIVE DEAL, BORIS!
YOU OWE ME, MAN, AND SINCE I'VE BEEN CLEANED OUT, YOU'RE GONNA HELP ME RE-STOCK FOR FREE!
NO, STAN... I CANNOT RETURN HOME WITHOUT MONEY OR EXPLOSIVES... MY EMPLOYERS WOULD TURN ME INTO BORSCHT!
MIKHAIL! ALEXEI!
WHACK
UT!
UT!

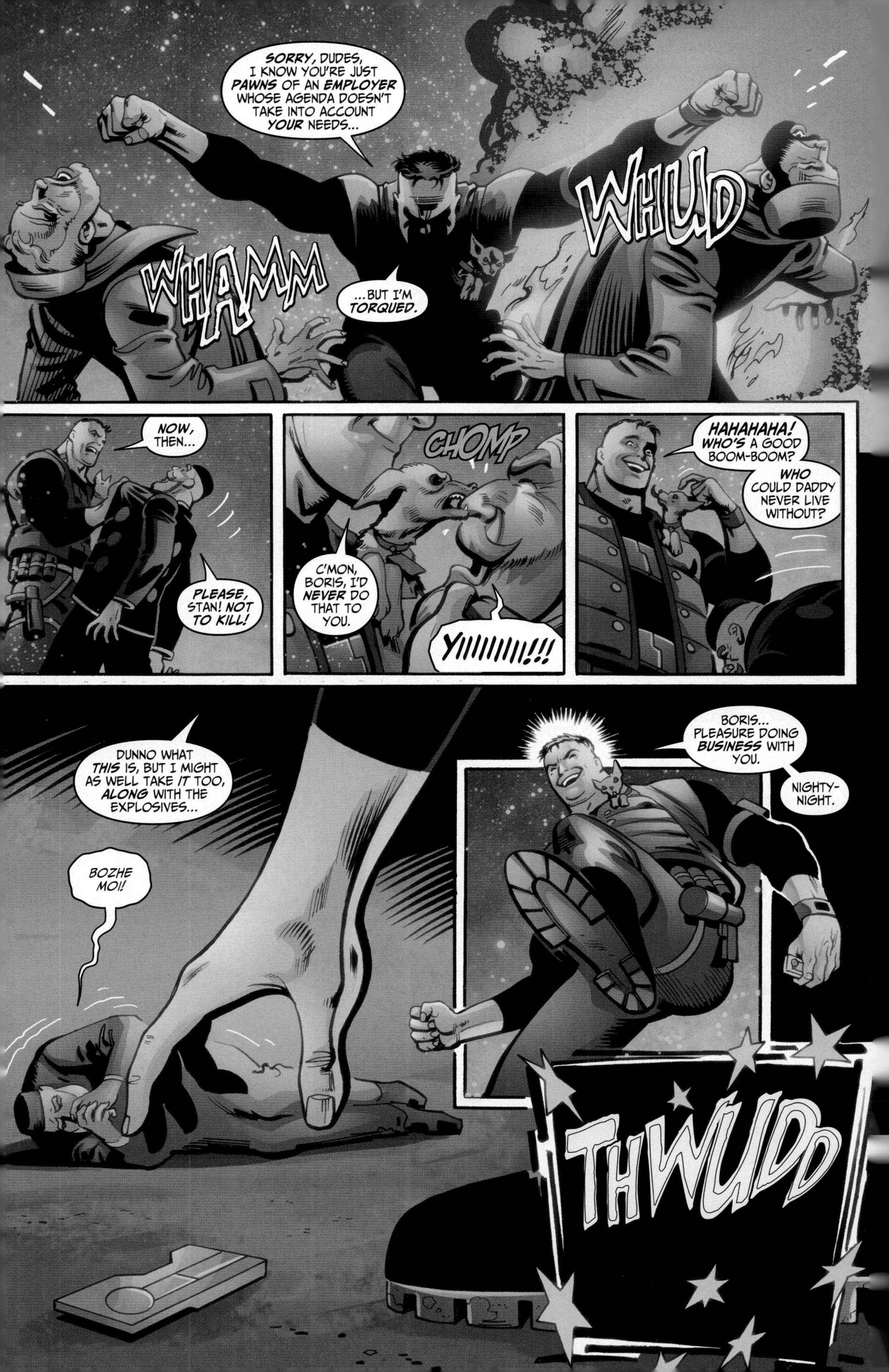
SORRY, DUDES, I KNOW YOU'RE JUST PAWNS OF AN EMPLOYER WHOSE AGENDA DOESN'T TAKE INTO ACCOUNT YOUR NEEDS...
WHAMM
WHUD
...BUT I'M TORQUED.
NOW, THEN...
PLEASE, STAN! NOT TO KILL!
CHOMP
C'MON, BORIS, I'D NEVER DO THAT TO YOU.
YIIIIIIIII!!!
HAHAHAHA! WHO'S A GOOD BOOM-BOOM?
WHO COULD DADDY NEVER LIVE WITHOUT?
DUNNO WHAT THIS IS, BUT I MIGHT AS WELL TAKE IT TOO, ALONG WITH THE EXPLOSIVES...
BOZHE MOI!
BORIS... PLEASURE DOING BUSINESS WITH YOU.
NIGHTY-NIGHT.
THWUDD

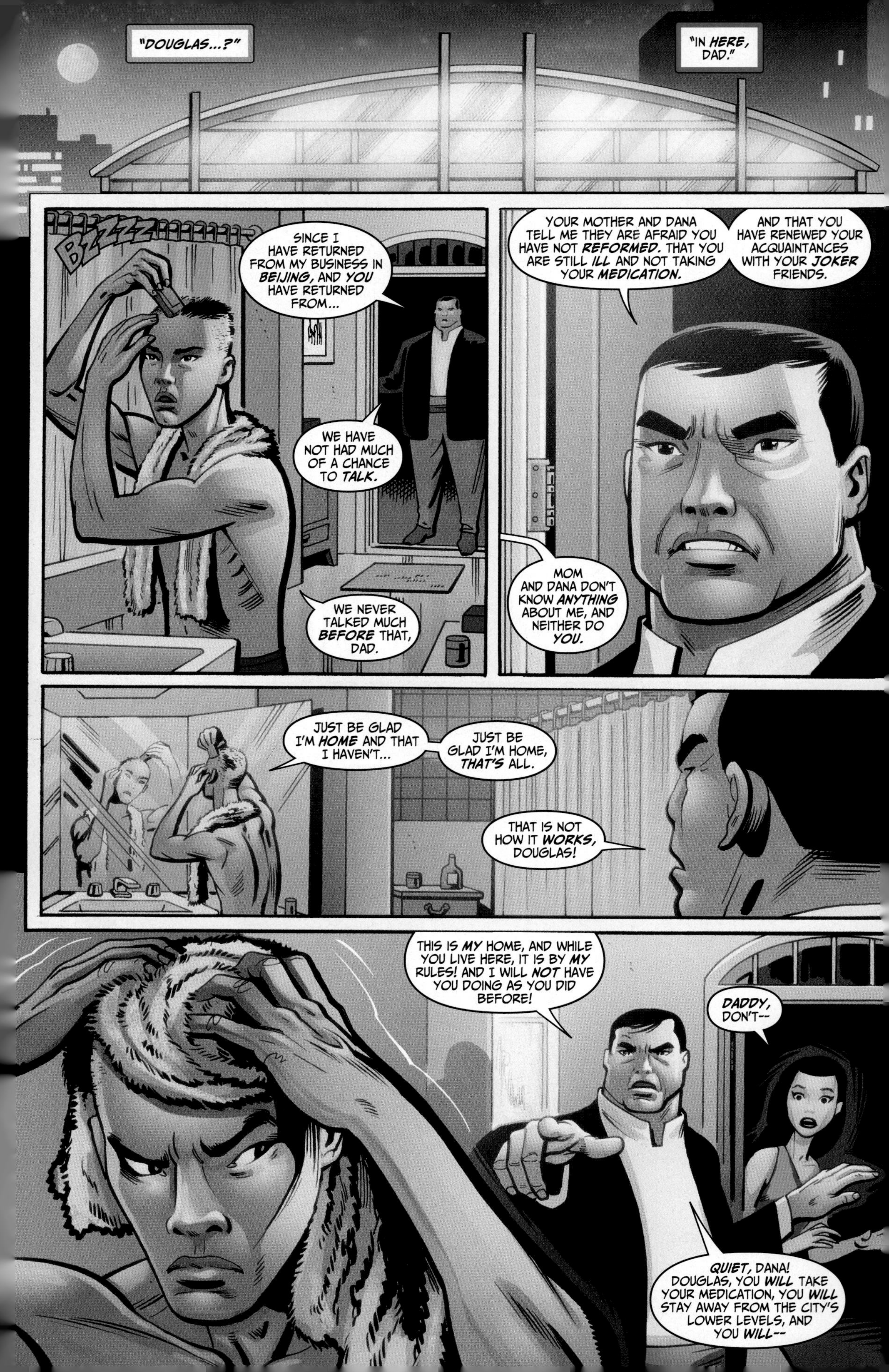
"DOUGLAS...?"
"IN HERE, DAD."
BZZZZ
SINCE I HAVE RETURNED FROM MY BUSINESS IN BEIJING, AND YOU HAVE RETURNED FROM...
WE HAVE NOT HAD MUCH OF A CHANCE TO TALK.
WE NEVER TALKED MUCH BEFORE THAT, DAD.
YOUR MOTHER AND DANA TELL ME THEY ARE AFRAID YOU HAVE NOT REFORMED. THAT YOU ARE STILL ILL AND NOT TAKING YOUR MEDICATION.
AND THAT YOU HAVE RENEWED YOUR ACQUAINTANCES WITH YOUR JOKER FRIENDS.
MOM AND DANA DON'T KNOW ANYTHING ABOUT ME, AND NEITHER DO YOU.
JUST BE GLAD I'M HOME AND THAT I HAVEN'T...
JUST BE GLAD I'M HOME, THAT'S ALL.
THAT IS NOT HOW IT WORKS, DOUGLAS!
THIS IS MY HOME, AND WHILE YOU LIVE HERE, IT IS BY MY RULES! AND I WILL NOT HAVE YOU DOING AS YOU DID BEFORE!
DADDY, DON'T--
QUIET, DANA! DOUGLAS, YOU WILL TAKE YOUR MEDICATION, YOU WILL STAY AWAY FROM THE CITY'S LOWER LEVELS, AND YOU WILL--

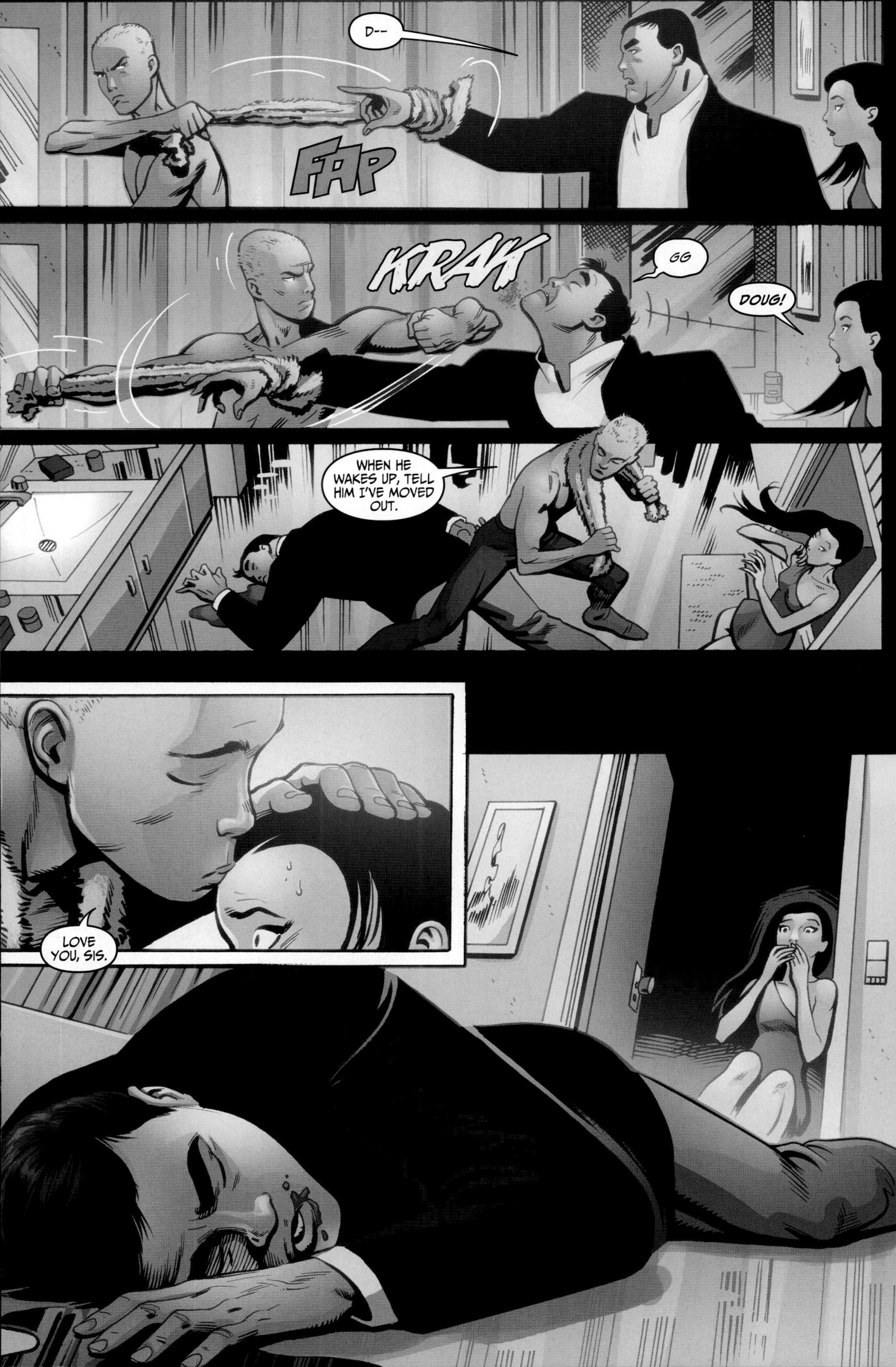
D--
FAP
KRAK
GG
DOUG!
WHEN HE WAKES UP, TELL HIM I'VE MOVED OUT.
LOVE YOU, SIS.

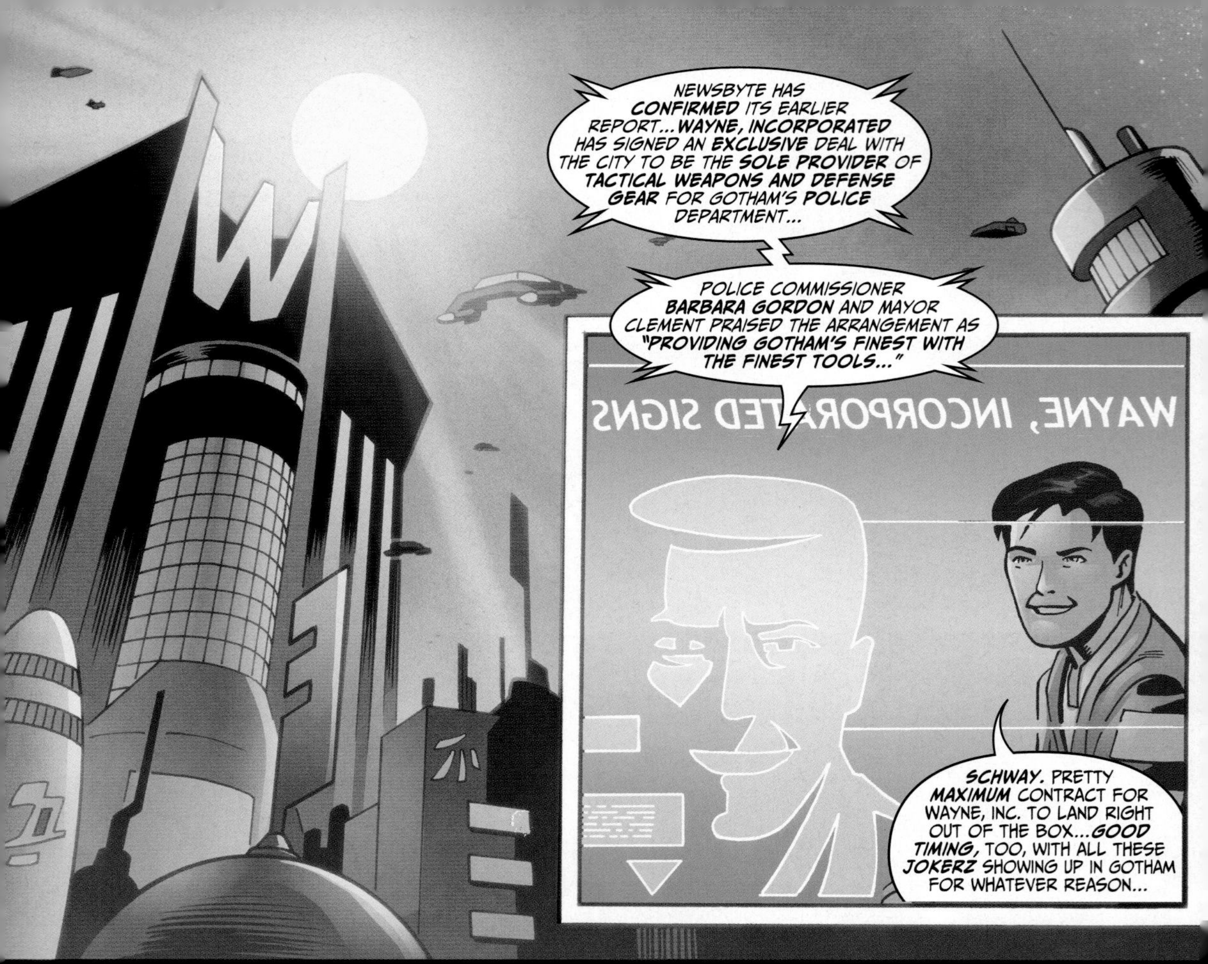

NEWSBYTE HAS CONFIRMED ITS EARLIER REPORT... WAYNE, INCORPORATED HAS SIGNED AN EXCLUSIVE DEAL WITH THE CITY TO BE THE SOLE PROVIDER OF TACTICAL WEAPONS AND DEFENSE GEAR FOR GOTHAM'S POLICE DEPARTMENT...
POLICE COMMISSIONER BARBARA GORDON AND MAYOR CLEMENT PRAISED THE ARRANGEMENT AS "PROVIDING GOTHAM'S FINEST WITH THE FINEST TOOLS..."
WAYNE, INCORPORATED SIGNS
SCHWAY. PRETTY MAXIMUM CONTRACT FOR WAYNE, INC. TO LAND RIGHT OUT OF THE BOX...GOOD TIMING, TOO, WITH ALL THESE JOKERZ SHOWING UP IN GOTHAM FOR WHATEVER REASON...

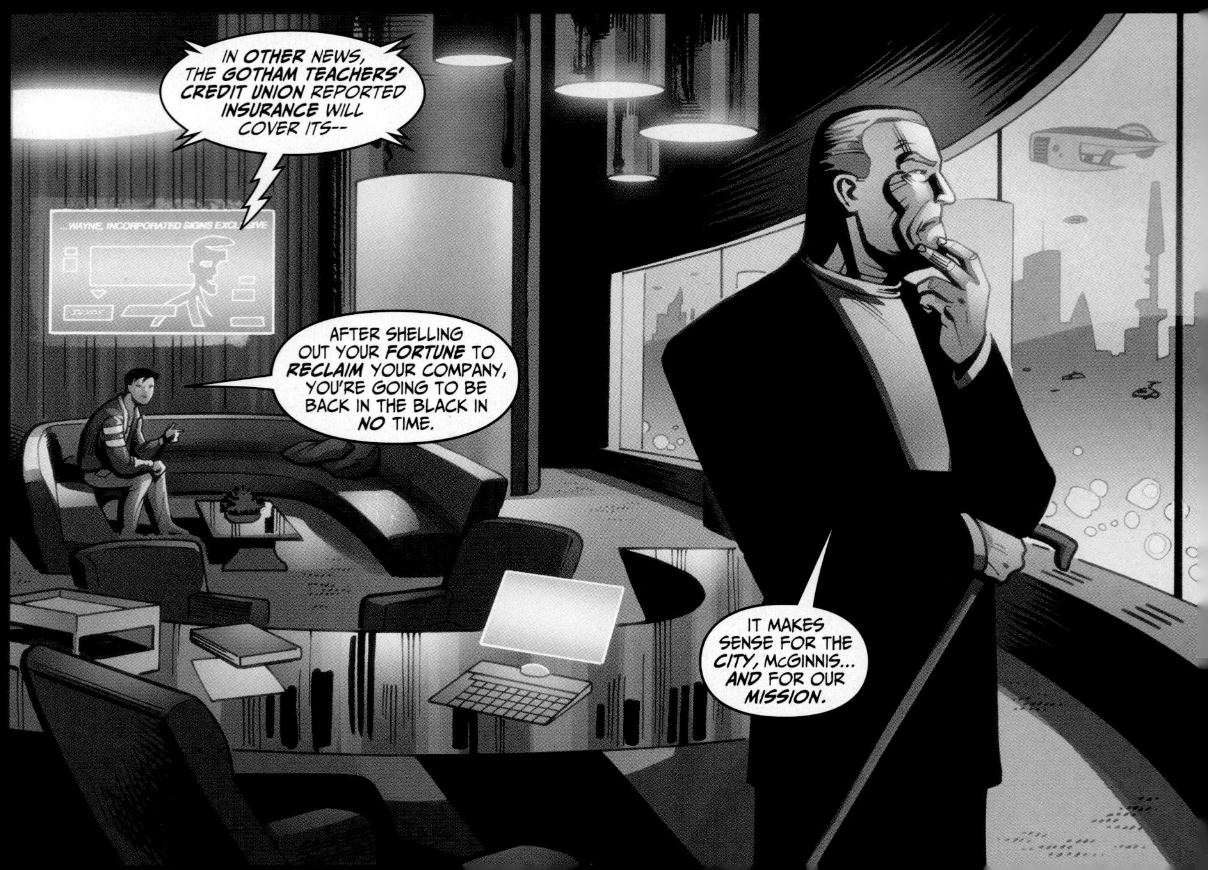

IN OTHER NEWS, THE GOTHAM TEACHERS' CREDIT UNION REPORTED INSURANCE WILL COVER ITS--
...WAYNE, INCORPORATED SIGNS EXCLUSIVE
AFTER SHELLING OUT YOUR FORTUNE TO RECLAIM YOUR COMPANY, YOU'RE GOING TO BE BACK IN THE BLACK IN NO TIME.
IT MAKES SENSE FOR THE CITY, McGINNIS... AND FOR OUR MISSION.

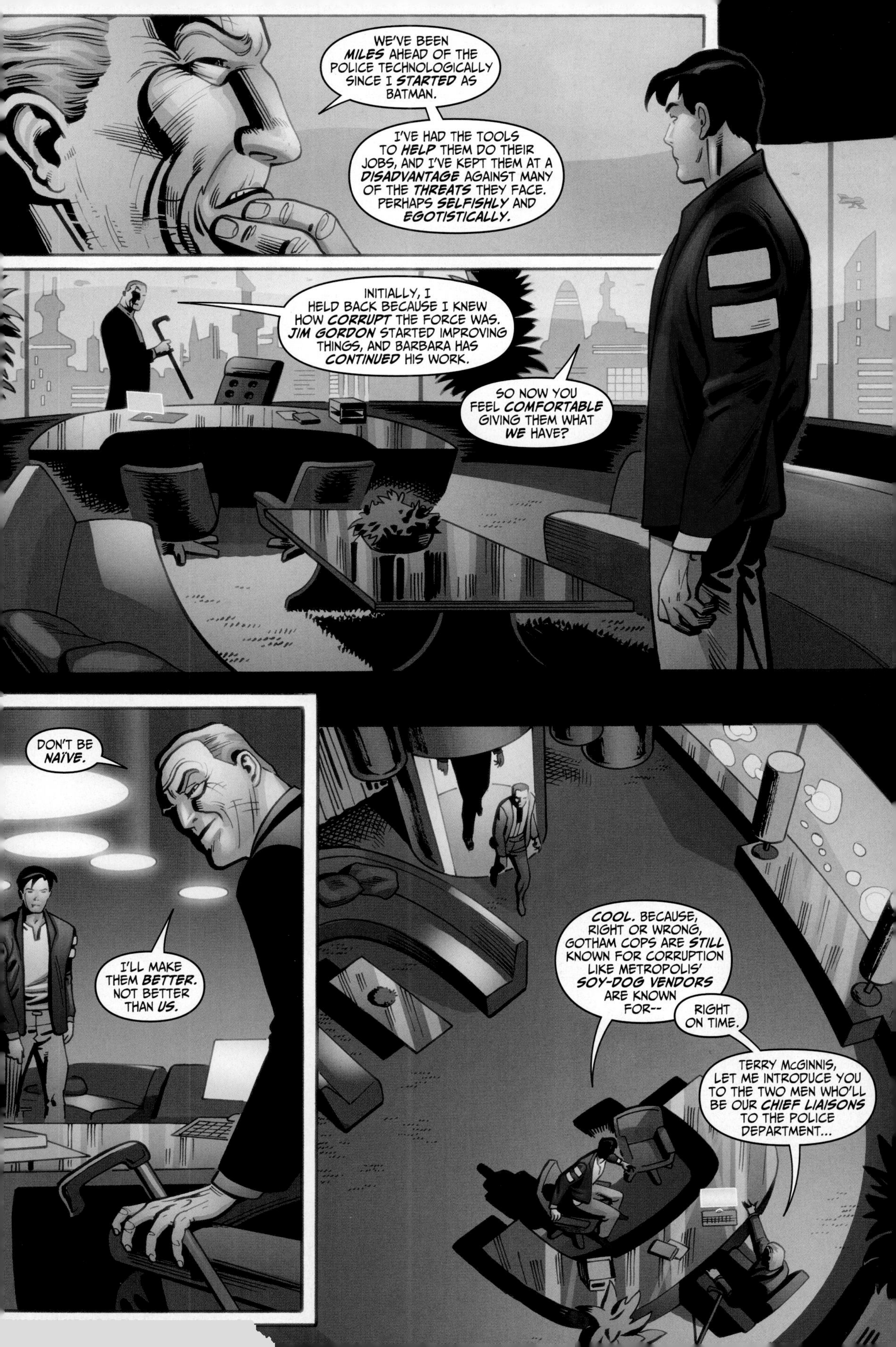
WE'VE BEEN MILES AHEAD OF THE POLICE TECHNOLOGICALLY SINCE I STARTED AS BATMAN.
I'VE HAD THE TOOLS TO HELP THEM DO THEIR JOBS, AND I'VE KEPT THEM AT A DISADVANTAGE AGAINST MANY OF THE THREATS THEY FACE. PERHAPS SELFISHLY AND EGOTISTICALLY.
INITIALLY, I HELD BACK BECAUSE I KNEW HOW CORRUPT THE FORCE WAS. JIM GORDON STARTED IMPROVING THINGS, AND BARBARA HAS CONTINUED HIS WORK.
SO NOW YOU FEEL COMFORTABLE GIVING THEM WHAT WE HAVE?
DON'T BE NAÏVE.
I'LL MAKE THEM BETTER. NOT BETTER THAN US.
COOL. BECAUSE, RIGHT OR WRONG, GOTHAM COPS ARE STILL KNOWN FOR CORRUPTION LIKE METROPOLIS' SOY-DOG VENDORS ARE KNOWN FOR--
RIGHT ON TIME.
TERRY McGINNIS, LET ME INTRODUCE YOU TO THE TWO MEN WHO'LL BE OUR CHIEF LIAISONS TO THE POLICE DEPARTMENT...

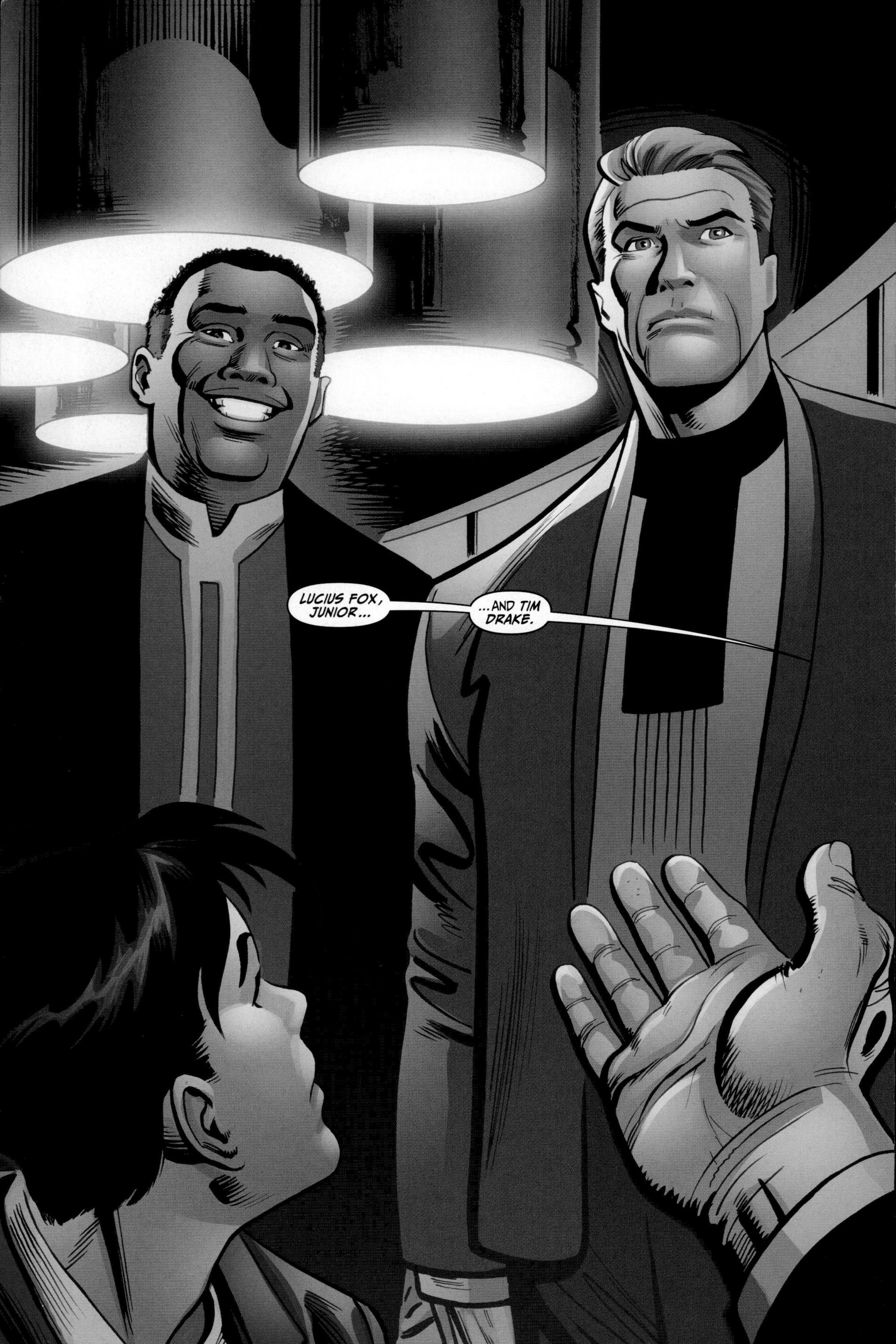
LUCIUS FOX, JUNIOR...
...AND TIM DRAKE.

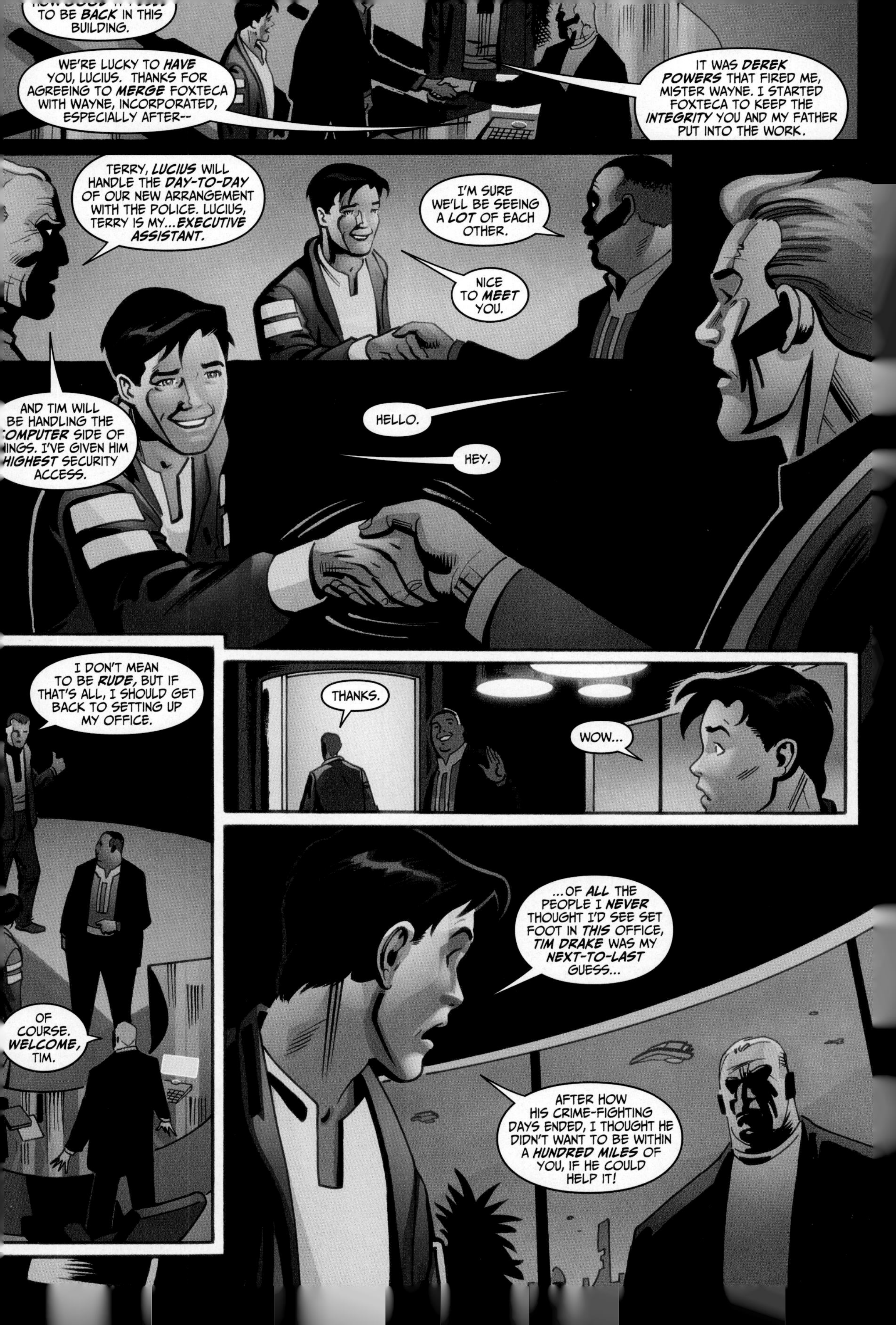
TO BE BACK IN THIS BUILDING.
WE'RE LUCKY TO HAVE YOU, LUCIUS. THANKS FOR AGREEING TO MERGE FOXTECA WITH WAYNE, INCORPORATED, ESPECIALLY AFTER--
IT WAS DEREK POWERS THAT FIRED ME, MISTER WAYNE. I STARTED FOXTECA TO KEEP THE INTEGRITY YOU AND MY FATHER PUT INTO THE WORK.
TERRY, LUCIUS WILL HANDLE THE DAY-TO-DAY OF OUR NEW ARRANGEMENT WITH THE POLICE. LUCIUS, TERRY IS MY...EXECUTIVE ASSISTANT.
I'M SURE WE'LL BE SEEING A LOT OF EACH OTHER.
NICE TO MEET YOU.
AND TIM WILL BE HANDLING THE OMPUTER SIDE OF INGS. I'VE GIVEN HIM HIGHEST SECURITY ACCESS.
HELLO.
HEY.
I DON'T MEAN TO BE RUDE, BUT IF THAT'S ALL, I SHOULD GET BACK TO SETTING UP MY OFFICE.
OF COURSE. WELCOME, TIM.
THANKS.
WOW...
...OF ALL THE PEOPLE I NEVER THOUGHT I'D SEE SET FOOT IN THIS OFFICE, TIM DRAKE WAS MY NEXT-TO-LAST GUESS...
AFTER HOW HIS CRIME-FIGHTING DAYS ENDED, I THOUGHT HE DIDN'T WANT TO BE WITHIN A HUNDRED MILES OF YOU, IF HE COULD HELP IT!

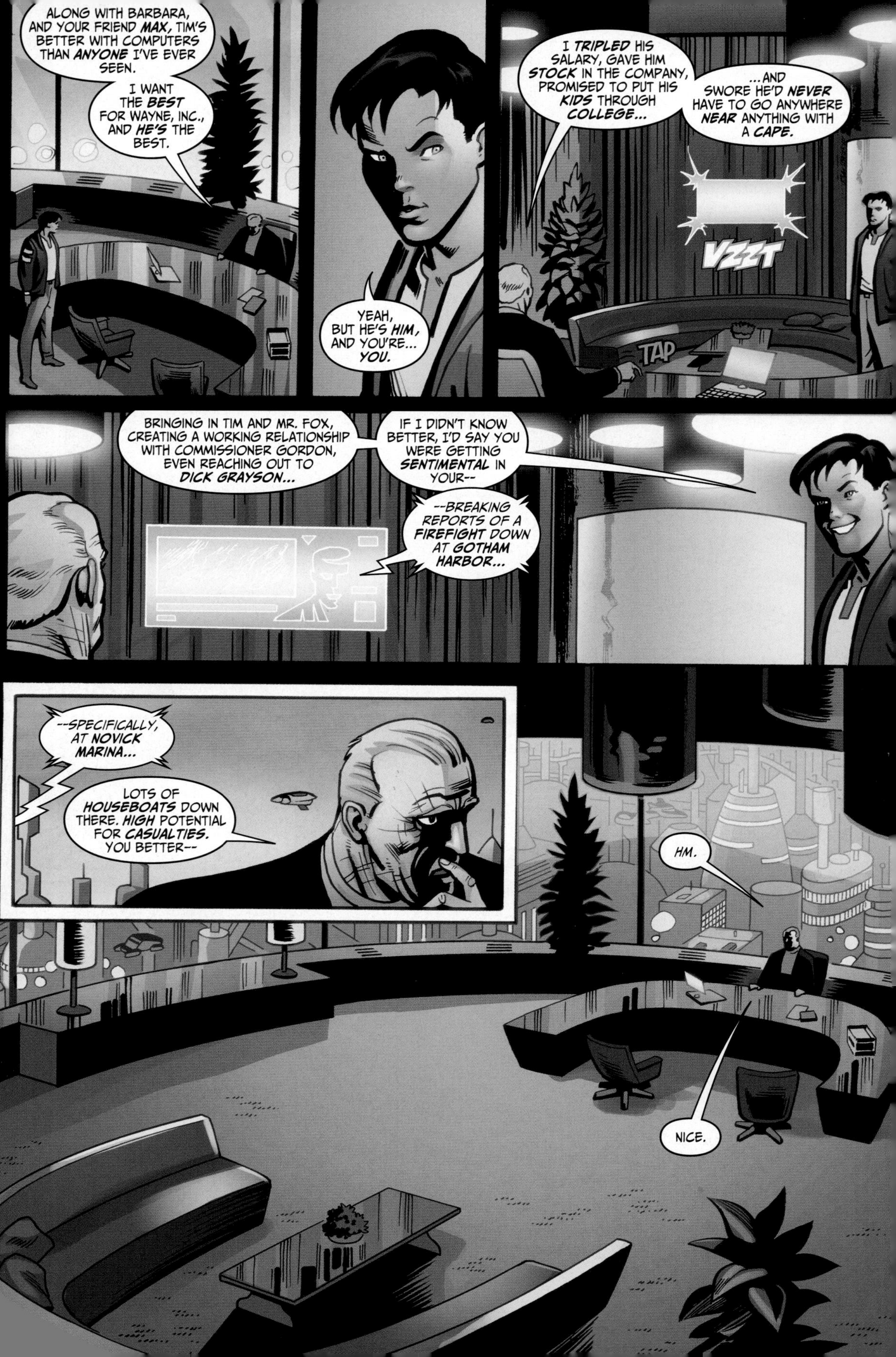
ALONG WITH BARBARA, AND YOUR FRIEND MAX, TIM'S BETTER WITH COMPUTERS THAN ANYONE I'VE EVER SEEN.
I WANT THE BEST FOR WAYNE, INC., AND HE'S THE BEST.
YEAH, BUT HE'S HIM, AND YOU'RE... YOU.
I TRIPLED HIS SALARY, GAVE HIM STOCK IN THE COMPANY, PROMISED TO PUT HIS KIDS THROUGH COLLEGE...
...AND SWORE HE'D NEVER HAVE TO GO ANYWHERE NEAR ANYTHING WITH A CAPE.
VZZT
TAP
BRINGING IN TIM AND MR. FOX, CREATING A WORKING RELATIONSHIP WITH COMMISSIONER GORDON, EVEN REACHING OUT TO DICK GRAYSON...
IF I DIDN'T KNOW BETTER, I'D SAY YOU WERE GETTING SENTIMENTAL IN YOUR--
--BREAKING REPORTS OF A FIREFIGHT DOWN AT GOTHAM HARBOR...
--SPECIFICALLY, AT NOVICK MARINA...
LOTS OF HOUSEBOATS DOWN THERE. HIGH POTENTIAL FOR CASUALTIES. YOU BETTER--
HM.
NICE.

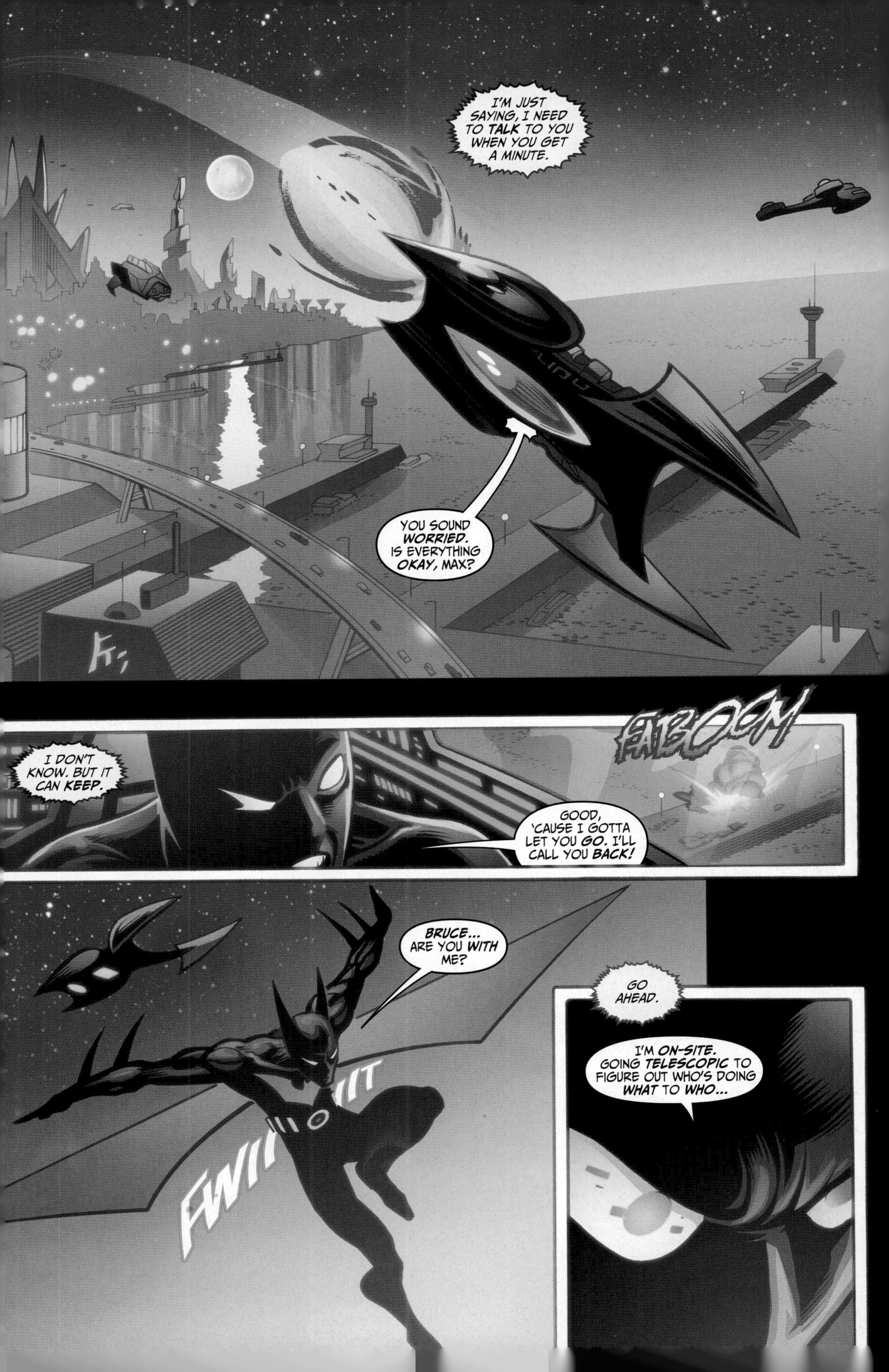
I'M JUST SAYING, I NEED TO TALK TO YOU WHEN YOU GET A MINUTE.
YOU SOUND WORRIED. IS EVERYTHING OKAY, MAX?
FABOOM
I DON'T KNOW. BUT IT CAN KEEP.
GOOD, 'CAUSE I GOTTA LET YOU GO. I'LL CALL YOU BACK!
BRUCE... ARE YOU WITH ME?
FWIIIIIT
GO AHEAD.
I'M ON-SITE. GOING TELESCOPIC TO FIGURE OUT WHO'S DOING WHAT TO WHO...

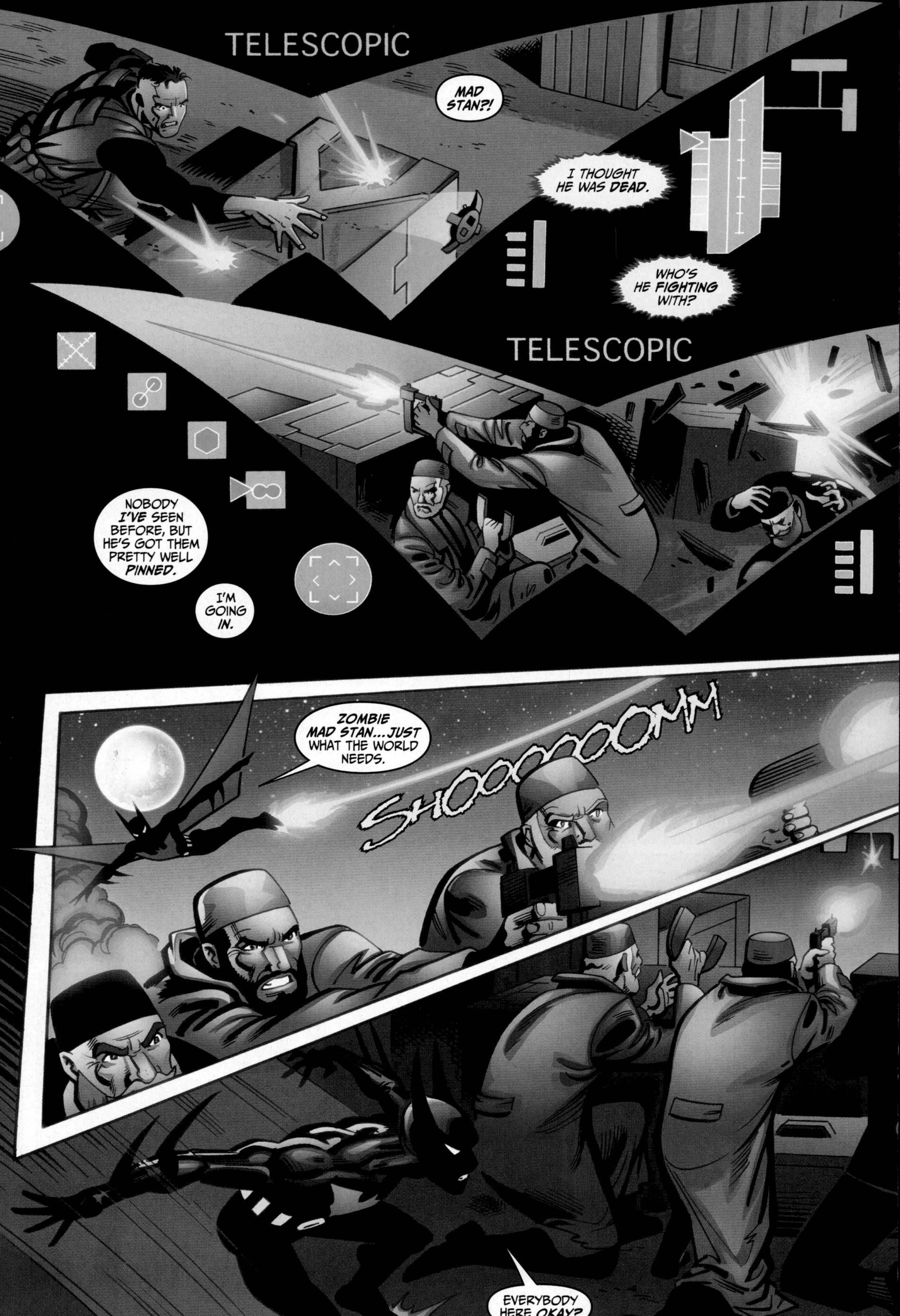
TELESCOPIC
MAD STAN?!
I THOUGHT HE WAS DEAD.
WHO'S HE FIGHTING WITH?
TELESCOPIC
NOBODY I'VE SEEN BEFORE, BUT HE'S GOT THEM PRETTY WELL PINNED.
I'M GOING IN.
ZOMBIE MAD STAN... JUST WHAT THE WORLD NEEDS.
SHOOOOOOOMM
EVERYBODY HERE OKAY?

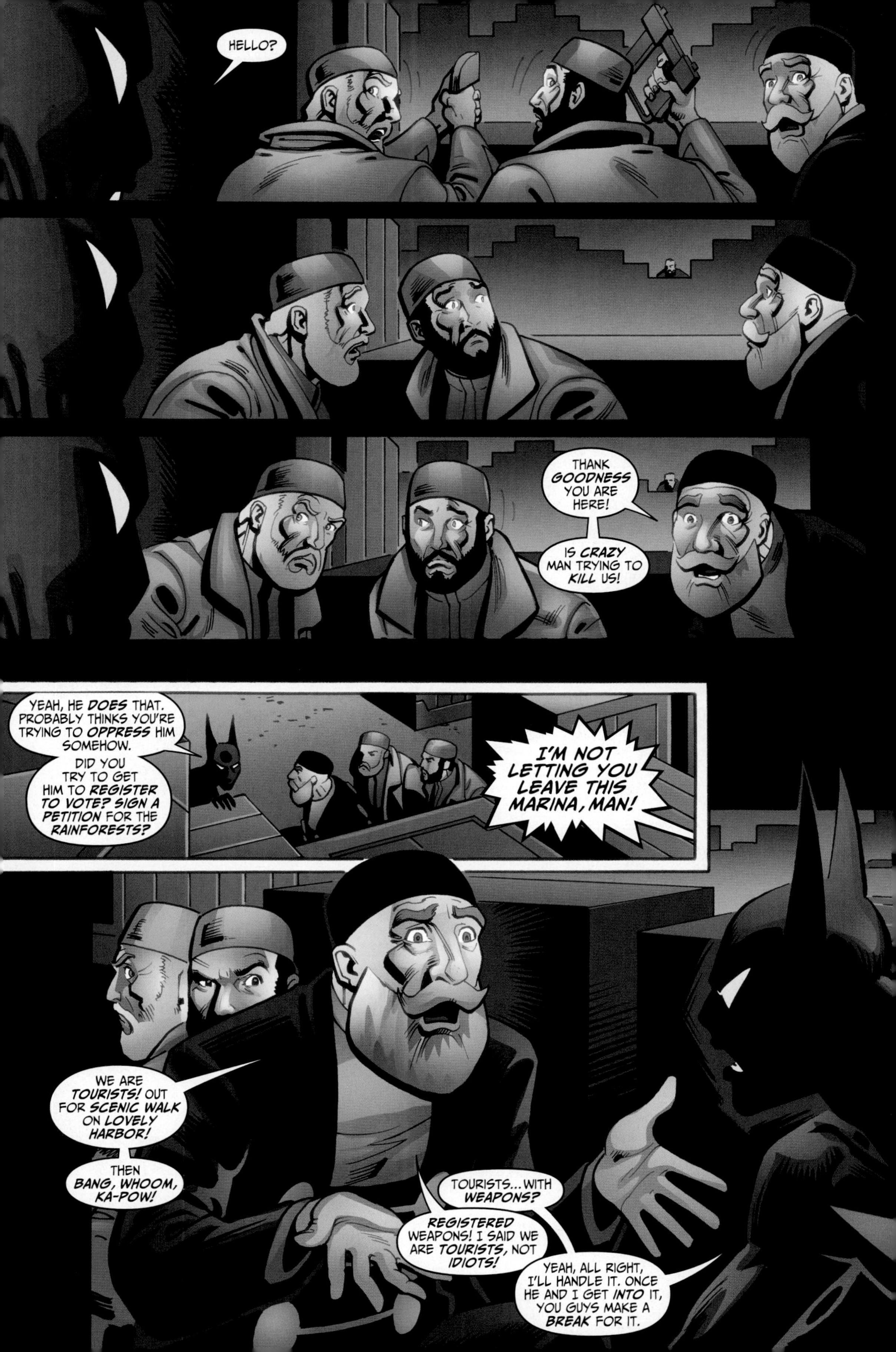
HELLO?
THANK GOODNESS YOU ARE HERE!
IS CRAZY MAN TRYING TO KILL US!
YEAH, HE DOES THAT. PROBABLY THINKS YOU'RE TRYING TO OPPRESS HIM SOMEHOW.
DID YOU TRY TO GET HIM TO REGISTER TO VOTE? SIGN A PETITION FOR THE RAINFORESTS?
I'M NOT LETTING YOU LEAVE THIS MARINA, MAN!
WE ARE TOURISTS! OUT FOR SCENIC WALK ON LOVELY HARBOR!
THEN BANG, WHOOM, KA-POW!
TOURISTS... WITH WEAPONS?
REGISTERED WEAPONS! I SAID WE ARE TOURISTS, NOT IDIOTS!
YEAH, ALL RIGHT, I'LL HANDLE IT. ONCE HE AND I GET INTO IT, YOU GUYS MAKE A BREAK FOR IT.

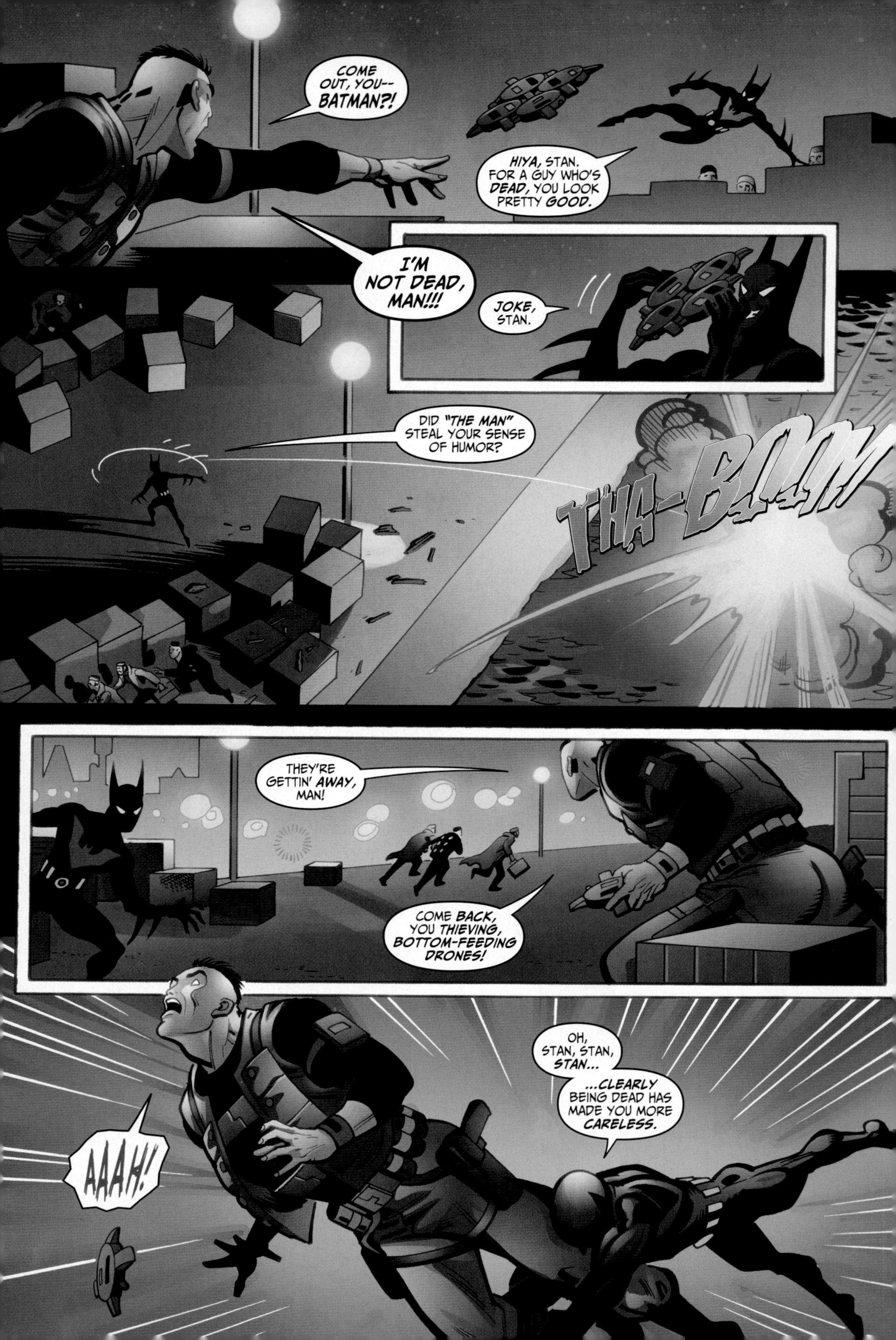
COME OUT, YOU-- BATMAN?!
HIYA, STAN. FOR A GUY WHO'S DEAD, YOU LOOK PRETTY GOOD.
I'M NOT DEAD, MAN!!!
JOKE, STAN.
DID "THE MAN" STEAL YOUR SENSE OF HUMOR?
THA-BOOM
THEY'RE GETTIN' AWAY, MAN!
COME BACK, YOU THIEVING, BOTTOM-FEEDING DRONES!
OH, STAN, STAN, STAN...
...CLEARLY BEING DEAD HAS MADE YOU MORE CARELESS.
AAAH!

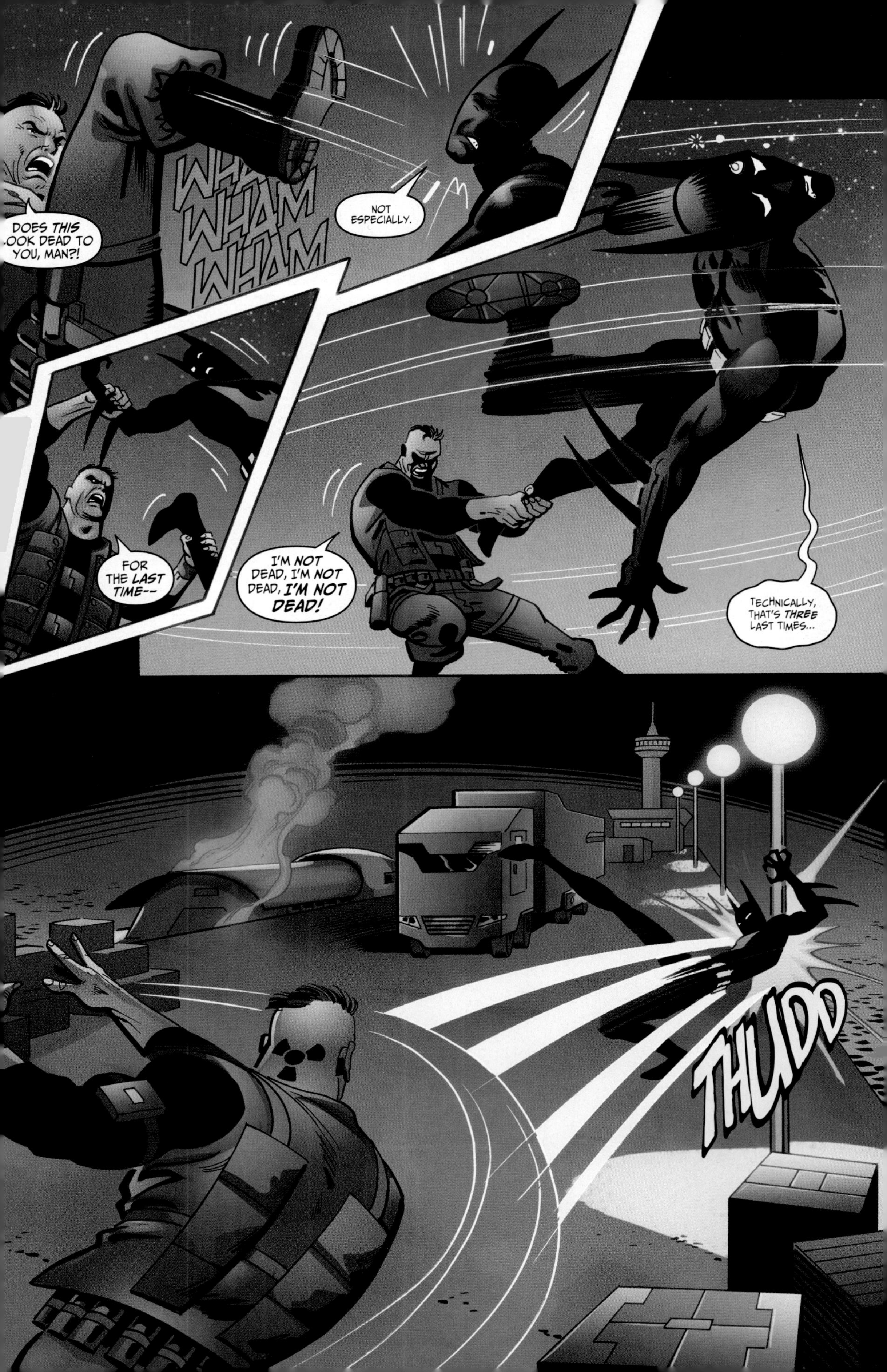
DOES THIS LOOK DEAD TO YOU, MAN?!
WHAM WHAM WHAM
NOT ESPECIALLY.
FOR THE LAST TIME--
I'M NOT DEAD, I'M NOT DEAD, I'M NOT DEAD!
TECHNICALLY, THAT'S THREE LAST TIMES...
THUDD

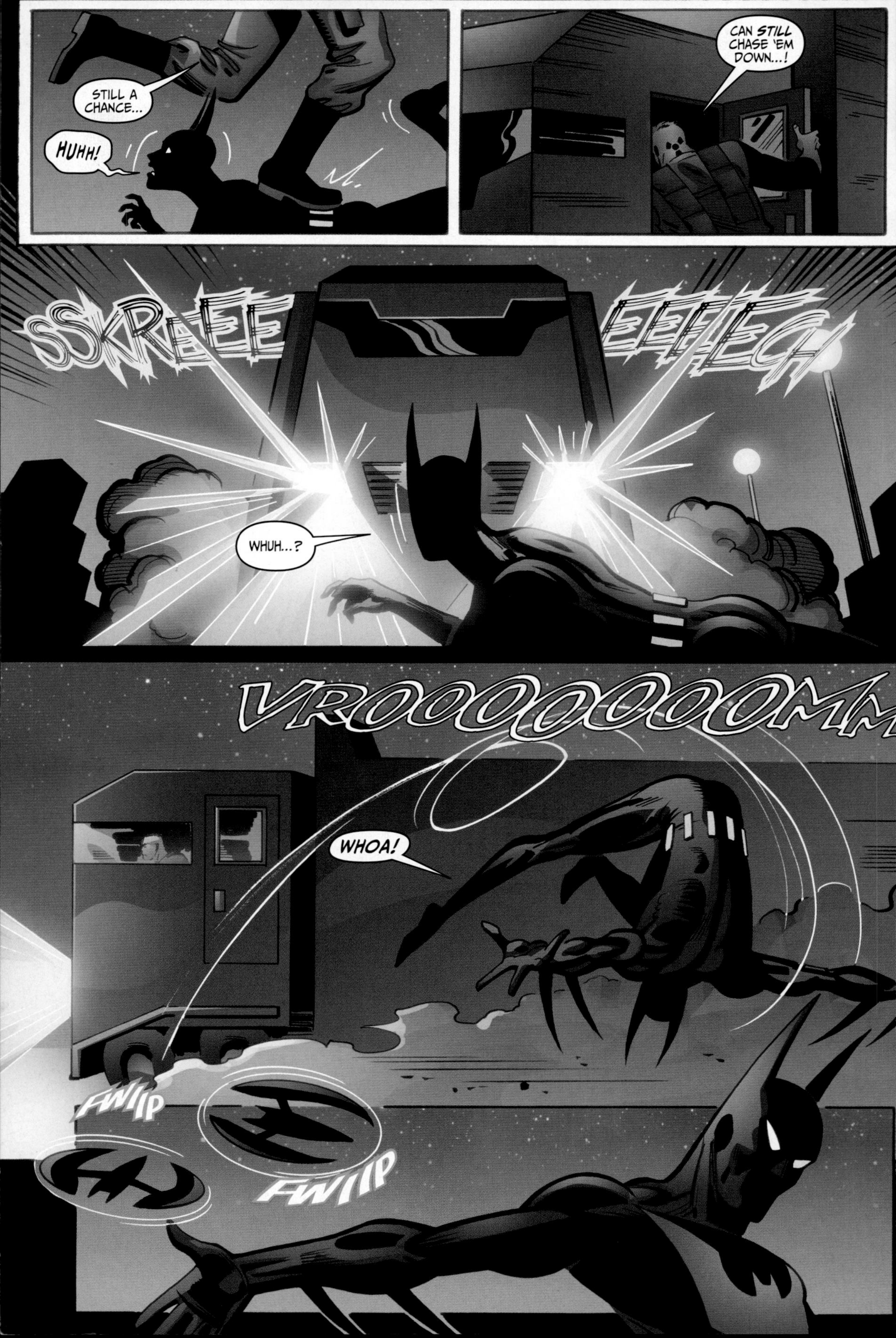
STILL A CHANCE...
HUHH!
CAN STILL CHASE 'EM DOWN...!
SSKREEEEEEEECH
WHUH...?
VROOOOOOOOMM
WHOA!
FWIIP
FWIIP

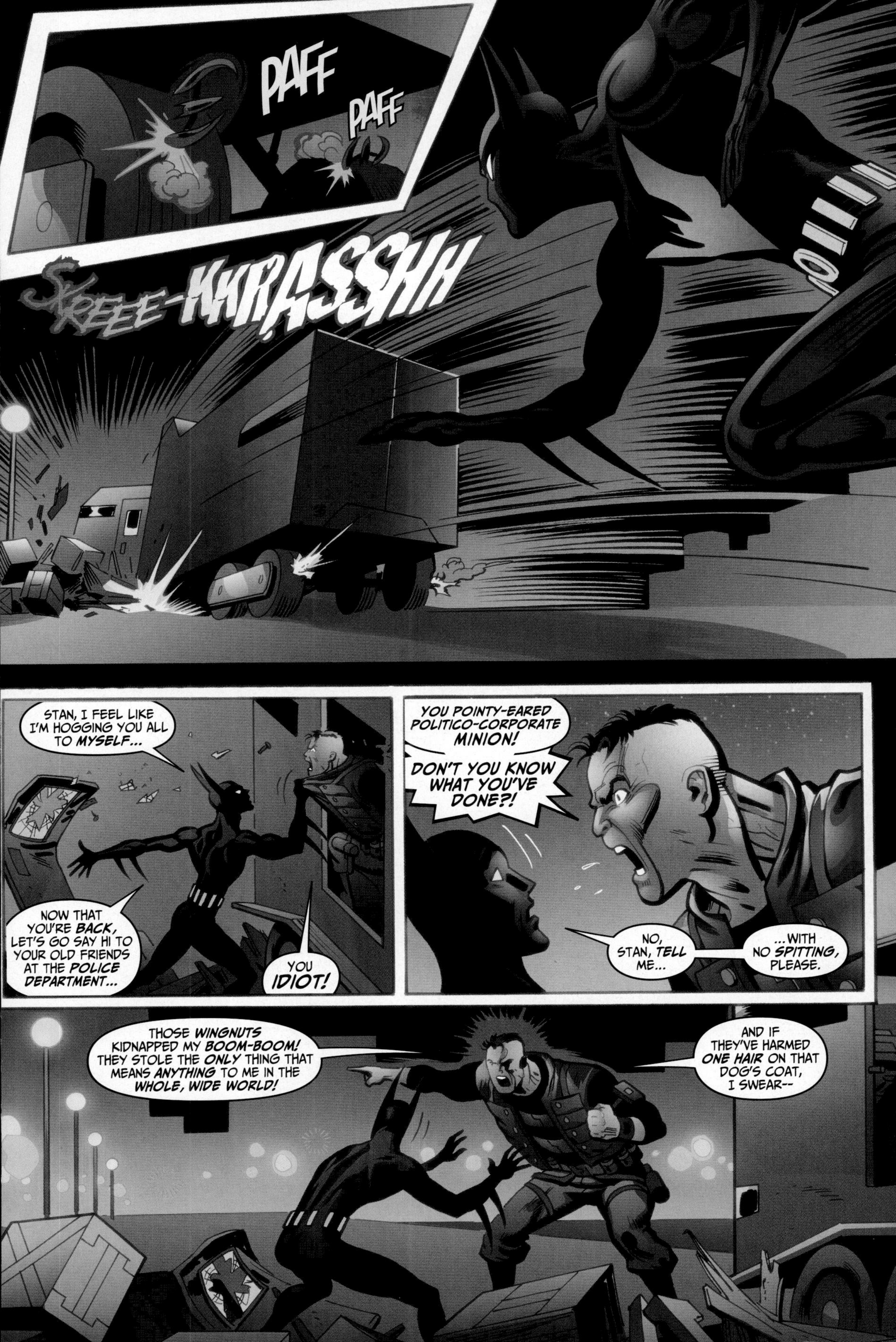
PAFF
PAFF
SKREEE-KKRASSHH
STAN, I FEEL LIKE I'M HOGGING YOU ALL TO MYSELF...
NOW THAT YOU'RE BACK, LET'S GO SAY HI TO YOUR OLD FRIENDS AT THE POLICE DEPARTMENT...
YOU IDIOT!
YOU POINTY-EARED POLITICO-CORPORATE MINION!
DON'T YOU KNOW WHAT YOU'VE DONE?!
NO, STAN, TELL ME...
...WITH NO SPITTING, PLEASE.
THOSE WINGNUTS KIDNAPPED MY BOOM-BOOM! THEY STOLE THE ONLY THING THAT MEANS ANYTHING TO ME IN THE WHOLE, WIDE WORLD!
AND IF THEY'VE HARMED ONE HAIR ON THAT DOG'S COAT, I SWEAR--

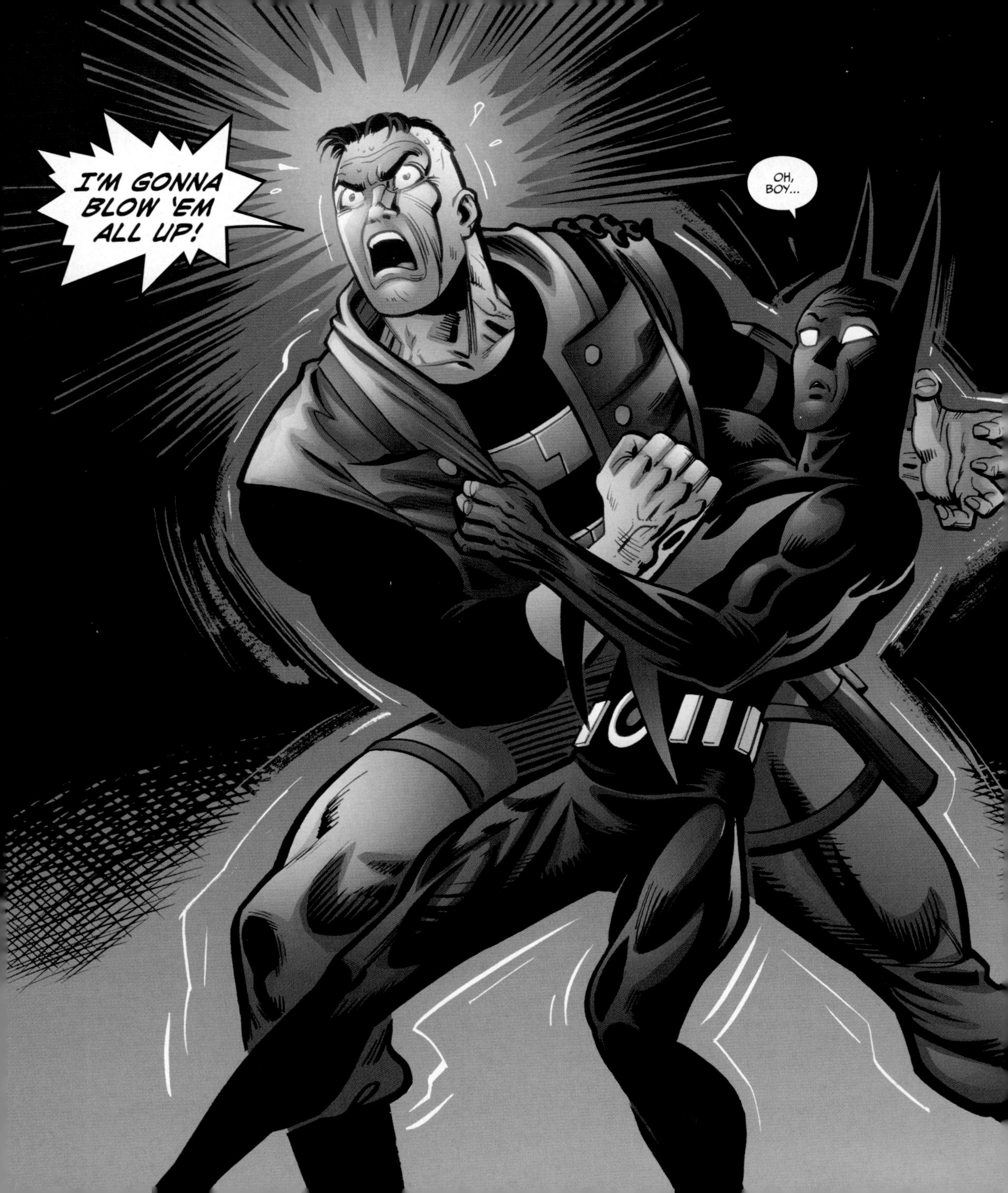
I'M GONNA BLOW 'EM ALL UP!
OH, BOY...

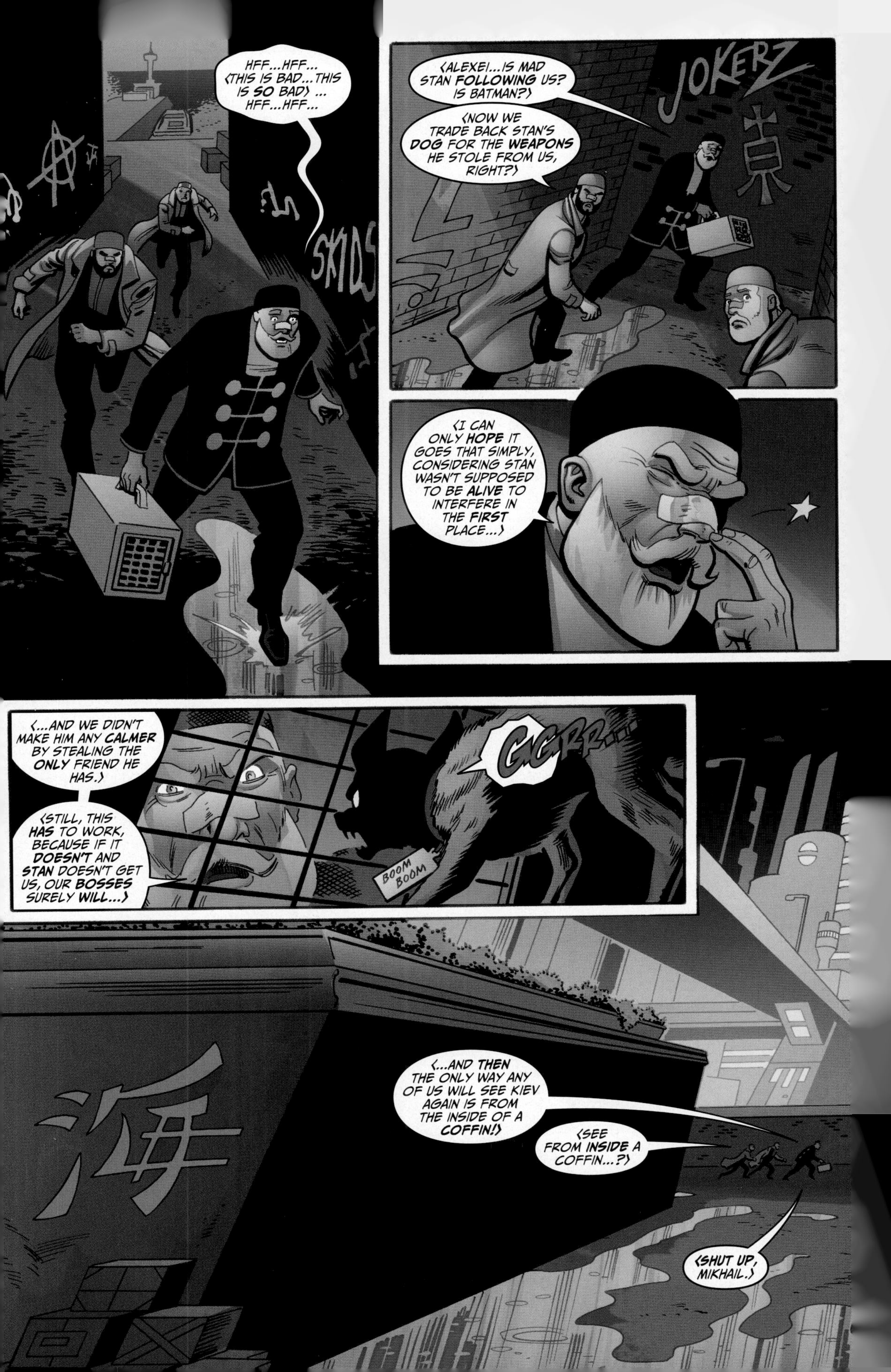
HFF...HFF... ‹THIS IS BAD...THIS IS SO BAD› ... HFF...HFF...
SKIDS
‹ALEXEI...IS MAD STAN FOLLOWING US? IS BATMAN?›
‹NOW WE TRADE BACK STAN'S DOG FOR THE WEAPONS HE STOLE FROM US, RIGHT?›
JOKERZ
‹I CAN ONLY HOPE IT GOES THAT SIMPLY, CONSIDERING STAN WASN'T SUPPOSED TO BE ALIVE TO INTERFERE IN THE FIRST PLACE...›
‹...AND WE DIDN'T MAKE HIM ANY CALMER BY STEALING THE ONLY FRIEND HE HAS.›
‹STILL, THIS HAS TO WORK, BECAUSE IF IT DOESN'T AND STAN DOESN'T GET US, OUR BOSSES SURELY WILL...›
GGRR...
BOOM BOOM
‹...AND THEN THE ONLY WAY ANY OF US WILL SEE KIEV AGAIN IS FROM THE INSIDE OF A COFFIN!›
‹SEE FROM INSIDE A COFFIN...?›
‹SHUT UP, MIKHAIL.›

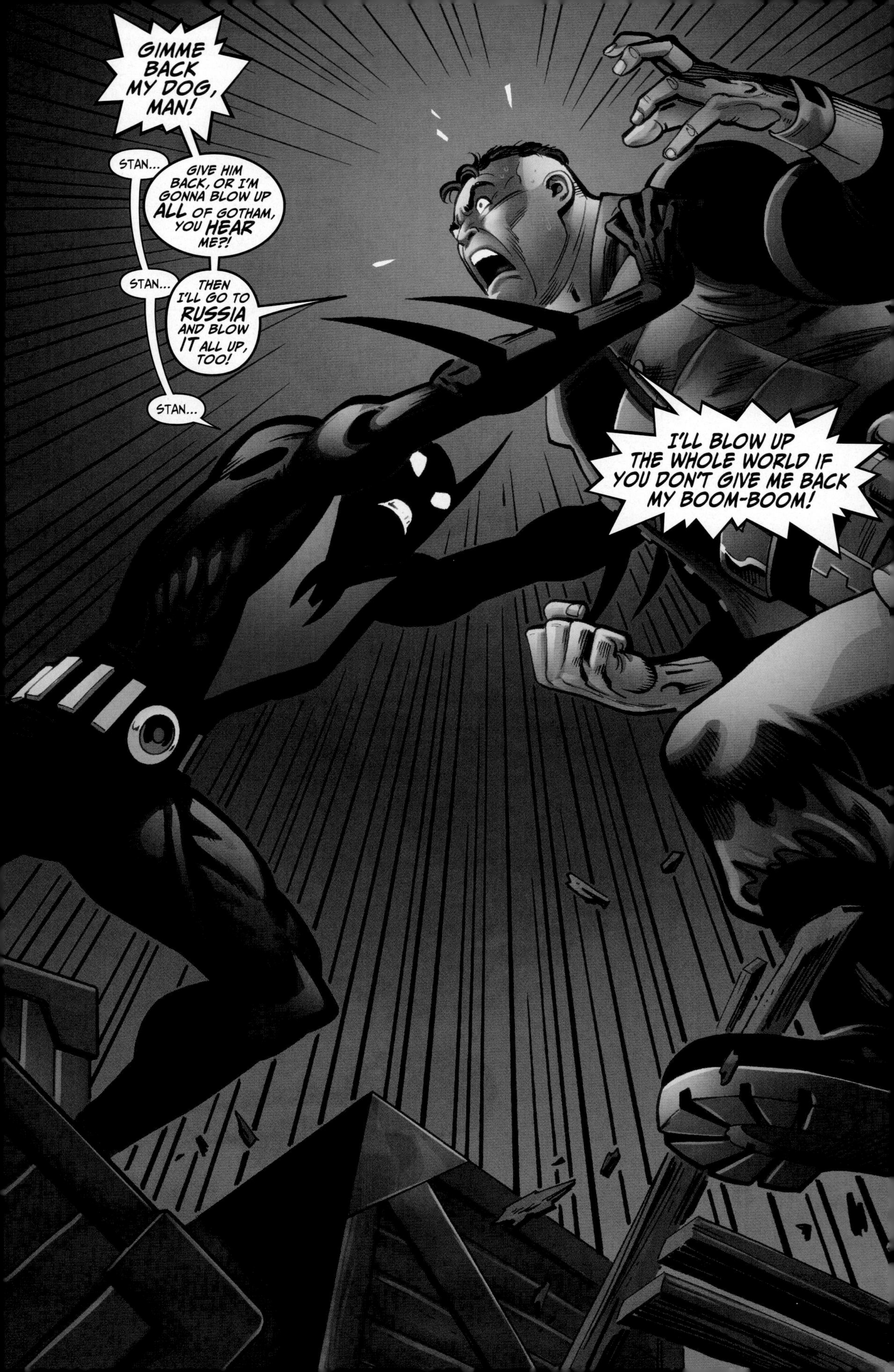
GIMME BACK MY DOG, MAN!
STAN...
GIVE HIM BACK, OR I'M GONNA BLOW UP ALL OF GOTHAM, YOU HEAR ME?!
STAN...
THEN I'LL GO TO RUSSIA AND BLOW IT ALL UP, TOO!
STAN...
I'LL BLOW UP THE WHOLE WORLD IF YOU DON'T GIVE ME BACK MY BOOM-BOOM!

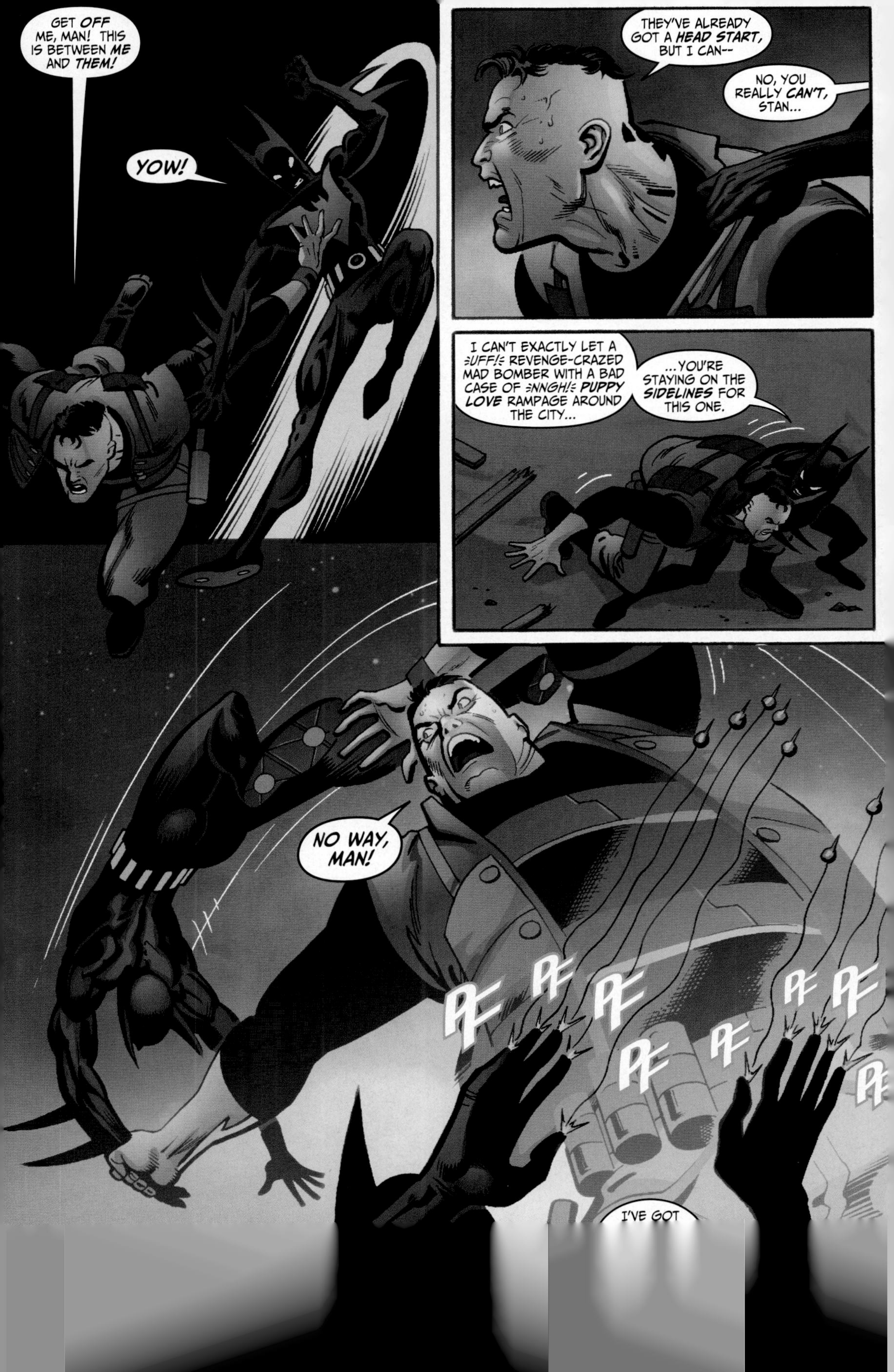

GET OFF ME, MAN! THIS IS BETWEEN ME AND THEM!
YOW!
THEY'VE ALREADY GOT A HEAD START, BUT I CAN--
NO, YOU REALLY CAN'T, STAN...
I CAN'T EXACTLY LET A UFF! REVENGE-CRAZED MAD BOMBER WITH A BAD CASE OF NNGH! PUPPY LOVE RAMPAGE AROUND THE CITY...
...YOU'RE STAYING ON THE SIDELINES FOR THIS ONE.
NO WAY, MAN!
PF
PF
PF
PF
PF
PF
PF
PF
I'VE GOT

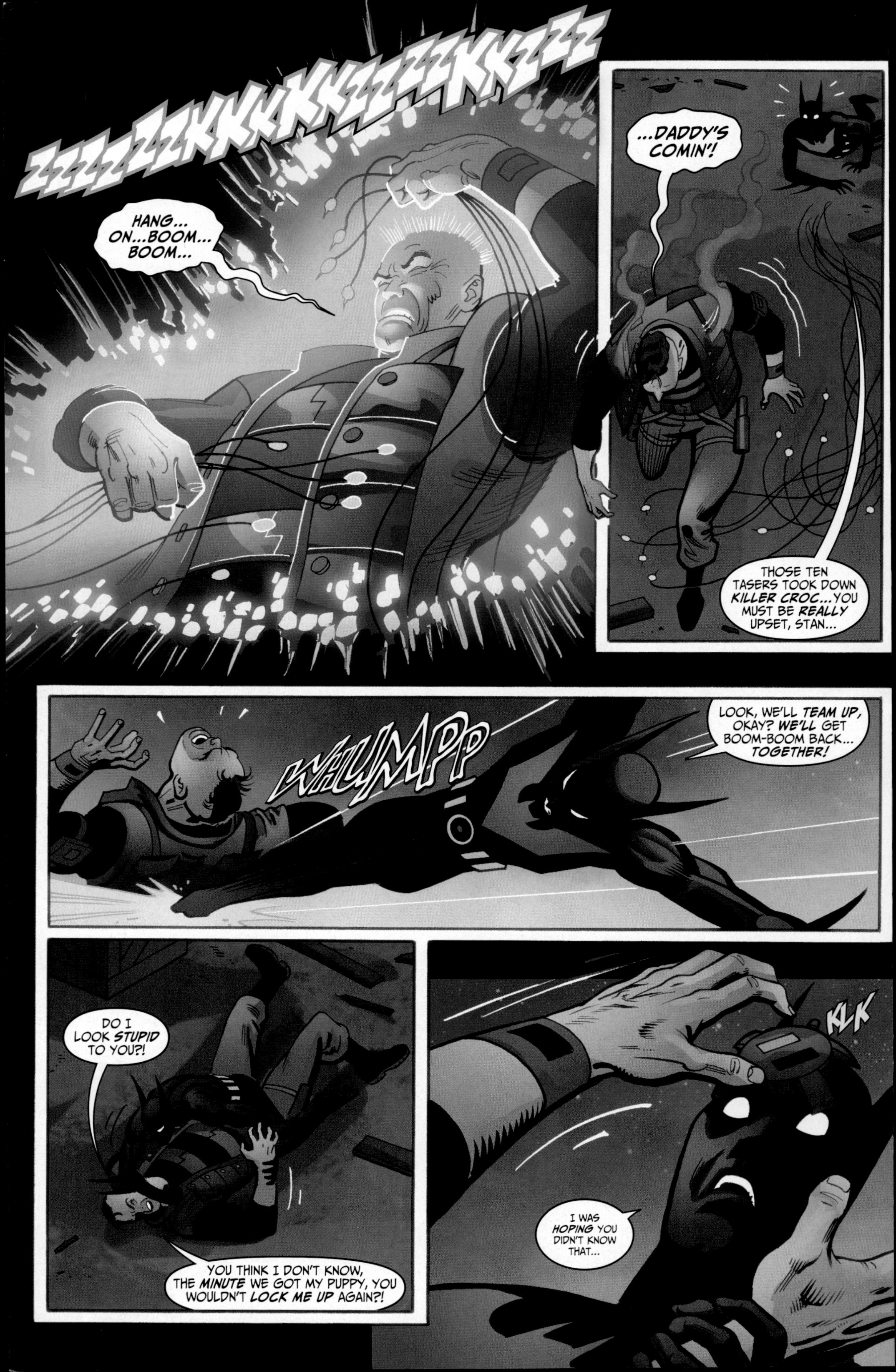
ZZZZZZZKKKKKKZZZZZZZKKZZZZ
HANG... ON...BOOM... BOOM...
...DADDY'S COMIN'!
THOSE TEN TASERS TOOK DOWN KILLER CROC...YOU MUST BE REALLY UPSET, STAN...
WHUMPP
LOOK, WE'LL TEAM UP, OKAY? WE'LL GET BOOM-BOOM BACK... TOGETHER!
DO I LOOK STUPID TO YOU?!
YOU THINK I DON'T KNOW, THE MINUTE WE GOT MY PUPPY, YOU WOULDN'T LOCK ME UP AGAIN?!
KLK
I WAS HOPING YOU DIDN'T KNOW THAT...

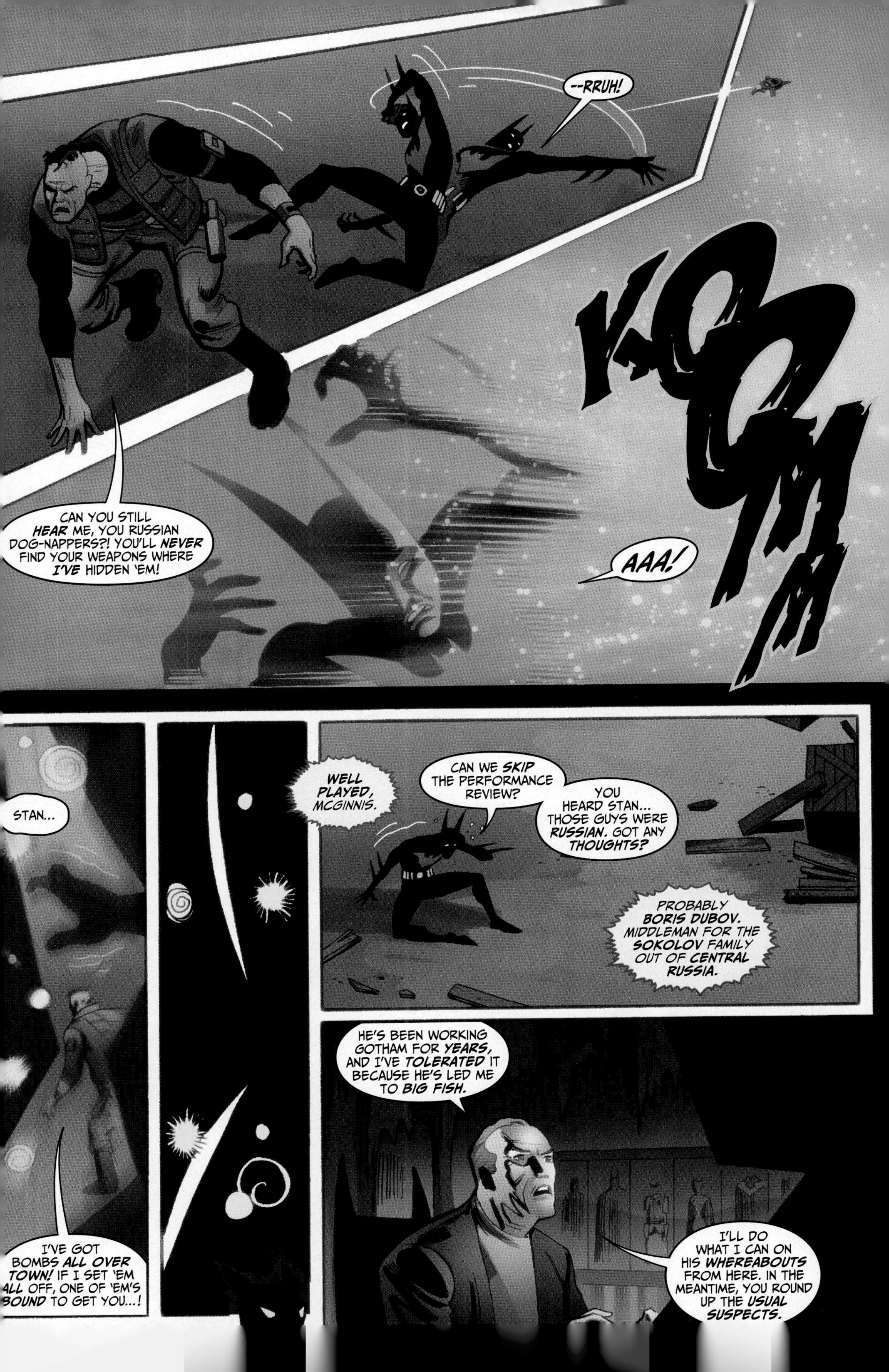
--RRUH!
CAN YOU STILL HEAR ME, YOU RUSSIAN DOG-NAPPERS?! YOU'LL NEVER FIND YOUR WEAPONS WHERE I'VE HIDDEN 'EM!
KOOMM
AAA!
STAN...
I'VE GOT BOMBS ALL OVER TOWN! IF I SET 'EM ALL OFF, ONE OF 'EM'S BOUND TO GET YOU...!
WELL PLAYED, MCGINNIS.
CAN WE SKIP THE PERFORMANCE REVIEW?
YOU HEARD STAN... THOSE GUYS WERE RUSSIAN. GOT ANY THOUGHTS?
PROBABLY BORIS DUBOV. MIDDLEMAN FOR THE SOKOLOV FAMILY OUT OF CENTRAL RUSSIA.
HE'S BEEN WORKING GOTHAM FOR YEARS, AND I'VE TOLERATED IT BECAUSE HE'S LED ME TO BIG FISH.
I'LL DO WHAT I CAN ON HIS WHEREABOUTS FROM HERE. IN THE MEANTIME, YOU ROUND UP THE USUAL SUSPECTS.

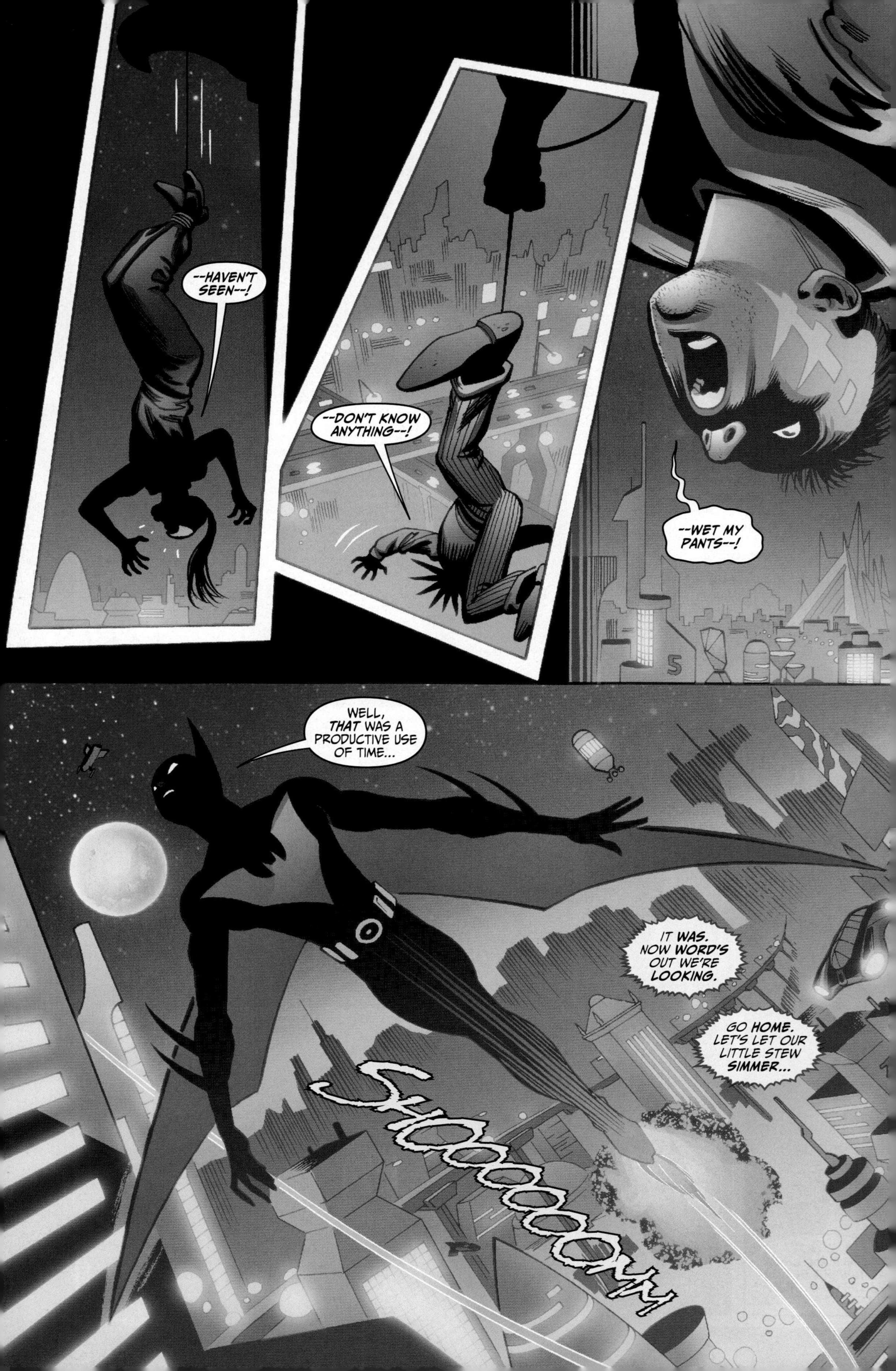
--HAVEN'T SEEN--!
--DON'T KNOW ANYTHING--!
--WET MY PANTS--!
WELL, THAT WAS A PRODUCTIVE USE OF TIME...
IT WAS. NOW WORD'S OUT WE'RE LOOKING.
GO HOME. LET'S LET OUR LITTLE STEW SIMMER...
SHOOOOOOM

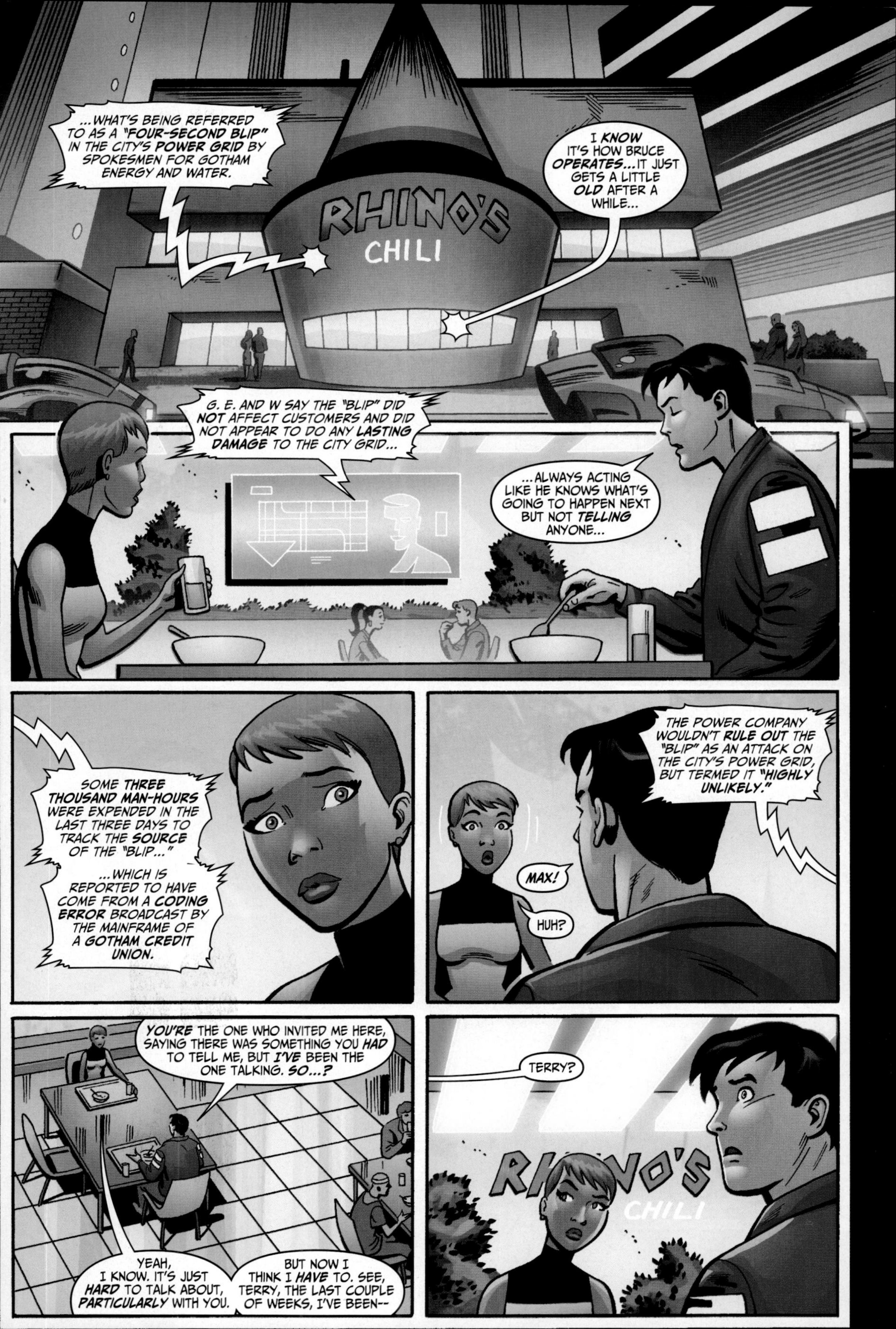
...WHAT'S BEING REFERRED TO AS A "FOUR-SECOND BLIP" IN THE CITY'S POWER GRID BY SPOKESMEN FOR GOTHAM ENERGY AND WATER.
I KNOW IT'S HOW BRUCE OPERATES...IT JUST GETS A LITTLE OLD AFTER A WHILE...
RHINO'S CHILI
G. E. AND W SAY THE "BLIP" DID NOT AFFECT CUSTOMERS AND DID NOT APPEAR TO DO ANY LASTING DAMAGE TO THE CITY GRID...
...ALWAYS ACTING LIKE HE KNOWS WHAT'S GOING TO HAPPEN NEXT BUT NOT TELLING ANYONE...
SOME THREE THOUSAND MAN-HOURS WERE EXPENDED IN THE LAST THREE DAYS TO TRACK THE SOURCE OF THE "BLIP..."
...WHICH IS REPORTED TO HAVE COME FROM A CODING ERROR BROADCAST BY THE MAINFRAME OF A GOTHAM CREDIT UNION.
THE POWER COMPANY WOULDN'T RULE OUT THE "BLIP" AS AN ATTACK ON THE CITY'S POWER GRID, BUT TERMED IT "HIGHLY UNLIKELY."
MAX!
HUH?
YOU'RE THE ONE WHO INVITED ME HERE, SAYING THERE WAS SOMETHING YOU HAD TO TELL ME, BUT I'VE BEEN THE ONE TALKING. SO...?
YEAH, I KNOW. IT'S JUST HARD TO TALK ABOUT, PARTICULARLY WITH YOU.
BUT NOW I THINK I HAVE TO. SEE, TERRY, THE LAST COUPLE OF WEEKS, I'VE BEEN--
TERRY?
RHINO'S CHILI

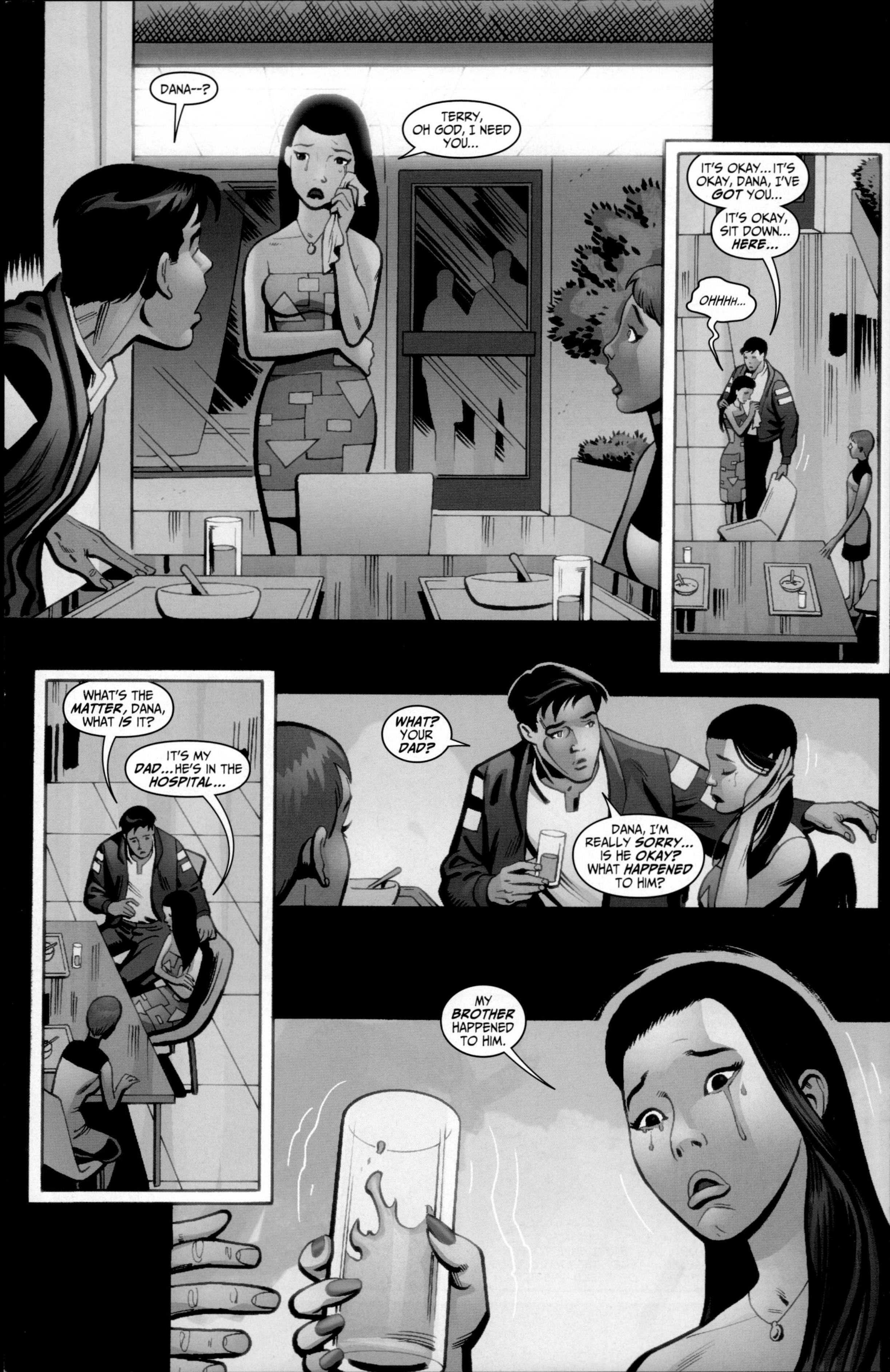
DANA--?
TERRY, OH GOD, I NEED YOU...
IT'S OKAY... IT'S OKAY, DANA, I'VE GOT YOU...
IT'S OKAY, SIT DOWN... HERE...
OHHHH...
WHAT'S THE MATTER, DANA, WHAT IS IT?
IT'S MY DAD... HE'S IN THE HOSPITAL...
WHAT? YOUR DAD?
DANA, I'M REALLY SORRY... IS HE OKAY? WHAT HAPPENED TO HIM?
MY BROTHER HAPPENED TO HIM.

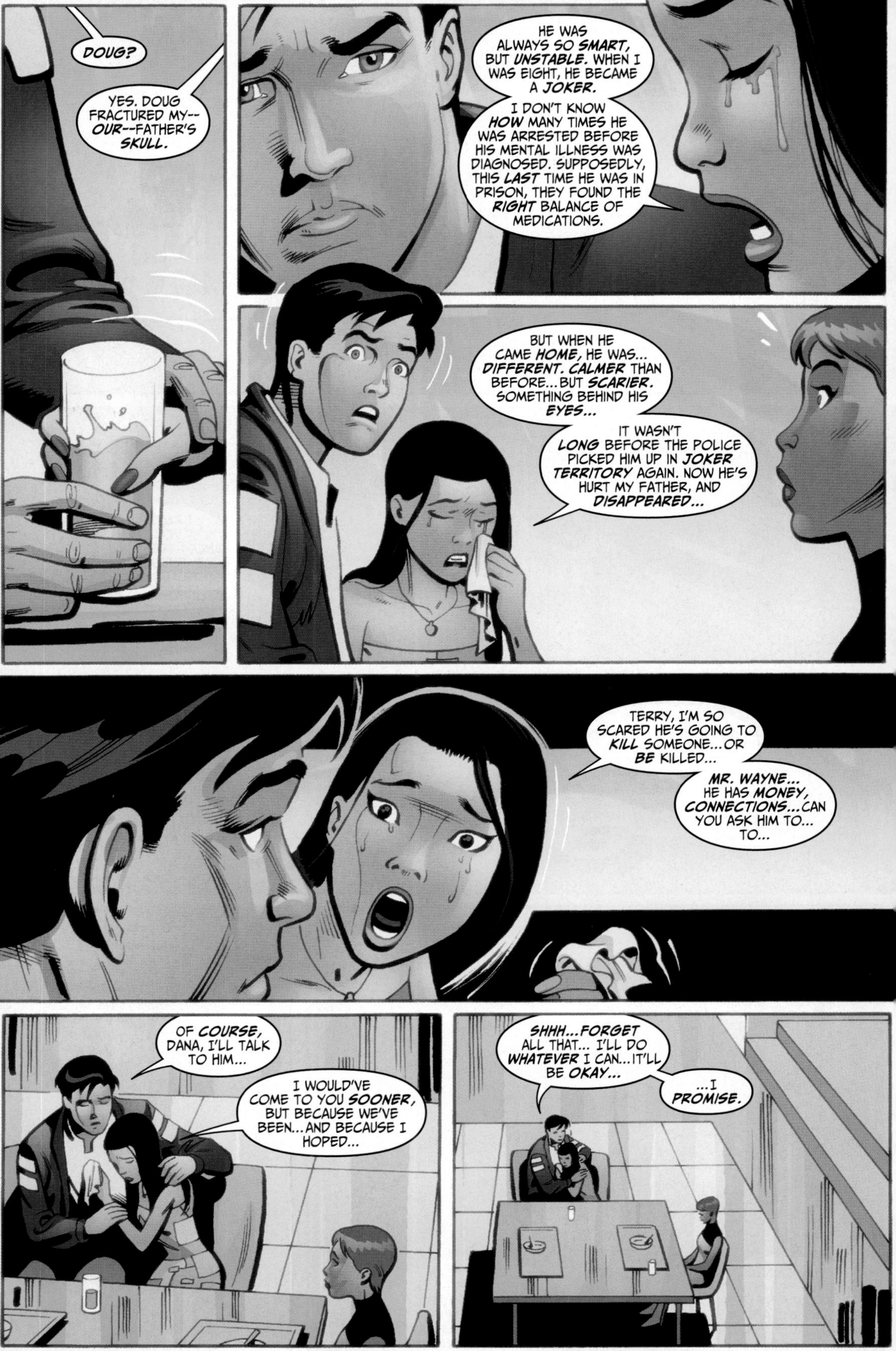
DOUG?
YES. DOUG FRACTURED MY--OUR--FATHER'S SKULL.
HE WAS ALWAYS SO SMART, BUT UNSTABLE. WHEN I WAS EIGHT, HE BECAME A JOKER.
I DON'T KNOW HOW MANY TIMES HE WAS ARRESTED BEFORE HIS MENTAL ILLNESS WAS DIAGNOSED. SUPPOSEDLY, THIS LAST TIME HE WAS IN PRISON, THEY FOUND THE RIGHT BALANCE OF MEDICATIONS.
BUT WHEN HE CAME HOME, HE WAS... DIFFERENT. CALMER THAN BEFORE...BUT SCARIER. SOMETHING BEHIND HIS EYES...
IT WASN'T LONG BEFORE THE POLICE PICKED HIM UP IN JOKER TERRITORY AGAIN. NOW HE'S HURT MY FATHER, AND DISAPPEARED...
TERRY, I'M SO SCARED HE'S GOING TO KILL SOMEONE...OR BE KILLED...
MR. WAYNE... HE HAS MONEY, CONNECTIONS...CAN YOU ASK HIM TO... TO...
OF COURSE, DANA, I'LL TALK TO HIM...
I WOULD'VE COME TO YOU SOONER, BUT BECAUSE WE'VE BEEN...AND BECAUSE I HOPED...
SHHH...FORGET ALL THAT... I'LL DO WHATEVER I CAN...IT'LL BE OKAY...
...I PROMISE.

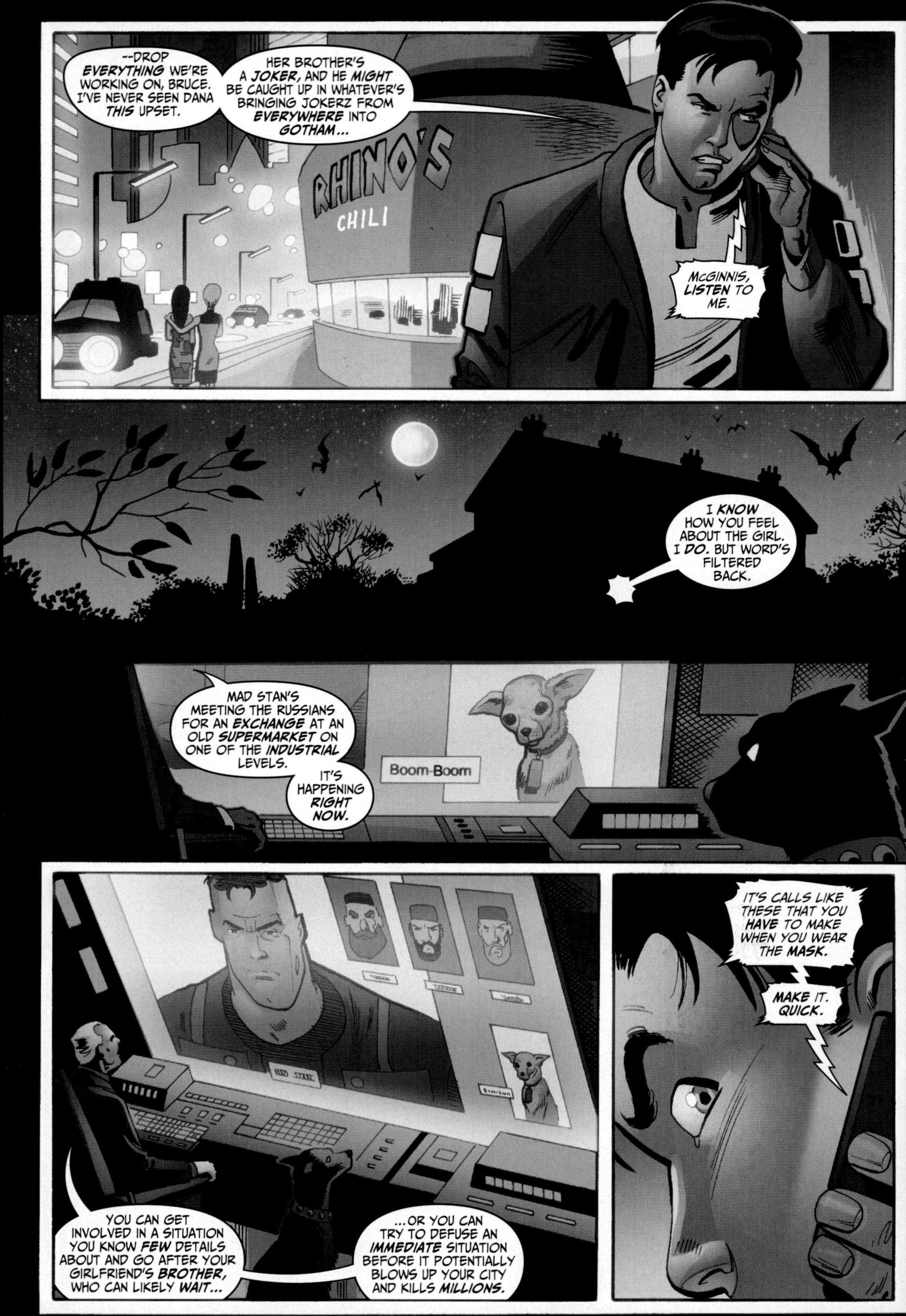
--DROP EVERYTHING WE'RE WORKING ON, BRUCE. I'VE NEVER SEEN DANA THIS UPSET.
HER BROTHER'S A JOKER, AND HE MIGHT BE CAUGHT UP IN WHATEVER'S BRINGING JOKERZ FROM EVERYWHERE INTO GOTHAM...
RHINO'S
CHILI
McGINNIS, LISTEN TO ME.
I KNOW HOW YOU FEEL ABOUT THE GIRL. I DO. BUT WORD'S FILTERED BACK.
MAD STAN'S MEETING THE RUSSIANS FOR AN EXCHANGE AT AN OLD SUPERMARKET ON ONE OF THE INDUSTRIAL LEVELS.
IT'S HAPPENING RIGHT NOW.
Boom-Boom
YOU CAN GET INVOLVED IN A SITUATION YOU KNOW FEW DETAILS ABOUT AND GO AFTER YOUR GIRLFRIEND'S BROTHER, WHO CAN LIKELY WAIT...
...OR YOU CAN TRY TO DEFUSE AN IMMEDIATE SITUATION BEFORE IT POTENTIALLY BLOWS UP YOUR CITY AND KILLS MILLIONS.
IT'S CALLS LIKE THESE THAT YOU HAVE TO MAKE WHEN YOU WEAR THE MASK.
MAKE IT. QUICK.

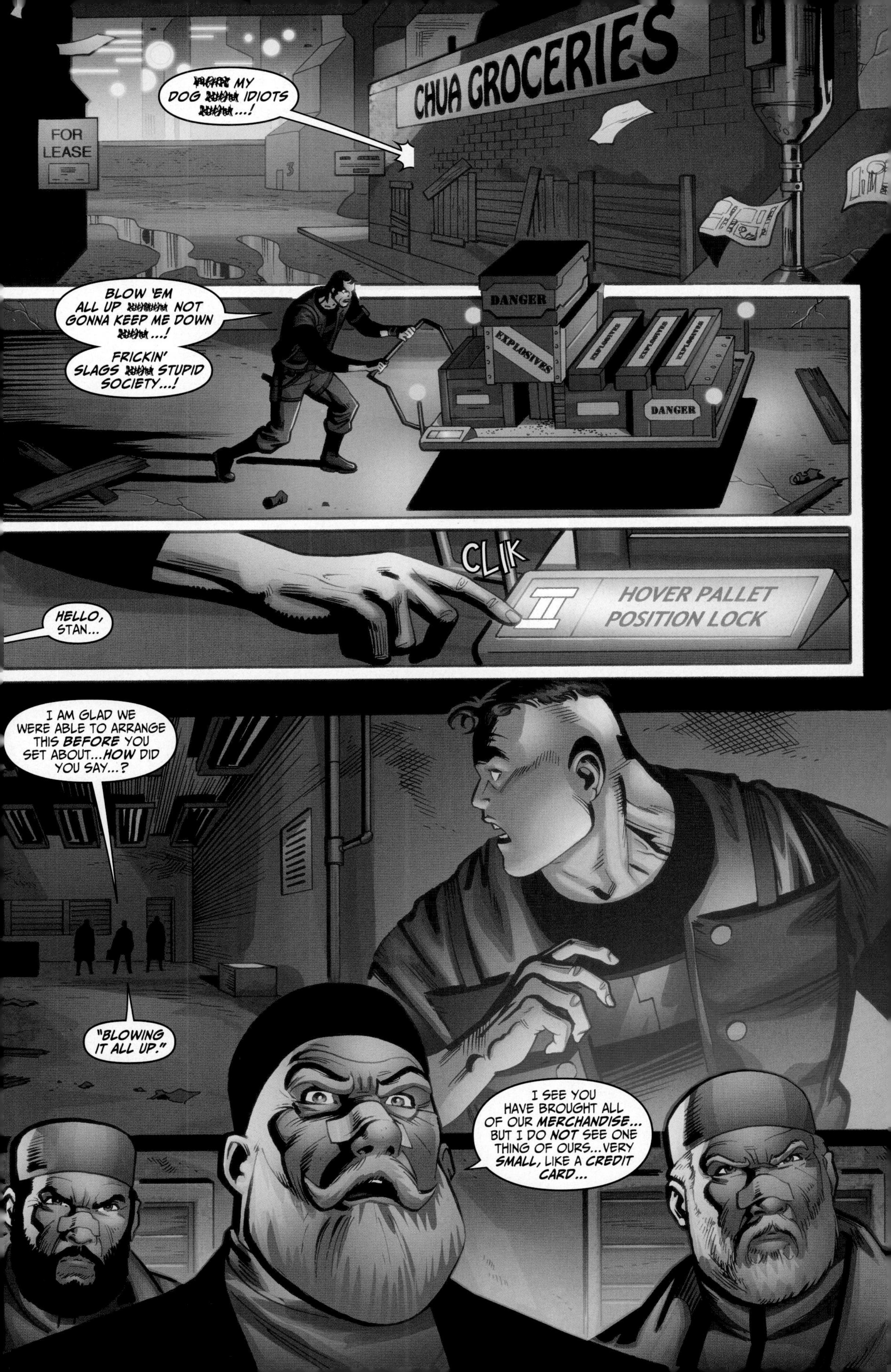

CHUA GROCERIES
FOR LEASE
MY DOG IDIOTS ...!
BLOW 'EM ALL UP NOT GONNA KEEP ME DOWN ...!
FRICKIN' SLAGS STUPID SOCIETY...!
DANGER
EXPLOSIVES
DANGER
CLIK
HOVER PALLET POSITION LOCK
HELLO, STAN...
I AM GLAD WE WERE ABLE TO ARRANGE THIS BEFORE YOU SET ABOUT...HOW DID YOU SAY...?
"BLOWING IT ALL UP."
I SEE YOU HAVE BROUGHT ALL OF OUR MERCHANDISE... BUT I DO NOT SEE ONE THING OF OURS...VERY SMALL, LIKE A CREDIT CARD...

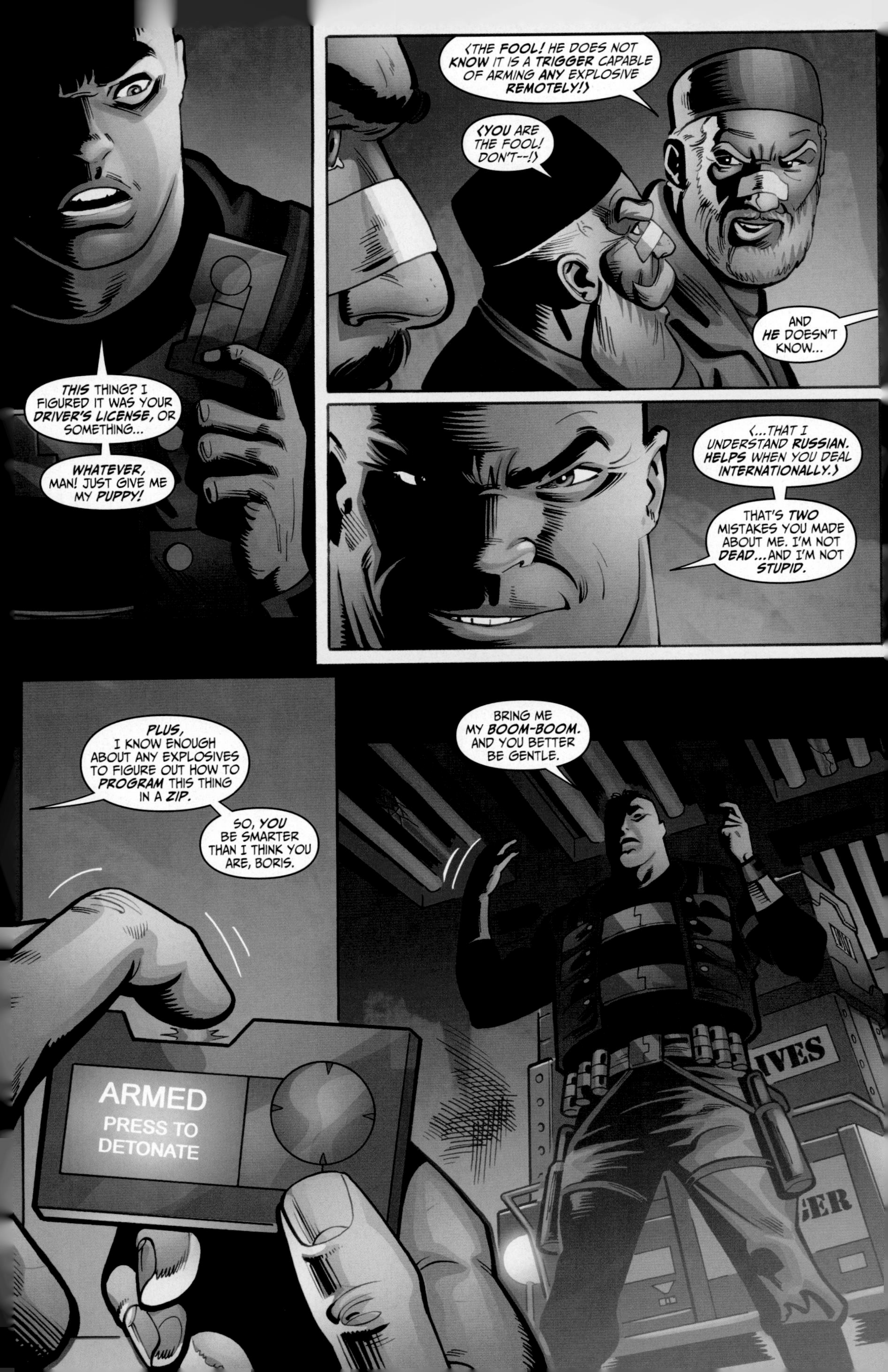

THIS THING? I FIGURED IT WAS YOUR DRIVER'S LICENSE, OR SOMETHING...
WHATEVER, MAN! JUST GIVE ME MY PUPPY!
‹THE FOOL! HE DOES NOT KNOW IT IS A TRIGGER CAPABLE OF ARMING ANY EXPLOSIVE REMOTELY!›
‹YOU ARE THE FOOL! DON'T--!›
AND HE DOESN'T KNOW...
‹...THAT I UNDERSTAND RUSSIAN. HELPS WHEN YOU DEAL INTERNATIONALLY.›
THAT'S TWO MISTAKES YOU MADE ABOUT ME. I'M NOT DEAD...AND I'M NOT STUPID.
PLUS, I KNOW ENOUGH ABOUT ANY EXPLOSIVES TO FIGURE OUT HOW TO PROGRAM THIS THING IN A ZIP.
SO, YOU BE SMARTER THAN I THINK YOU ARE, BORIS.
BRING ME MY BOOM-BOOM. AND YOU BETTER BE GENTLE.
ARMED
PRESS TO DETONATE
IVES
ER

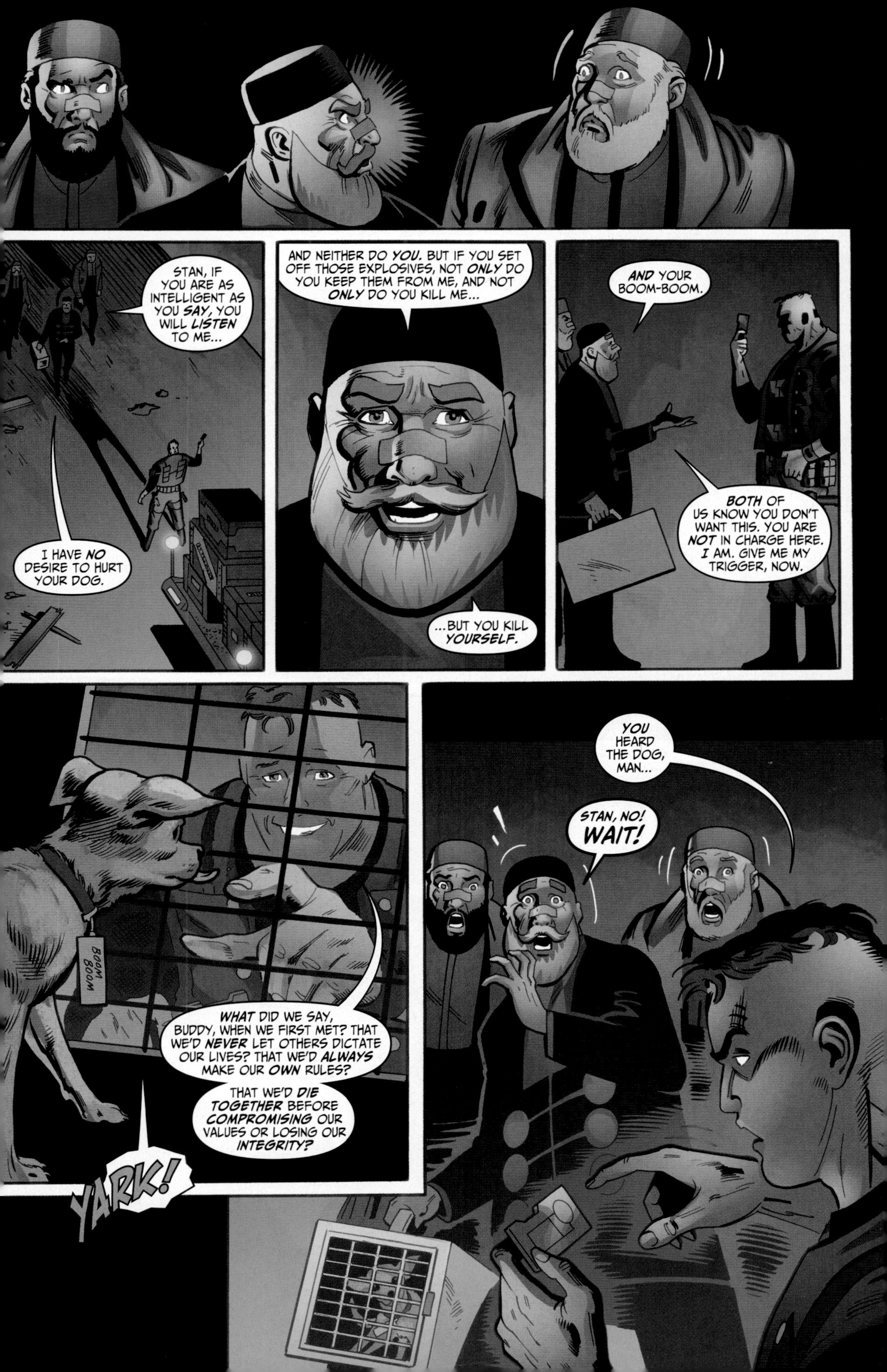

STAN, IF YOU ARE AS INTELLIGENT AS YOU SAY, YOU WILL LISTEN TO ME...
I HAVE NO DESIRE TO HURT YOUR DOG.
AND NEITHER DO YOU. BUT IF YOU SET OFF THOSE EXPLOSIVES, NOT ONLY DO YOU KEEP THEM FROM ME, AND NOT ONLY DO YOU KILL ME...
...BUT YOU KILL YOURSELF.
AND YOUR BOOM-BOOM.
BOTH OF US KNOW YOU DON'T WANT THIS. YOU ARE NOT IN CHARGE HERE. I AM. GIVE ME MY TRIGGER, NOW.
BOOM BOOM
WHAT DID WE SAY, BUDDY, WHEN WE FIRST MET? THAT WE'D NEVER LET OTHERS DICTATE OUR LIVES? THAT WE'D ALWAYS MAKE OUR OWN RULES?
THAT WE'D DIE TOGETHER BEFORE COMPROMISING OUR VALUES OR LOSING OUR INTEGRITY?
YARK!
YOU HEARD THE DOG, MAN...
STAN, NO! WAIT!

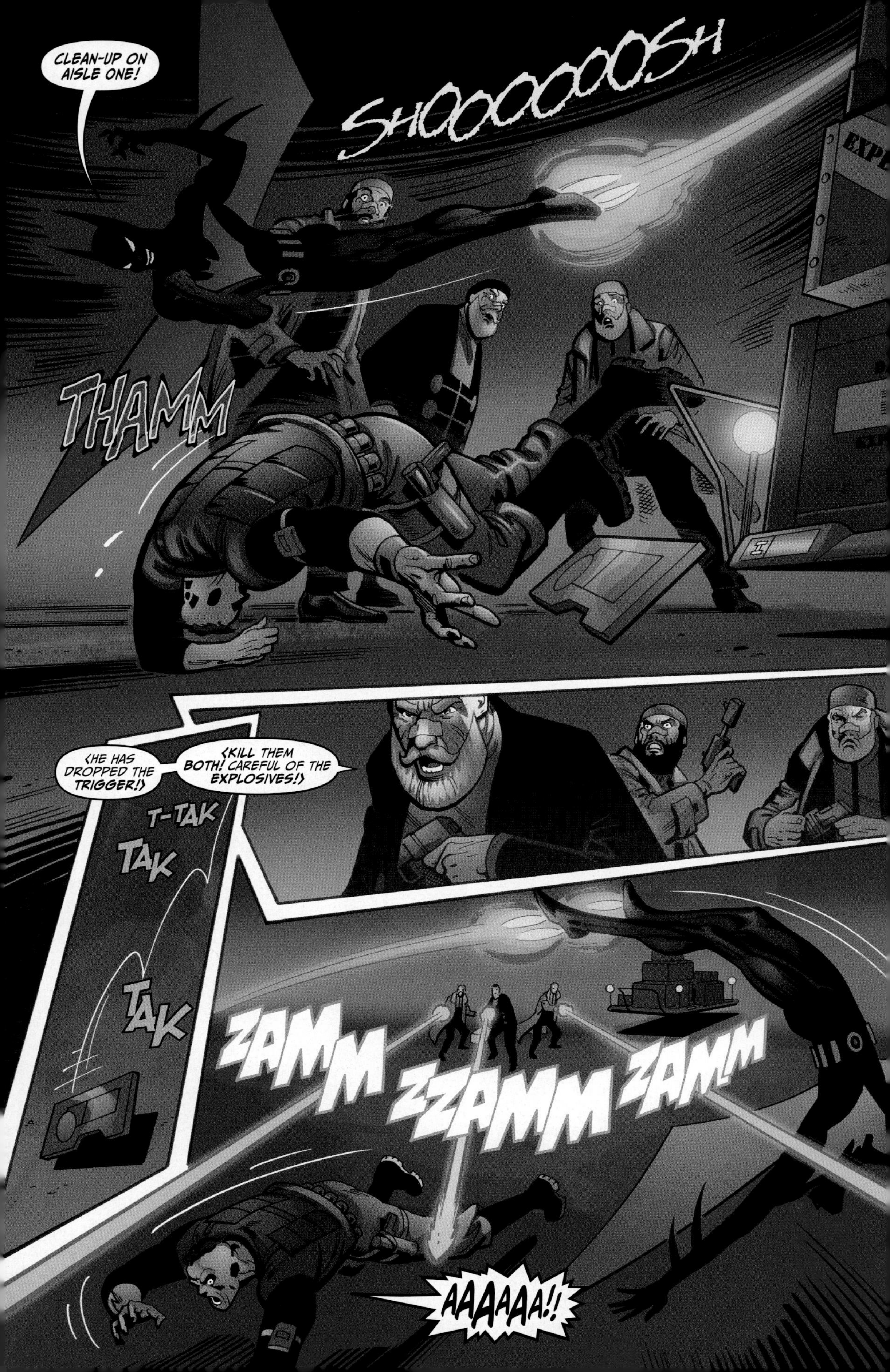
CLEAN-UP ON AISLE ONE!
SHOOOOOOOSH
THAMM
<HE HAS DROPPED THE TRIGGER!>
<KILL THEM BOTH! CAREFUL OF THE EXPLOSIVES!>
T-TAK
TAK
TAK
ZAMM
ZZAMM
ZAMM
AAAAAA!!

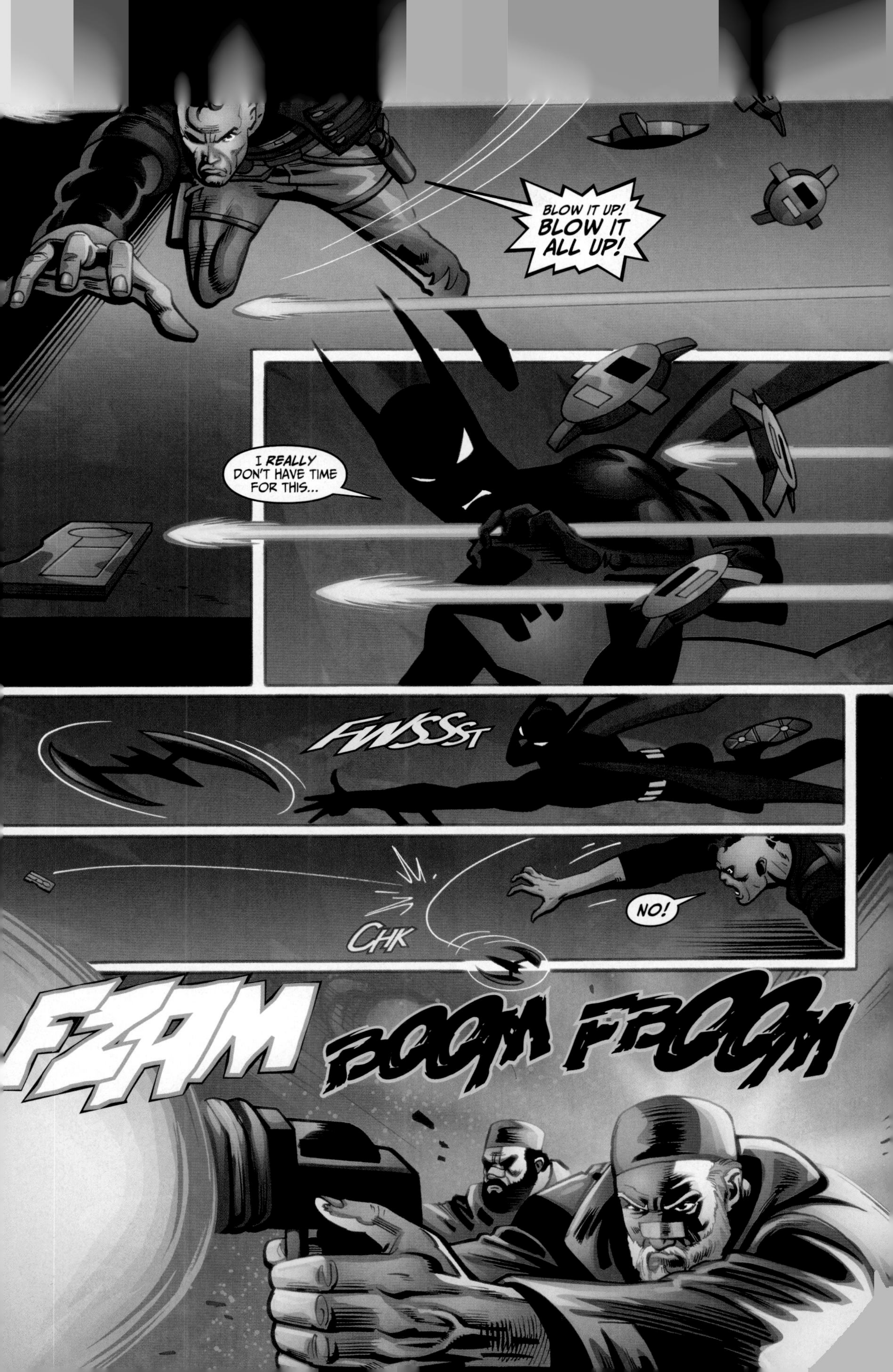

BLOW IT UP! BLOW IT ALL UP!
I REALLY DON'T HAVE TIME FOR THIS...
FWSSST
CHK
NO!
FZAM
BOOM
FROOM

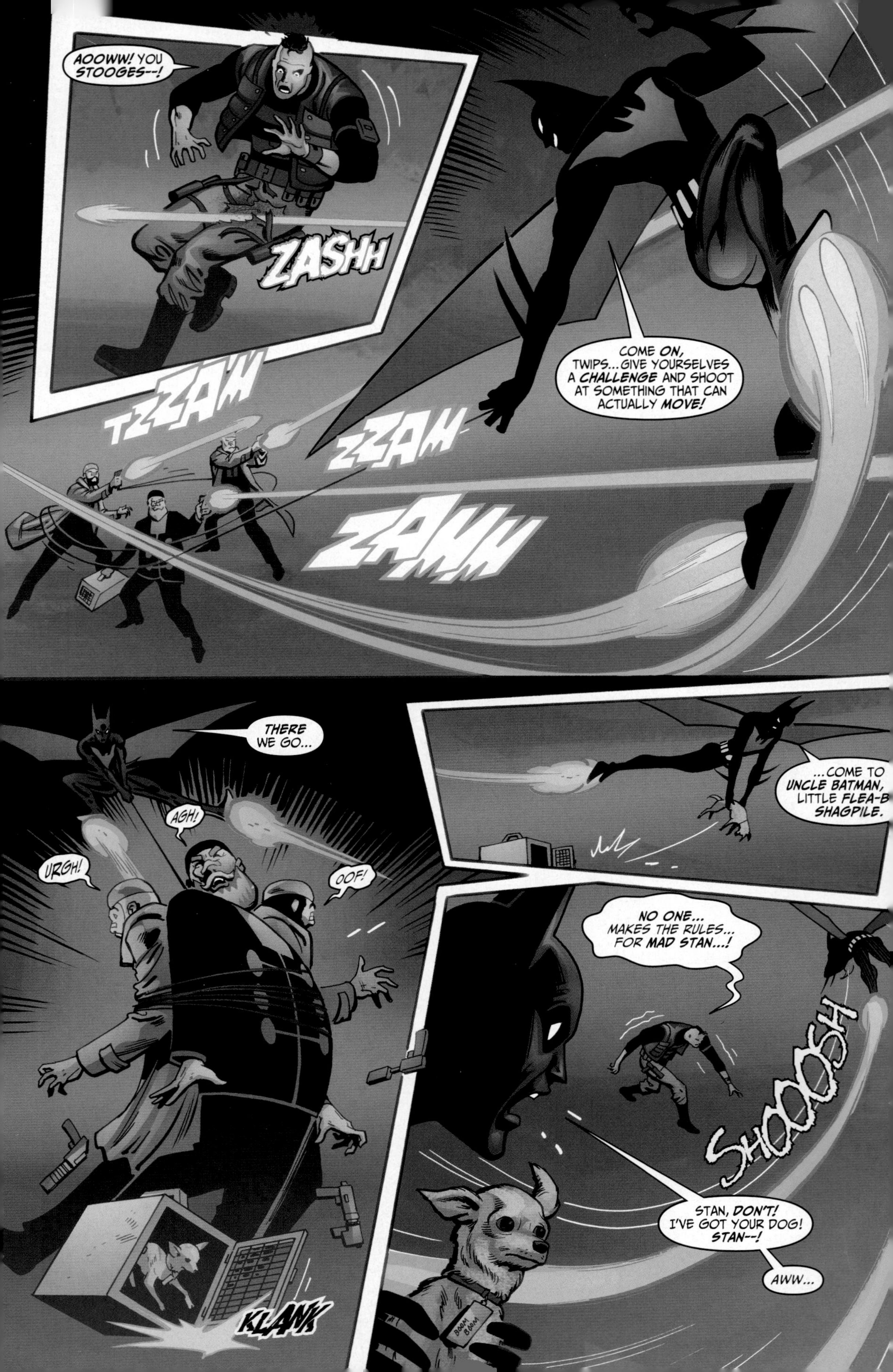
AOOWW! YOU STOOGES--!
ZASHH
COME ON, TWIPS...GIVE YOURSELVES A CHALLENGE AND SHOOT AT SOMETHING THAT CAN ACTUALLY MOVE!
TZZAM
ZZAM
ZAMM
THERE WE GO...
AGH!
URGH!
OOF!
KLANK
...COME TO UNCLE BATMAN, LITTLE FLEA-B SHAGPILE.
NO ONE... MAKES THE RULES... FOR MAD STAN...!
SHOOOSH
STAN, DON'T! I'VE GOT YOUR DOG! STAN--!
AWW...

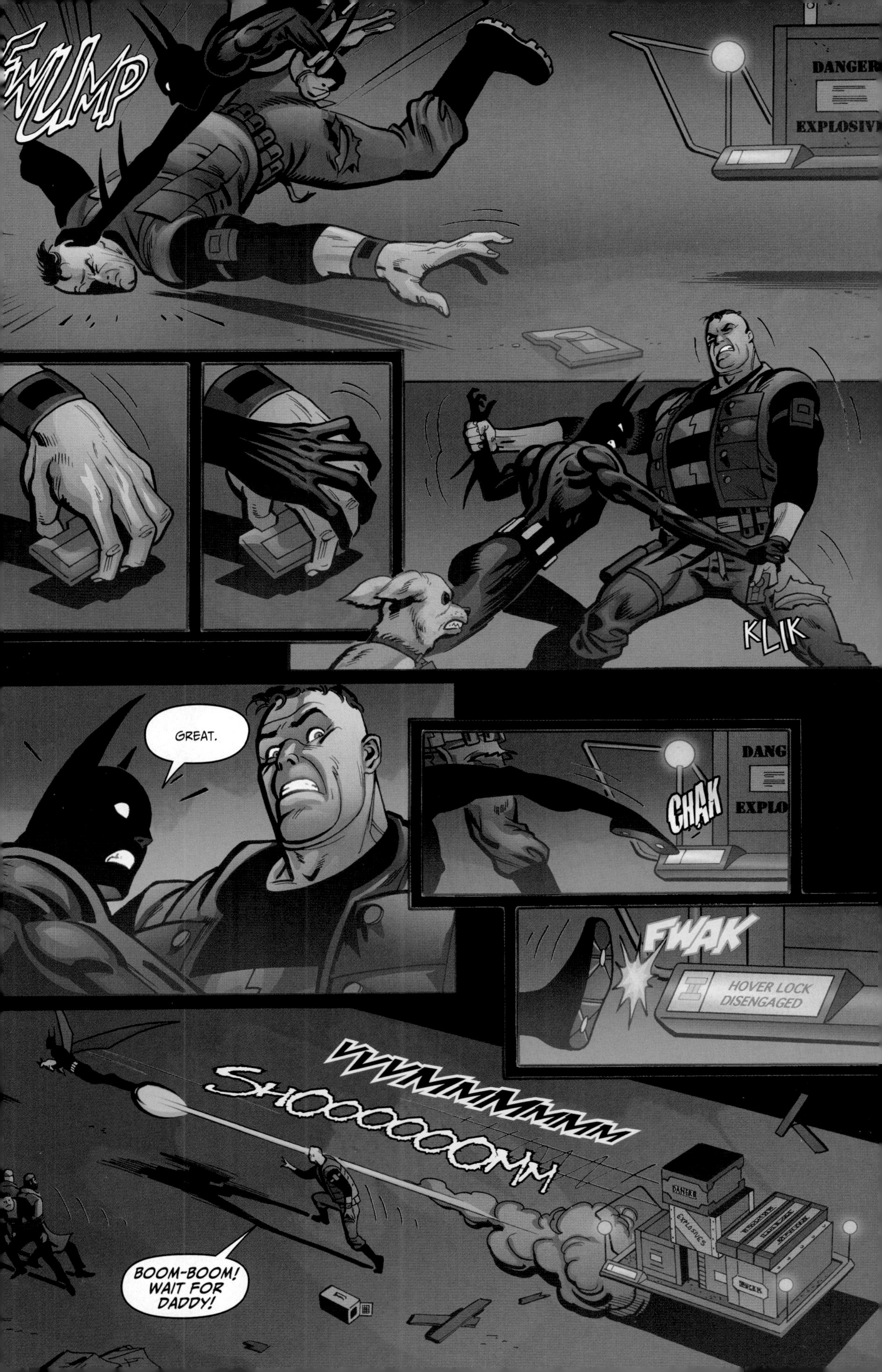
FWUMP
DANGER
EXPLOSIVE
KLIK
GREAT.
DANG
EXPLO
CHAK
FWAK
HOVER LOCK
DISENGAGED
VVVMMMMMMMM
SHOOOOOOOMM
BOOM-BOOM! WAIT FOR DADDY!

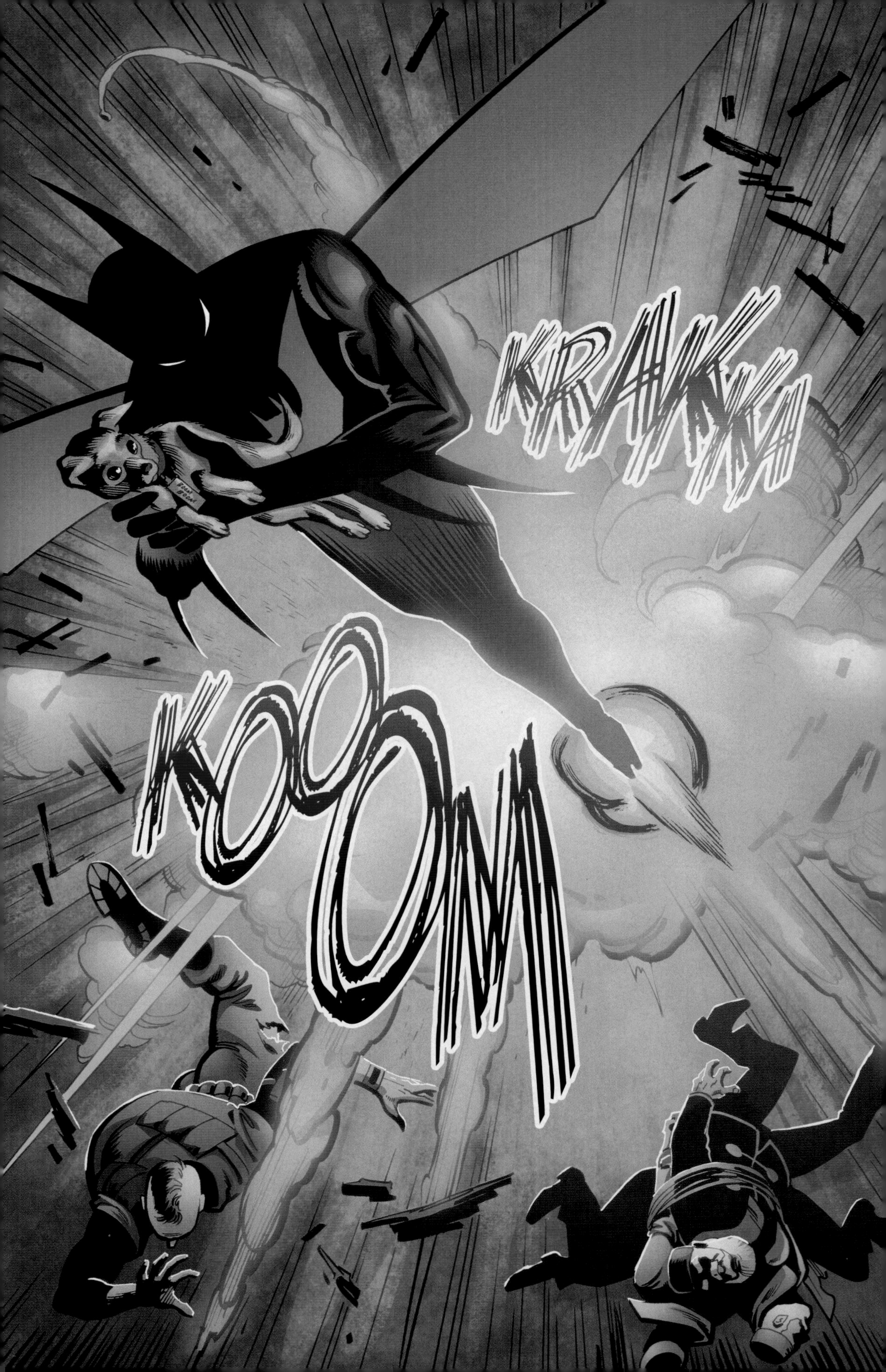
KRAKKA
BOOM BOOM
KOOOOM

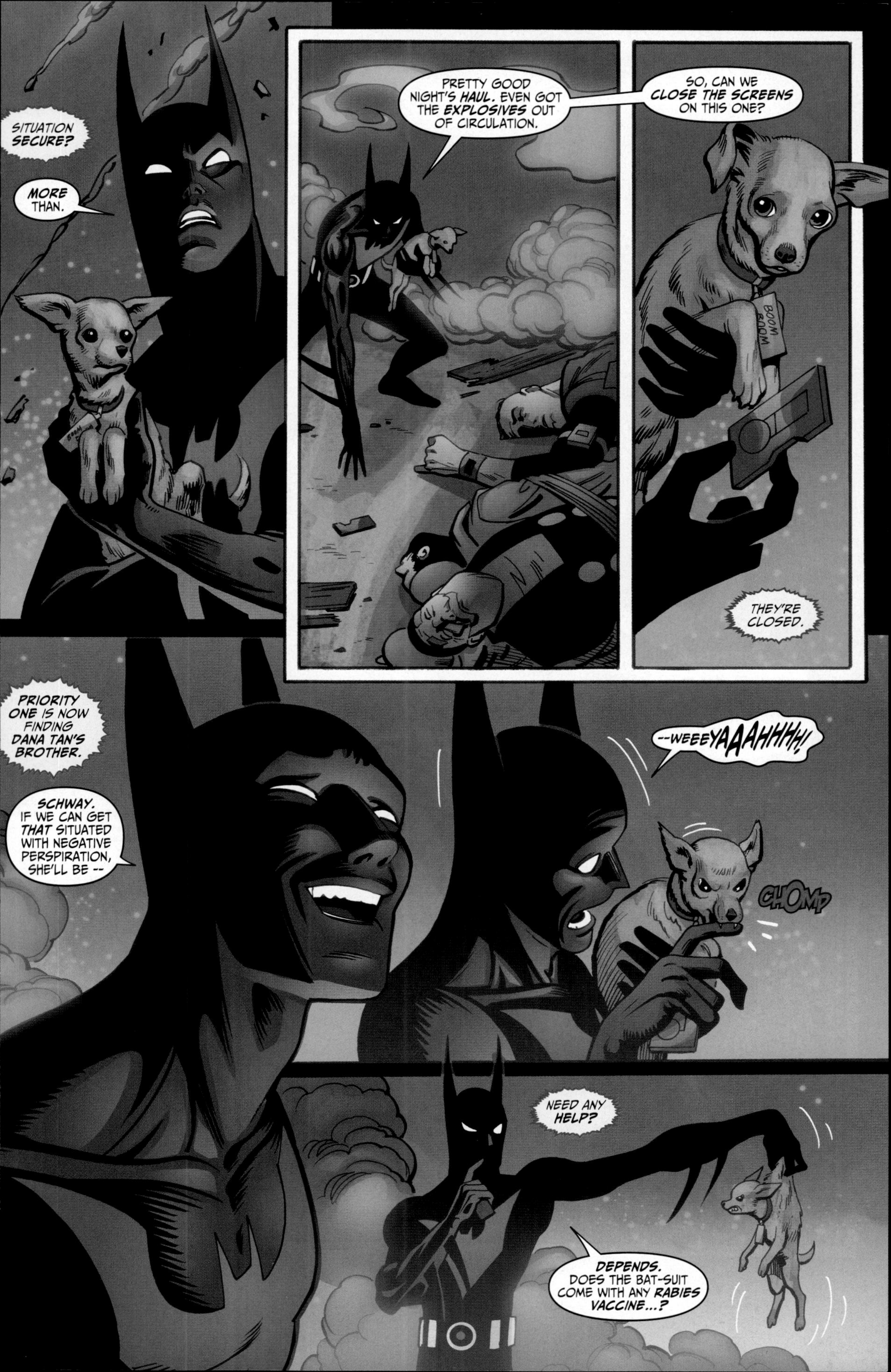
SITUATION SECURE?
MORE THAN.
PRETTY GOOD NIGHT'S HAUL. EVEN GOT THE EXPLOSIVES OUT OF CIRCULATION.
SO, CAN WE CLOSE THE SCREENS ON THIS ONE?
BOOM BOOM
THEY'RE CLOSED.
PRIORITY ONE IS NOW FINDING DANA TAN'S BROTHER.
SCHWAY. IF WE CAN GET THAT SITUATED WITH NEGATIVE PERSPIRATION, SHE'LL BE --
--WEEEYAAAHHHH!
CHOMP
NEED ANY HELP?
DEPENDS. DOES THE BAT-SUIT COME WITH ANY RABIES VACCINE...?

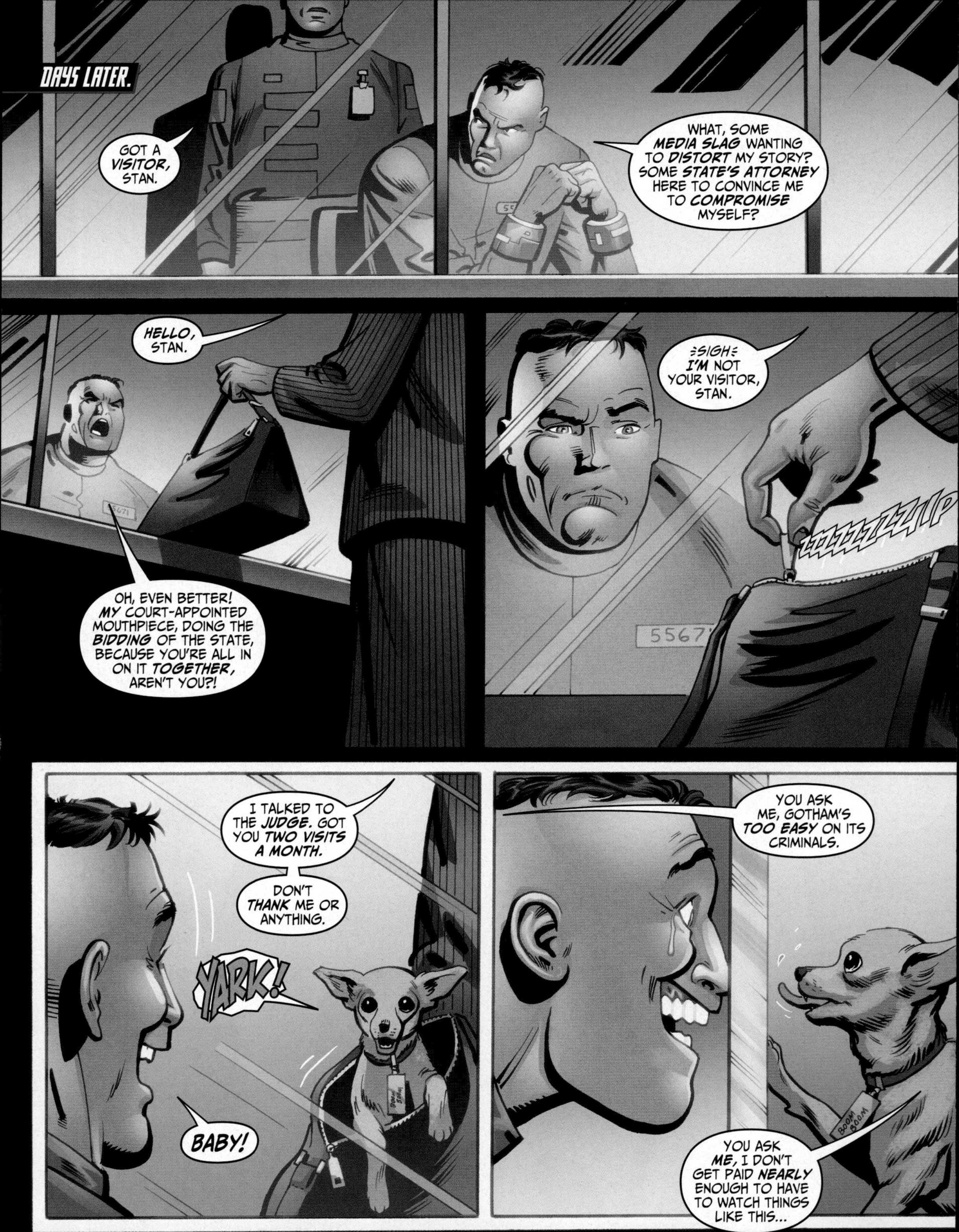
DAYS LATER.
GOT A VISITOR, STAN.
WHAT, SOME MEDIA SLAG WANTING TO DISTORT MY STORY? SOME STATE'S ATTORNEY HERE TO CONVINCE ME TO COMPROMISE MYSELF?
HELLO, STAN.
OH, EVEN BETTER! MY COURT-APPOINTED MOUTHPIECE, DOING THE BIDDING OF THE STATE, BECAUSE YOU'RE ALL IN ON IT TOGETHER, AREN'T YOU?!
SIGH I'M NOT YOUR VISITOR, STAN.
ZZZZZZZZIP
I TALKED TO THE JUDGE. GOT YOU TWO VISITS A MONTH.
DON'T THANK ME OR ANYTHING.
YARK!
BABY!
YOU ASK ME, GOTHAM'S TOO EASY ON ITS CRIMINALS.
YOU ASK ME, I DON'T GET PAID NEARLY ENOUGH TO HAVE TO WATCH THINGS LIKE THIS...

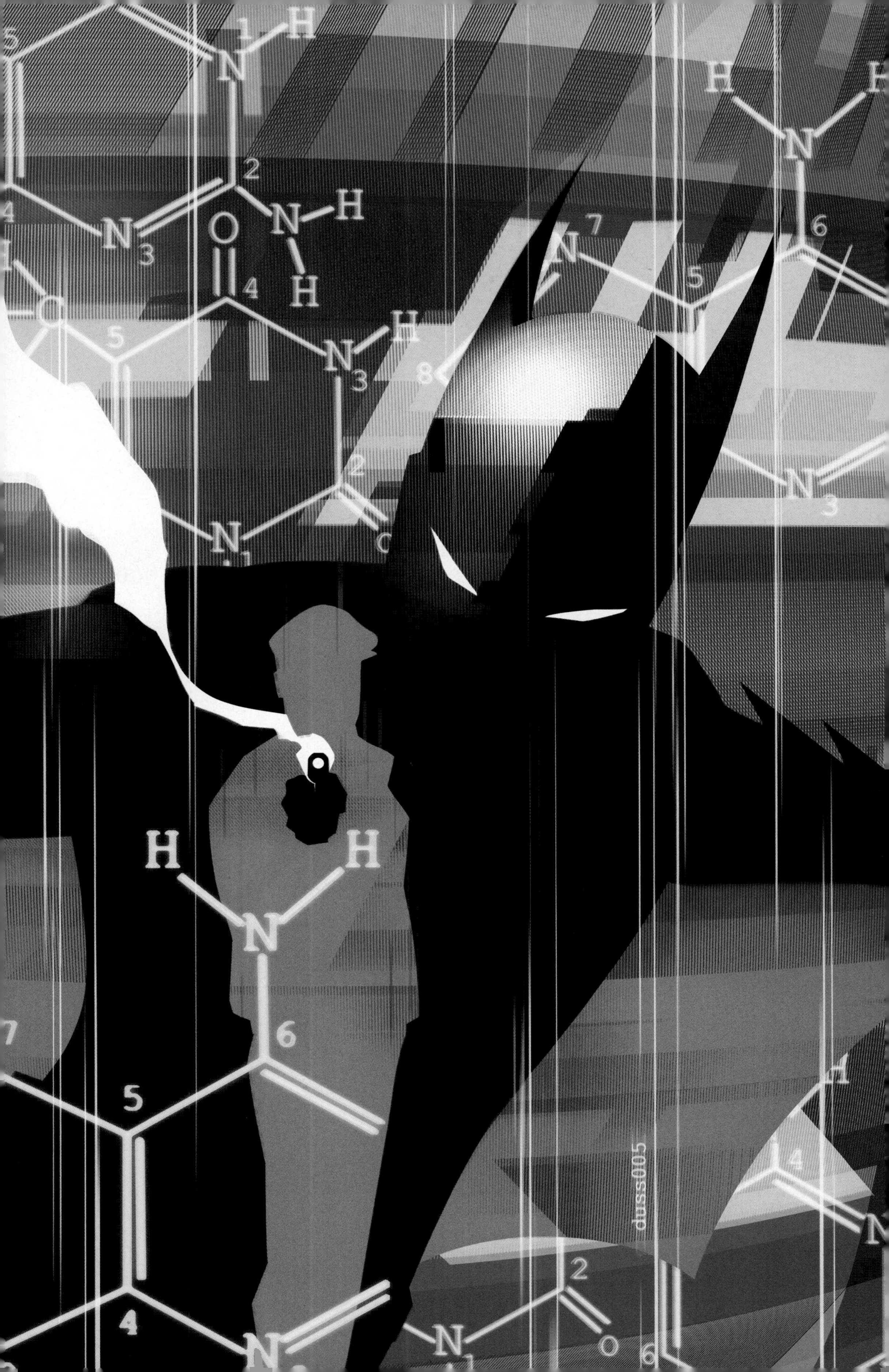
duss005

LEGENDS OF THE DARK KNIGHT: **JAKE**

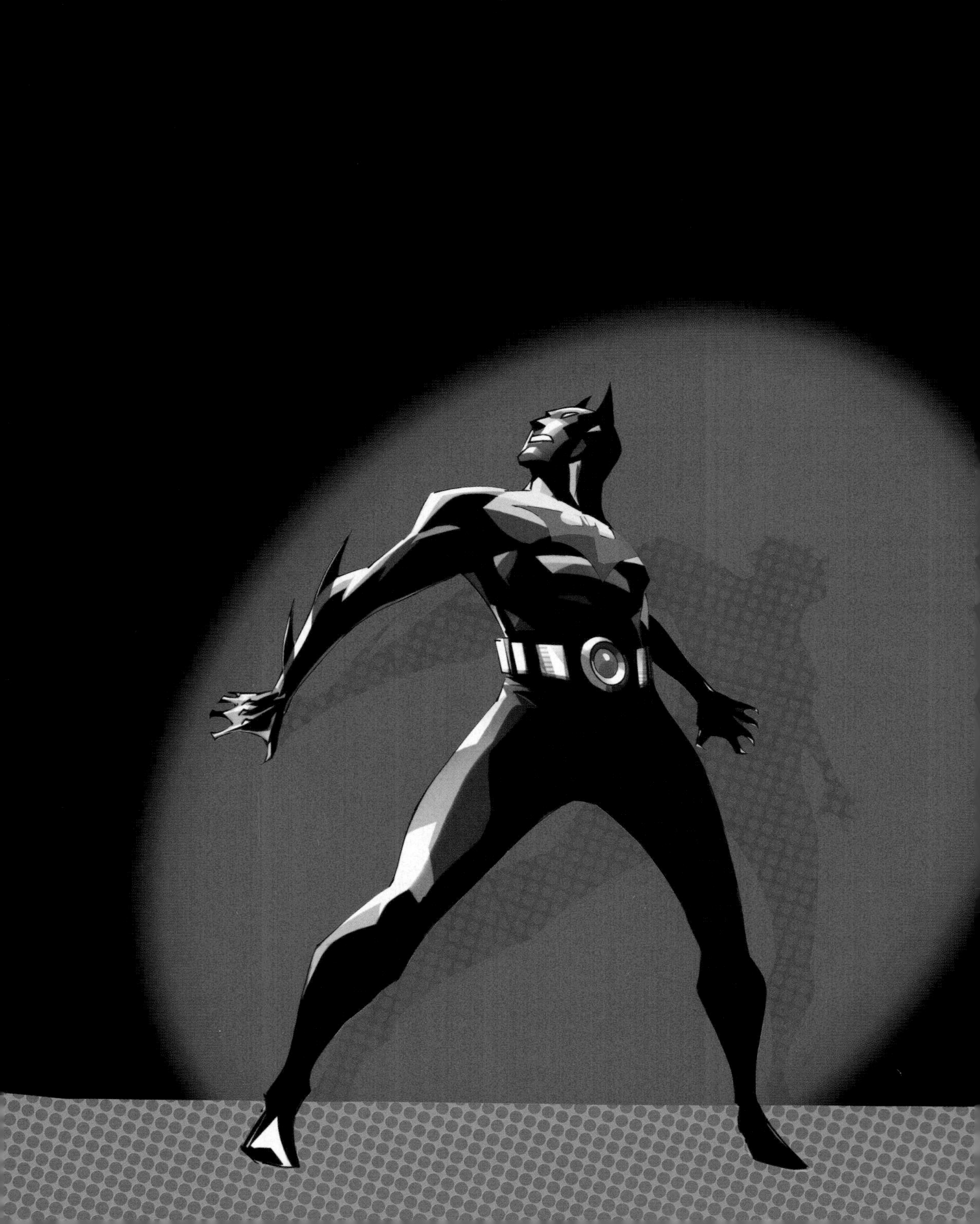

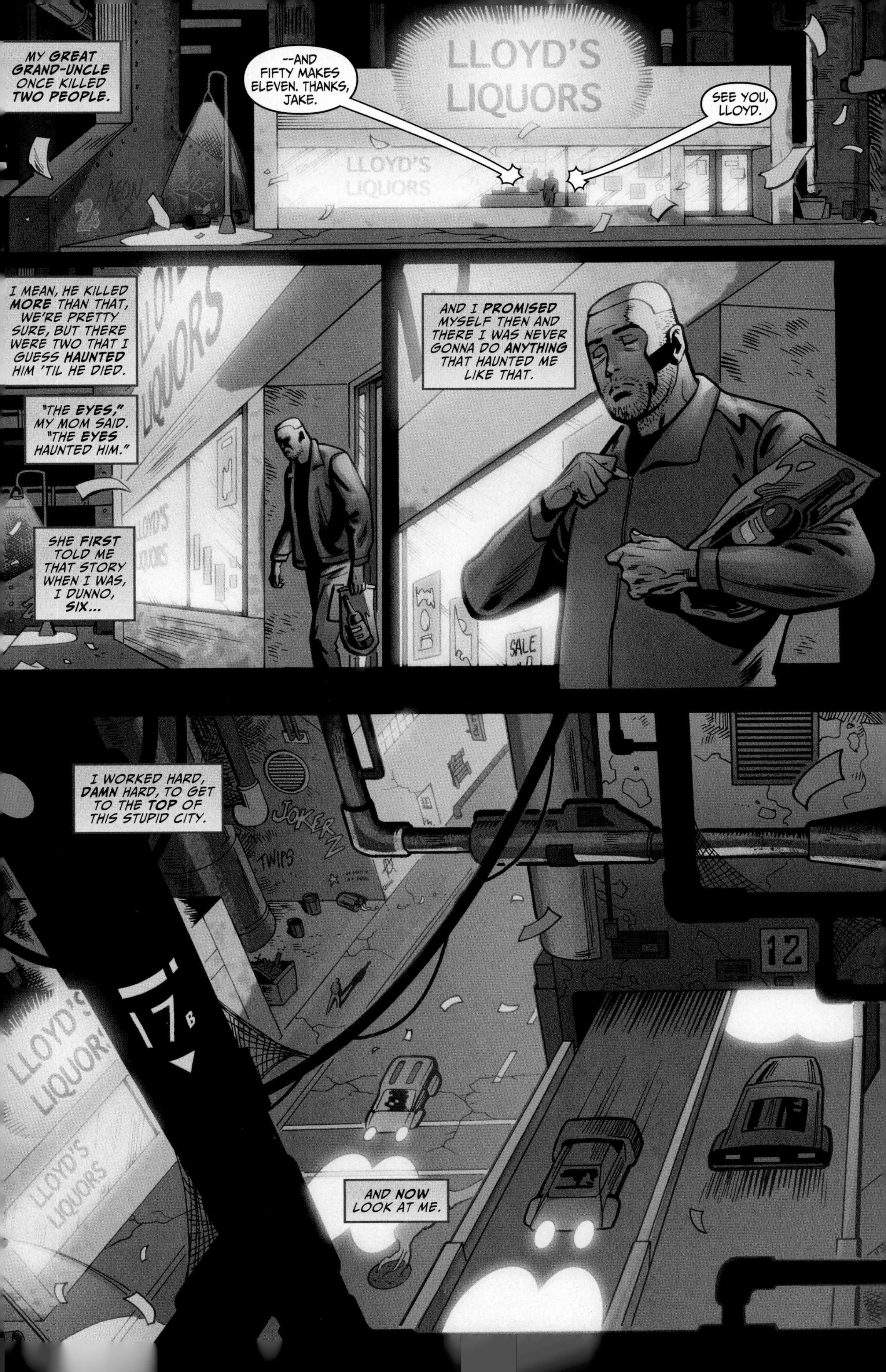

MY GREAT GRAND-UNCLE ONCE KILLED TWO PEOPLE.
LLOYD'S LIQUORS
--AND FIFTY MAKES ELEVEN. THANKS, JAKE.
SEE YOU, LLOYD.
I MEAN, HE KILLED MORE THAN THAT, WE'RE PRETTY SURE, BUT THERE WERE TWO THAT I GUESS HAUNTED HIM 'TIL HE DIED.
"THE EYES," MY MOM SAID. "THE EYES HAUNTED HIM."
SHE FIRST TOLD ME THAT STORY WHEN I WAS, I DUNNO, SIX...
AND I PROMISED MYSELF THEN AND THERE I WAS NEVER GONNA DO ANYTHING THAT HAUNTED ME LIKE THAT.
SALE
I WORKED HARD, DAMN HARD, TO GET TO THE TOP OF THIS STUPID CITY.
JOKERZ
TWIPS
12
17B
LLOYD'S LIQUORS
AND NOW LOOK AT ME.

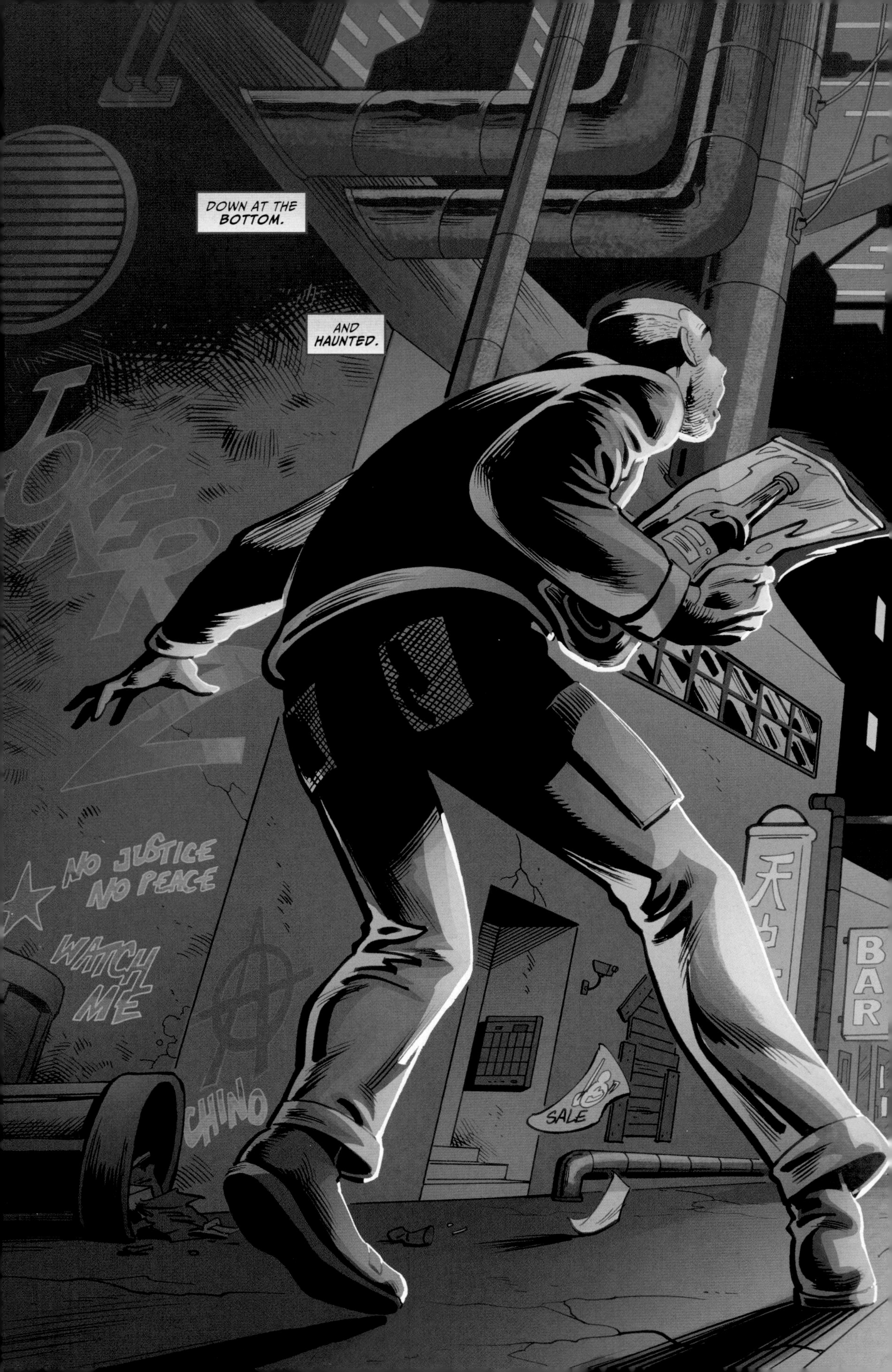
DOWN AT THE BOTTOM.
AND HAUNTED.
JOKER
NO JUSTICE NO PEACE
WATCH ME
CHINO
SALE
BAR

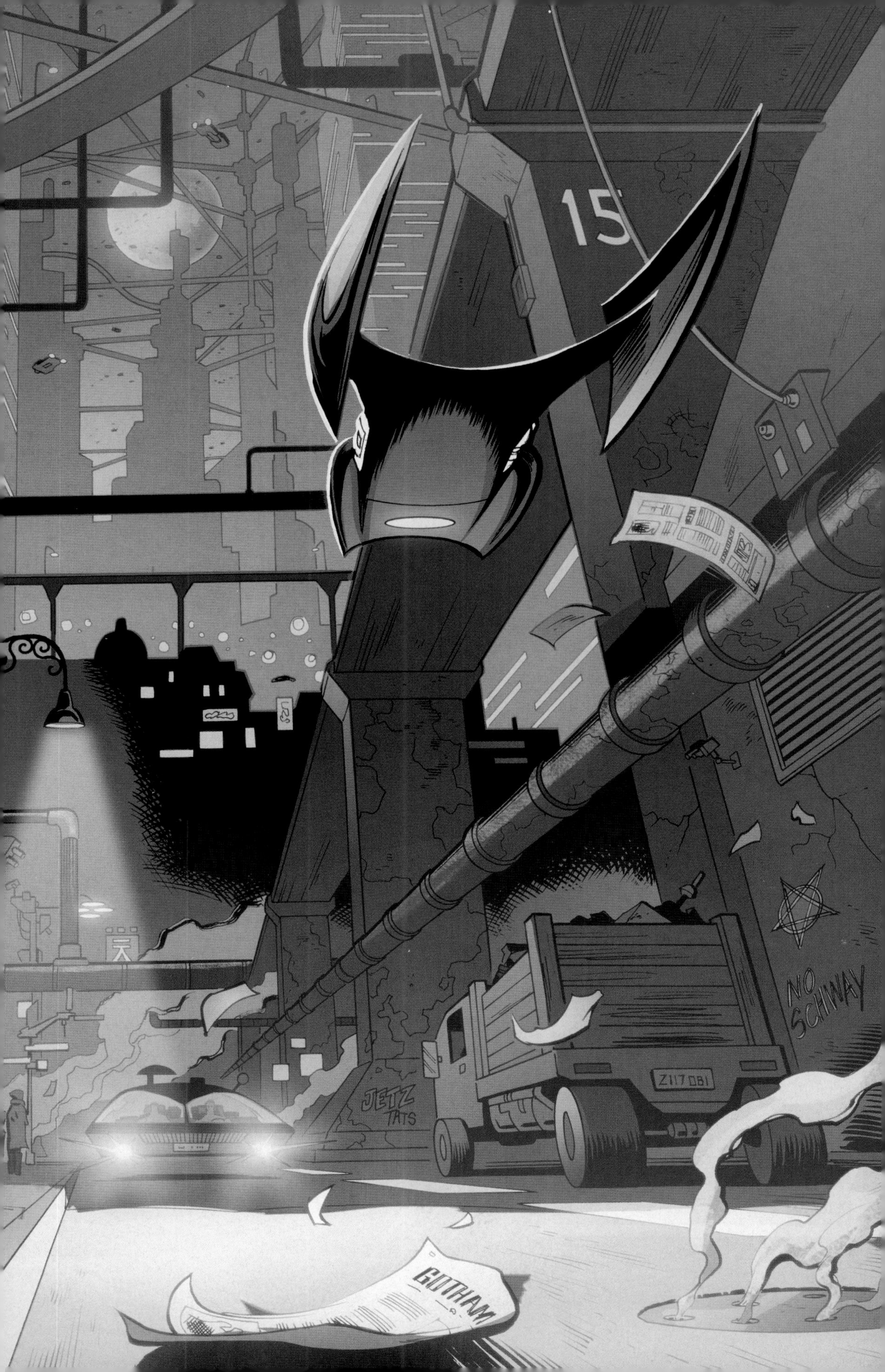
15
NO SCHWAY
JETZ
TATS
Z117 OBI
GOTHAM

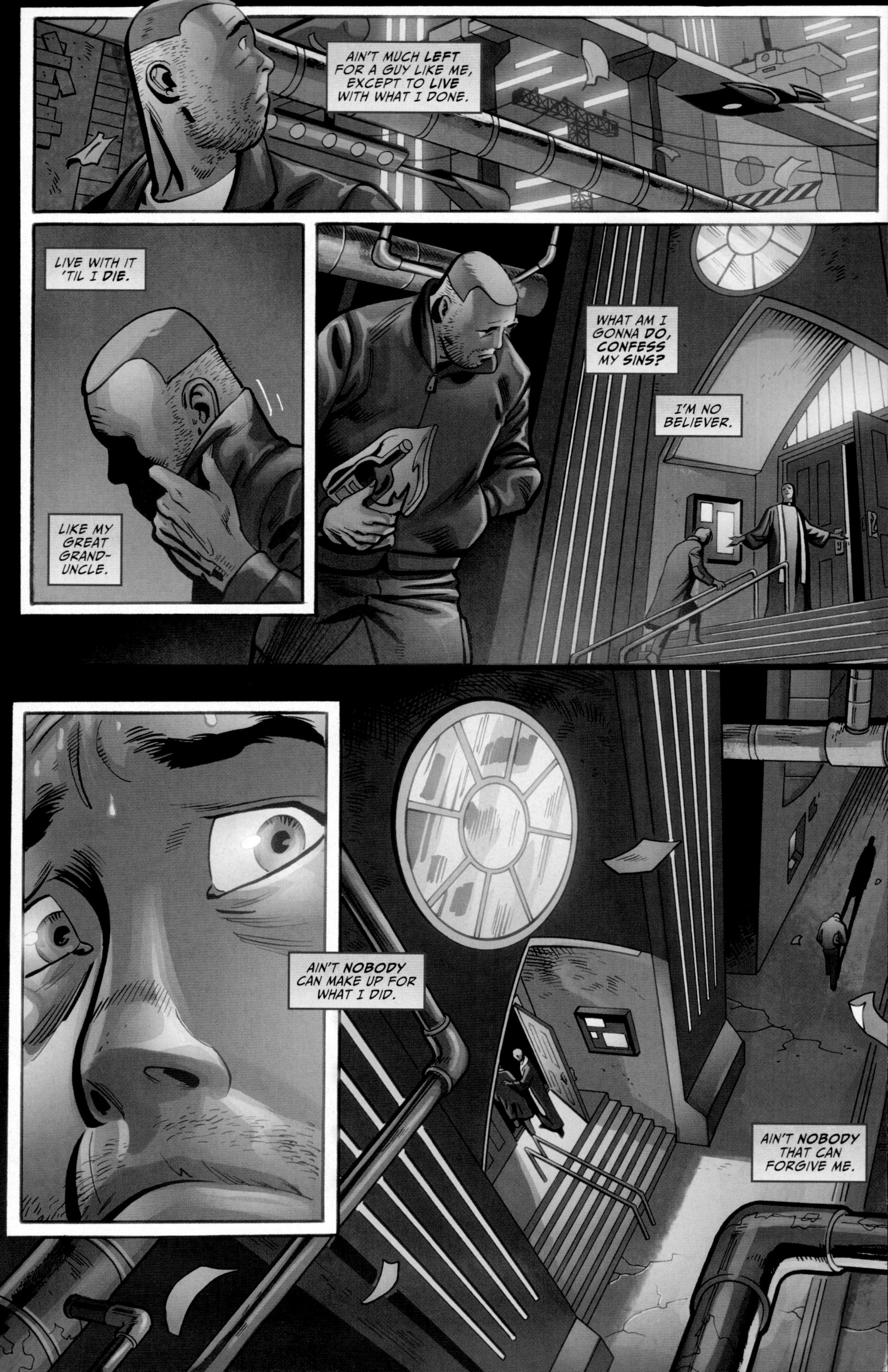
AIN'T MUCH LEFT FOR A GUY LIKE ME, EXCEPT TO LIVE WITH WHAT I DONE.
LIVE WITH IT 'TIL I DIE.
LIKE MY GREAT GRAND-UNCLE.
WHAT AM I GONNA DO, CONFESS MY SINS?
I'M NO BELIEVER.
AIN'T NOBODY CAN MAKE UP FOR WHAT I DID.
AIN'T NOBODY THAT CAN FORGIVE ME.

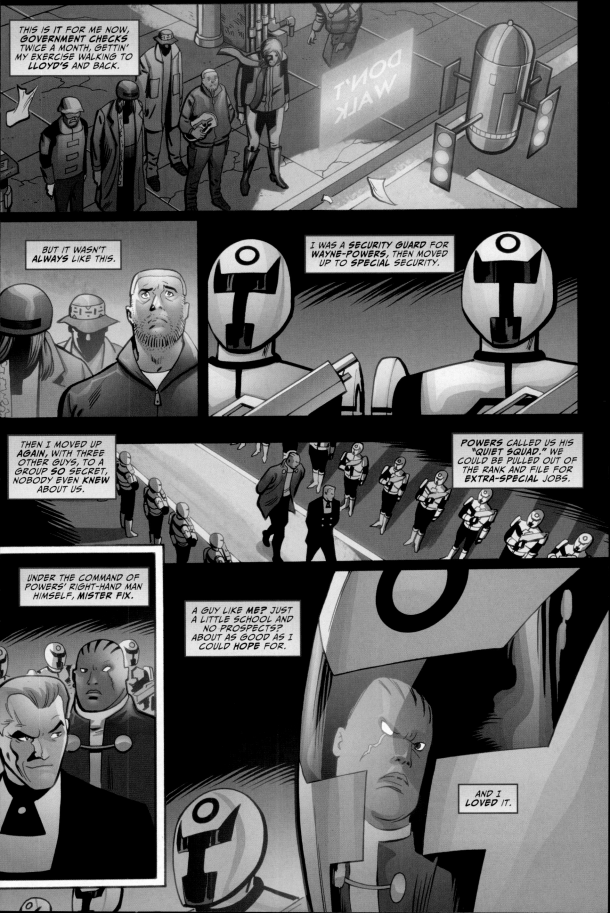

THIS IS IT FOR ME NOW, GOVERNMENT CHECKS TWICE A MONTH, GETTIN' MY EXERCISE WALKING TO LLOYD'S AND BACK.

BUT IT WASN'T ALWAYS LIKE THIS.

I WAS A SECURITY GUARD FOR WAYNE-POWERS, THEN MOVED UP TO SPECIAL SECURITY.

THEN I MOVED UP AGAIN, WITH THREE OTHER GUYS, TO A GROUP SO SECRET, NOBODY EVEN KNEW ABOUT US.

POWERS CALLED US HIS "QUIET SQUAD." WE COULD BE PULLED OUT OF THE RANK AND FILE FOR EXTRA-SPECIAL JOBS.

UNDER THE COMMAND OF POWERS' RIGHT-HAND MAN HIMSELF, MISTER FIX.

A GUY LIKE ME? JUST A LITTLE SCHOOL AND NO PROSPECTS? ABOUT AS GOOD AS I COULD HOPE FOR.

AND I LOVED IT.

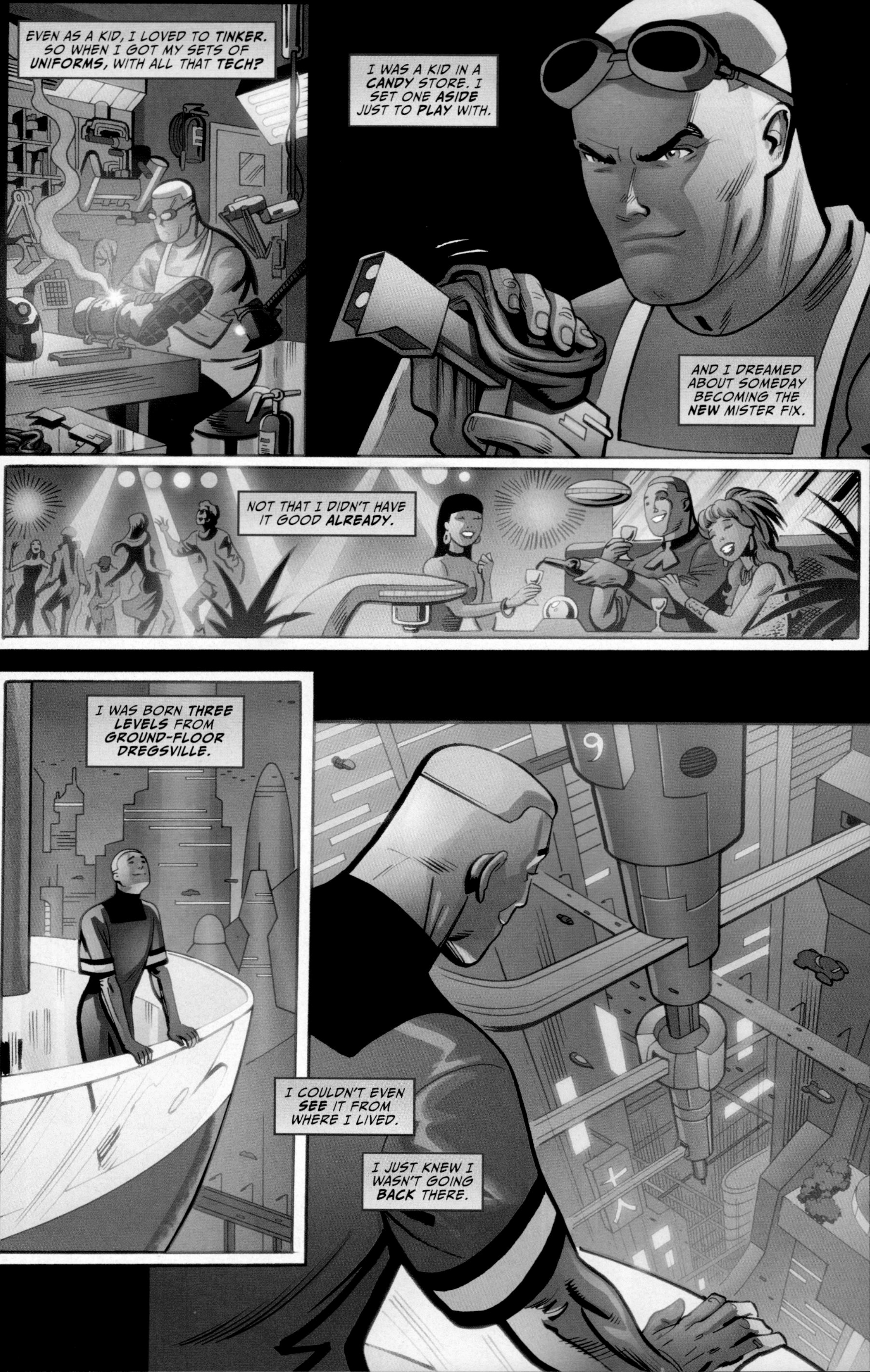
EVEN AS A KID, I LOVED TO TINKER. SO WHEN I GOT MY SETS OF UNIFORMS, WITH ALL THAT TECH?
I WAS A KID IN A CANDY STORE. I SET ONE ASIDE JUST TO PLAY WITH.
AND I DREAMED ABOUT SOMEDAY BECOMING THE NEW MISTER FIX.
NOT THAT I DIDN'T HAVE IT GOOD ALREADY.
I WAS BORN THREE LEVELS FROM GROUND-FLOOR DREGSVILLE.
I COULDN'T EVEN SEE IT FROM WHERE I LIVED.
I JUST KNEW I WASN'T GOING BACK THERE.

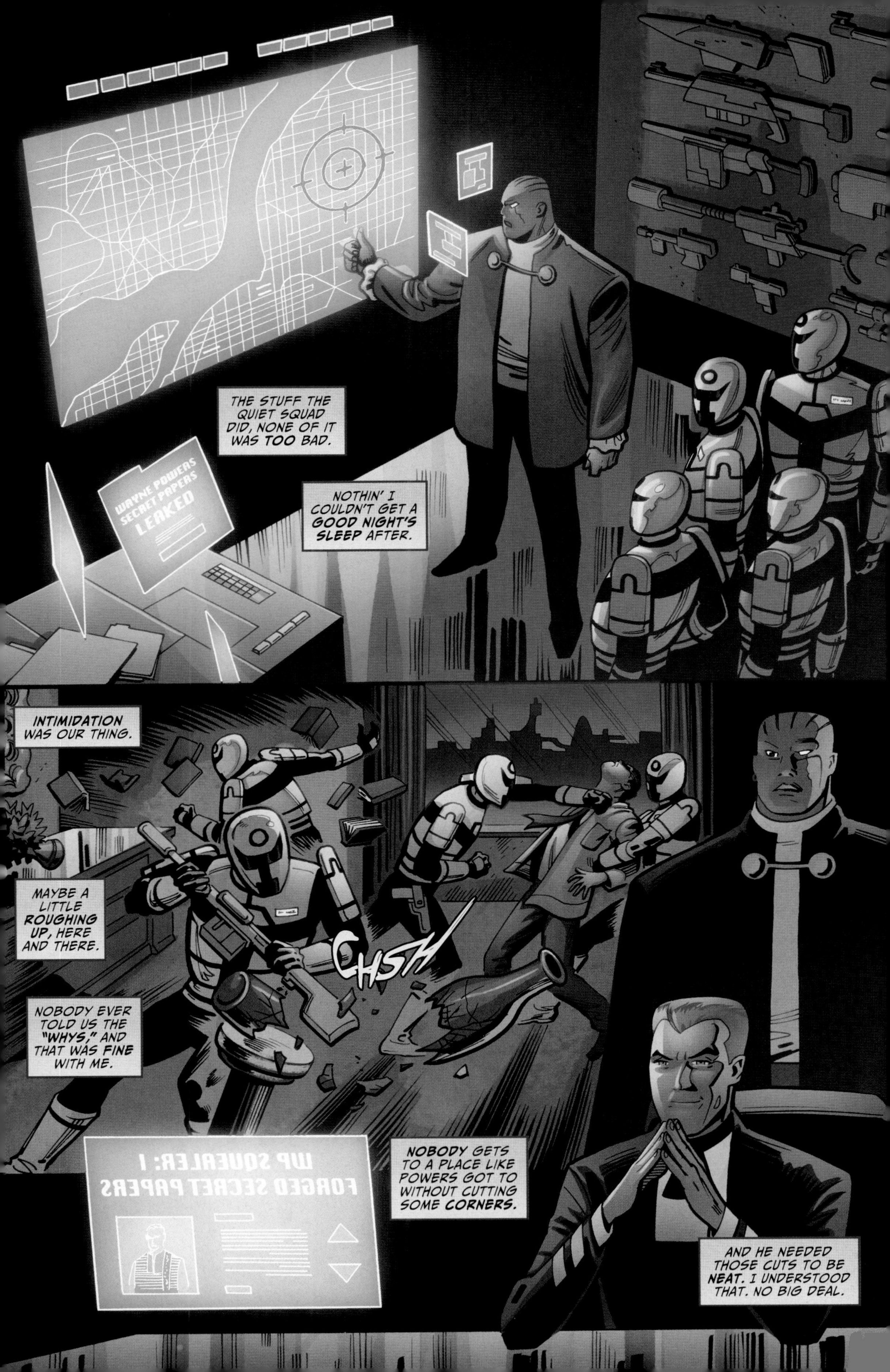
THE STUFF THE QUIET SQUAD DID, NONE OF IT WAS TOO BAD.
WAYNE POWERS SECRET PAPERS LEAKED
NOTHIN' I COULDN'T GET A GOOD NIGHT'S SLEEP AFTER.
INTIMIDATION WAS OUR THING.
MAYBE A LITTLE ROUGHING UP, HERE AND THERE.
CHSH
NOBODY EVER TOLD US THE "WHYS," AND THAT WAS FINE WITH ME.
WP SQUEALER: I FORGED SECRET PAPERS
NOBODY GETS TO A PLACE LIKE POWERS GOT TO WITHOUT CUTTING SOME CORNERS.
AND HE NEEDED THOSE CUTS TO BE NEAT. I UNDERSTOOD THAT. NO BIG DEAL.

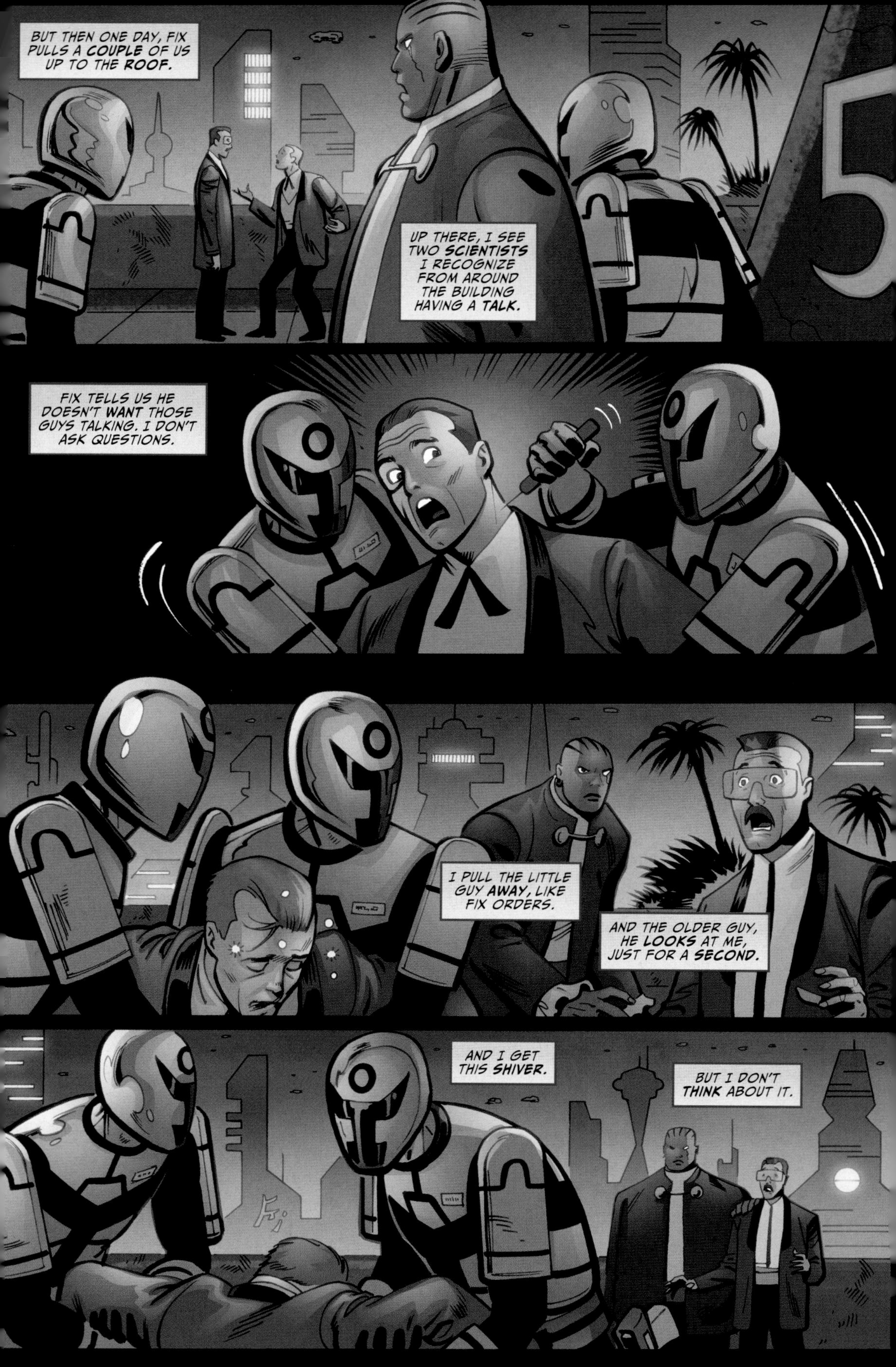
BUT THEN ONE DAY, FIX PULLS A COUPLE OF US UP TO THE ROOF.
UP THERE, I SEE TWO SCIENTISTS I RECOGNIZE FROM AROUND THE BUILDING HAVING A TALK.
FIX TELLS US HE DOESN'T WANT THOSE GUYS TALKING. I DON'T ASK QUESTIONS.
I PULL THE LITTLE GUY AWAY, LIKE FIX ORDERS.
AND THE OLDER GUY, HE LOOKS AT ME, JUST FOR A SECOND.
AND I GET THIS SHIVER.
BUT I DON'T THINK ABOUT IT.

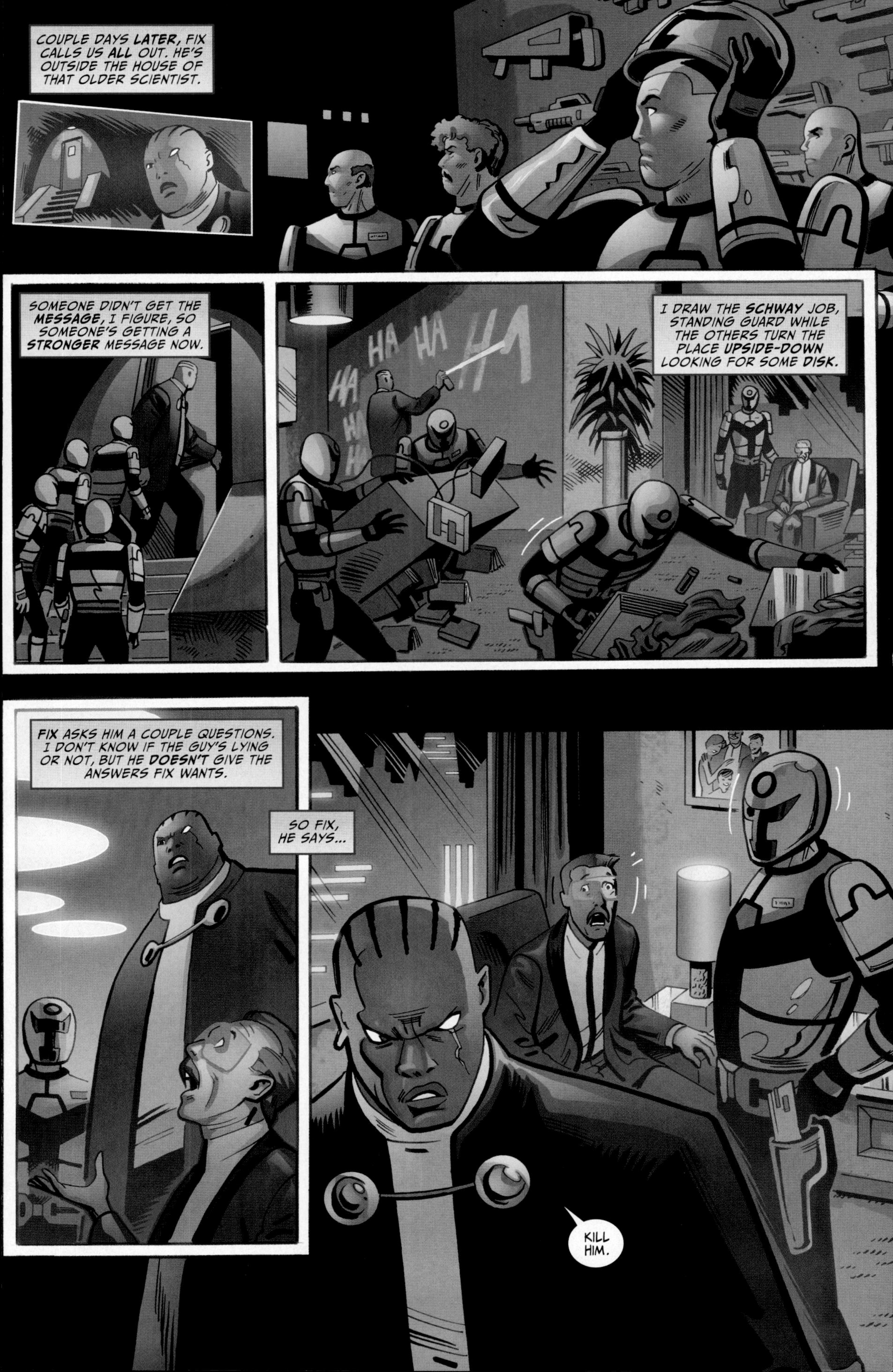

COUPLE DAYS LATER, FIX CALLS US ALL OUT. HE'S OUTSIDE THE HOUSE OF THAT OLDER SCIENTIST.
SOMEONE DIDN'T GET THE MESSAGE, I FIGURE, SO SOMEONE'S GETTING A STRONGER MESSAGE NOW.
HA HA HA HA HA HA HA
I DRAW THE SCHWAY JOB, STANDING GUARD WHILE THE OTHERS TURN THE PLACE UPSIDE-DOWN LOOKING FOR SOME DISK.
FIX ASKS HIM A COUPLE QUESTIONS. I DON'T KNOW IF THE GUY'S LYING OR NOT, BUT HE DOESN'T GIVE THE ANSWERS FIX WANTS.
SO FIX, HE SAYS...
KILL HIM.

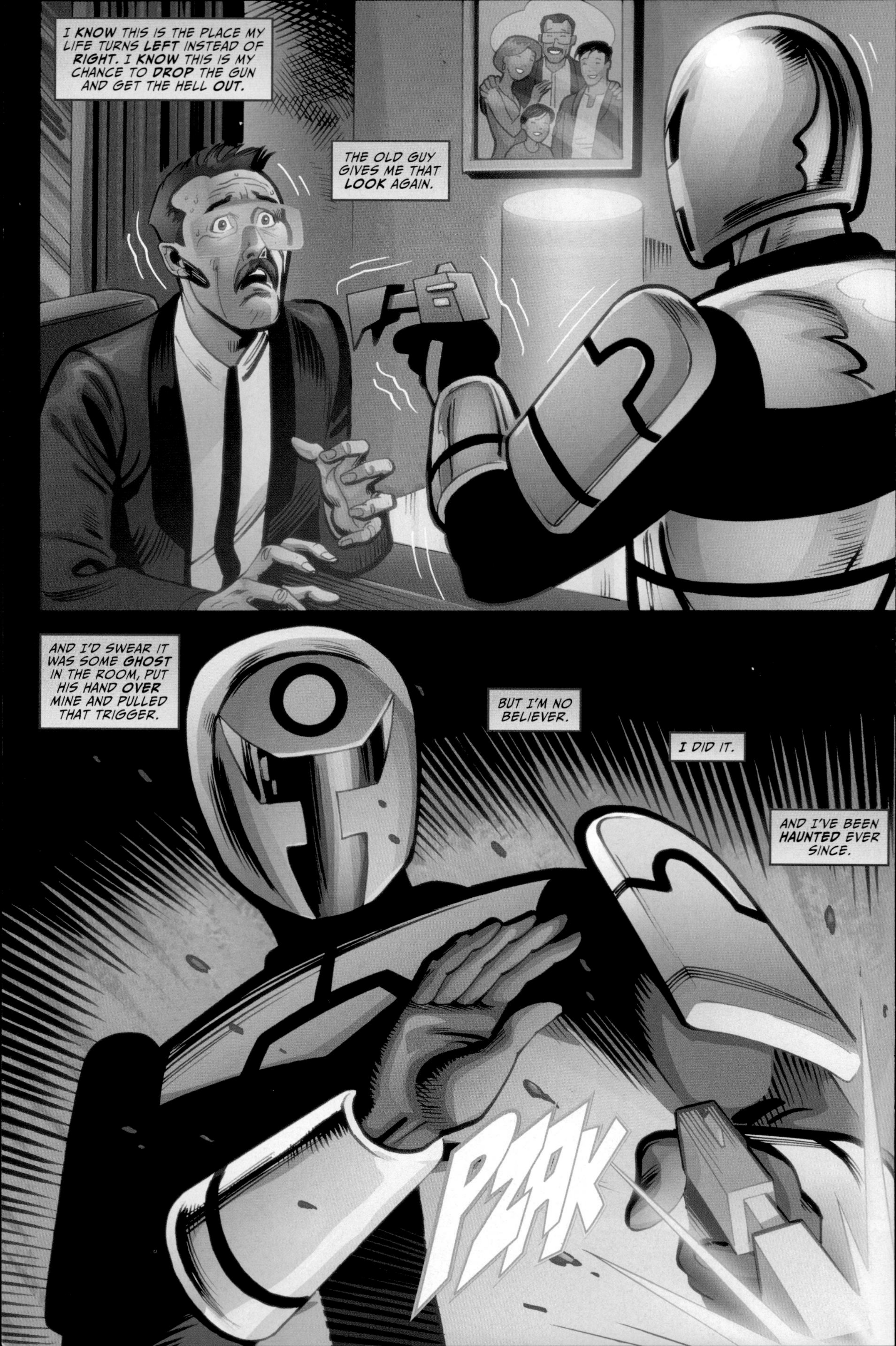
I KNOW THIS IS THE PLACE MY LIFE TURNS LEFT INSTEAD OF RIGHT. I KNOW THIS IS MY CHANCE TO DROP THE GUN AND GET THE HELL OUT.
THE OLD GUY GIVES ME THAT LOOK AGAIN.
AND I'D SWEAR IT WAS SOME GHOST IN THE ROOM, PUT HIS HAND OVER MINE AND PULLED THAT TRIGGER.
BUT I'M NO BELIEVER.
I DID IT.
AND I'VE BEEN HAUNTED EVER SINCE.
PZAK

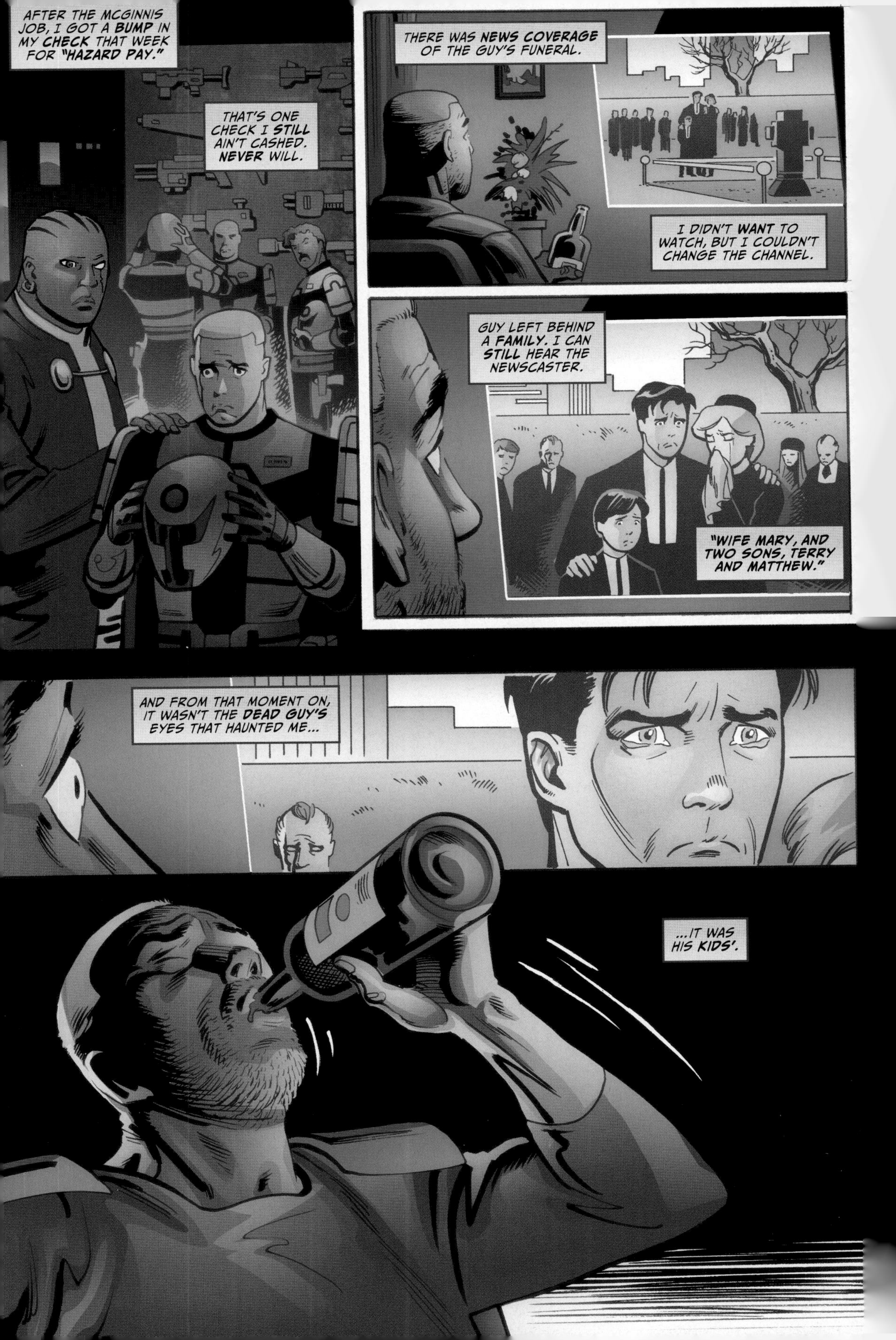
AFTER THE MCGINNIS JOB, I GOT A BUMP IN MY CHECK THAT WEEK FOR "HAZARD PAY."
THAT'S ONE CHECK I STILL AIN'T CASHED. NEVER WILL.
THERE WAS NEWS COVERAGE OF THE GUY'S FUNERAL.
I DIDN'T WANT TO WATCH, BUT I COULDN'T CHANGE THE CHANNEL.
GUY LEFT BEHIND A FAMILY. I CAN STILL HEAR THE NEWSCASTER.
"WIFE MARY, AND TWO SONS, TERRY AND MATTHEW."
AND FROM THAT MOMENT ON, IT WASN'T THE DEAD GUY'S EYES THAT HAUNTED ME...
...IT WAS HIS KIDS'.

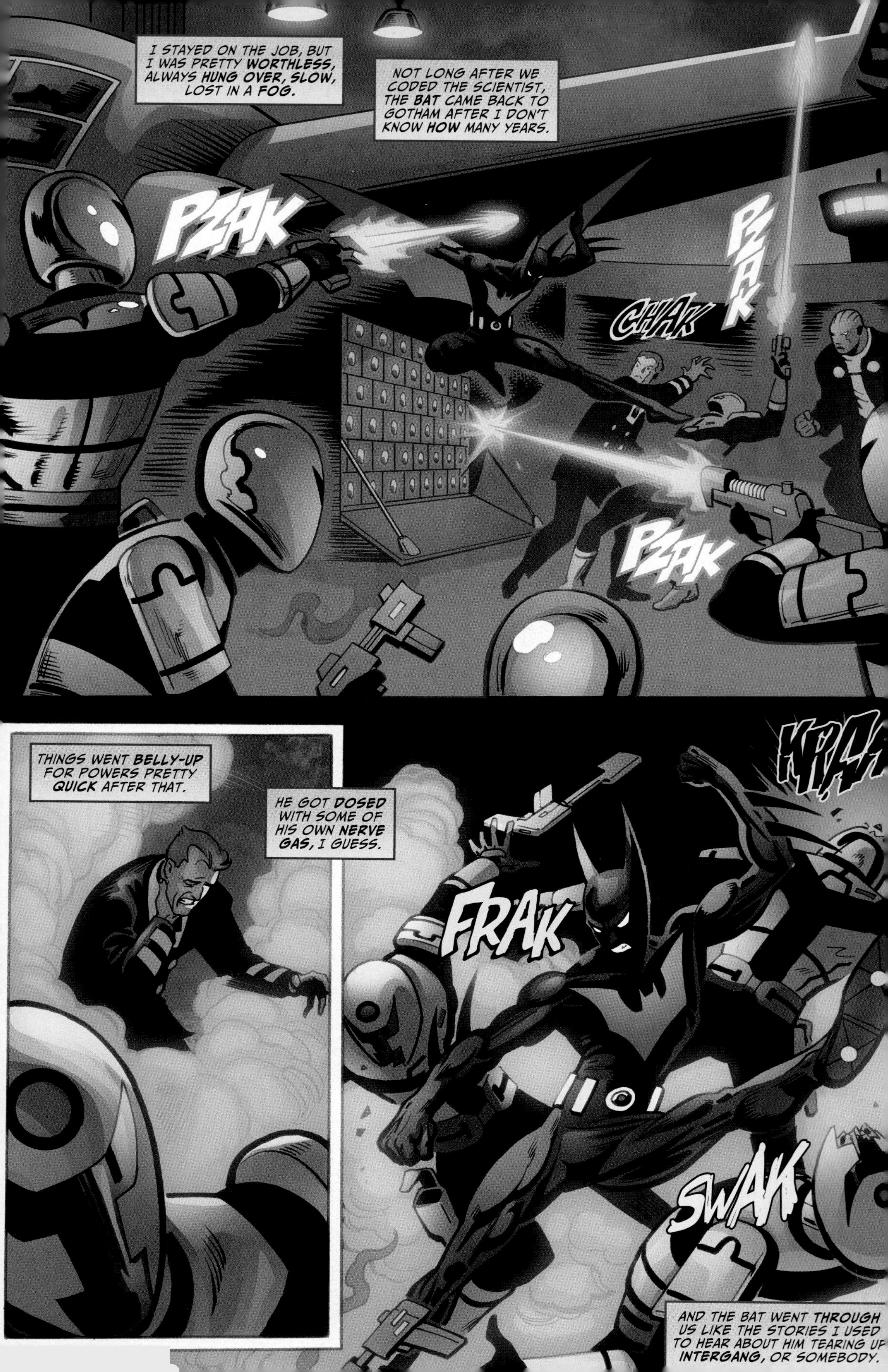
I STAYED ON THE JOB, BUT I WAS PRETTY WORTHLESS, ALWAYS HUNG OVER, SLOW, LOST IN A FOG.
NOT LONG AFTER WE CODED THE SCIENTIST, THE BAT CAME BACK TO GOTHAM AFTER I DON'T KNOW HOW MANY YEARS.
PZAK
PZAK
CHAK
PZAK
THINGS WENT BELLY-UP FOR POWERS PRETTY QUICK AFTER THAT.
HE GOT DOSED WITH SOME OF HIS OWN NERVE GAS, I GUESS.
FRAK
SWAK
AND THE BAT WENT THROUGH US LIKE THE STORIES I USED TO HEAR ABOUT HIM TEARING UP INTERGANG, OR SOMEBODY.

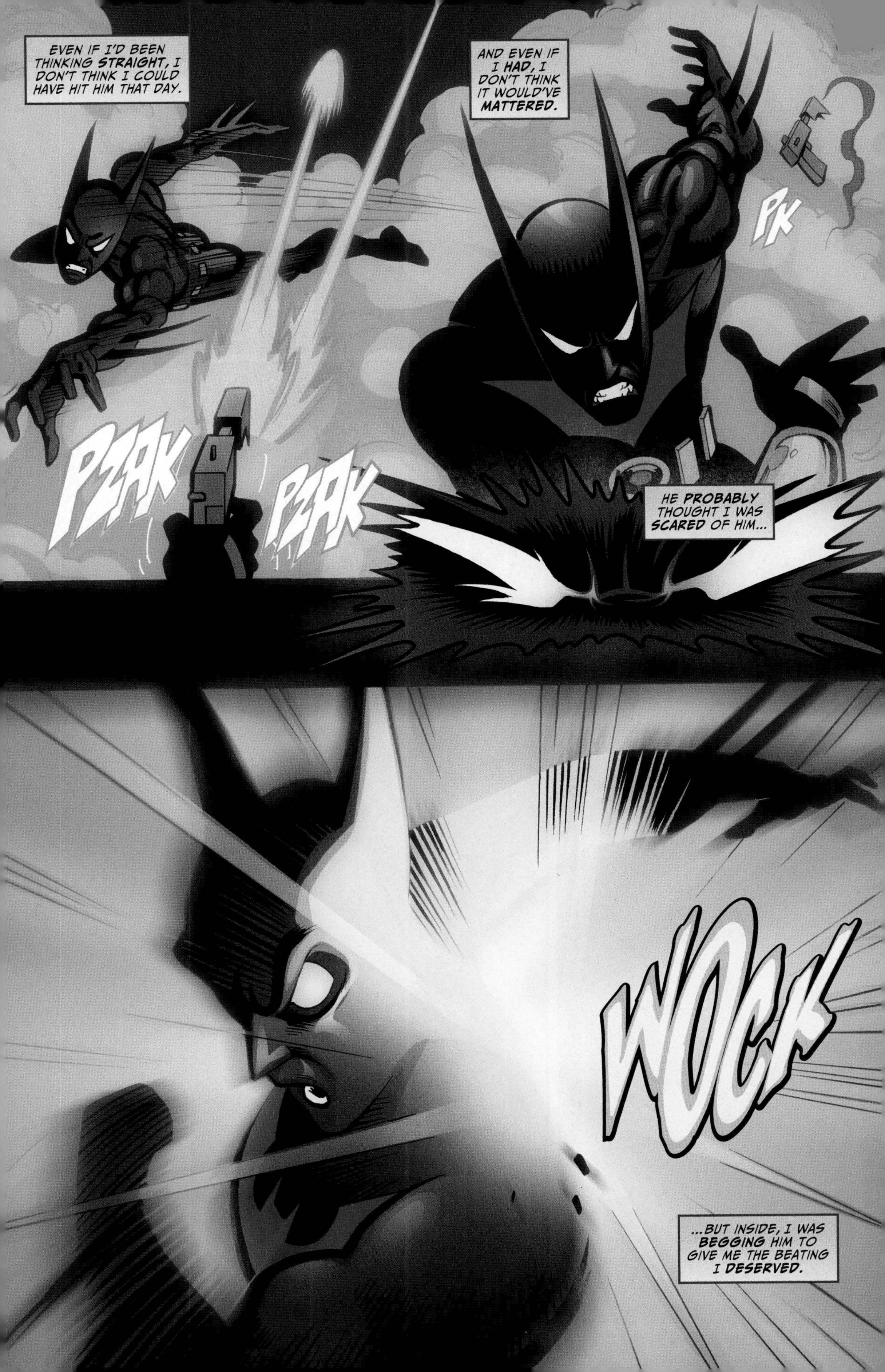
EVEN IF I'D BEEN THINKING STRAIGHT, I DON'T THINK I COULD HAVE HIT HIM THAT DAY.
AND EVEN IF I HAD, I DON'T THINK IT WOULD'VE MATTERED.
PK
PZAK
PZAK
HE PROBABLY THOUGHT I WAS SCARED OF HIM...
WOCK
...BUT INSIDE, I WAS BEGGING HIM TO GIVE ME THE BEATING I DESERVED.

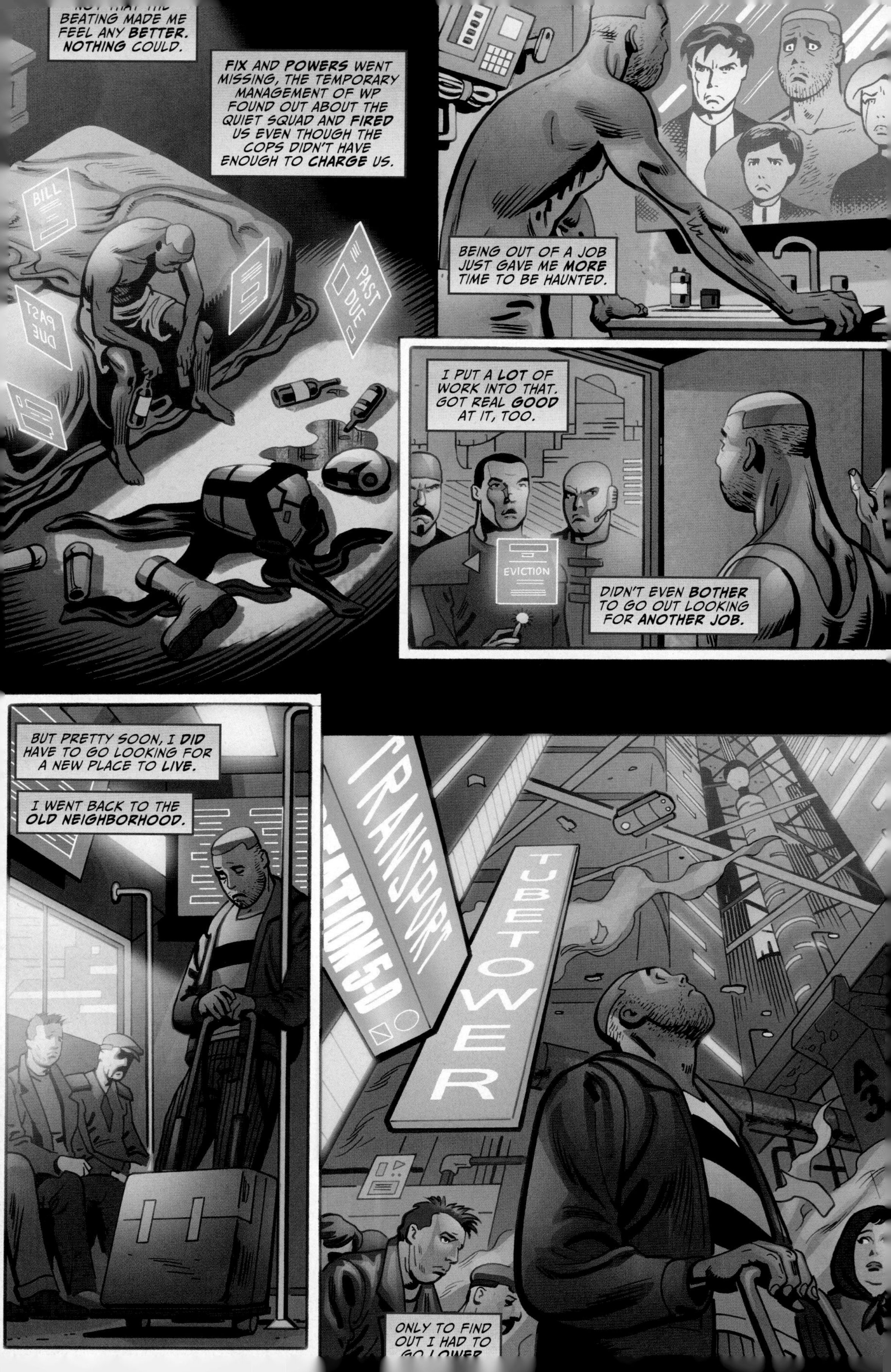

BEATING MADE ME FEEL ANY BETTER. NOTHING COULD.
FIX AND POWERS WENT MISSING, THE TEMPORARY MANAGEMENT OF WP FOUND OUT ABOUT THE QUIET SQUAD AND FIRED US EVEN THOUGH THE COPS DIDN'T HAVE ENOUGH TO CHARGE US.
BILL
PAST DUE
PAST DUE
BEING OUT OF A JOB JUST GAVE ME MORE TIME TO BE HAUNTED.
I PUT A LOT OF WORK INTO THAT. GOT REAL GOOD AT IT, TOO.
EVICTION
DIDN'T EVEN BOTHER TO GO OUT LOOKING FOR ANOTHER JOB.
BUT PRETTY SOON, I DID HAVE TO GO LOOKING FOR A NEW PLACE TO LIVE.
I WENT BACK TO THE OLD NEIGHBORHOOD.
TRANSPORT
STATION 5-D
TUBE TOWER
ONLY TO FIND OUT I HAD TO GO LOWER

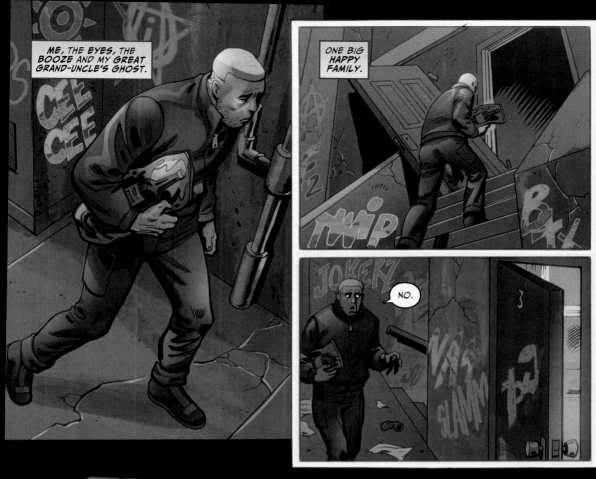

ME, THE EYES, THE BOOZE AND MY GREAT GRAND-UNCLE'S GHOST.

ONE BIG HAPPY FAMILY.

NO.

NO!

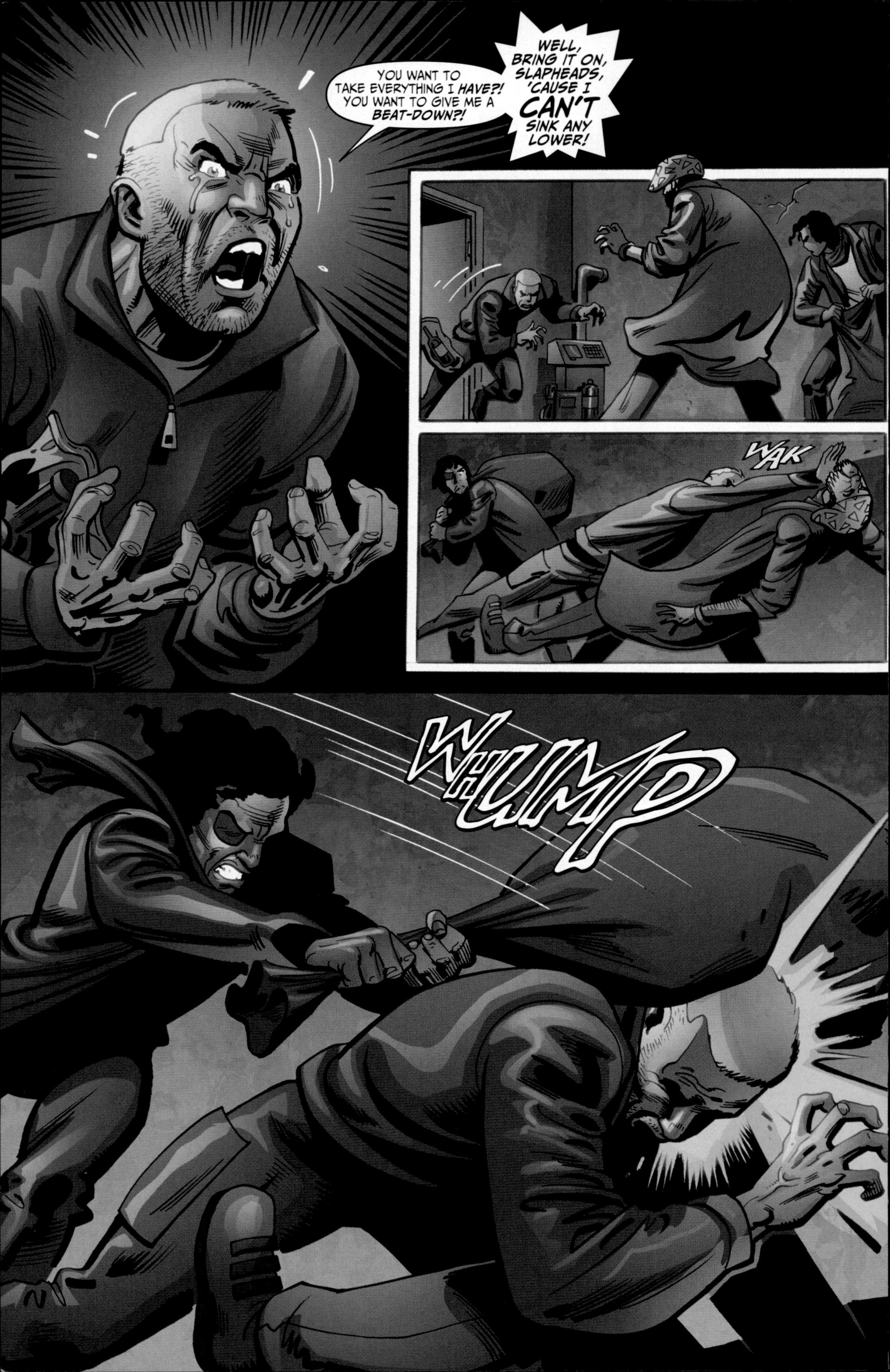
YOU WANT TO TAKE EVERYTHING I HAVE?! YOU WANT TO GIVE ME A BEAT-DOWN?!
WELL, BRING IT ON, SLAPHEADS, 'CAUSE I CAN'T SINK ANY LOWER!
WAK
WHUMP

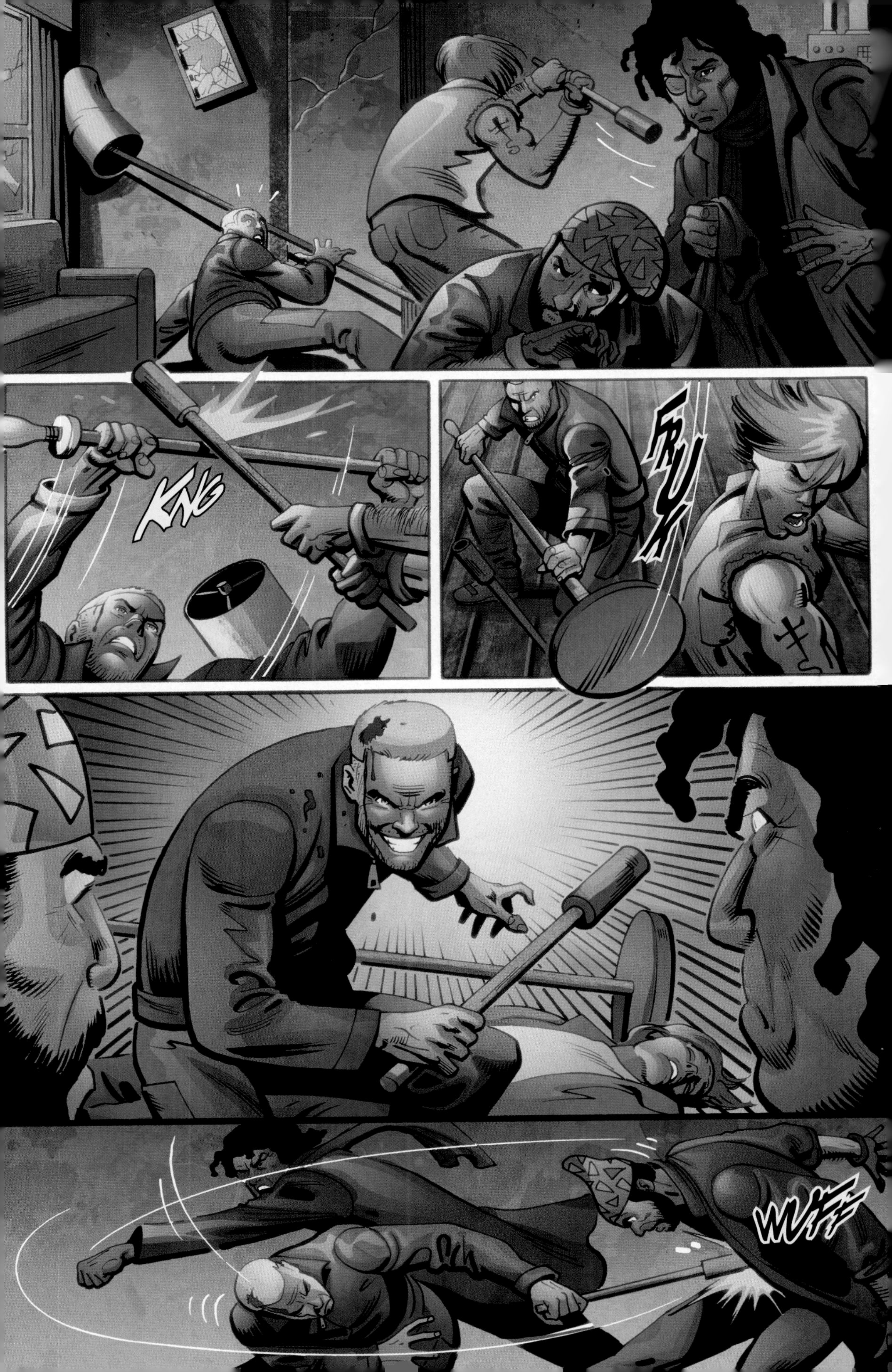
KNG
FRUK
WUFF

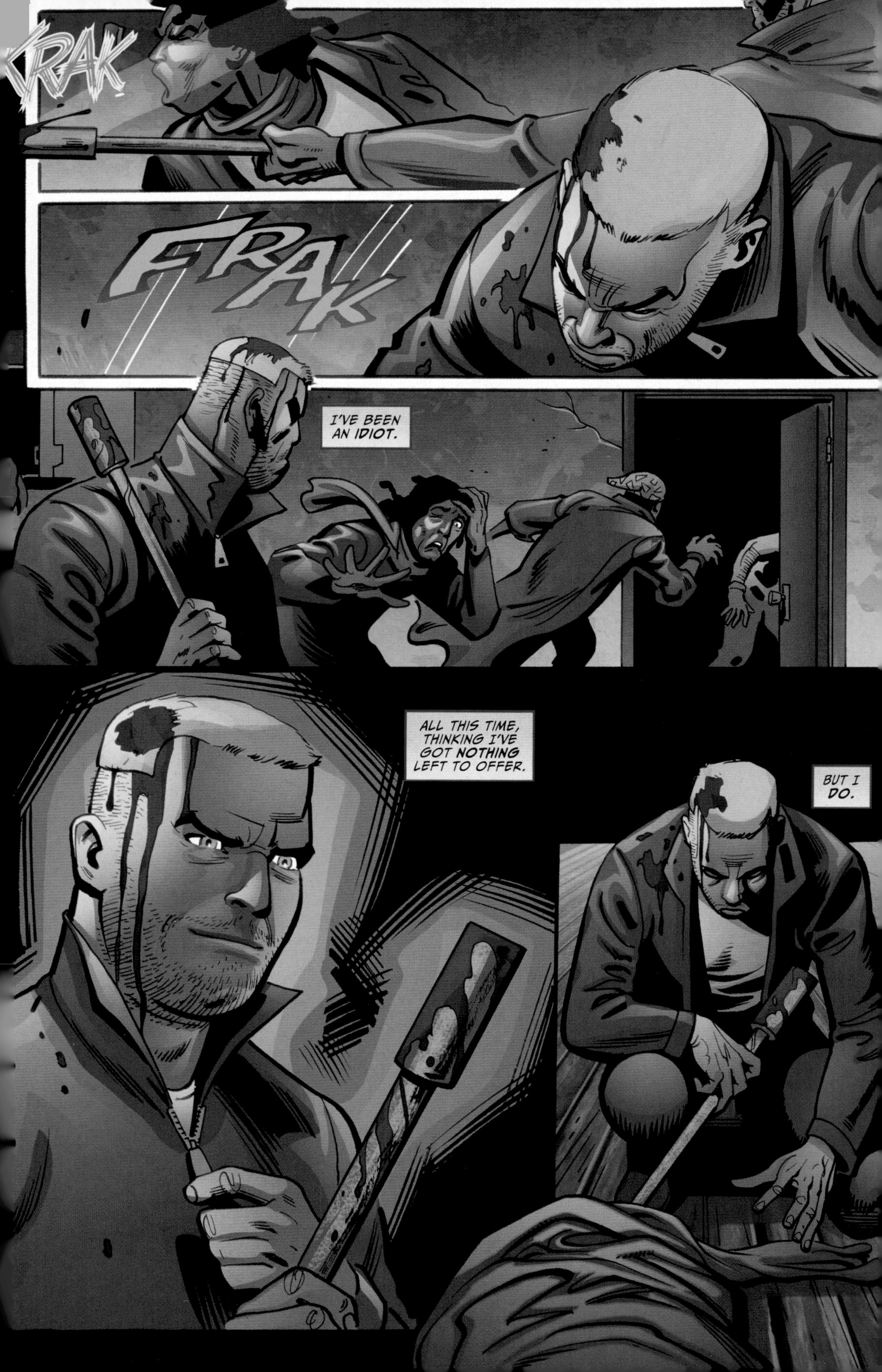
KRAK
FRAK
I'VE BEEN AN IDIOT.
ALL THIS TIME, THINKING I'VE GOT NOTHING LEFT TO OFFER.
BUT I DO.

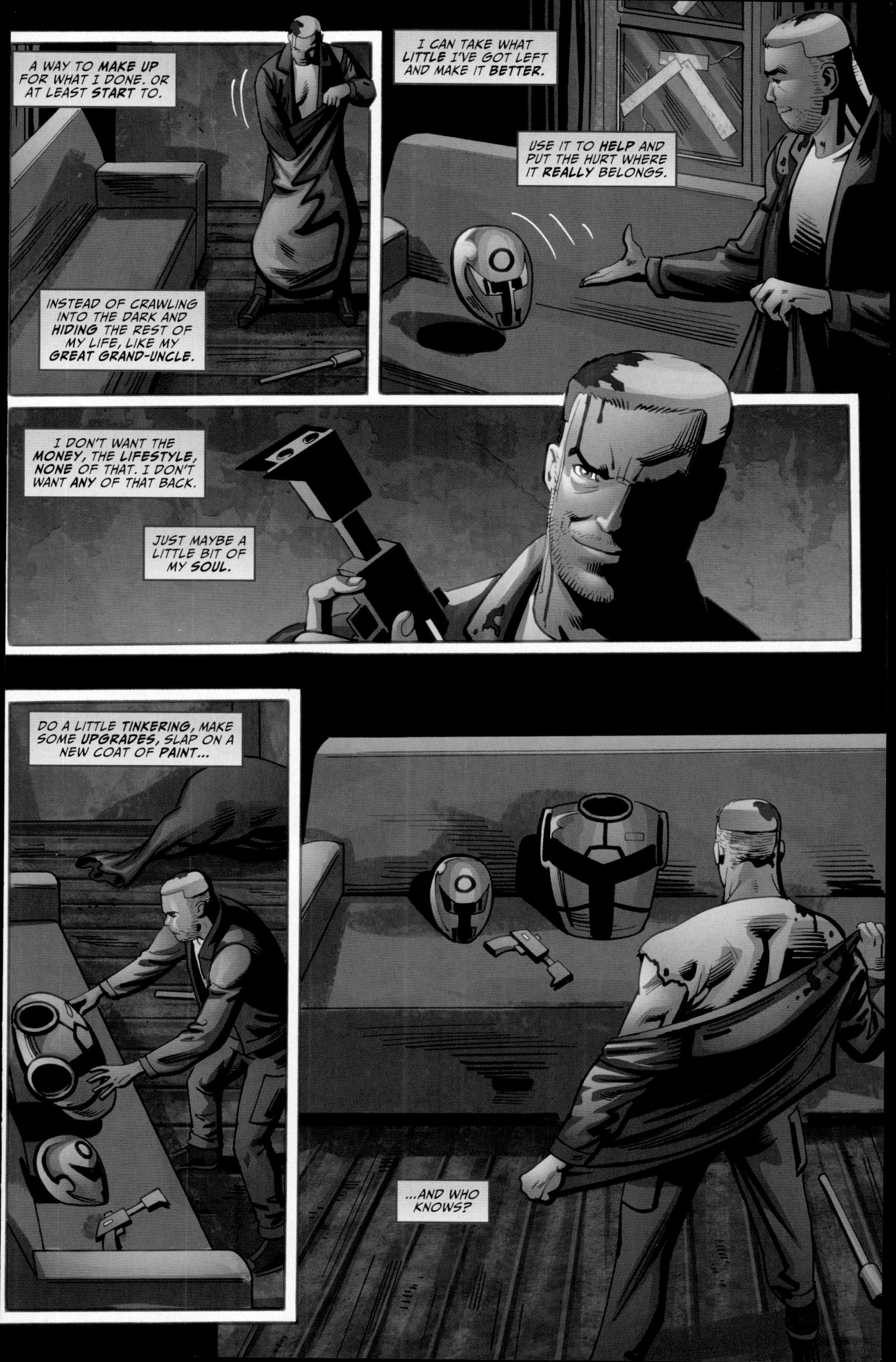
A WAY TO MAKE UP FOR WHAT I DONE. OR AT LEAST START TO.
INSTEAD OF CRAWLING INTO THE DARK AND HIDING THE REST OF MY LIFE, LIKE MY GREAT GRAND-UNCLE.
I CAN TAKE WHAT LITTLE I'VE GOT LEFT AND MAKE IT BETTER.
USE IT TO HELP AND PUT THE HURT WHERE IT REALLY BELONGS.
I DON'T WANT THE MONEY, THE LIFESTYLE, NONE OF THAT. I DON'T WANT ANY OF THAT BACK.
JUST MAYBE A LITTLE BIT OF MY SOUL.
DO A LITTLE TINKERING, MAKE SOME UPGRADES, SLAP ON A NEW COAT OF PAINT...
...AND WHO KNOWS?

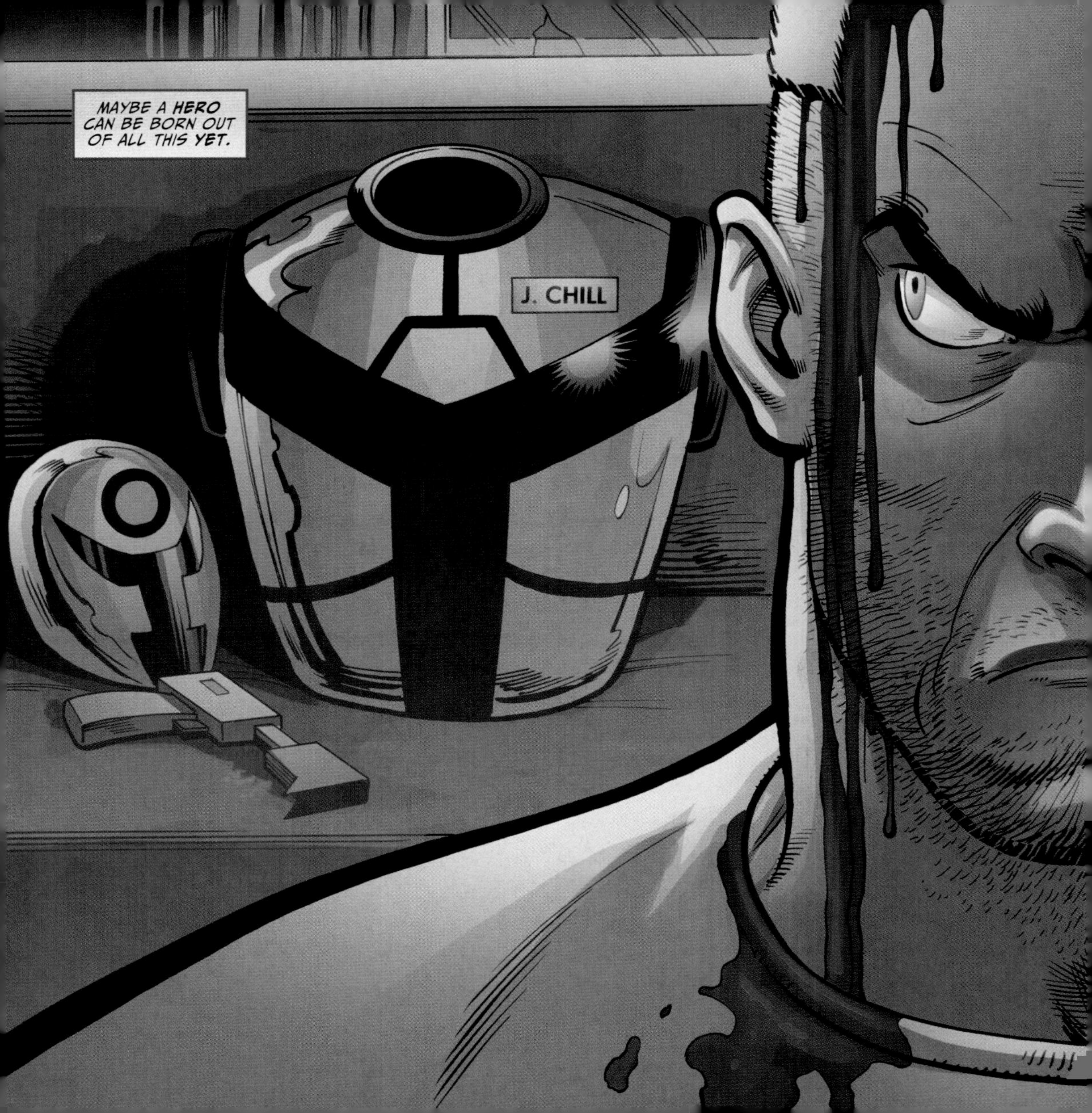
MAYBE A HERO CAN BE BORN OUT OF ALL THIS YET.
J. CHILL

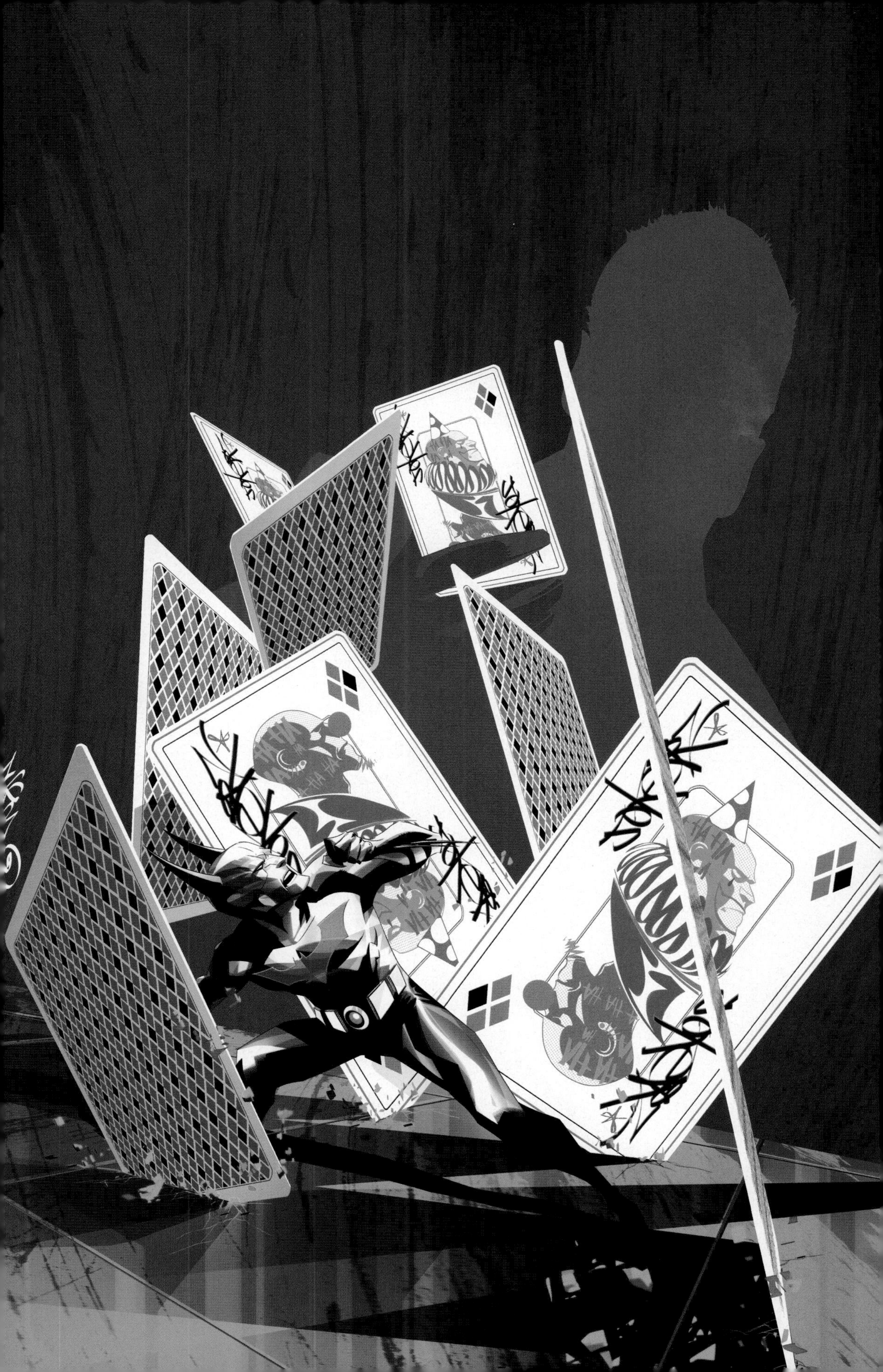

10,000 CLOWNS

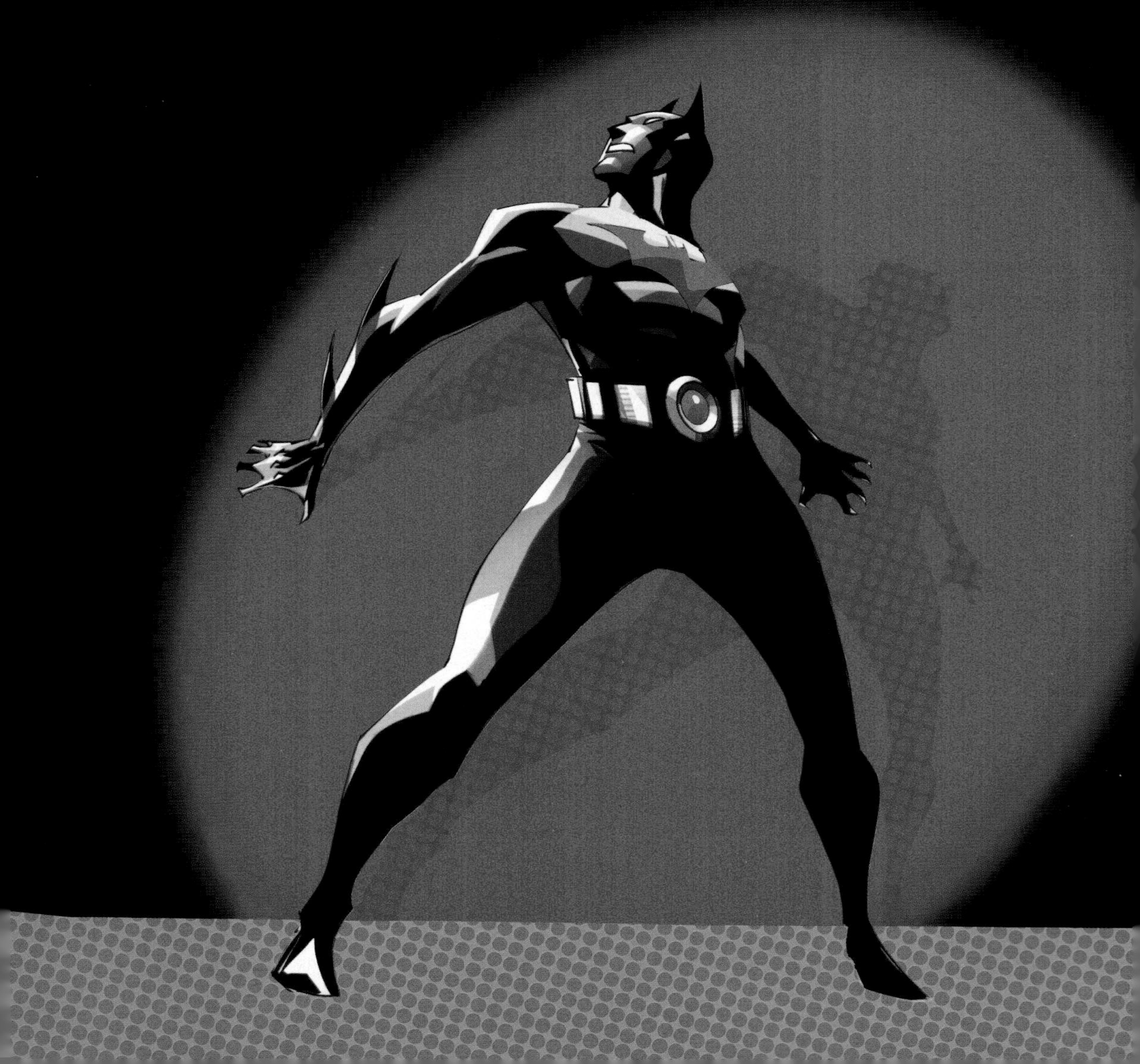

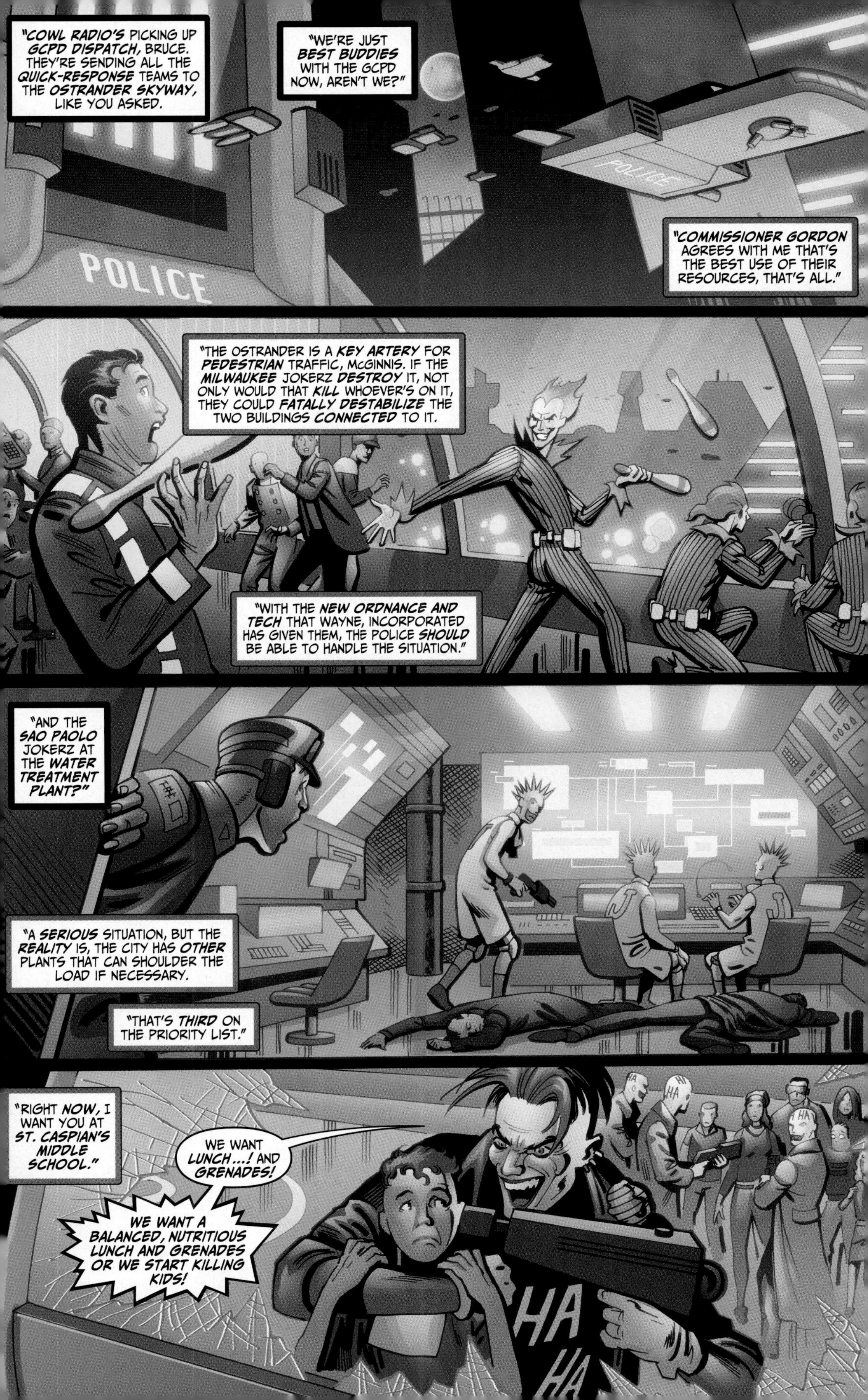
"COWL RADIO'S PICKING UP GCPD DISPATCH, BRUCE. THEY'RE SENDING ALL THE QUICK-RESPONSE TEAMS TO THE OSTRANDER SKYWAY, LIKE YOU ASKED.
"WE'RE JUST BEST BUDDIES WITH THE GCPD NOW, AREN'T WE?"
POLICE
POLICE
"COMMISSIONER GORDON AGREES WITH ME THAT'S THE BEST USE OF THEIR RESOURCES, THAT'S ALL."
"THE OSTRANDER IS A KEY ARTERY FOR PEDESTRIAN TRAFFIC, McGINNIS. IF THE MILWAUKEE JOKERZ DESTROY IT, NOT ONLY WOULD THAT KILL WHOEVER'S ON IT, THEY COULD FATALLY DESTABILIZE THE TWO BUILDINGS CONNECTED TO IT.
"WITH THE NEW ORDNANCE AND TECH THAT WAYNE, INCORPORATED HAS GIVEN THEM, THE POLICE SHOULD BE ABLE TO HANDLE THE SITUATION."
"AND THE SAO PAOLO JOKERZ AT THE WATER TREATMENT PLANT?"
"A SERIOUS SITUATION, BUT THE REALITY IS, THE CITY HAS OTHER PLANTS THAT CAN SHOULDER THE LOAD IF NECESSARY.
"THAT'S THIRD ON THE PRIORITY LIST."
"RIGHT NOW, I WANT YOU AT ST. CASPIAN'S MIDDLE SCHOOL."
WE WANT LUNCH...! AND GRENADES!
WE WANT A BALANCED, NUTRITIOUS LUNCH AND GRENADES OR WE START KILLING KIDS!
HA
HA
HA
HA
HA

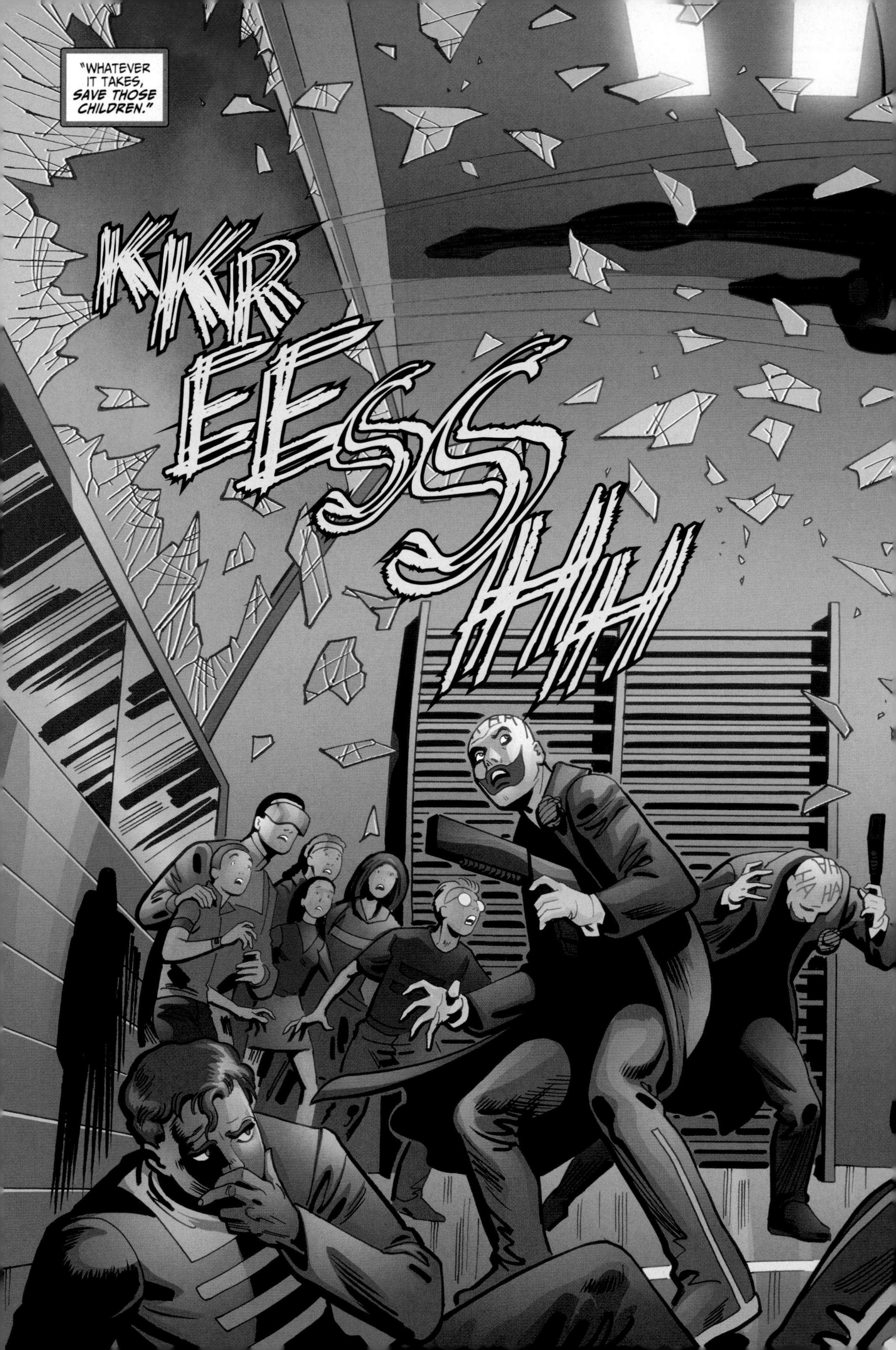
"WHATEVER IT TAKES, SAVE THOSE CHILDREN."
KKR EESSHH

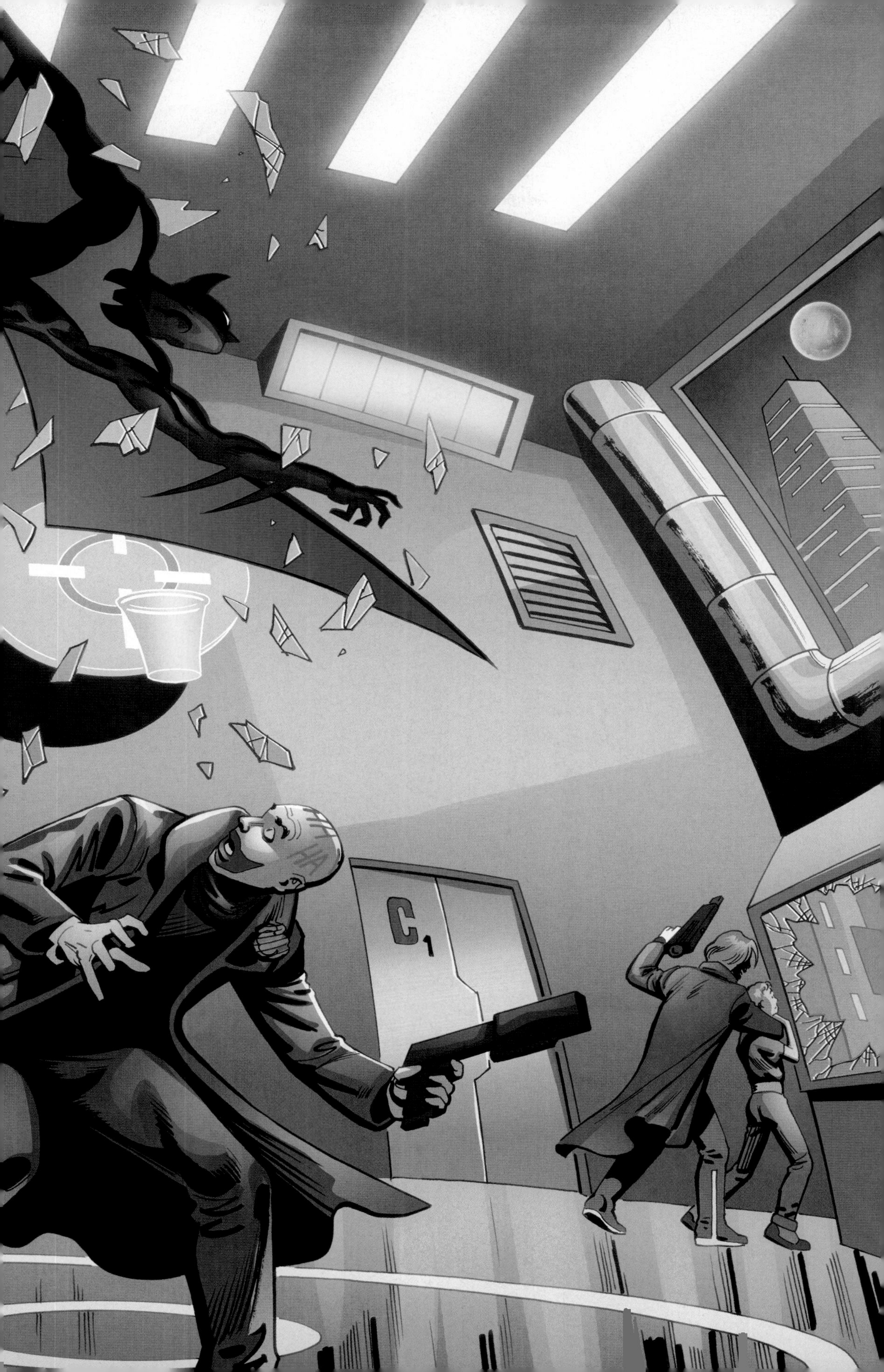
HA
HA
C1

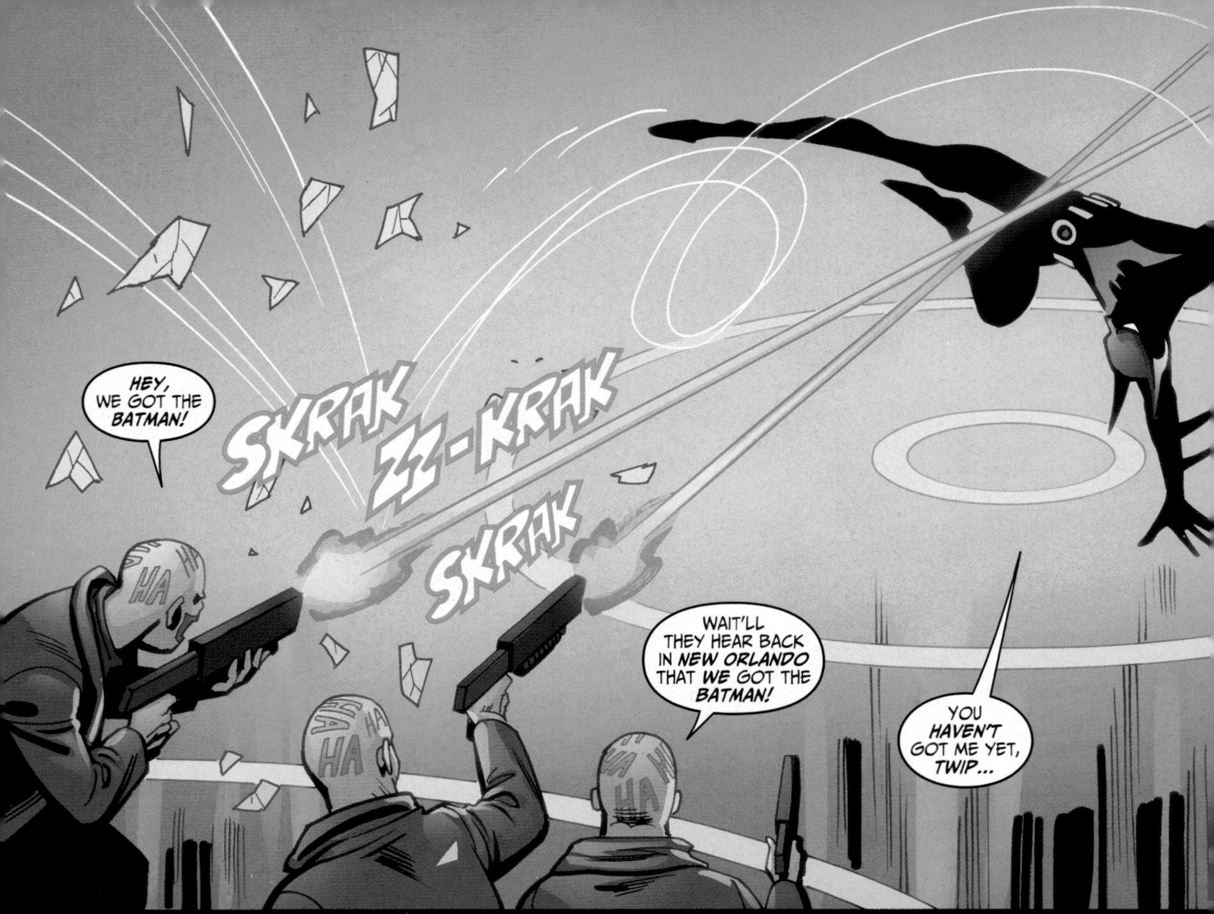
HEY, WE GOT THE BATMAN!
SKRAK
ZZ-KRAK
SKRAK
WAIT'LL THEY HEAR BACK IN NEW ORLANDO THAT WE GOT THE BATMAN!
YOU HAVEN'T GOT ME YET, TWIP...

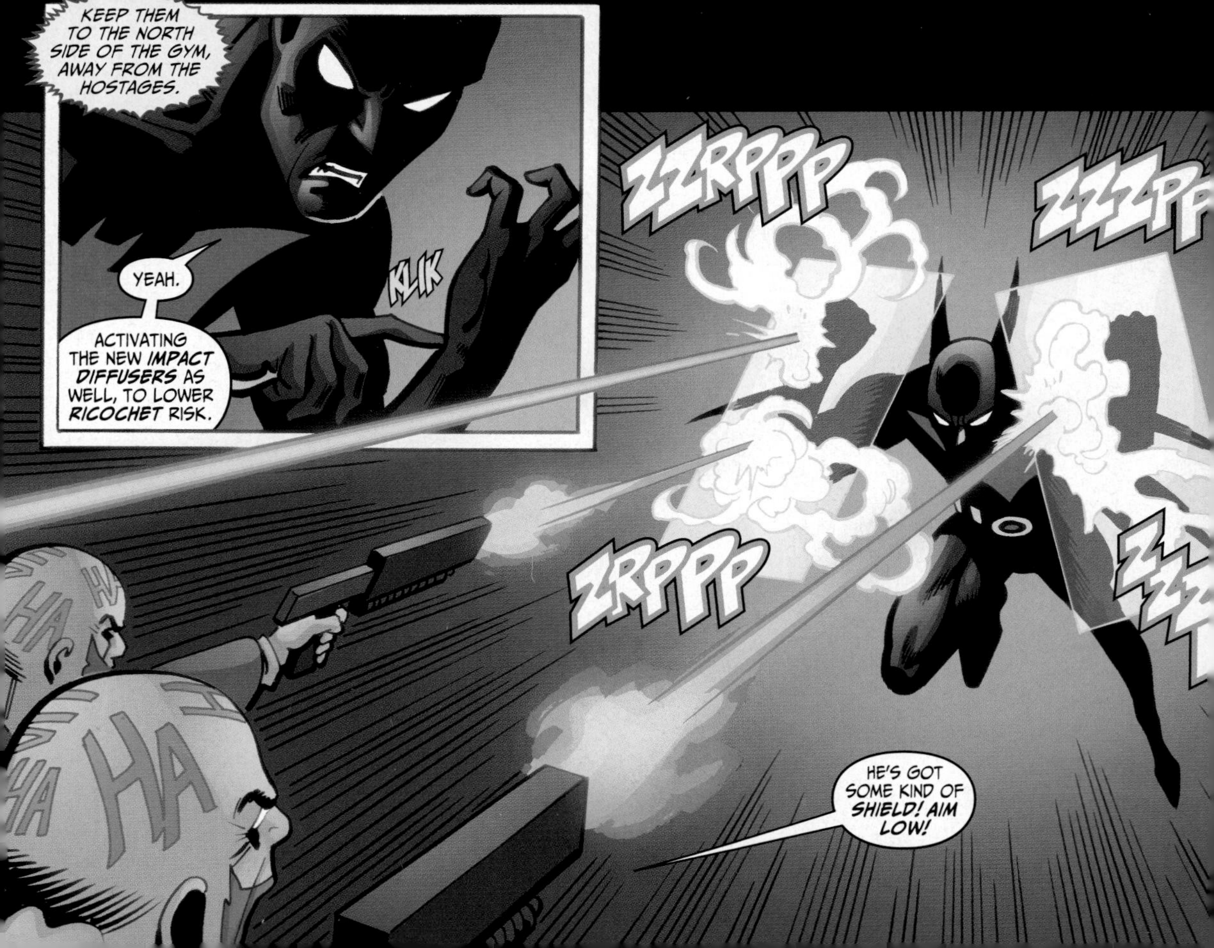
KEEP THEM TO THE NORTH SIDE OF THE GYM, AWAY FROM THE HOSTAGES.
YEAH.
KLIK
ACTIVATING THE NEW IMPACT DIFFUSERS AS WELL, TO LOWER RICOCHET RISK.
ZZRPPPP
ZZZZPP
ZRPPP
HE'S GOT SOME KIND OF SHIELD! AIM LOW!

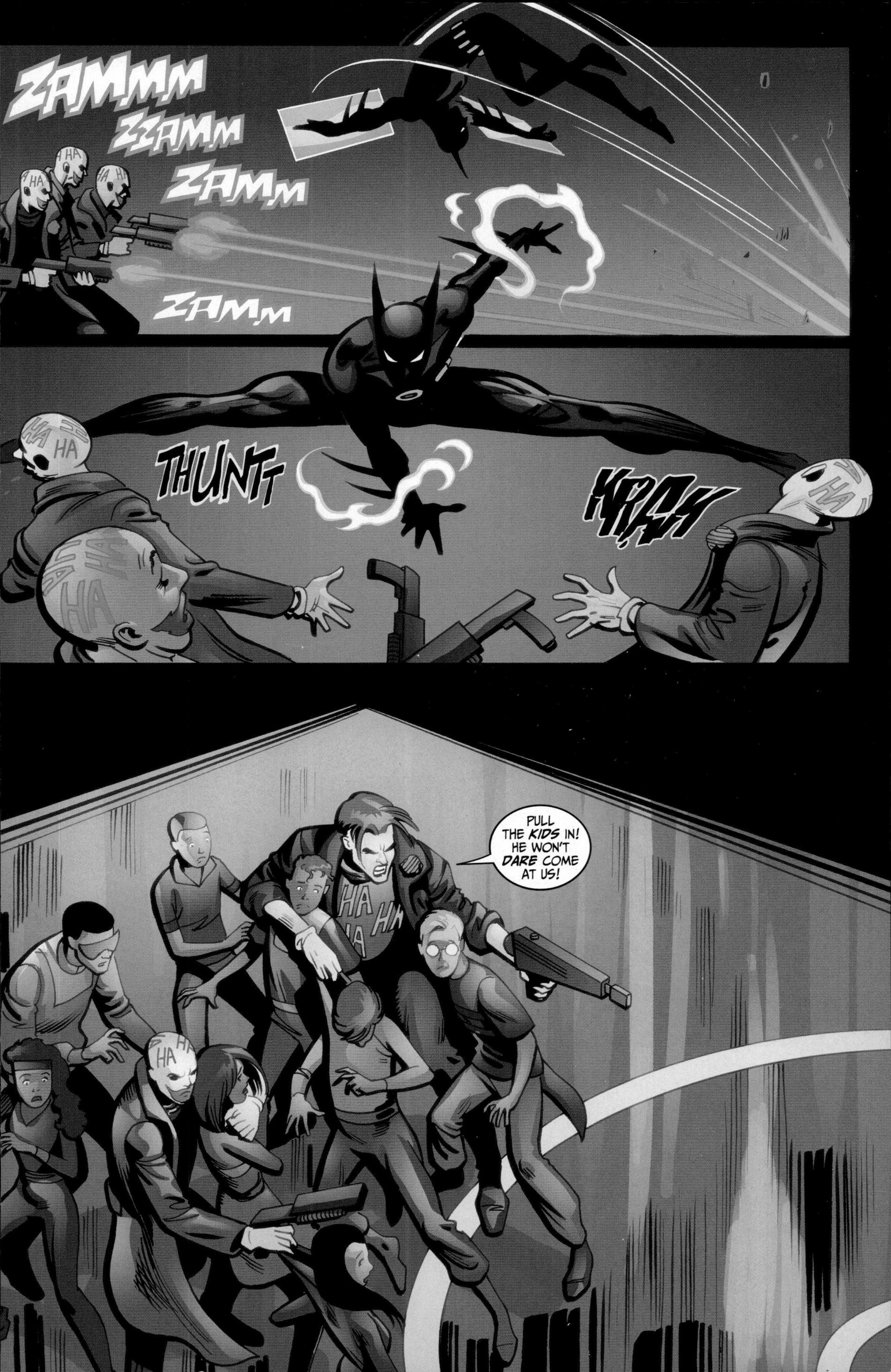
ZAMMM
ZZAMM
ZAMM
ZAMM
THUNTT
KRACK
PULL THE KIDS IN! HE WON'T DARE COME AT US!

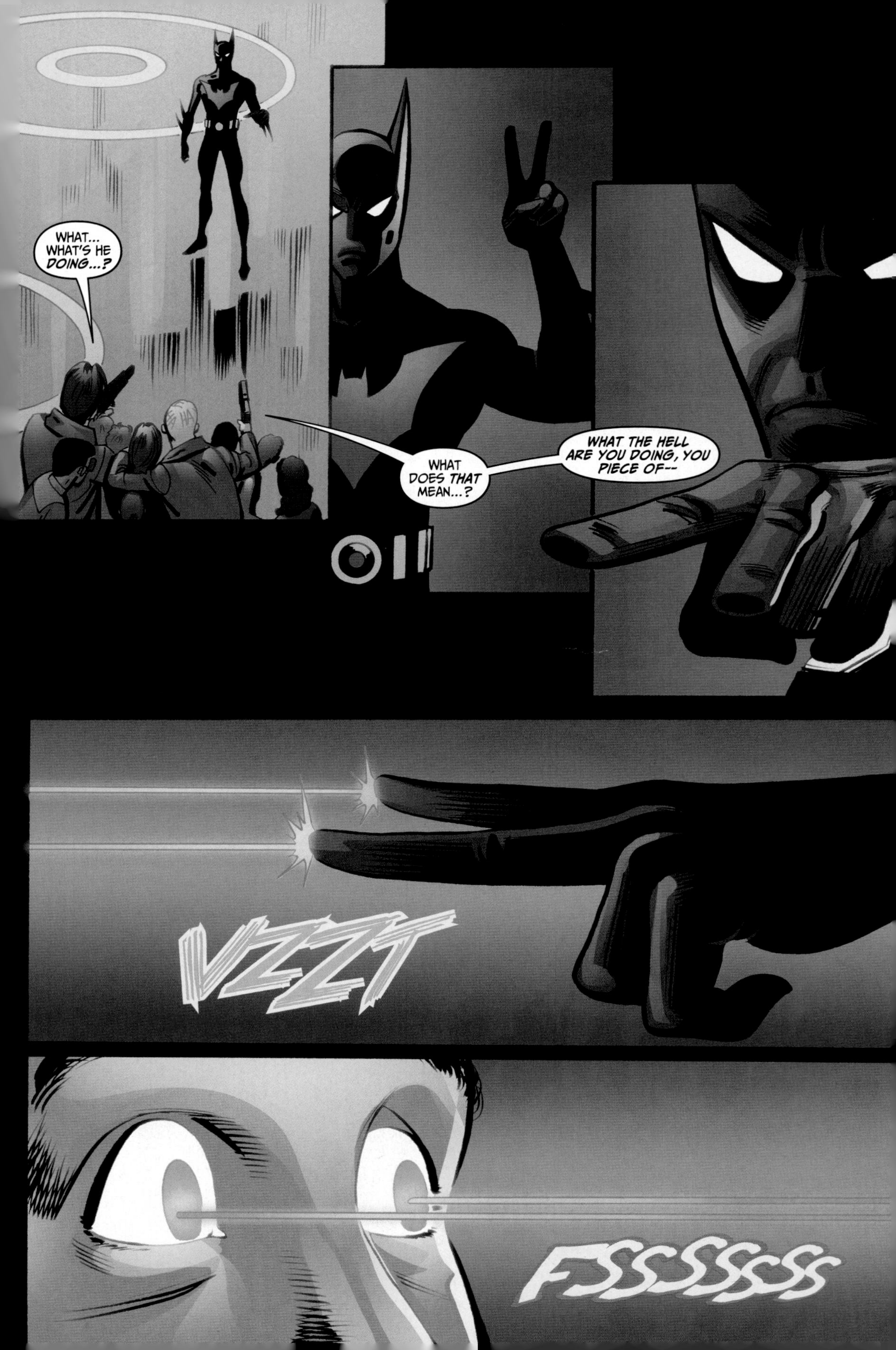
WHAT... WHAT'S HE DOING...?
WHAT DOES THAT MEAN...?
WHAT THE HELL ARE YOU DOING, YOU PIECE OF--
VZZT
FSSSSSSS

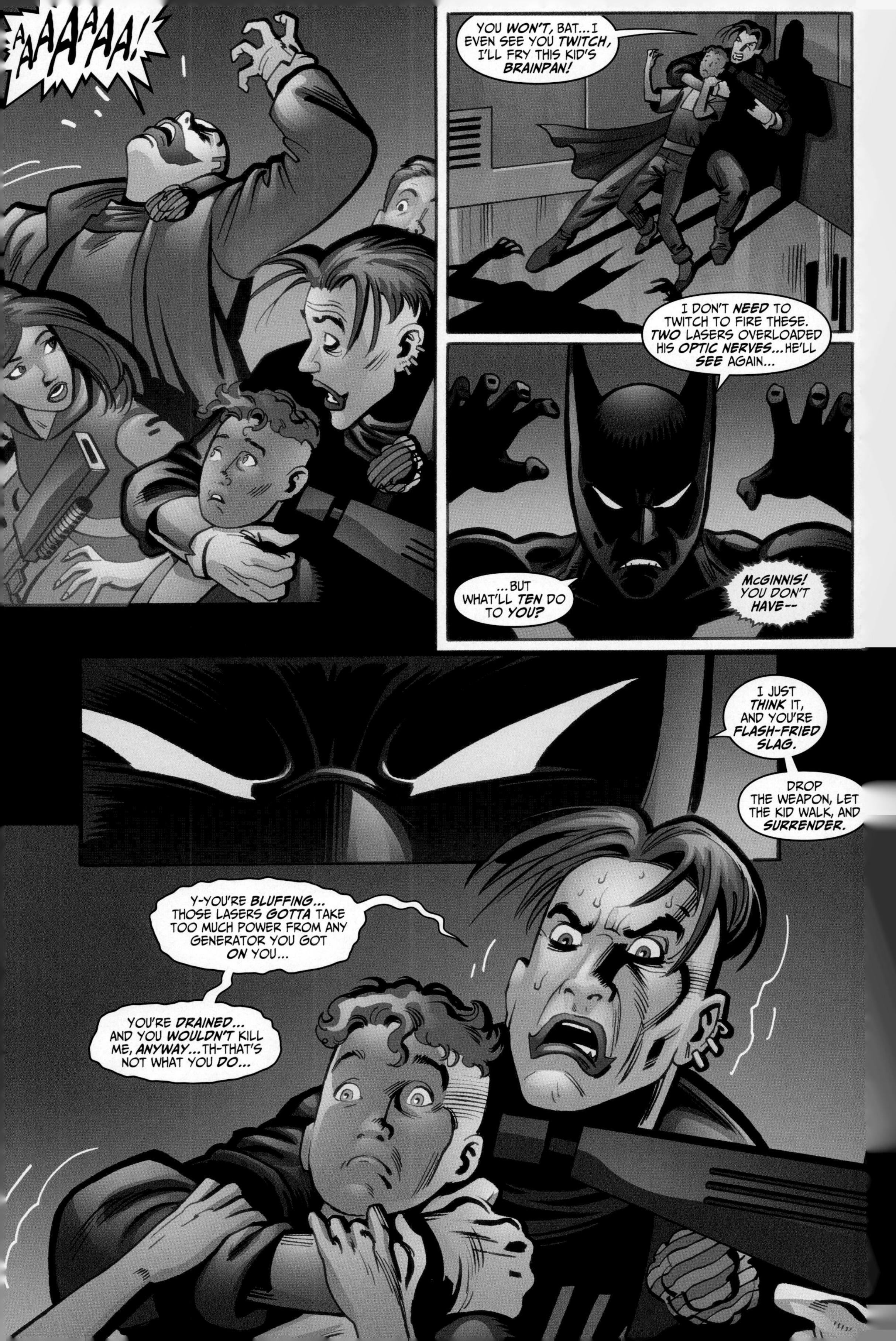
AAAAAAA!
YOU WON'T, BAT... I EVEN SEE YOU TWITCH, I'LL FRY THIS KID'S BRAINPAN!
I DON'T NEED TO TWITCH TO FIRE THESE. TWO LASERS OVERLOADED HIS OPTIC NERVES... HE'LL SEE AGAIN...
...BUT WHAT'LL TEN DO TO YOU?
McGINNIS! YOU DON'T HAVE--
I JUST THINK IT, AND YOU'RE FLASH-FRIED SLAG.
DROP THE WEAPON, LET THE KID WALK, AND SURRENDER.
Y-YOU'RE BLUFFING... THOSE LASERS GOTTA TAKE TOO MUCH POWER FROM ANY GENERATOR YOU GOT ON YOU...
YOU'RE DRAINED... AND YOU WOULDN'T KILL ME, ANYWAY... TH-THAT'S NOT WHAT YOU DO...

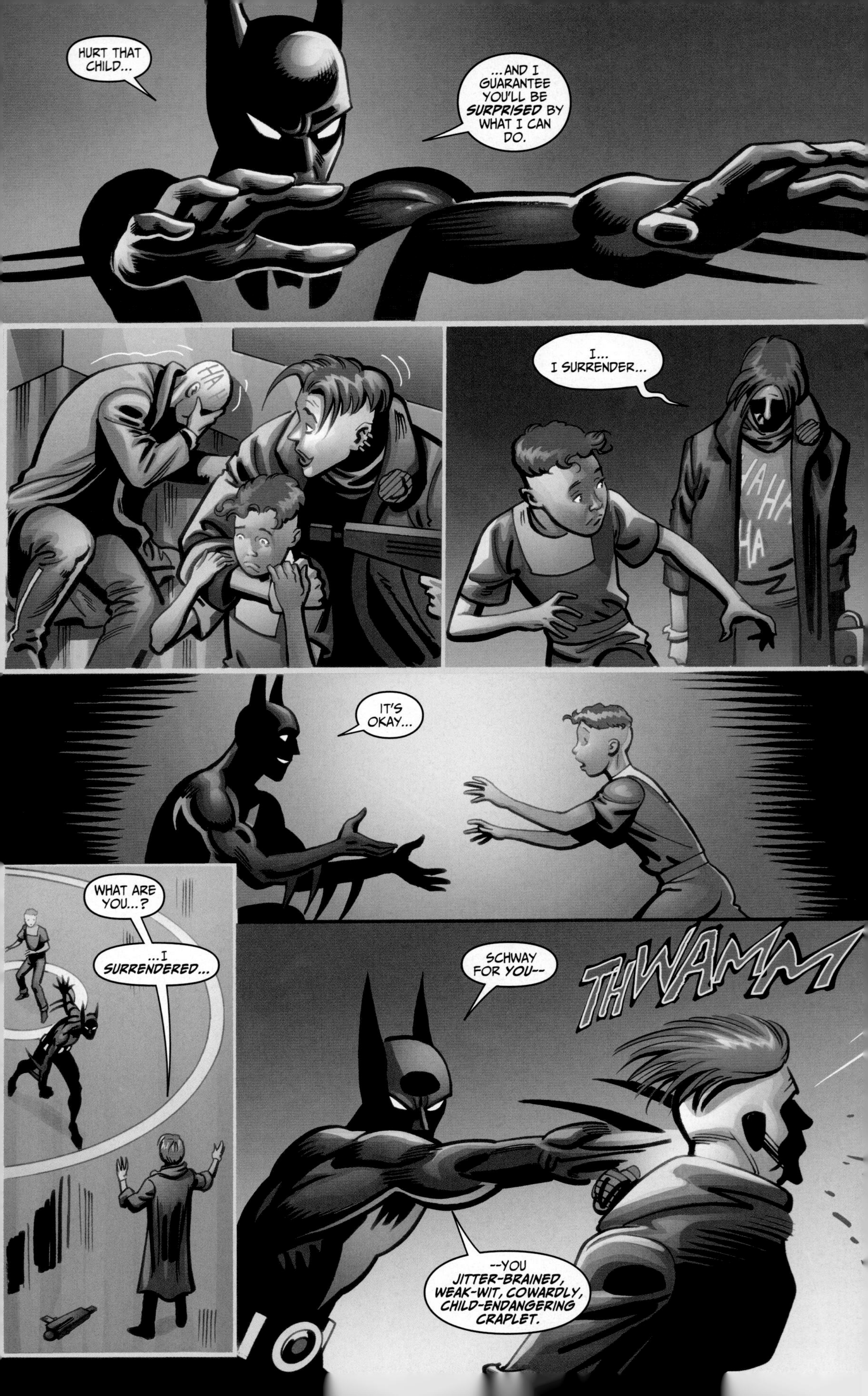
HURT THAT CHILD...
...AND I GUARANTEE YOU'LL BE SURPRISED BY WHAT I CAN DO.
HA
I... I SURRENDER...
HA HA HA HA
IT'S OKAY...
WHAT ARE YOU...?
...I SURRENDERED...
SCHWAY FOR YOU--
THWAMM
--YOU JITTER-BRAINED, WEAK-WIT, COWARDLY, CHILD-ENDANGERING CRAPLET.

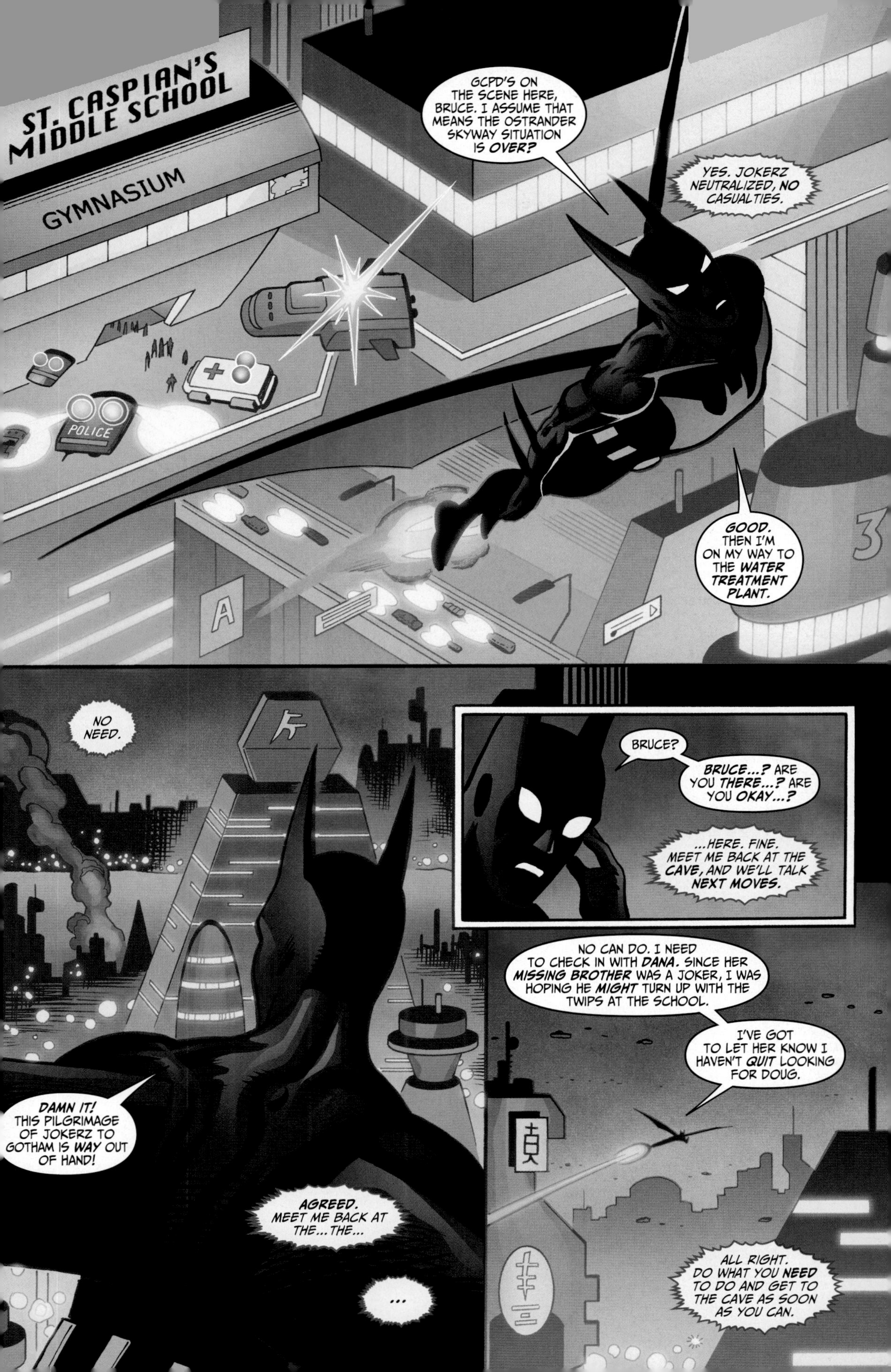
ST. CASPIAN'S MIDDLE SCHOOL
GYMNASIUM
POLICE
GCPD'S ON THE SCENE HERE, BRUCE. I ASSUME THAT MEANS THE OSTRANDER SKYWAY SITUATION IS OVER?
YES. JOKERZ NEUTRALIZED, NO CASUALTIES.
GOOD. THEN I'M ON MY WAY TO THE WATER TREATMENT PLANT.
NO NEED.
DAMN IT! THIS PILGRIMAGE OF JOKERZ TO GOTHAM IS WAY OUT OF HAND!
AGREED. MEET ME BACK AT THE...THE...
...
BRUCE?
BRUCE...? ARE YOU THERE...? ARE YOU OKAY...?
...HERE. FINE. MEET ME BACK AT THE CAVE, AND WE'LL TALK NEXT MOVES.
NO CAN DO. I NEED TO CHECK IN WITH DANA. SINCE HER MISSING BROTHER WAS A JOKER, I WAS HOPING HE MIGHT TURN UP WITH THE TWIPS AT THE SCHOOL.
I'VE GOT TO LET HER KNOW I HAVEN'T QUIT LOOKING FOR DOUG.
ALL RIGHT. DO WHAT YOU NEED TO DO AND GET TO THE CAVE AS SOON AS YOU CAN.

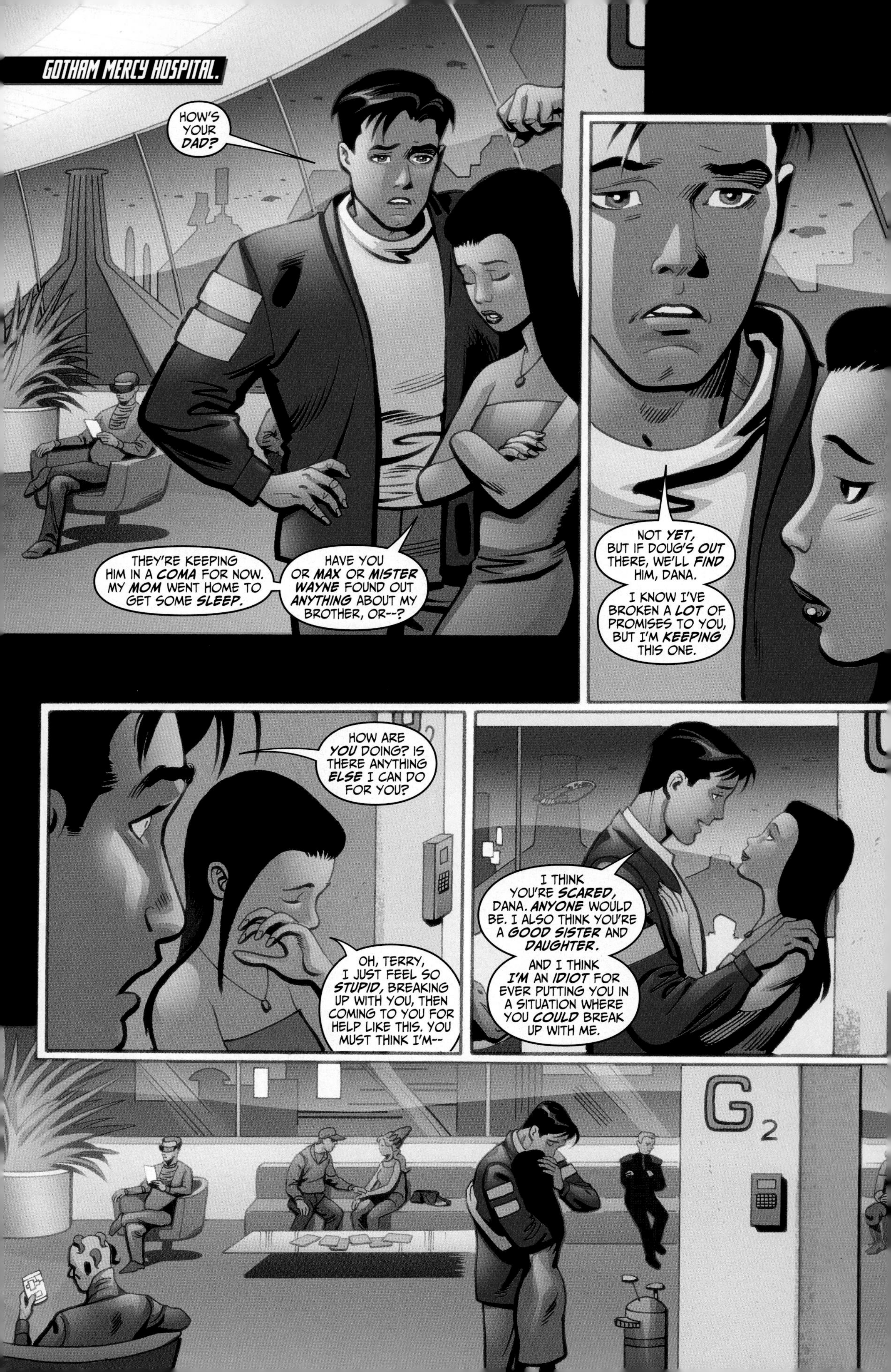
GOTHAM MERCY HOSPITAL.
HOW'S YOUR DAD?
THEY'RE KEEPING HIM IN A COMA FOR NOW. MY MOM WENT HOME TO GET SOME SLEEP.
HAVE YOU OR MAX OR MISTER WAYNE FOUND OUT ANYTHING ABOUT MY BROTHER, OR--?
NOT YET, BUT IF DOUG'S OUT THERE, WE'LL FIND HIM, DANA.
I KNOW I'VE BROKEN A LOT OF PROMISES TO YOU, BUT I'M KEEPING THIS ONE.
HOW ARE YOU DOING? IS THERE ANYTHING ELSE I CAN DO FOR YOU?
OH, TERRY, I JUST FEEL SO STUPID, BREAKING UP WITH YOU, THEN COMING TO YOU FOR HELP LIKE THIS. YOU MUST THINK I'M--
I THINK YOU'RE SCARED, DANA. ANYONE WOULD BE. I ALSO THINK YOU'RE A GOOD SISTER AND DAUGHTER.
AND I THINK I'M AN IDIOT FOR EVER PUTTING YOU IN A SITUATION WHERE YOU COULD BREAK UP WITH ME.
G2

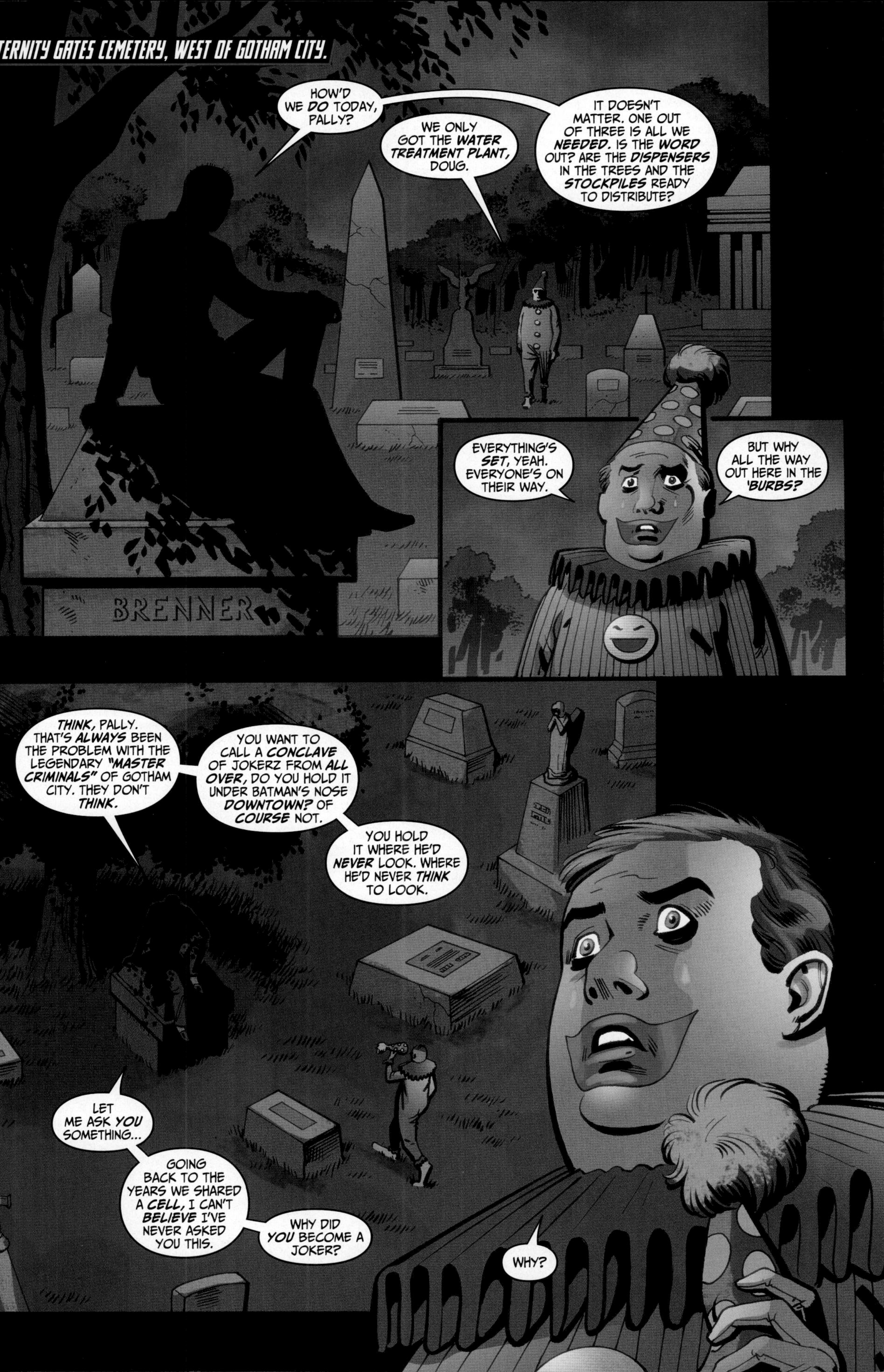
TERNITY GATES CEMETERY, WEST OF GOTHAM CITY.
HOW'D WE DO TODAY, PALLY?
WE ONLY GOT THE WATER TREATMENT PLANT, DOUG.
IT DOESN'T MATTER. ONE OUT OF THREE IS ALL WE NEEDED. IS THE WORD OUT? ARE THE DISPENSERS IN THE TREES AND THE STOCKPILES READY TO DISTRIBUTE?
BRENNER
EVERYTHING'S SET, YEAH. EVERYONE'S ON THEIR WAY.
BUT WHY ALL THE WAY OUT HERE IN THE 'BURBS?
THINK, PALLY. THAT'S ALWAYS BEEN THE PROBLEM WITH THE LEGENDARY "MASTER CRIMINALS" OF GOTHAM CITY. THEY DON'T THINK.
YOU WANT TO CALL A CONCLAVE OF JOKERZ FROM ALL OVER, DO YOU HOLD IT UNDER BATMAN'S NOSE DOWNTOWN? OF COURSE NOT.
YOU HOLD IT WHERE HE'D NEVER LOOK. WHERE HE'D NEVER THINK TO LOOK.
LET ME ASK YOU SOMETHING...
GOING BACK TO THE YEARS WE SHARED A CELL, I CAN'T BELIEVE I'VE NEVER ASKED YOU THIS.
WHY DID YOU BECOME A JOKER?
WHY?

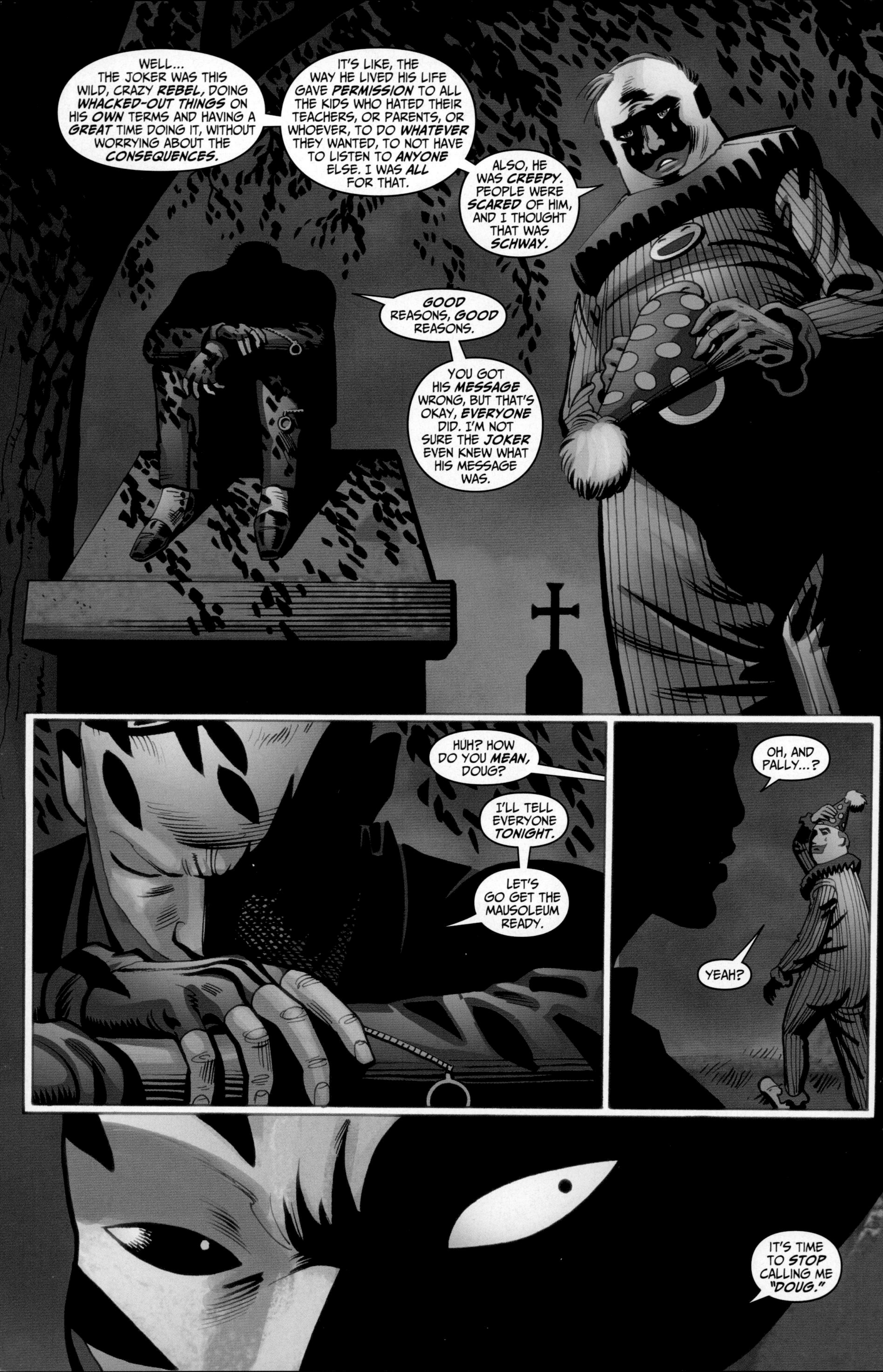
WELL... THE JOKER WAS THIS WILD, CRAZY REBEL, DOING WHACKED-OUT THINGS ON HIS OWN TERMS AND HAVING A GREAT TIME DOING IT, WITHOUT WORRYING ABOUT THE CONSEQUENCES.
IT'S LIKE, THE WAY HE LIVED HIS LIFE GAVE PERMISSION TO ALL THE KIDS WHO HATED THEIR TEACHERS, OR PARENTS, OR WHOEVER, TO DO WHATEVER THEY WANTED, TO NOT HAVE TO LISTEN TO ANYONE ELSE. I WAS ALL FOR THAT.
ALSO, HE WAS CREEPY. PEOPLE WERE SCARED OF HIM, AND I THOUGHT THAT WAS SCHWAY.
GOOD REASONS, GOOD REASONS.
YOU GOT HIS MESSAGE WRONG, BUT THAT'S OKAY, EVERYONE DID. I'M NOT SURE THE JOKER EVEN KNEW WHAT HIS MESSAGE WAS.
HUH? HOW DO YOU MEAN, DOUG?
I'LL TELL EVERYONE TONIGHT.
LET'S GO GET THE MAUSOLEUM READY.
OH, AND PALLY...?
YEAH?
IT'S TIME TO STOP CALLING ME "DOUG."

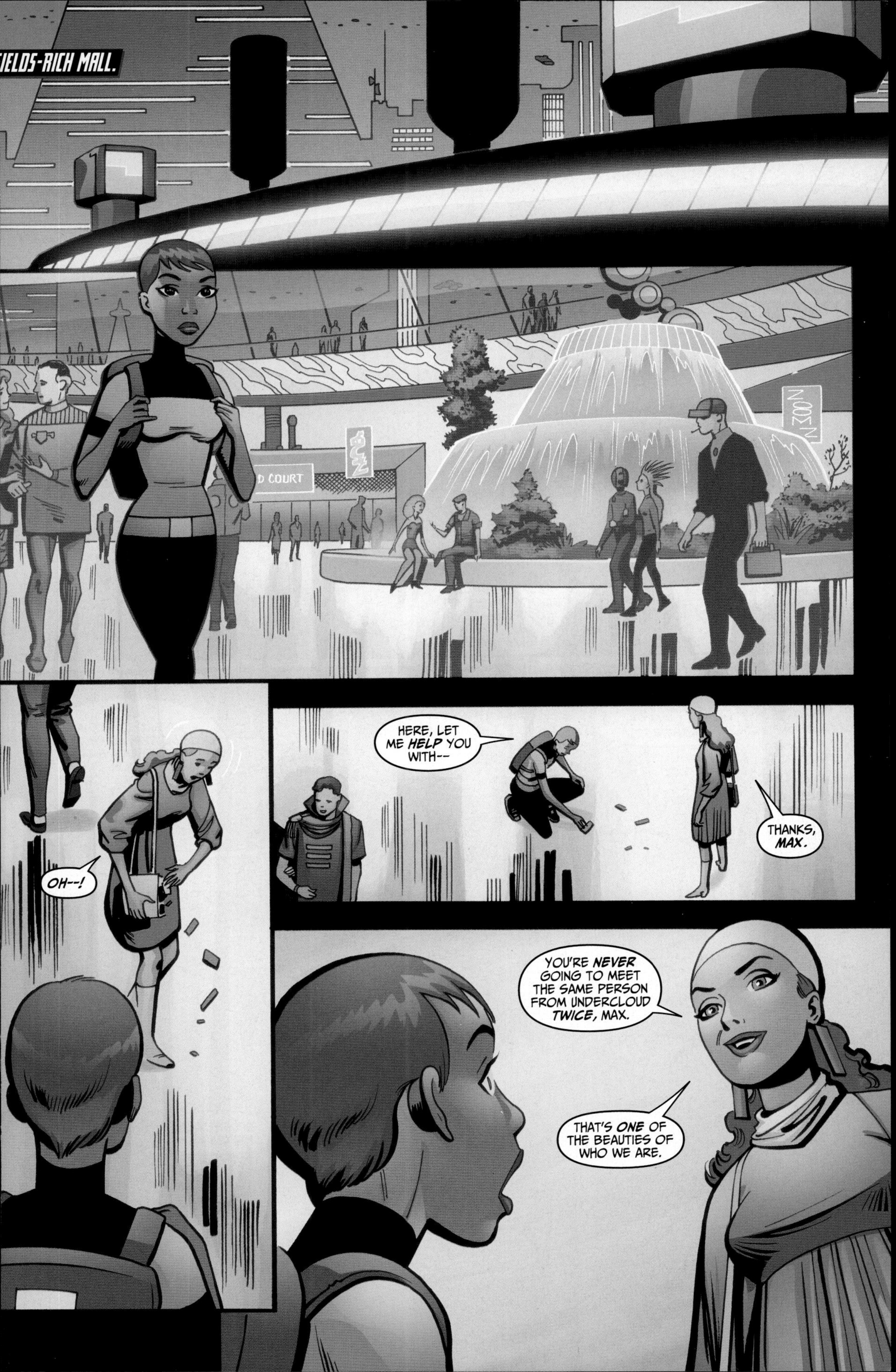

...IELDS-RICH MALL.
D COURT
ZOOM
OH--!
HERE, LET ME HELP YOU WITH--
THANKS, MAX.
YOU'RE NEVER GOING TO MEET THE SAME PERSON FROM UNDERCLOUD TWICE, MAX.
THAT'S ONE OF THE BEAUTIES OF WHO WE ARE.

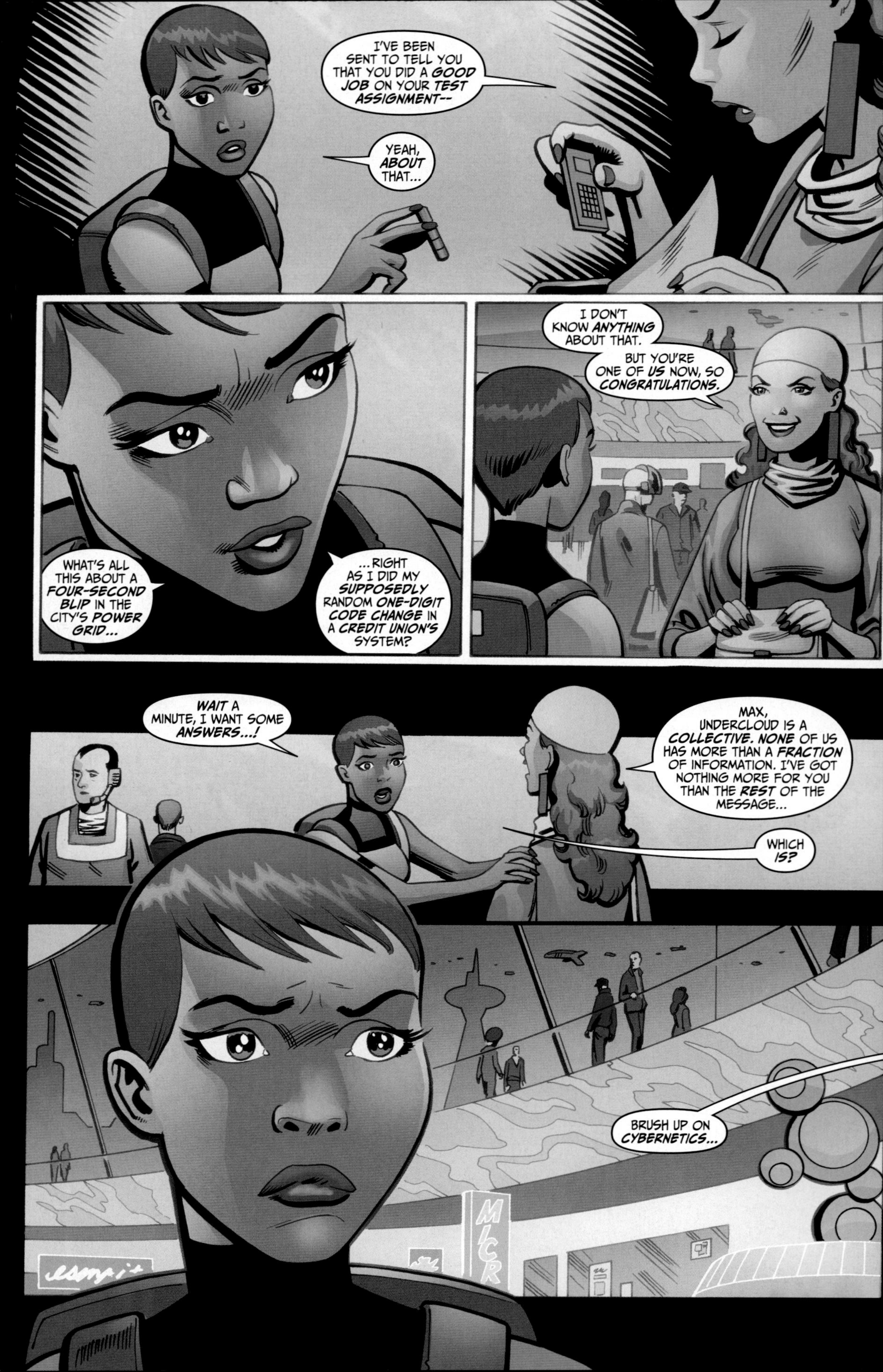
I'VE BEEN SENT TO TELL YOU THAT YOU DID A GOOD JOB ON YOUR TEST ASSIGNMENT--
YEAH, ABOUT THAT...
WHAT'S ALL THIS ABOUT A FOUR-SECOND BLIP IN THE CITY'S POWER GRID...
...RIGHT AS I DID MY SUPPOSEDLY RANDOM ONE-DIGIT CODE CHANGE IN A CREDIT UNION'S SYSTEM?
I DON'T KNOW ANYTHING ABOUT THAT.
BUT YOU'RE ONE OF US NOW, SO CONGRATULATIONS.
WAIT A MINUTE, I WANT SOME ANSWERS...!
MAX, UNDERCLOUD IS A COLLECTIVE. NONE OF US HAS MORE THAN A FRACTION OF INFORMATION. I'VE GOT NOTHING MORE FOR YOU THAN THE REST OF THE MESSAGE...
WHICH IS?
BRUSH UP ON CYBERNETICS...
MICR

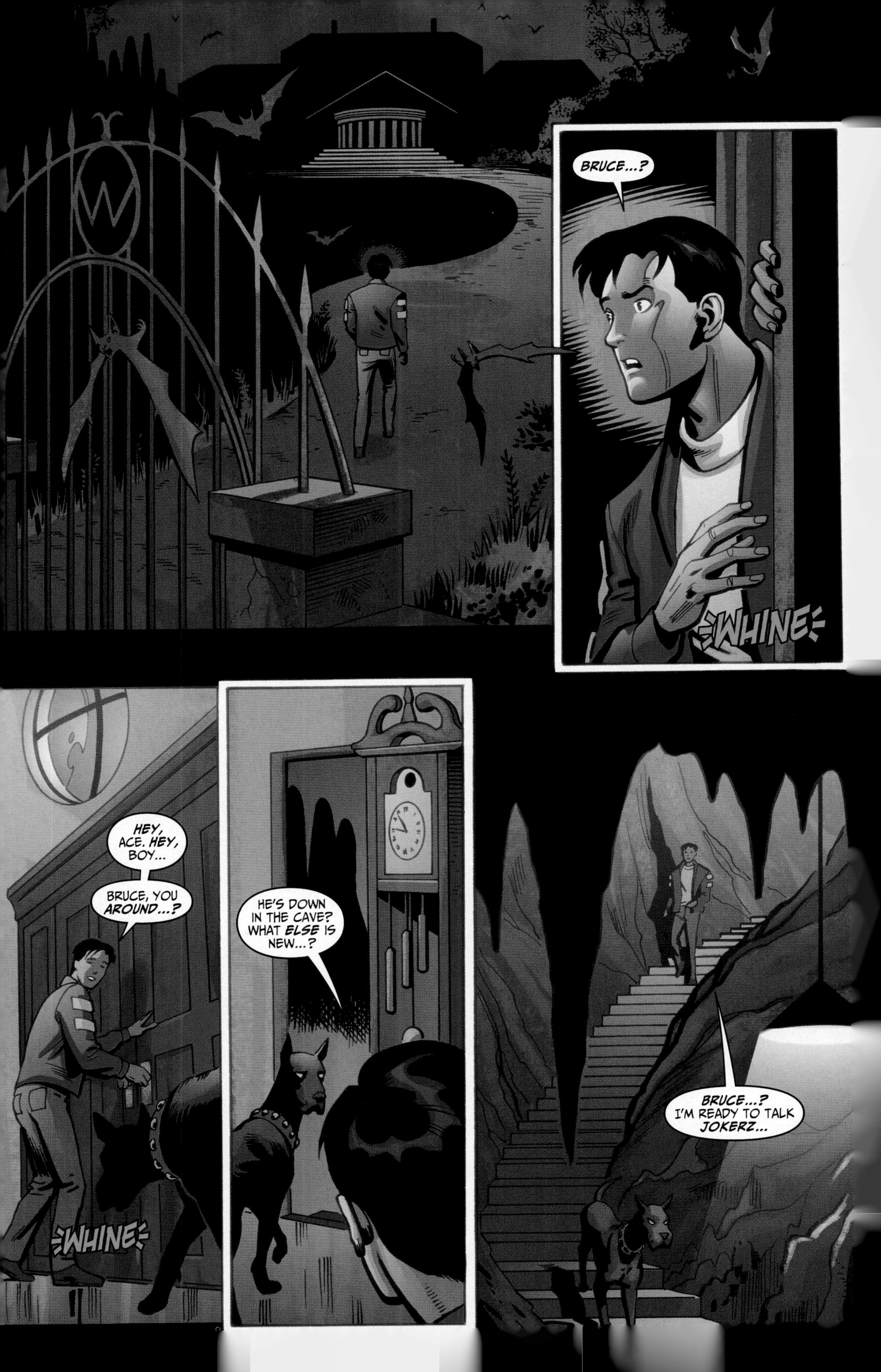
BRUCE...?
WHINE
HEY, ACE. HEY, BOY...
BRUCE, YOU AROUND...?
WHINE
HE'S DOWN IN THE CAVE? WHAT ELSE IS NEW...?
BRUCE...? I'M READY TO TALK JOKERZ...

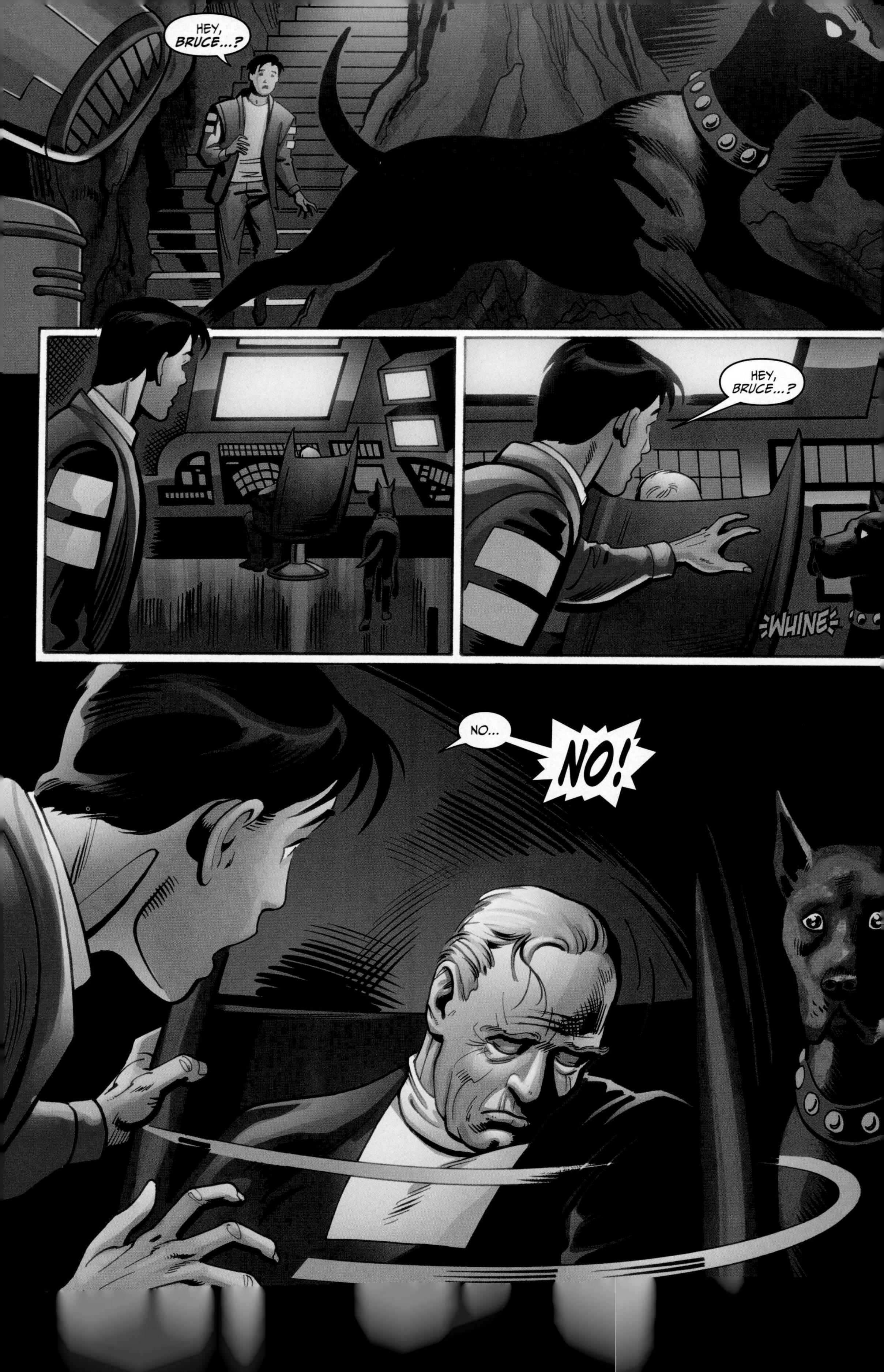

HEY, BRUCE...?
HEY, BRUCE...?
WHINE
NO...
NO!

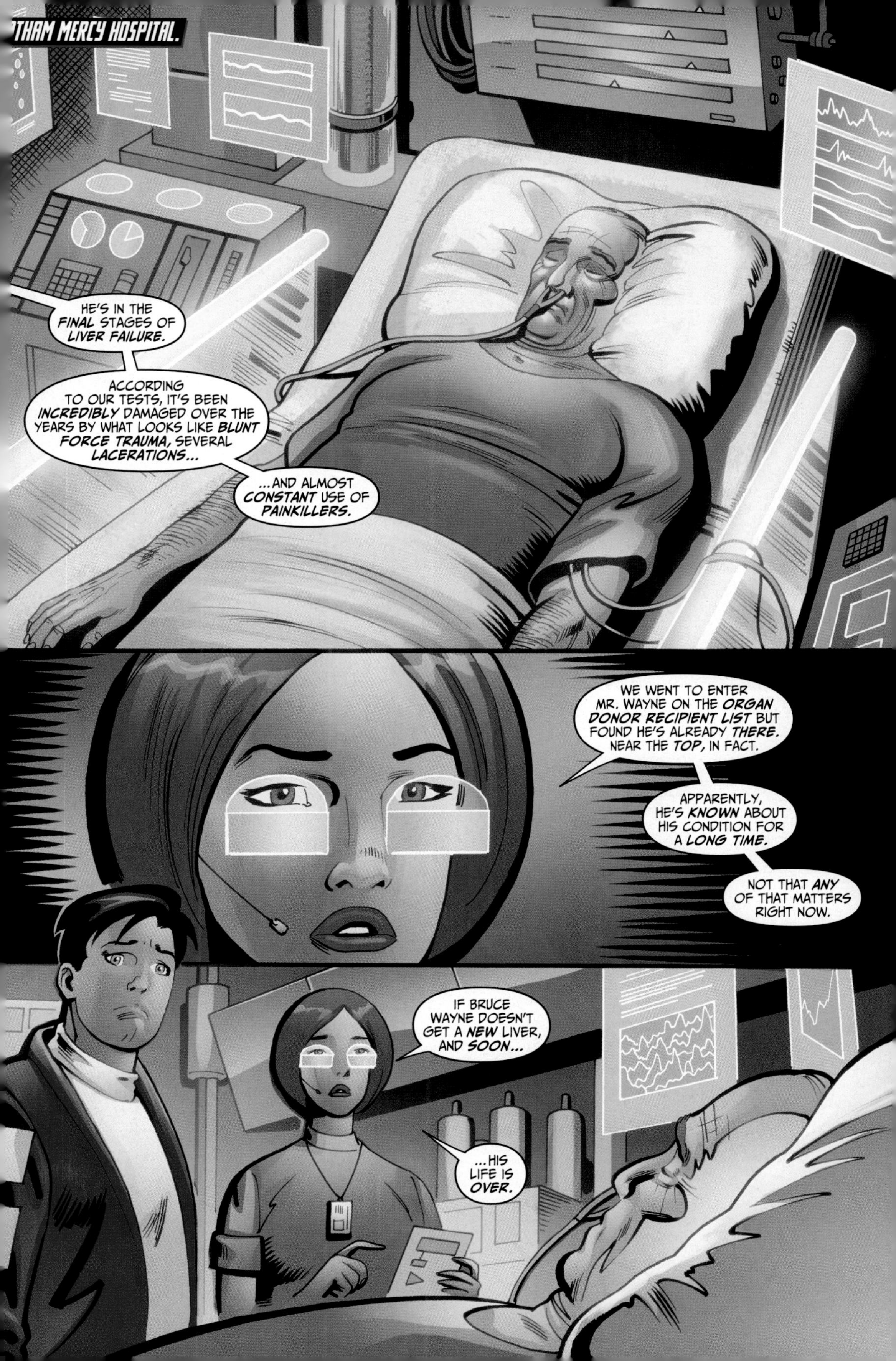
THAM MERCY HOSPITAL.
HE'S IN THE FINAL STAGES OF LIVER FAILURE.
ACCORDING TO OUR TESTS, IT'S BEEN INCREDIBLY DAMAGED OVER THE YEARS BY WHAT LOOKS LIKE BLUNT FORCE TRAUMA, SEVERAL LACERATIONS...
...AND ALMOST CONSTANT USE OF PAINKILLERS.
WE WENT TO ENTER MR. WAYNE ON THE ORGAN DONOR RECIPIENT LIST BUT FOUND HE'S ALREADY THERE. NEAR THE TOP, IN FACT.
APPARENTLY, HE'S KNOWN ABOUT HIS CONDITION FOR A LONG TIME.
NOT THAT ANY OF THAT MATTERS RIGHT NOW.
IF BRUCE WAYNE DOESN'T GET A NEW LIVER, AND SOON...
...HIS LIFE IS OVER.

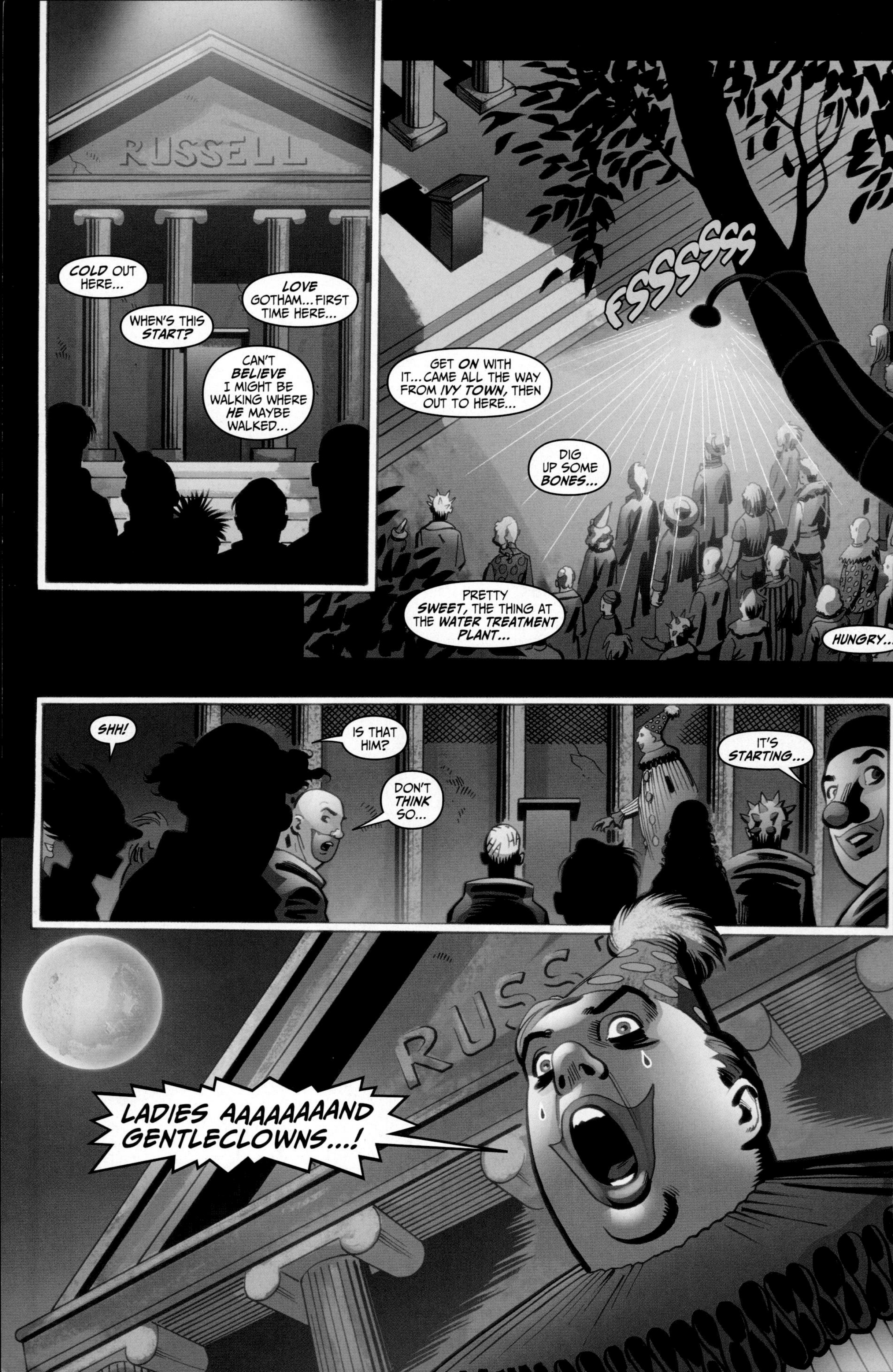
RUSSELL
COLD OUT HERE...
WHEN'S THIS START?
LOVE GOTHAM... FIRST TIME HERE...
CAN'T BELIEVE I MIGHT BE WALKING WHERE HE MAYBE WALKED...
FSSSSSSS
GET ON WITH IT... CAME ALL THE WAY FROM IVY TOWN, THEN OUT TO HERE...
DIG UP SOME BONES...
PRETTY SWEET, THE THING AT THE WATER TREATMENT PLANT...
HUNGRY...
SHH!
IS THAT HIM?
DON'T THINK SO...
IT'S STARTING...
LADIES AAAAAAAAND GENTLECLOWNS...!

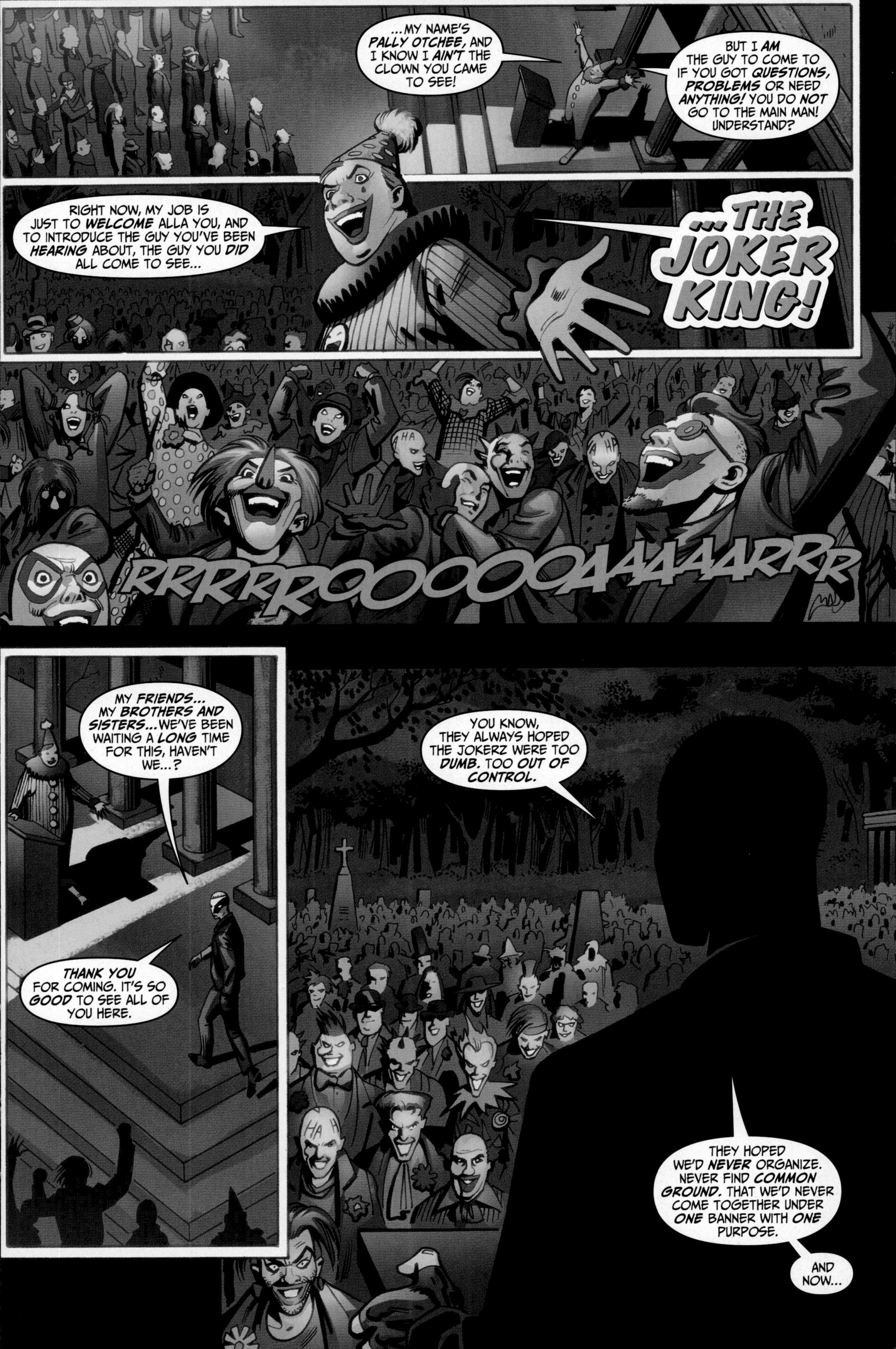
...MY NAME'S PALLY OTCHEE, AND I KNOW I AIN'T THE CLOWN YOU CAME TO SEE!
BUT I AM THE GUY TO COME TO IF YOU GOT QUESTIONS, PROBLEMS OR NEED ANYTHING! YOU DO NOT GO TO THE MAIN MAN! UNDERSTAND?
RIGHT NOW, MY JOB IS JUST TO WELCOME ALLA YOU, AND TO INTRODUCE THE GUY YOU'VE BEEN HEARING ABOUT, THE GUY YOU DID ALL COME TO SEE...
...THE JOKER KING!
RRRRROOOOOOAAAAARRRR
MY FRIENDS... MY BROTHERS AND SISTERS... WE'VE BEEN WAITING A LONG TIME FOR THIS, HAVEN'T WE...?
THANK YOU FOR COMING. IT'S SO GOOD TO SEE ALL OF YOU HERE.
YOU KNOW, THEY ALWAYS HOPED THE JOKERZ WERE TOO DUMB. TOO OUT OF CONTROL.
THEY HOPED WE'D NEVER ORGANIZE. NEVER FIND COMMON GROUND. THAT WE'D NEVER COME TOGETHER UNDER ONE BANNER WITH ONE PURPOSE.
AND NOW...

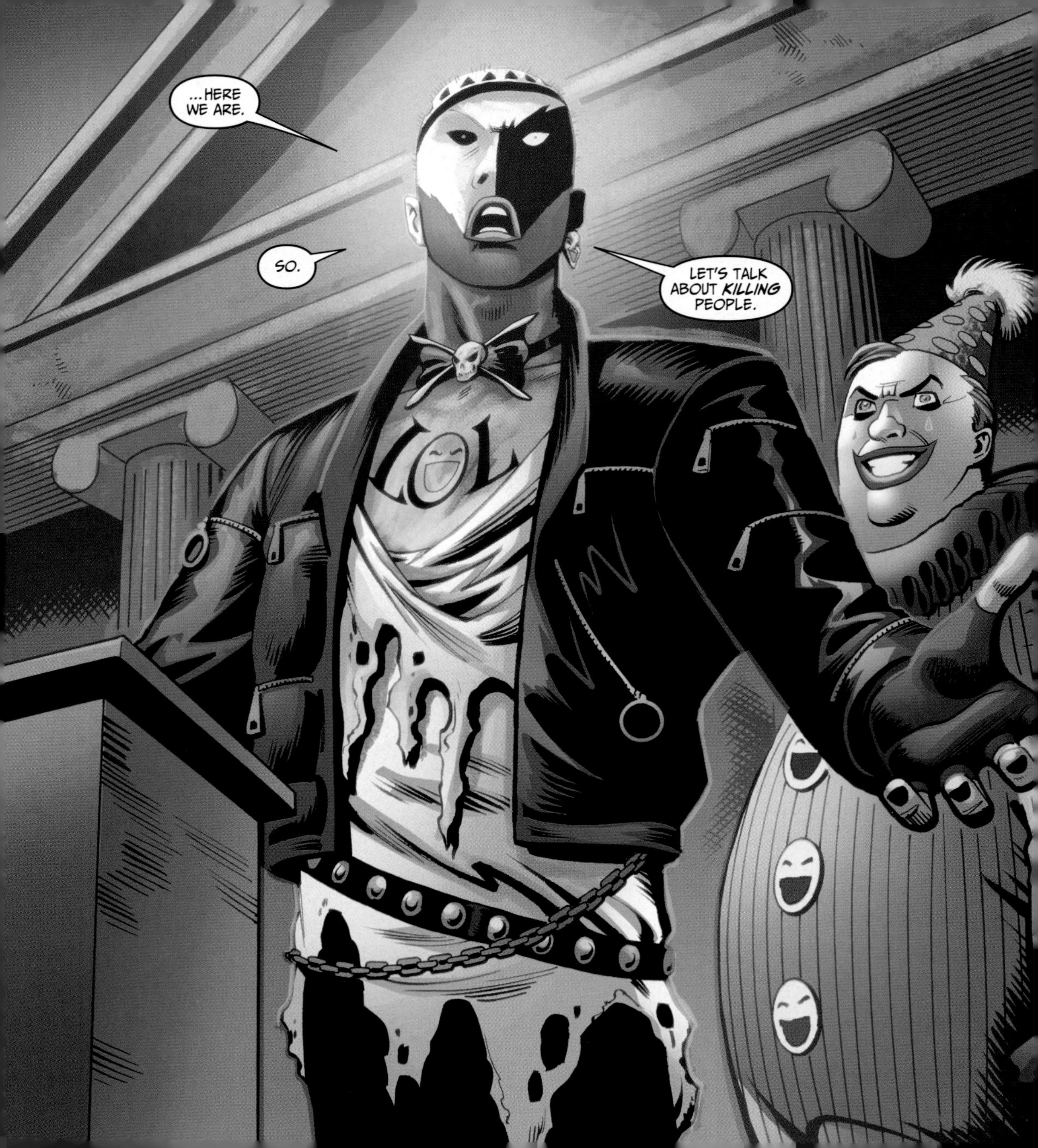
...HERE WE ARE.
SO.
LET'S TALK ABOUT *KILLING* PEOPLE.

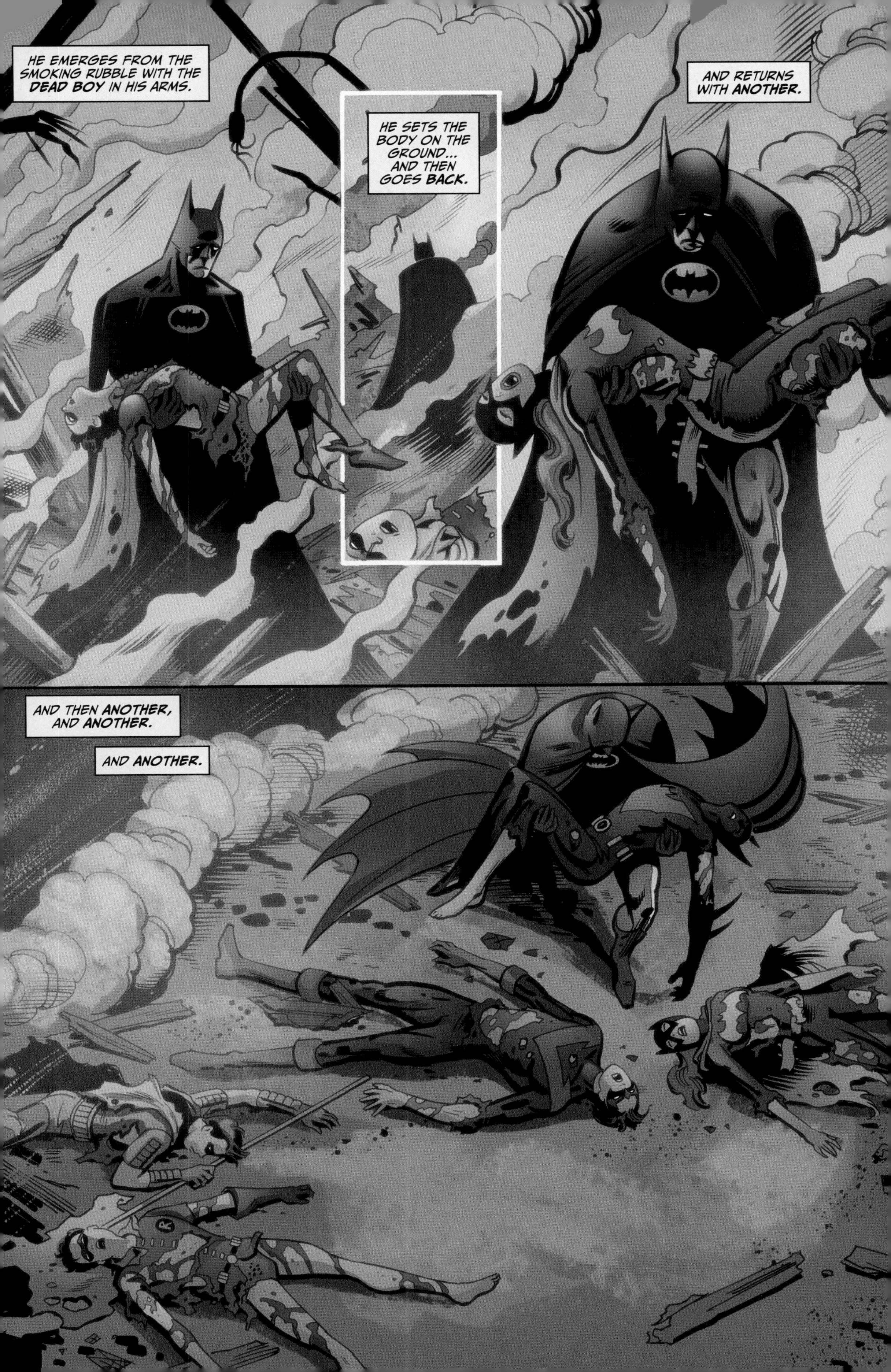
HE EMERGES FROM THE SMOKING RUBBLE WITH THE DEAD BOY IN HIS ARMS.
HE SETS THE BODY ON THE GROUND... AND THEN GOES BACK.
AND RETURNS WITH ANOTHER.
AND THEN ANOTHER, AND ANOTHER.
AND ANOTHER.

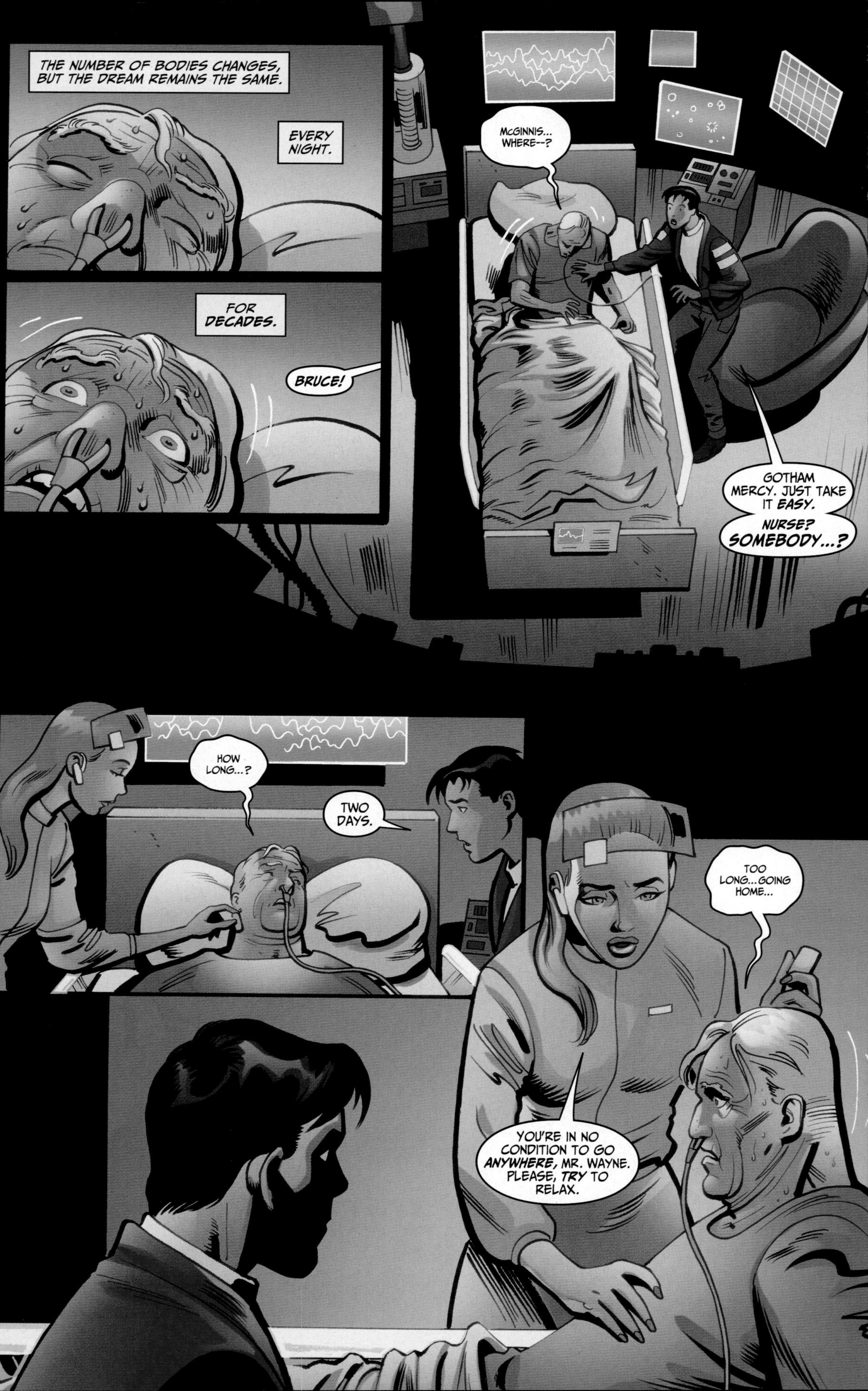
THE NUMBER OF BODIES CHANGES, BUT THE DREAM REMAINS THE SAME.
EVERY NIGHT.
FOR DECADES.
BRUCE!
McGINNIS... WHERE--?
GOTHAM MERCY. JUST TAKE IT EASY.
NURSE? SOMEBODY...?
HOW LONG...?
TWO DAYS.
TOO LONG...GOING HOME...
YOU'RE IN NO CONDITION TO GO ANYWHERE, MR. WAYNE. PLEASE, TRY TO RELAX.

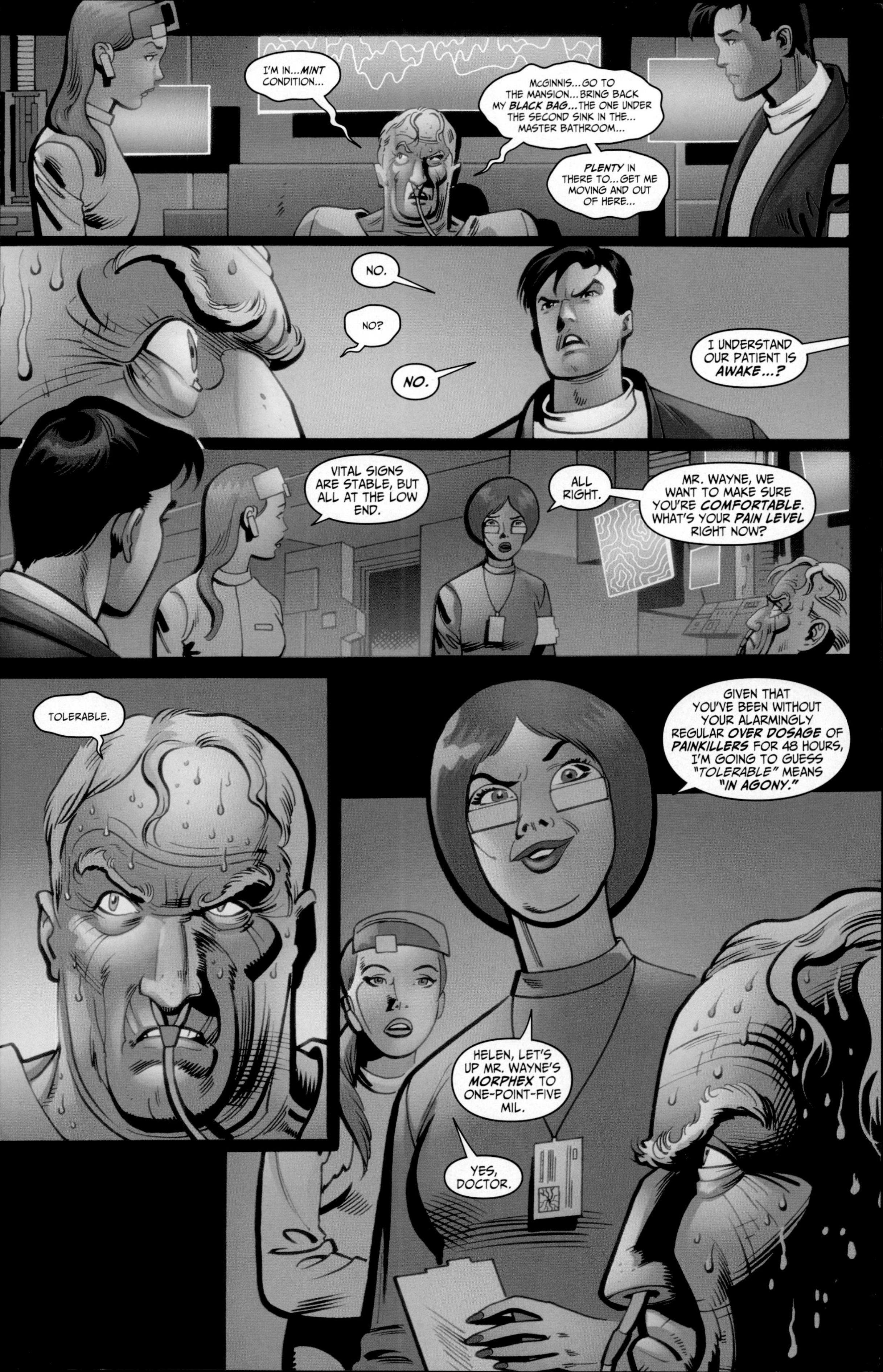
I'M IN...MINT CONDITION...
McGINNIS...GO TO THE MANSION...BRING BACK MY BLACK BAG...THE ONE UNDER THE SECOND SINK IN THE... MASTER BATHROOM...
PLENTY IN THERE TO...GET ME MOVING AND OUT OF HERE...
NO.
NO?
NO.
I UNDERSTAND OUR PATIENT IS AWAKE...?
VITAL SIGNS ARE STABLE, BUT ALL AT THE LOW END.
ALL RIGHT.
MR. WAYNE, WE WANT TO MAKE SURE YOU'RE COMFORTABLE. WHAT'S YOUR PAIN LEVEL RIGHT NOW?
TOLERABLE.
GIVEN THAT YOU'VE BEEN WITHOUT YOUR ALARMINGLY REGULAR OVER DOSAGE OF PAINKILLERS FOR 48 HOURS, I'M GOING TO GUESS "TOLERABLE" MEANS "IN AGONY."
HELEN, LET'S UP MR. WAYNE'S MORPHEX TO ONE-POINT-FIVE MIL.
YES, DOCTOR.

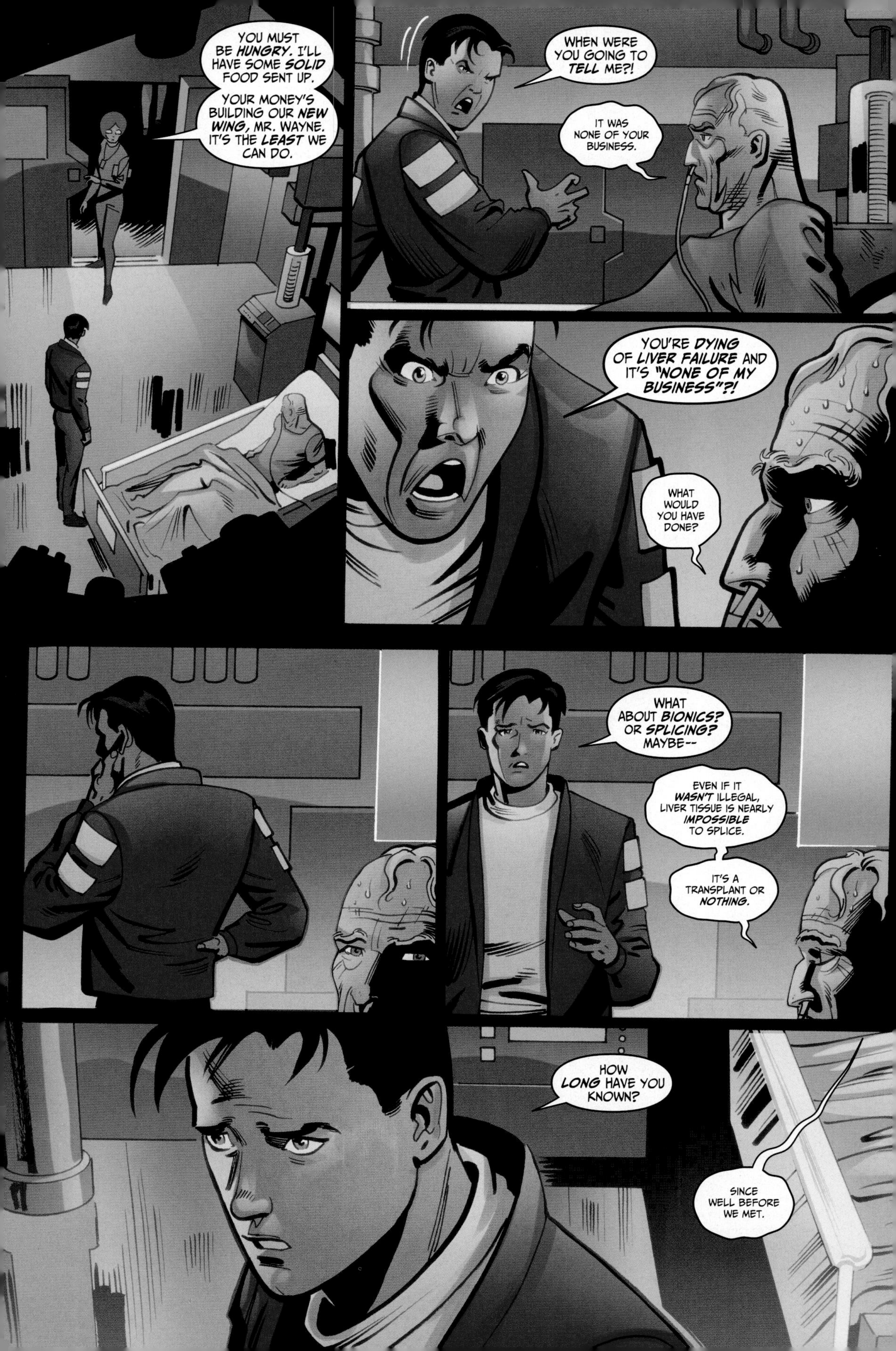
YOU MUST BE HUNGRY. I'LL HAVE SOME SOLID FOOD SENT UP.
YOUR MONEY'S BUILDING OUR NEW WING, MR. WAYNE. IT'S THE LEAST WE CAN DO.
WHEN WERE YOU GOING TO TELL ME?!
IT WAS NONE OF YOUR BUSINESS.
YOU'RE DYING OF LIVER FAILURE AND IT'S "NONE OF MY BUSINESS"?!
WHAT WOULD YOU HAVE DONE?
WHAT ABOUT BIONICS? OR SPLICING? MAYBE--
EVEN IF IT WASN'T ILLEGAL, LIVER TISSUE IS NEARLY IMPOSSIBLE TO SPLICE.
IT'S A TRANSPLANT OR NOTHING.
HOW LONG HAVE YOU KNOWN?
SINCE WELL BEFORE WE MET.

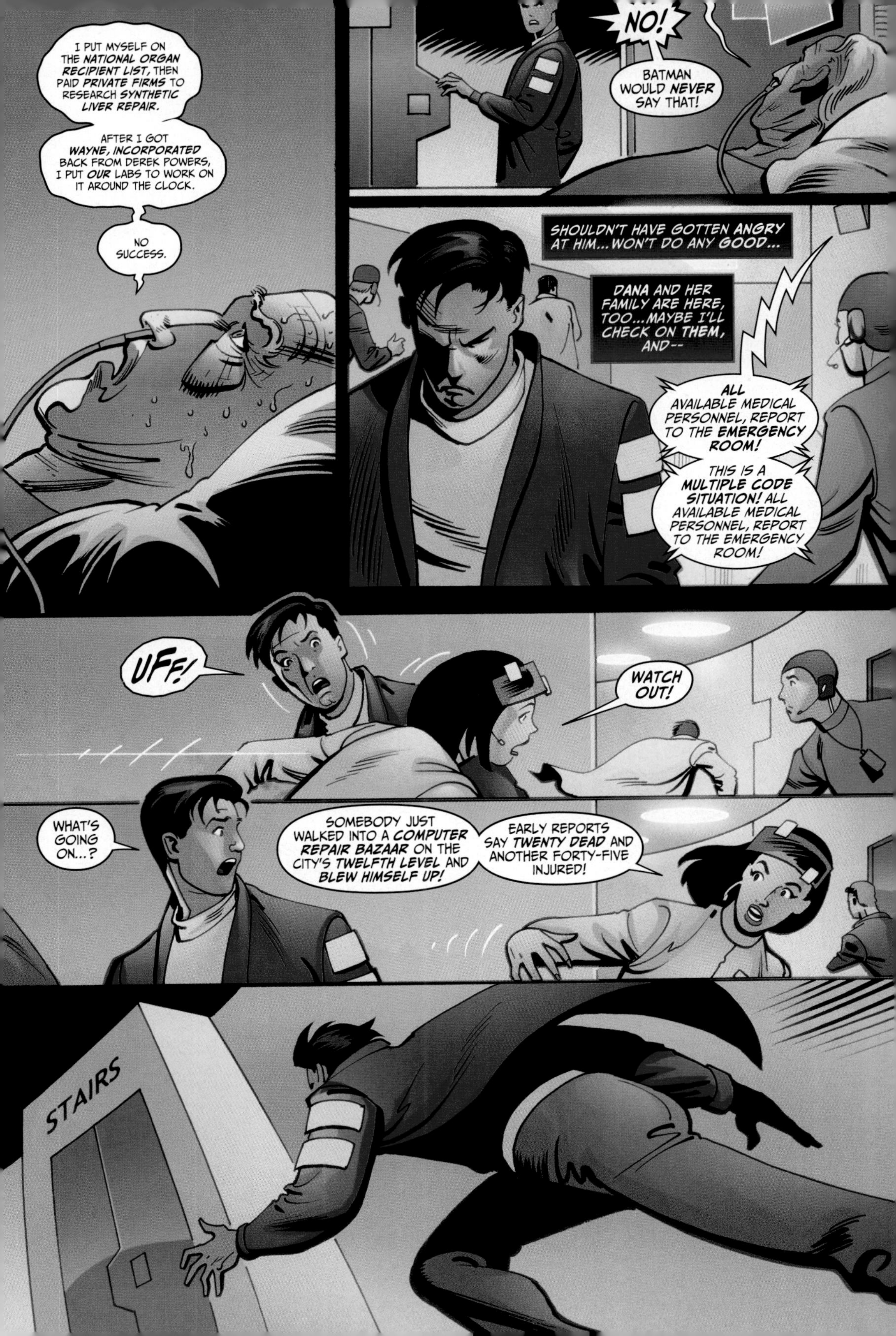
I PUT MYSELF ON THE NATIONAL ORGAN RECIPIENT LIST, THEN PAID PRIVATE FIRMS TO RESEARCH SYNTHETIC LIVER REPAIR.
AFTER I GOT WAYNE, INCORPORATED BACK FROM DEREK POWERS, I PUT OUR LABS TO WORK ON IT AROUND THE CLOCK.
NO SUCCESS.
NO!
BATMAN WOULD NEVER SAY THAT!
SHOULDN'T HAVE GOTTEN ANGRY AT HIM...WON'T DO ANY GOOD...
DANA AND HER FAMILY ARE HERE, TOO...MAYBE I'LL CHECK ON THEM, AND--
ALL AVAILABLE MEDICAL PERSONNEL, REPORT TO THE EMERGENCY ROOM!
THIS IS A MULTIPLE CODE SITUATION! ALL AVAILABLE MEDICAL PERSONNEL, REPORT TO THE EMERGENCY ROOM!
UFF!
WATCH OUT!
WHAT'S GOING ON...?
SOMEBODY JUST WALKED INTO A COMPUTER REPAIR BAZAAR ON THE CITY'S TWELFTH LEVEL AND BLEW HIMSELF UP!
EARLY REPORTS SAY TWENTY DEAD AND ANOTHER FORTY-FIVE INJURED!
STAIRS

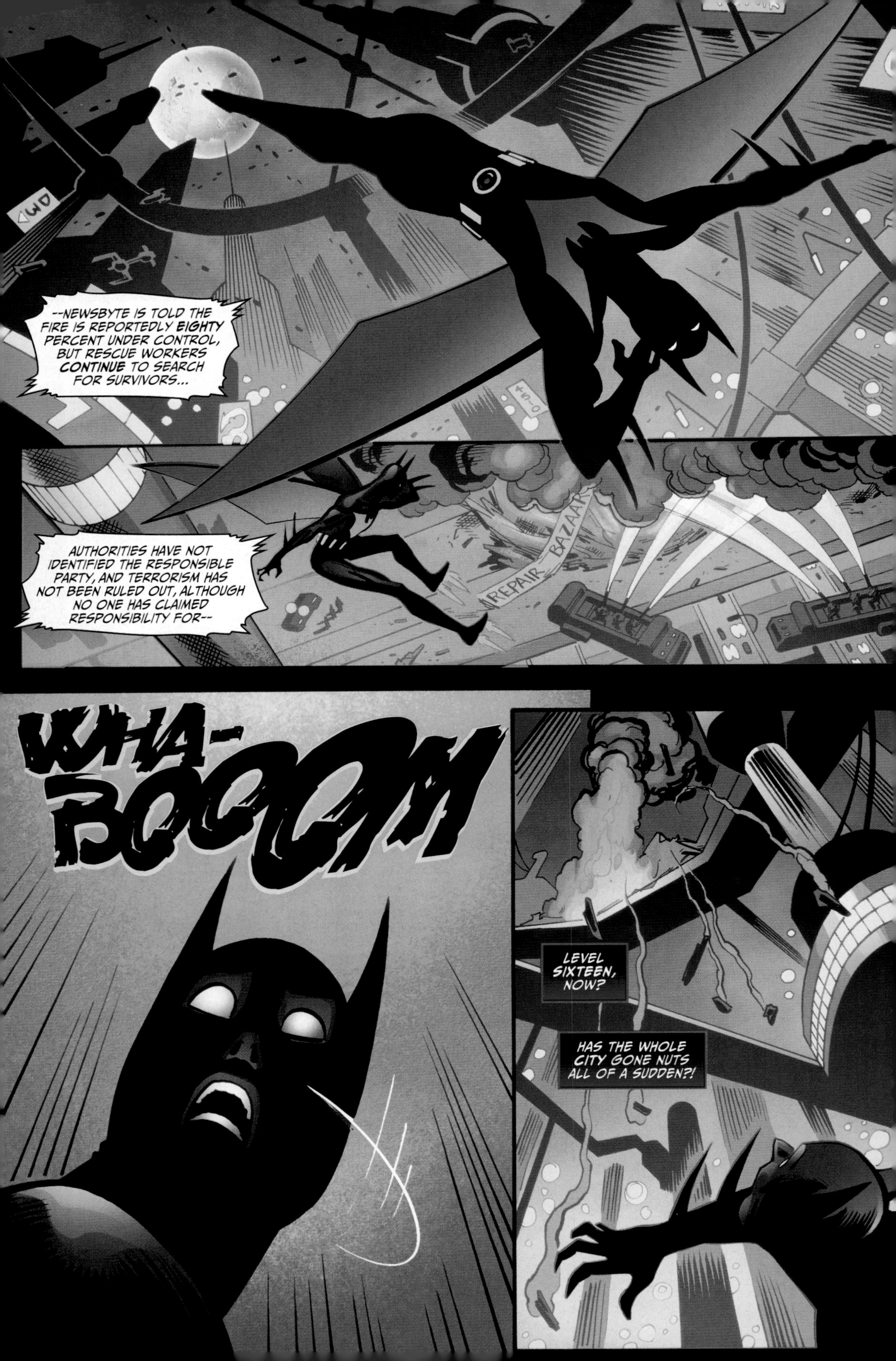
--NEWSBYTE IS TOLD THE FIRE IS REPORTEDLY EIGHTY PERCENT UNDER CONTROL, BUT RESCUE WORKERS CONTINUE TO SEARCH FOR SURVIVORS...
REPAIR BAZAAR
AUTHORITIES HAVE NOT IDENTIFIED THE RESPONSIBLE PARTY, AND TERRORISM HAS NOT BEEN RULED OUT, ALTHOUGH NO ONE HAS CLAIMED RESPONSIBILITY FOR--
WHA-BOOOM
LEVEL SIXTEEN, NOW?
HAS THE WHOLE CITY GONE NUTS ALL OF A SUDDEN?!

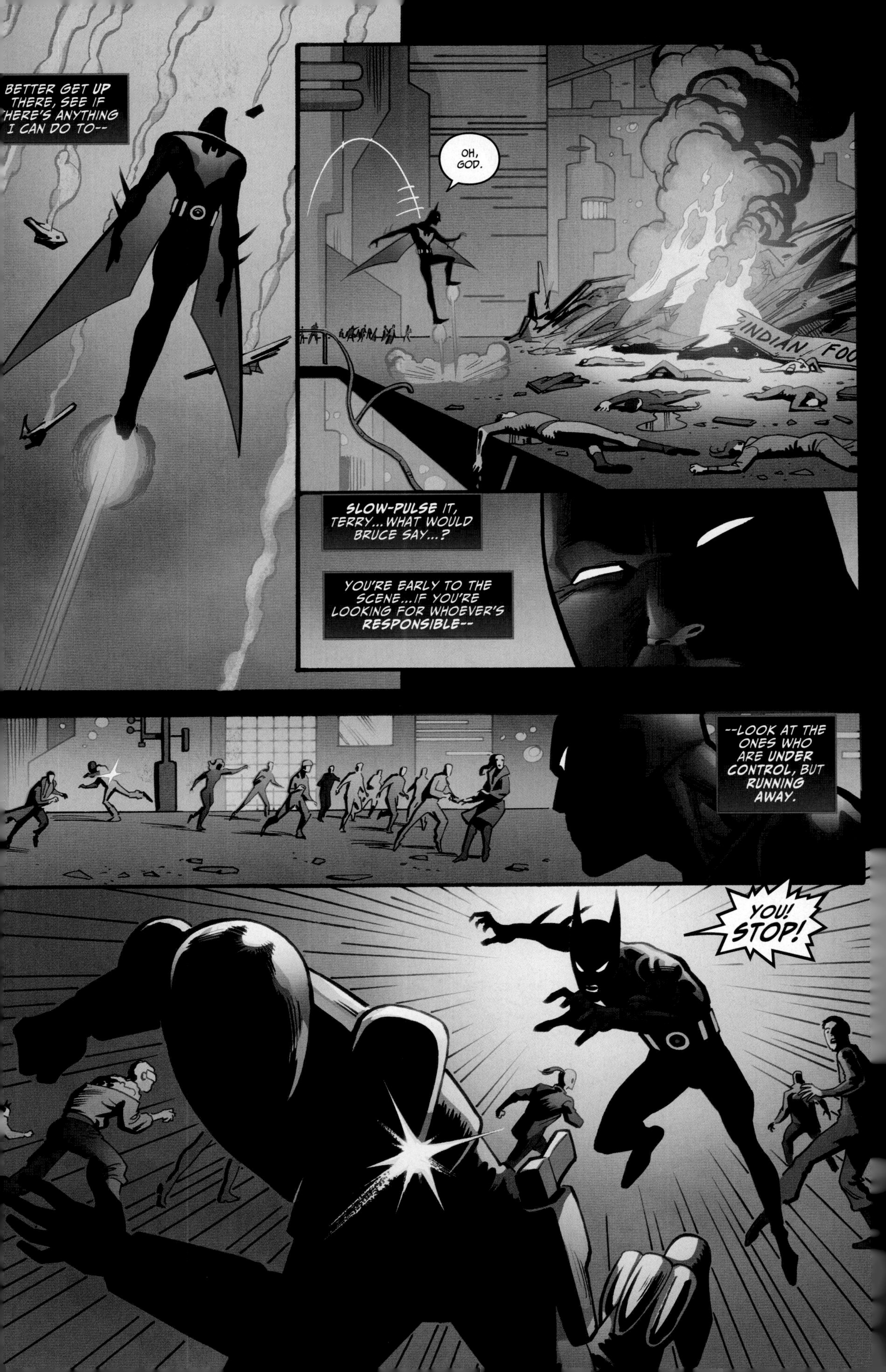
BETTER GET UP THERE, SEE IF THERE'S ANYTHING I CAN DO TO--
OH, GOD.
SLOW-PULSE IT, TERRY...WHAT WOULD BRUCE SAY...?
YOU'RE EARLY TO THE SCENE...IF YOU'RE LOOKING FOR WHOEVER'S RESPONSIBLE--
--LOOK AT THE ONES WHO ARE UNDER CONTROL, BUT RUNNING AWAY.
YOU! STOP!
INDIAN FOO

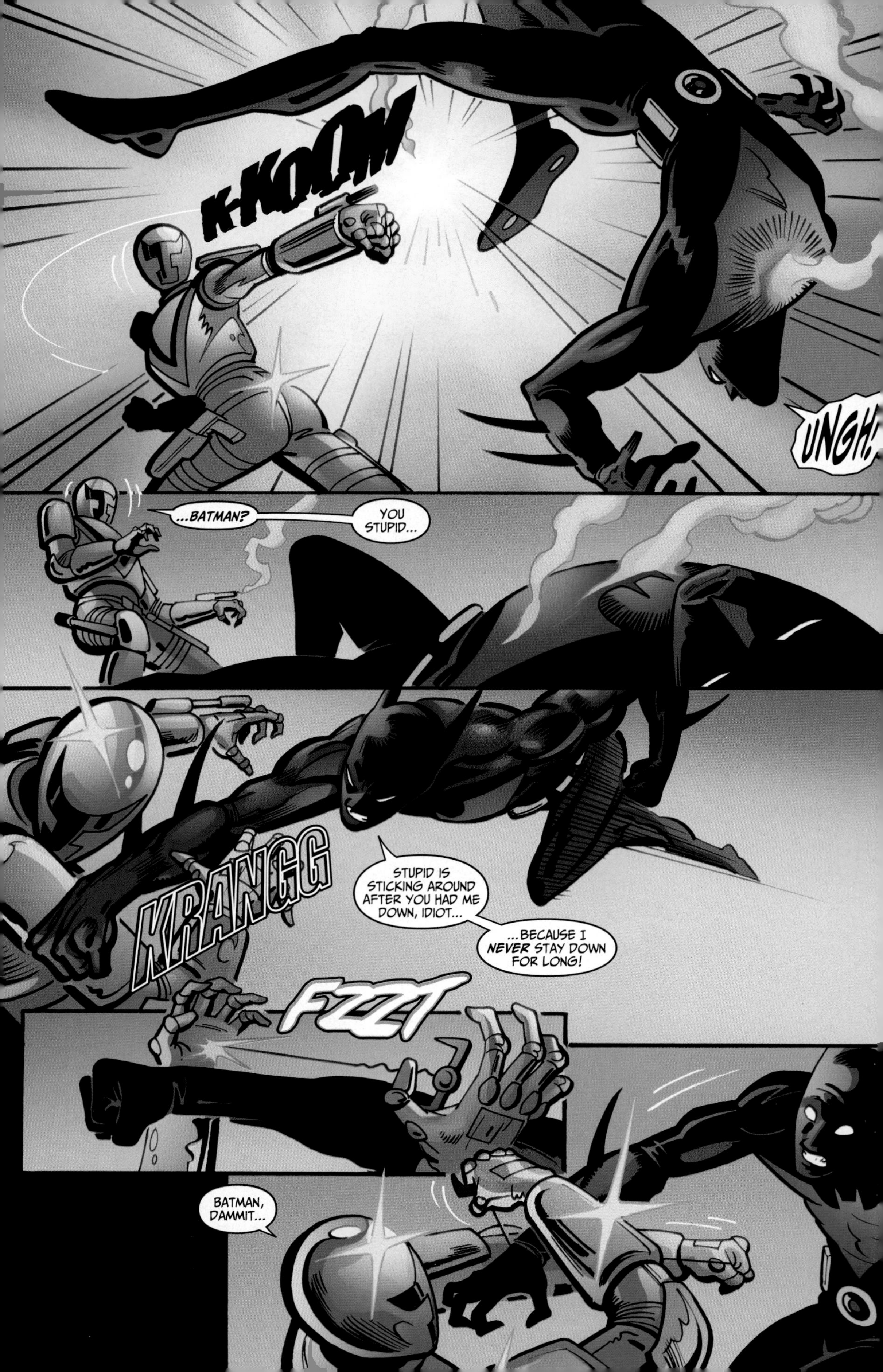
K-KOOM
UNGH!
...BATMAN?
YOU STUPID...
KRANGG
STUPID IS STICKING AROUND AFTER YOU HAD ME DOWN, IDIOT...
...BECAUSE I NEVER STAY DOWN FOR LONG!
FZZT
BATMAN, DAMMIT...

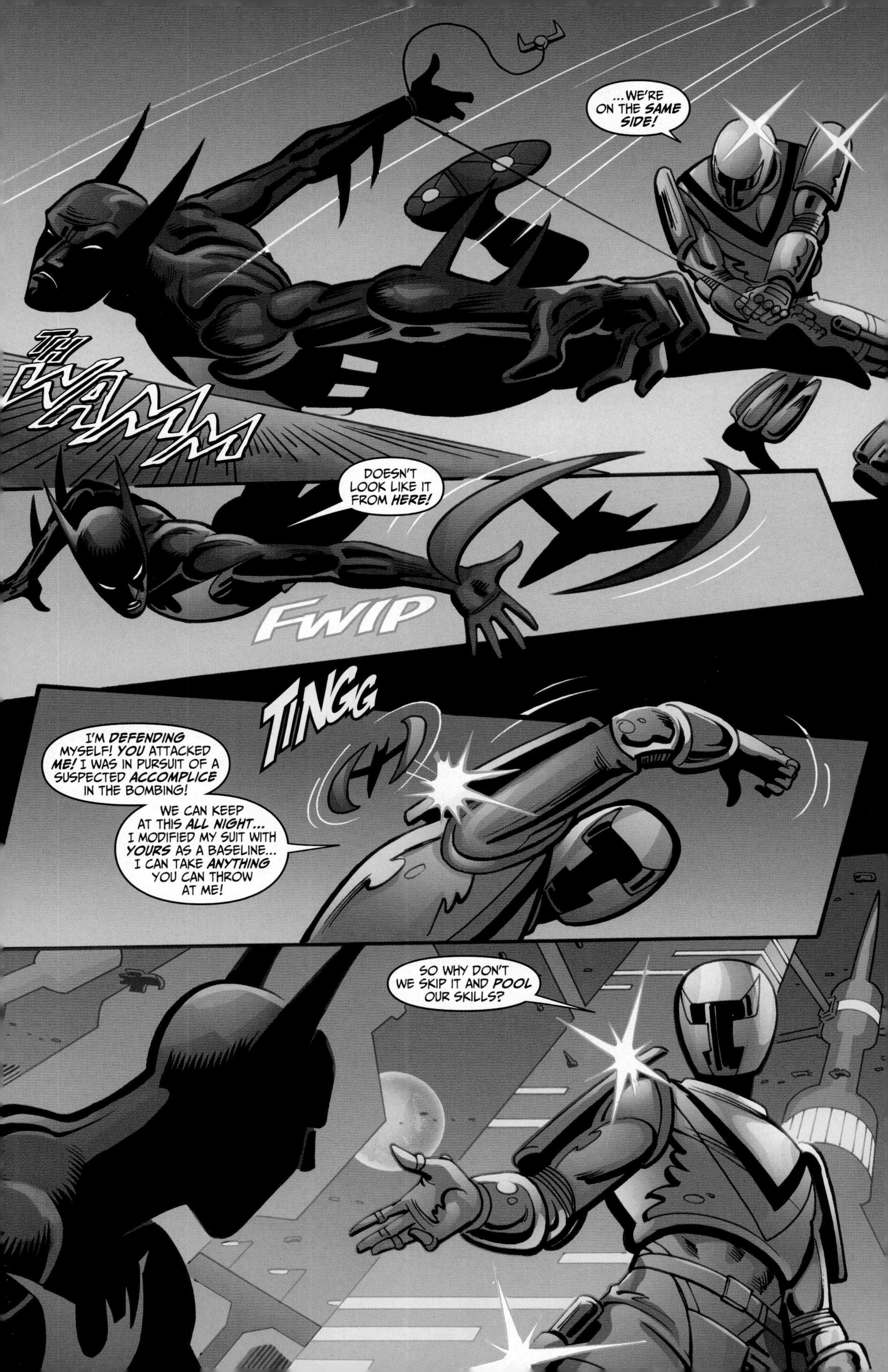
...WE'RE ON THE SAME SIDE!
THWAMM
DOESN'T LOOK LIKE IT FROM HERE!
FWIP
TINGG
I'M DEFENDING MYSELF! YOU ATTACKED ME! I WAS IN PURSUIT OF A SUSPECTED ACCOMPLICE IN THE BOMBING!
WE CAN KEEP AT THIS ALL NIGHT... I MODIFIED MY SUIT WITH YOURS AS A BASELINE... I CAN TAKE ANYTHING YOU CAN THROW AT ME!
SO WHY DON'T WE SKIP IT AND POOL OUR SKILLS?

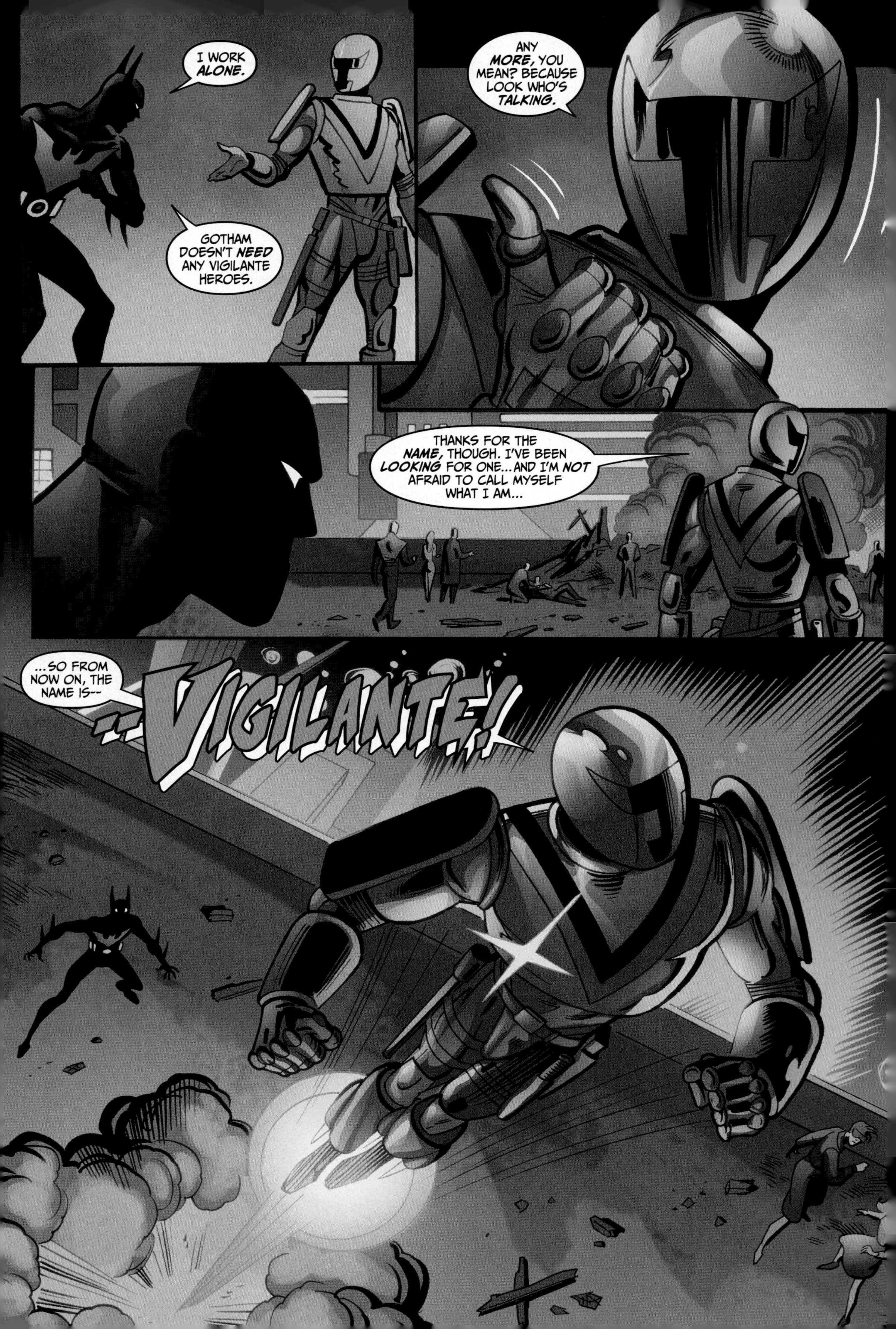
I WORK ALONE.
GOTHAM DOESN'T NEED ANY VIGILANTE HEROES.
ANY MORE, YOU MEAN? BECAUSE LOOK WHO'S TALKING.
THANKS FOR THE NAME, THOUGH. I'VE BEEN LOOKING FOR ONE...AND I'M NOT AFRAID TO CALL MYSELF WHAT I AM...
...SO FROM NOW ON, THE NAME IS--
--VIGILANTE!

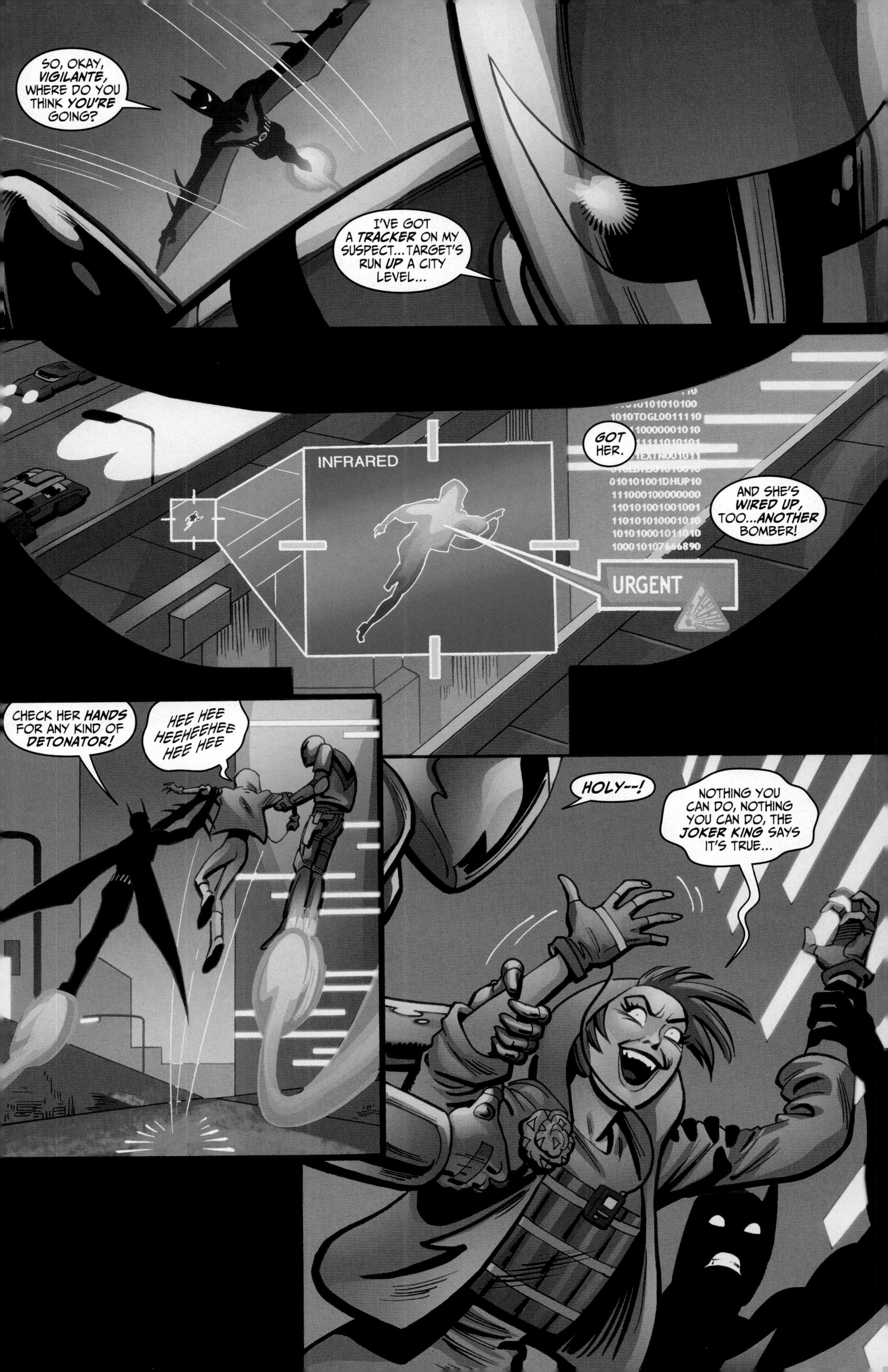
SO, OKAY, VIGILANTE, WHERE DO YOU THINK YOU'RE GOING?
I'VE GOT A TRACKER ON MY SUSPECT...TARGET'S RUN UP A CITY LEVEL...
INFRARED
GOT HER.
AND SHE'S WIRED UP, TOO...ANOTHER BOMBER!
URGENT
CHECK HER HANDS FOR ANY KIND OF DETONATOR!
HEE HEE HEEHEEHEE HEE HEE
HOLY--!
NOTHING YOU CAN DO, NOTHING YOU CAN DO, THE JOKER KING SAYS IT'S TRUE...

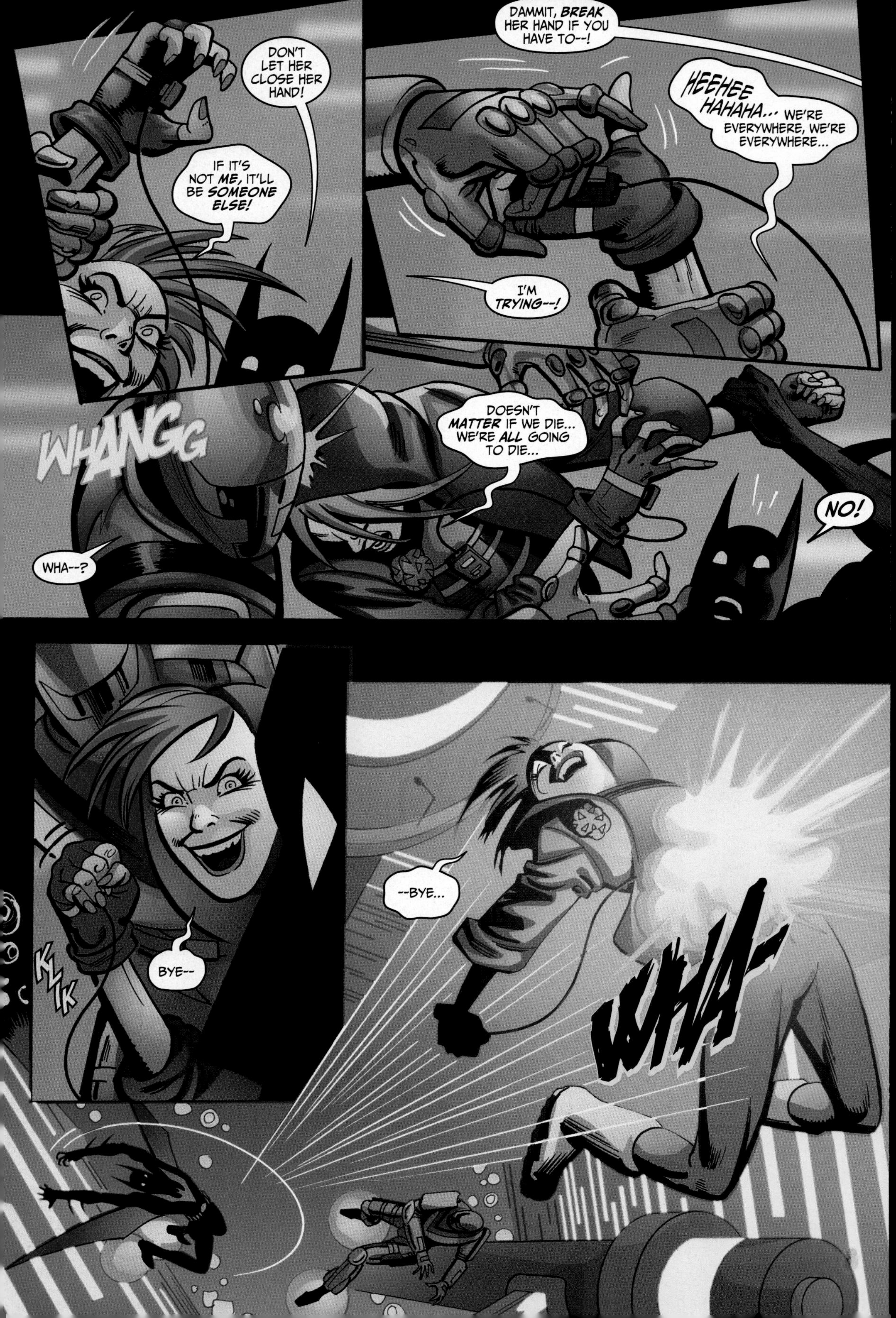
DON'T LET HER CLOSE HER HAND!
IF IT'S NOT ME, IT'LL BE SOMEONE ELSE!
DAMMIT, BREAK HER HAND IF YOU HAVE TO--!
HEEHEE HAHAHA... WE'RE EVERYWHERE, WE'RE EVERYWHERE...
I'M TRYING--!
WHANGG
DOESN'T MATTER IF WE DIE... WE'RE ALL GOING TO DIE...
NO!
WHA--?
KLIK
BYE--
--BYE...
WHA-

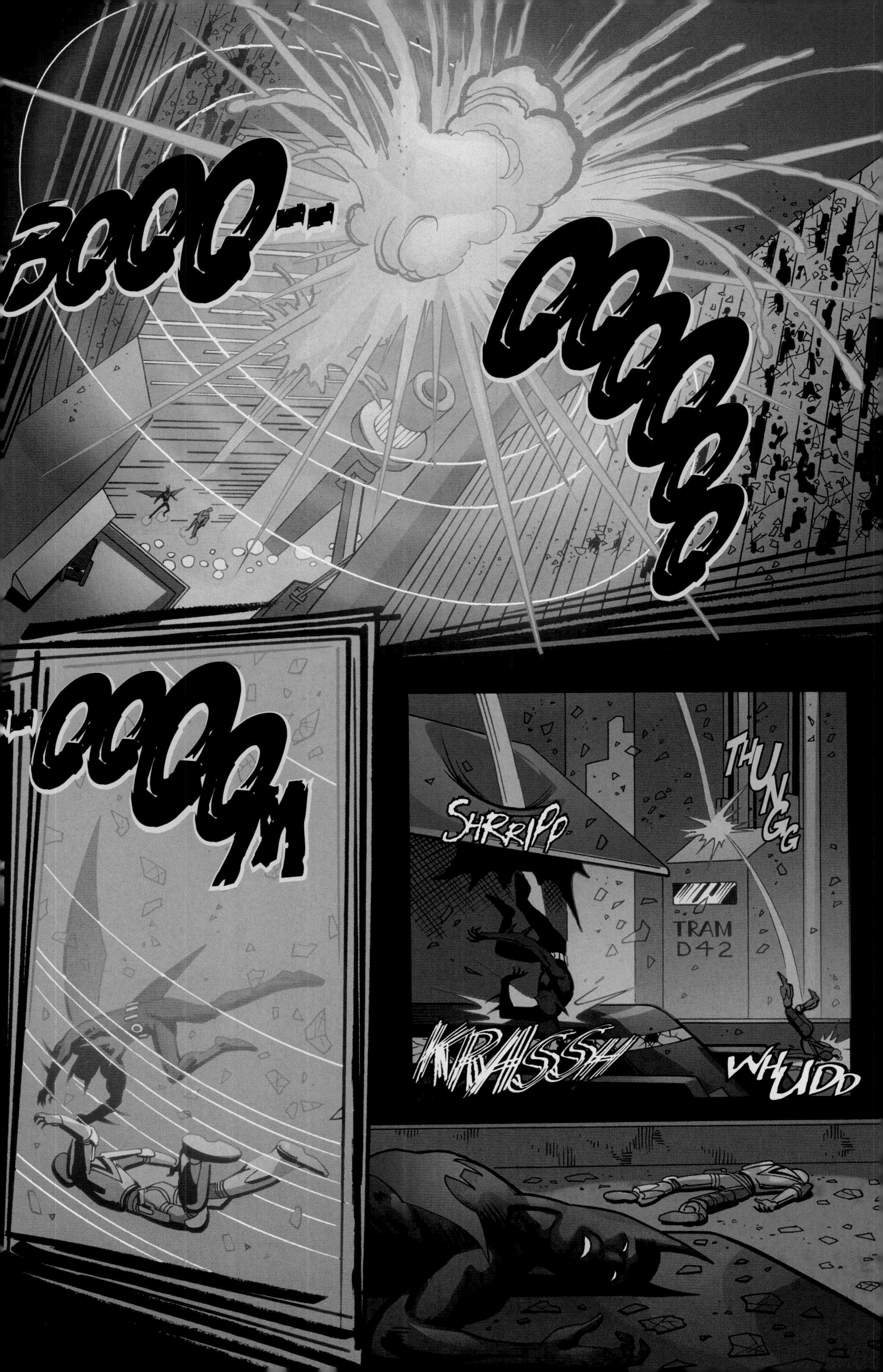
BOOO--
OOOOOO
--OOOOOM
SHRRIPP
THUNGG
TRAM D42
KRASSSH
WHUDD

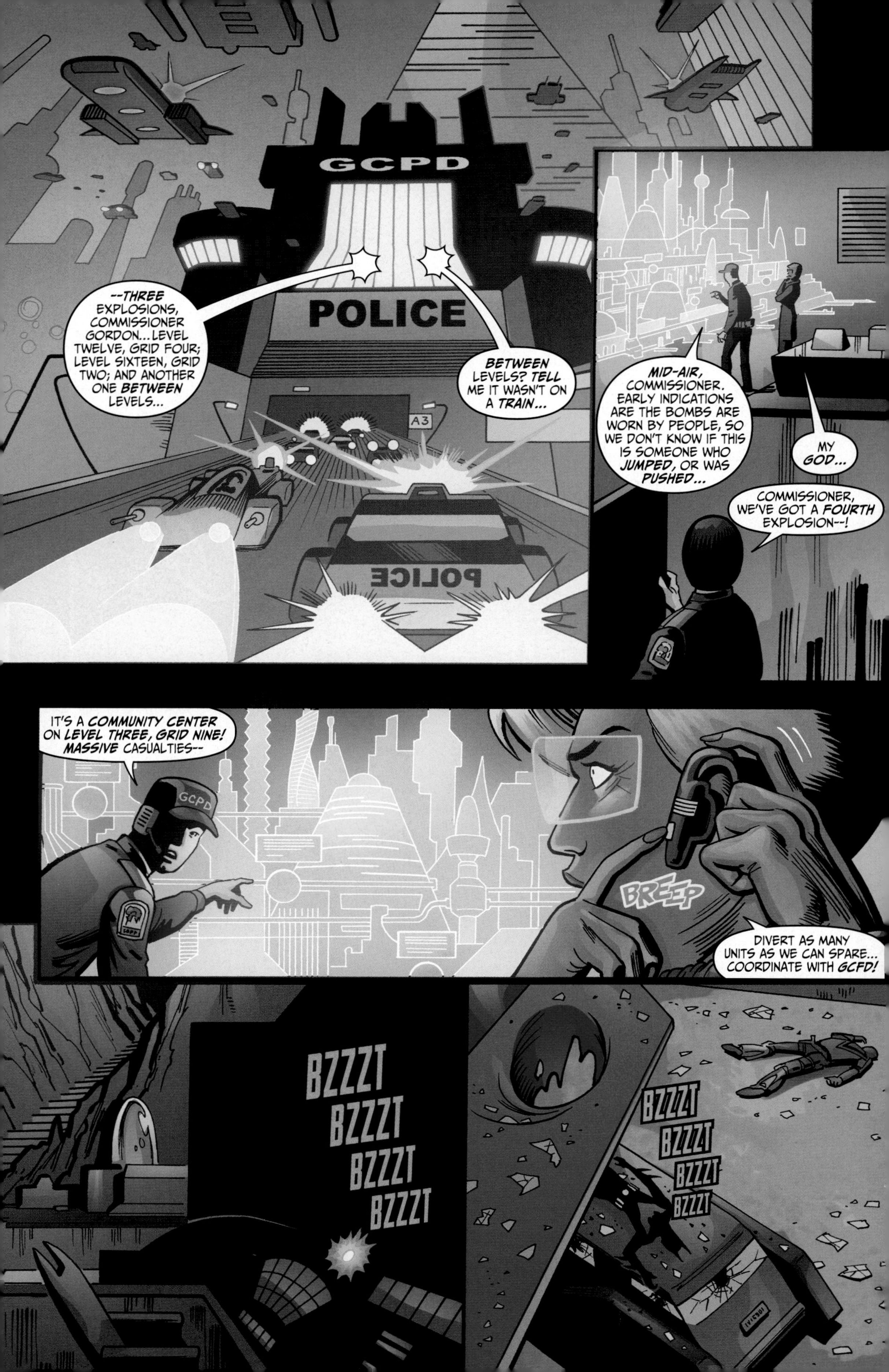
GCPD
POLICE
--THREE EXPLOSIONS, COMMISSIONER GORDON...LEVEL TWELVE, GRID FOUR; LEVEL SIXTEEN, GRID TWO; AND ANOTHER ONE BETWEEN LEVELS...
BETWEEN LEVELS? TELL ME IT WASN'T ON A TRAIN...
A3
POLICE
MID-AIR, COMMISSIONER. EARLY INDICATIONS ARE THE BOMBS ARE WORN BY PEOPLE, SO WE DON'T KNOW IF THIS IS SOMEONE WHO JUMPED, OR WAS PUSHED...
MY GOD...
COMMISSIONER, WE'VE GOT A FOURTH EXPLOSION--!
IT'S A COMMUNITY CENTER ON LEVEL THREE, GRID NINE! MASSIVE CASUALTIES--
GCPD
BREEP
DIVERT AS MANY UNITS AS WE CAN SPARE... COORDINATE WITH GCFD!
BZZZT
BZZZT
BZZZT
BZZZT
BZZZT
BZZZT
BZZZT
BZZZT

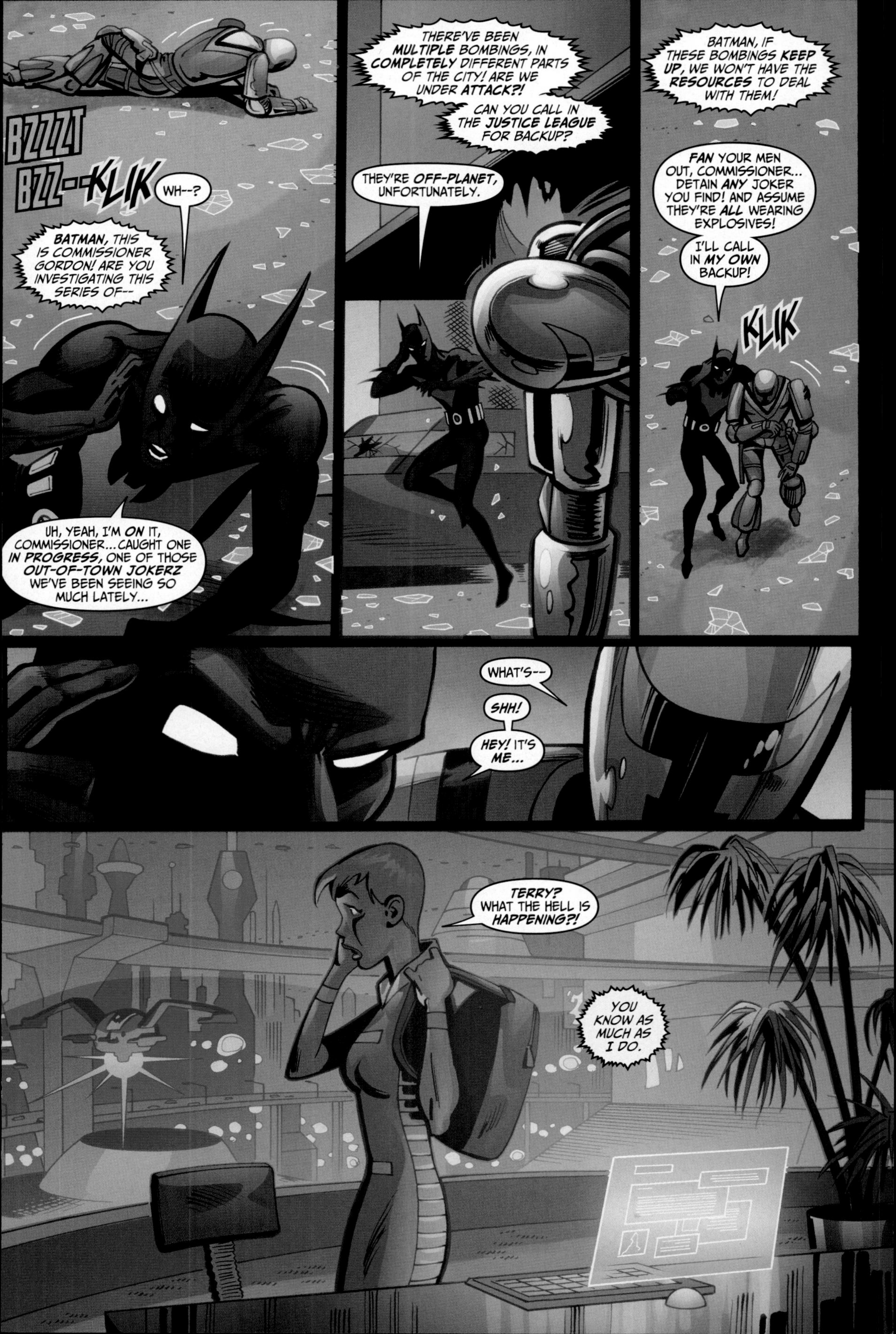
BZZZZT
BZZ--KLIK
WH--?
BATMAN, THIS IS COMMISSIONER GORDON! ARE YOU INVESTIGATING THIS SERIES OF--
UH, YEAH, I'M ON IT, COMMISSIONER...CAUGHT ONE IN PROGRESS, ONE OF THOSE OUT-OF-TOWN JOKERZ WE'VE BEEN SEEING SO MUCH LATELY...
THERE'VE BEEN MULTIPLE BOMBINGS, IN COMPLETELY DIFFERENT PARTS OF THE CITY! ARE WE UNDER ATTACK?!
CAN YOU CALL IN THE JUSTICE LEAGUE FOR BACKUP?
THEY'RE OFF-PLANET, UNFORTUNATELY.
BATMAN, IF THESE BOMBINGS KEEP UP, WE WON'T HAVE THE RESOURCES TO DEAL WITH THEM!
FAN YOUR MEN OUT, COMMISSIONER... DETAIN ANY JOKER YOU FIND! AND ASSUME THEY'RE ALL WEARING EXPLOSIVES!
I'LL CALL IN MY OWN BACKUP!
KLIK
WHAT'S--
SHH!
HEY! IT'S ME...
TERRY? WHAT THE HELL IS HAPPENING?!
YOU KNOW AS MUCH AS I DO.

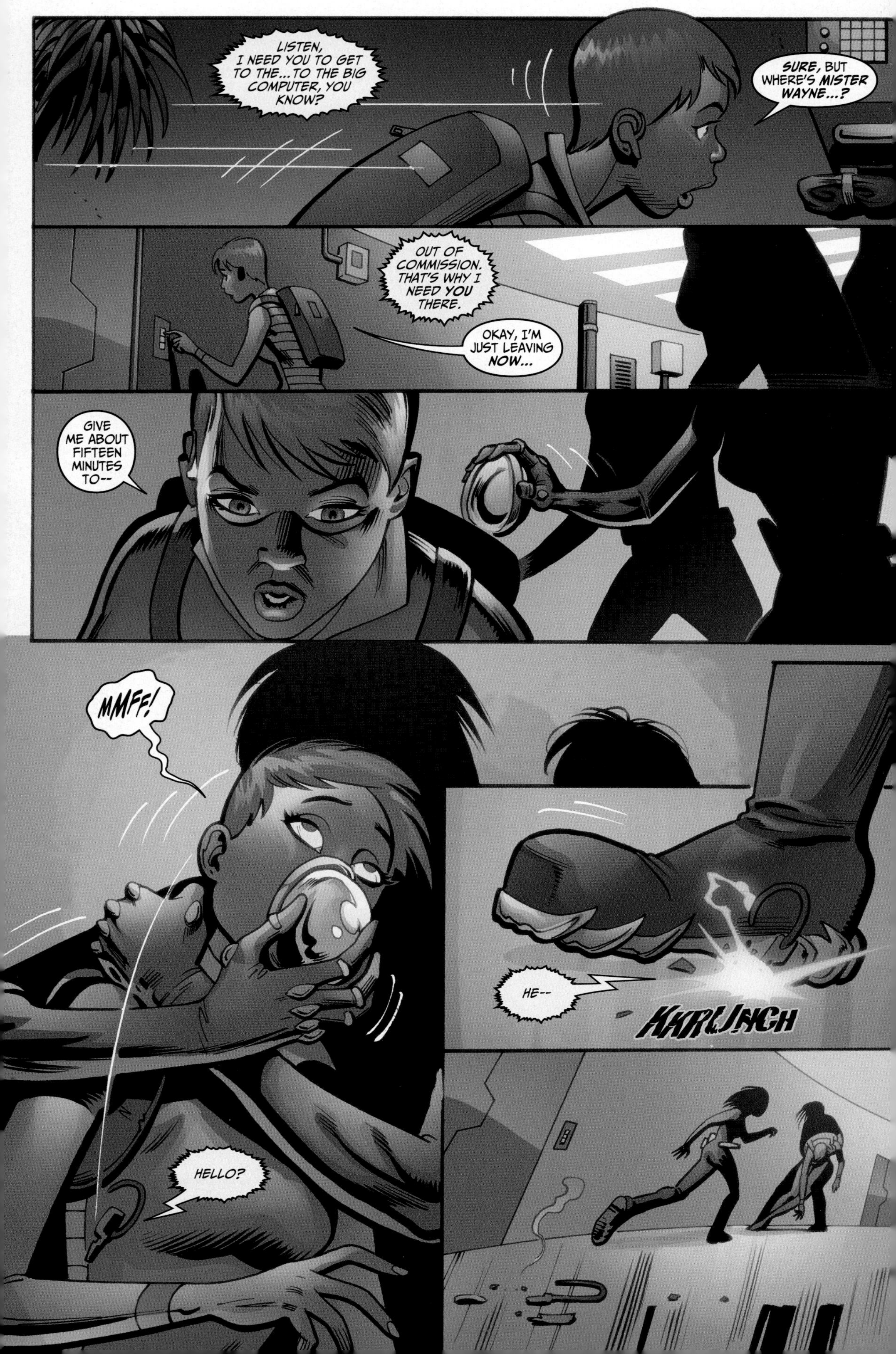
LISTEN, I NEED YOU TO GET TO THE...TO THE BIG COMPUTER, YOU KNOW?
SURE, BUT WHERE'S MISTER WAYNE...?
OUT OF COMMISSION. THAT'S WHY I NEED YOU THERE.
OKAY, I'M JUST LEAVING NOW...
GIVE ME ABOUT FIFTEEN MINUTES TO--
MMFF!
OKAY, I'M HE--
KKRUNCH
HELLO?

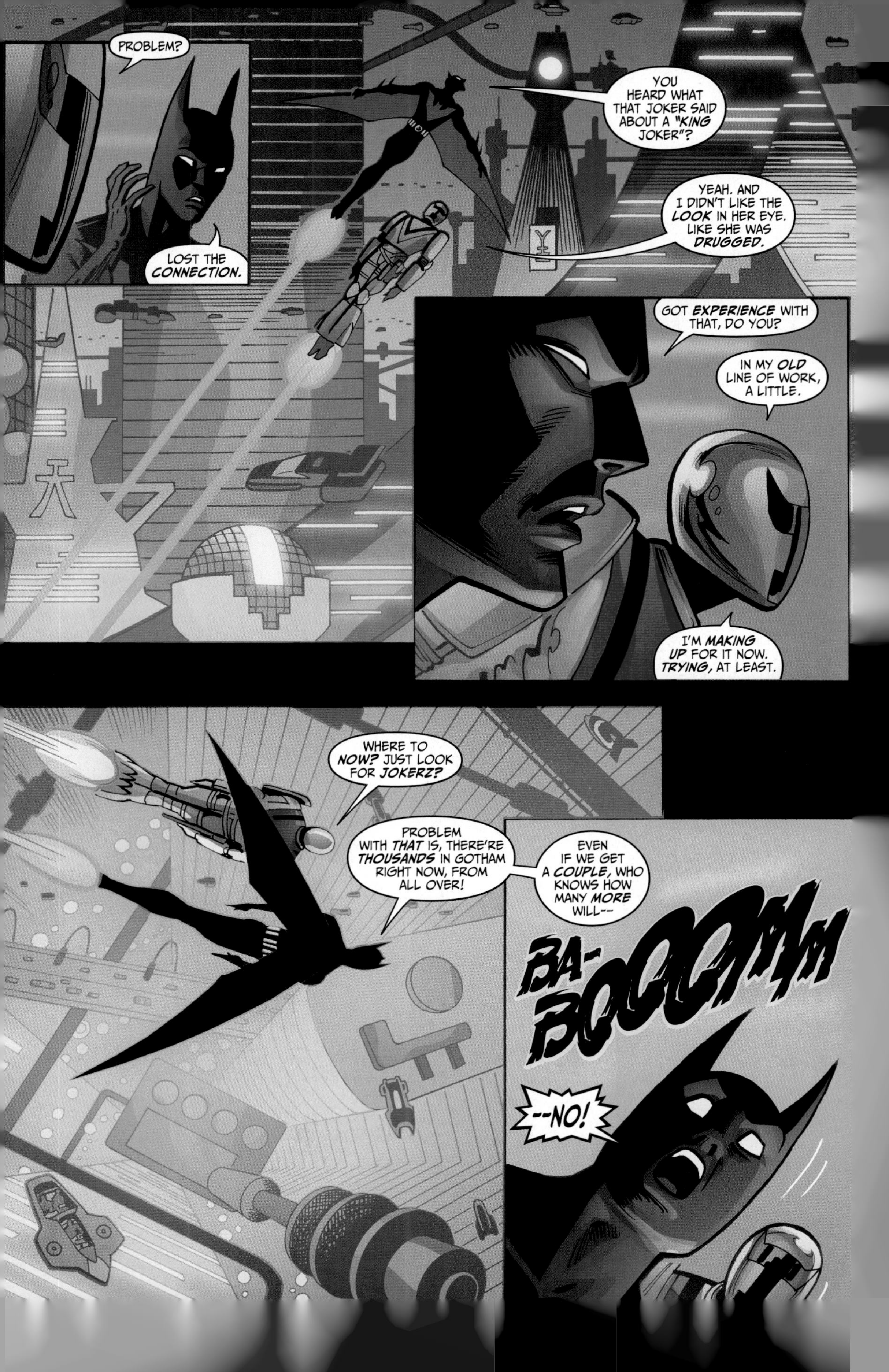
PROBLEM?
LOST THE CONNECTION.
YOU HEARD WHAT THAT JOKER SAID ABOUT A "KING JOKER"?
YEAH. AND I DIDN'T LIKE THE LOOK IN HER EYE. LIKE SHE WAS DRUGGED.
GOT EXPERIENCE WITH THAT, DO YOU?
IN MY OLD LINE OF WORK, A LITTLE.
I'M MAKING UP FOR IT NOW. TRYING, AT LEAST.
WHERE TO NOW? JUST LOOK FOR JOKERZ?
PROBLEM WITH THAT IS, THERE'RE THOUSANDS IN GOTHAM RIGHT NOW, FROM ALL OVER!
EVEN IF WE GET A COUPLE, WHO KNOWS HOW MANY MORE WILL--
BA-BOOOMM
--NO!

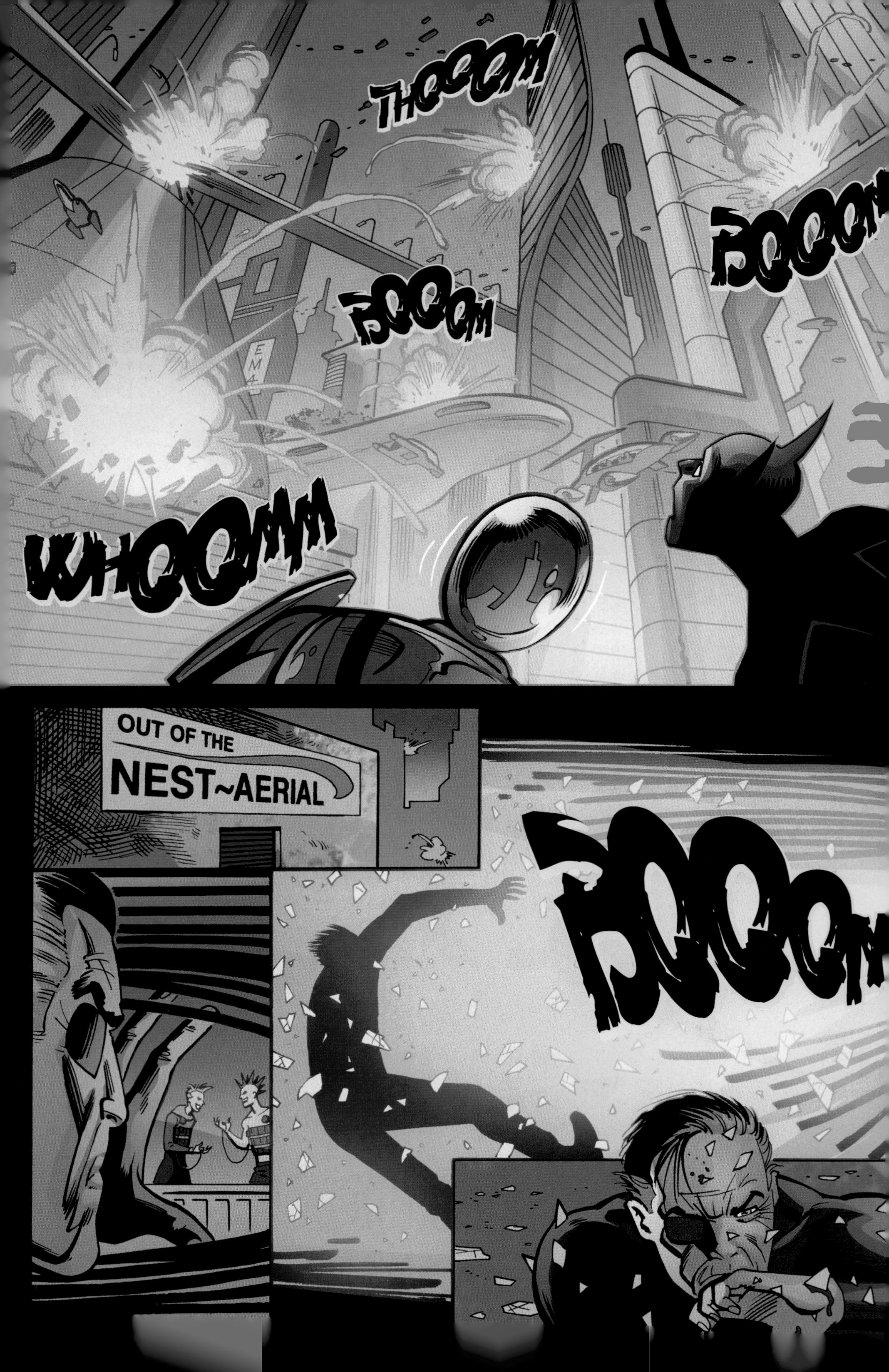
THOOOM
BOOOOM
BOOOM
WHOOMM
OUT OF THE
NEST~AERIAL
BOOOM

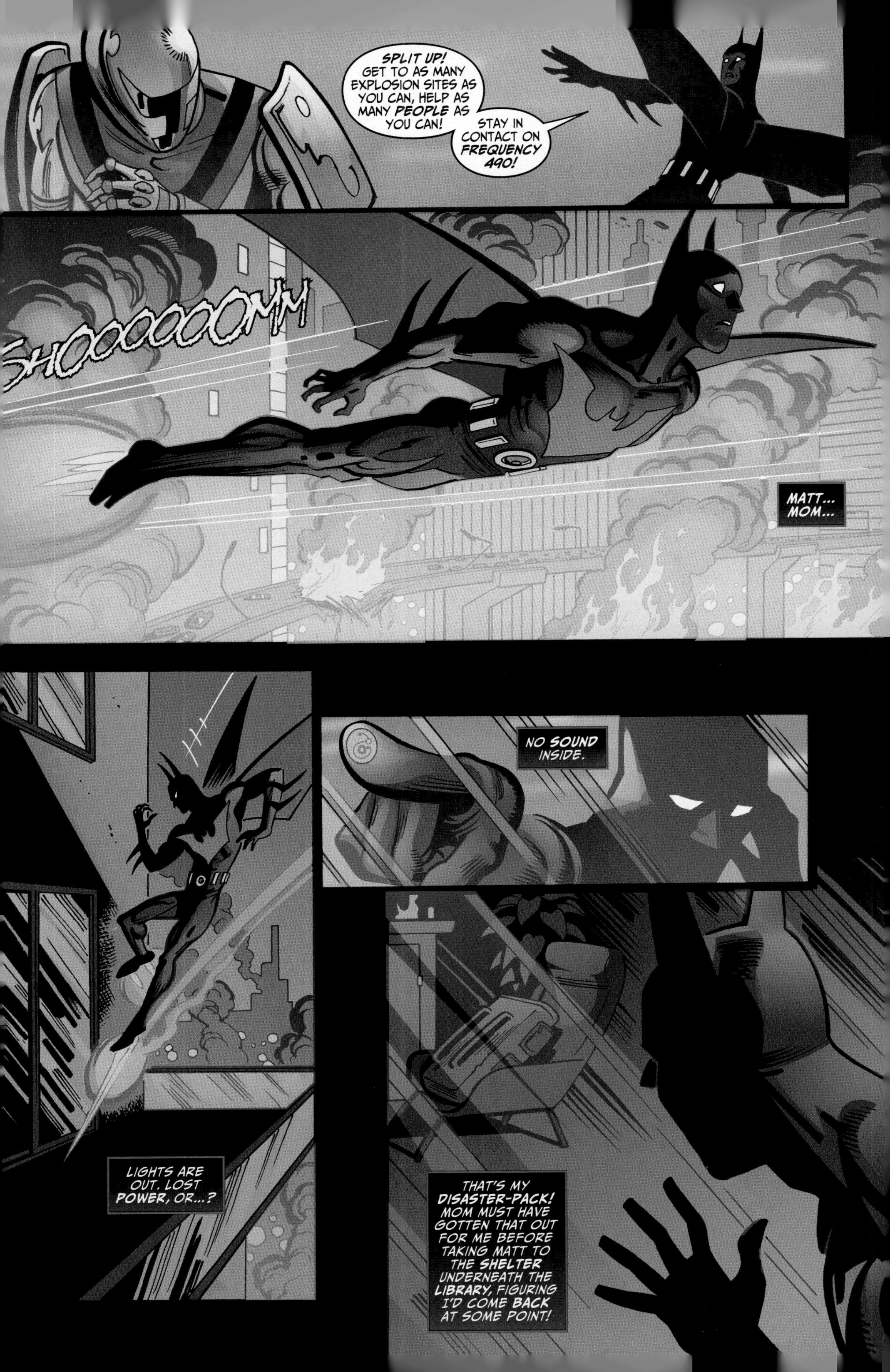
SPLIT UP! GET TO AS MANY EXPLOSION SITES AS YOU CAN, HELP AS MANY PEOPLE AS YOU CAN!
STAY IN CONTACT ON FREQUENCY 490!
SHOOOOOOOOMM
MATT... MOM...
LIGHTS ARE OUT. LOST POWER, OR...?
NO SOUND INSIDE.
THAT'S MY DISASTER-PACK! MOM MUST HAVE GOTTEN THAT OUT FOR ME BEFORE TAKING MATT TO THE SHELTER UNDERNEATH THE LIBRARY, FIGURING I'D COME BACK AT SOME POINT!

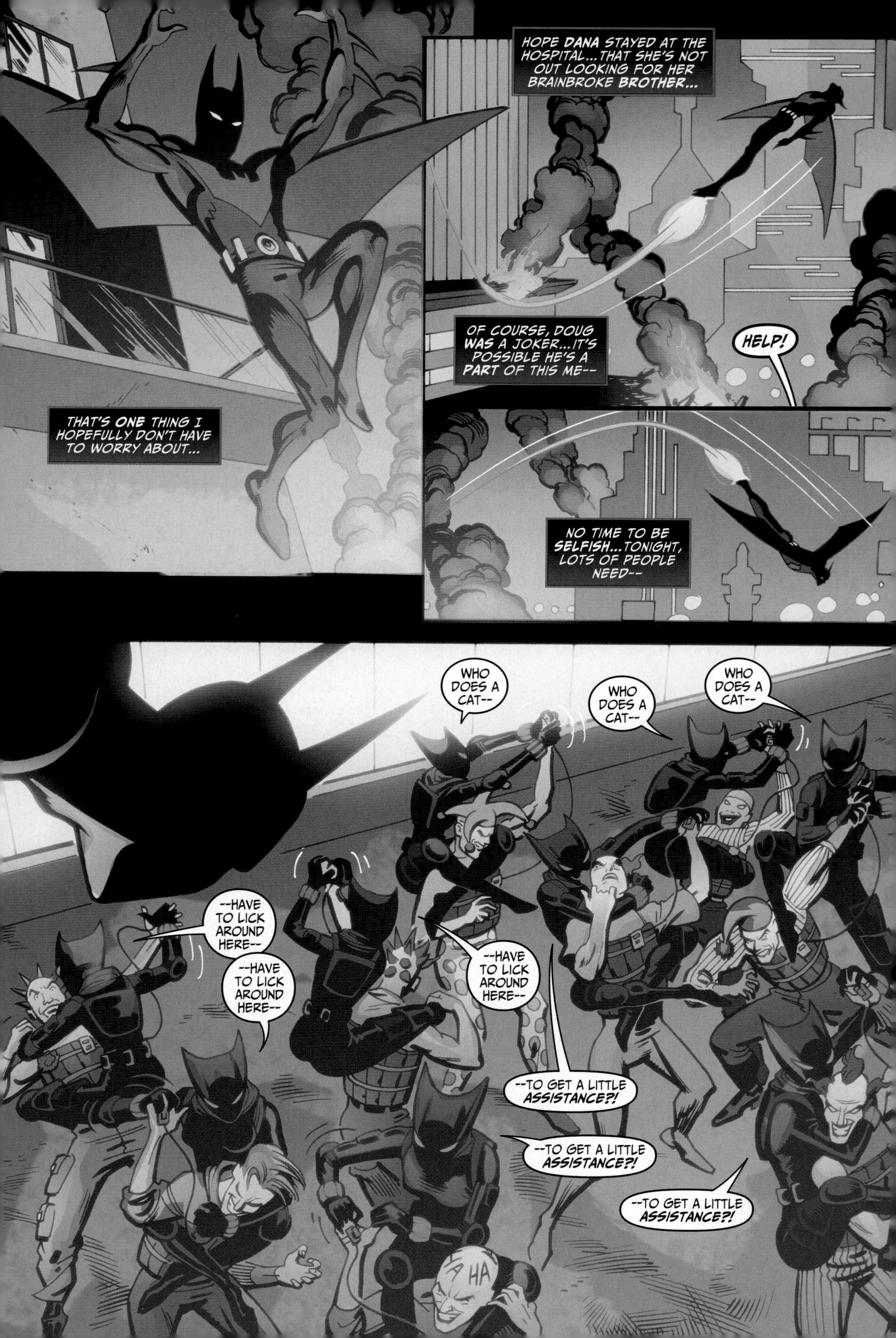
THAT'S ONE THING I HOPEFULLY DON'T HAVE TO WORRY ABOUT...
HOPE DANA STAYED AT THE HOSPITAL...THAT SHE'S NOT OUT LOOKING FOR HER BRAINBROKE BROTHER...
OF COURSE, DOUG WAS A JOKER...IT'S POSSIBLE HE'S A PART OF THIS ME--
HELP!
NO TIME TO BE SELFISH...TONIGHT, LOTS OF PEOPLE NEED--
WHO DOES A CAT--
WHO DOES A CAT--
WHO DOES A CAT--
--HAVE TO LICK AROUND HERE--
--HAVE TO LICK AROUND HERE--
--HAVE TO LICK AROUND HERE--
--TO GET A LITTLE ASSISTANCE?!
--TO GET A LITTLE ASSISTANCE?!
--TO GET A LITTLE ASSISTANCE?!

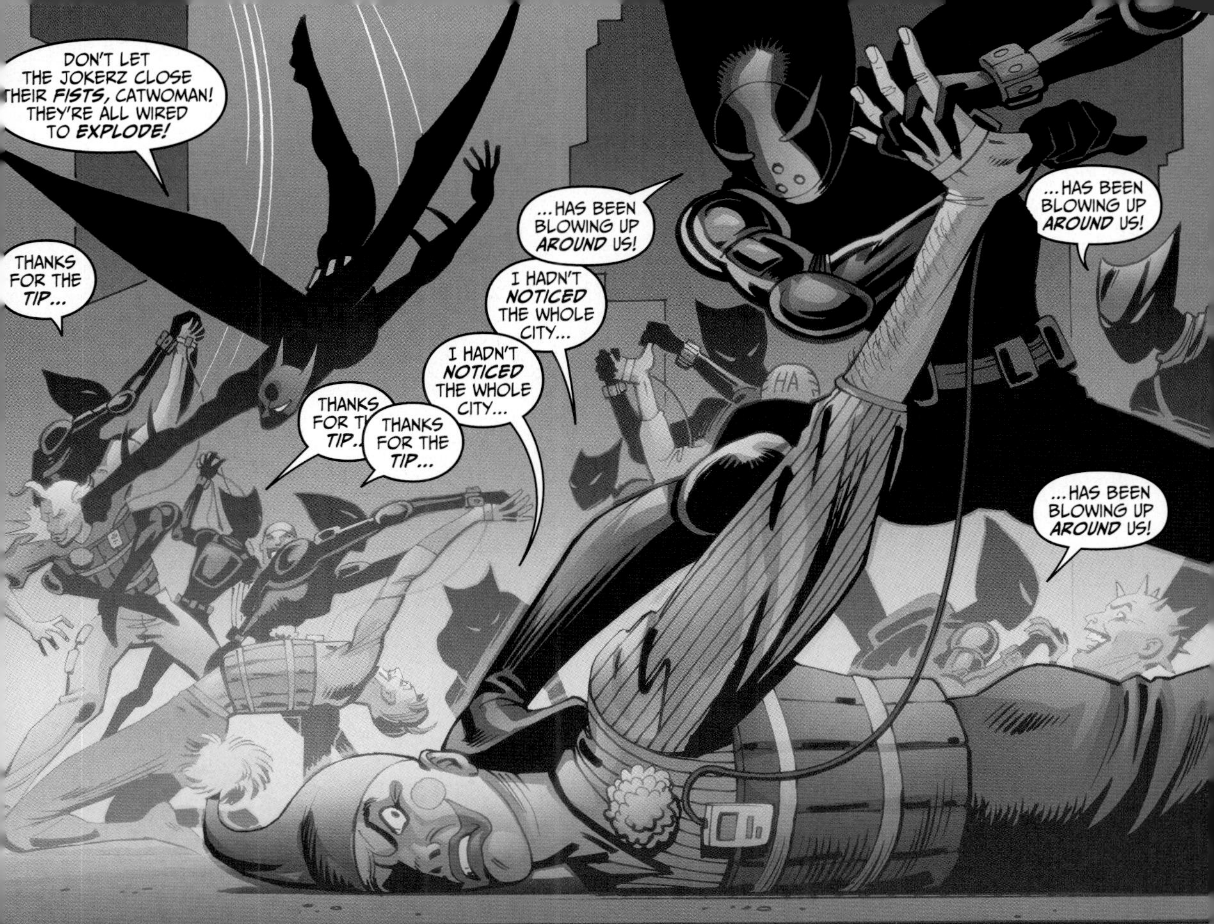
DON'T LET THE JOKERZ CLOSE THEIR FISTS, CATWOMAN! THEY'RE ALL WIRED TO EXPLODE!
THANKS FOR THE TIP...
...HAS BEEN BLOWING UP AROUND US!
I HADN'T NOTICED THE WHOLE CITY...
I HADN'T NOTICED THE WHOLE CITY...
THANKS FOR THE TIP...
THANKS FOR THE TIP...
...HAS BEEN BLOWING UP AROUND US!
...HAS BEEN BLOWING UP AROUND US!

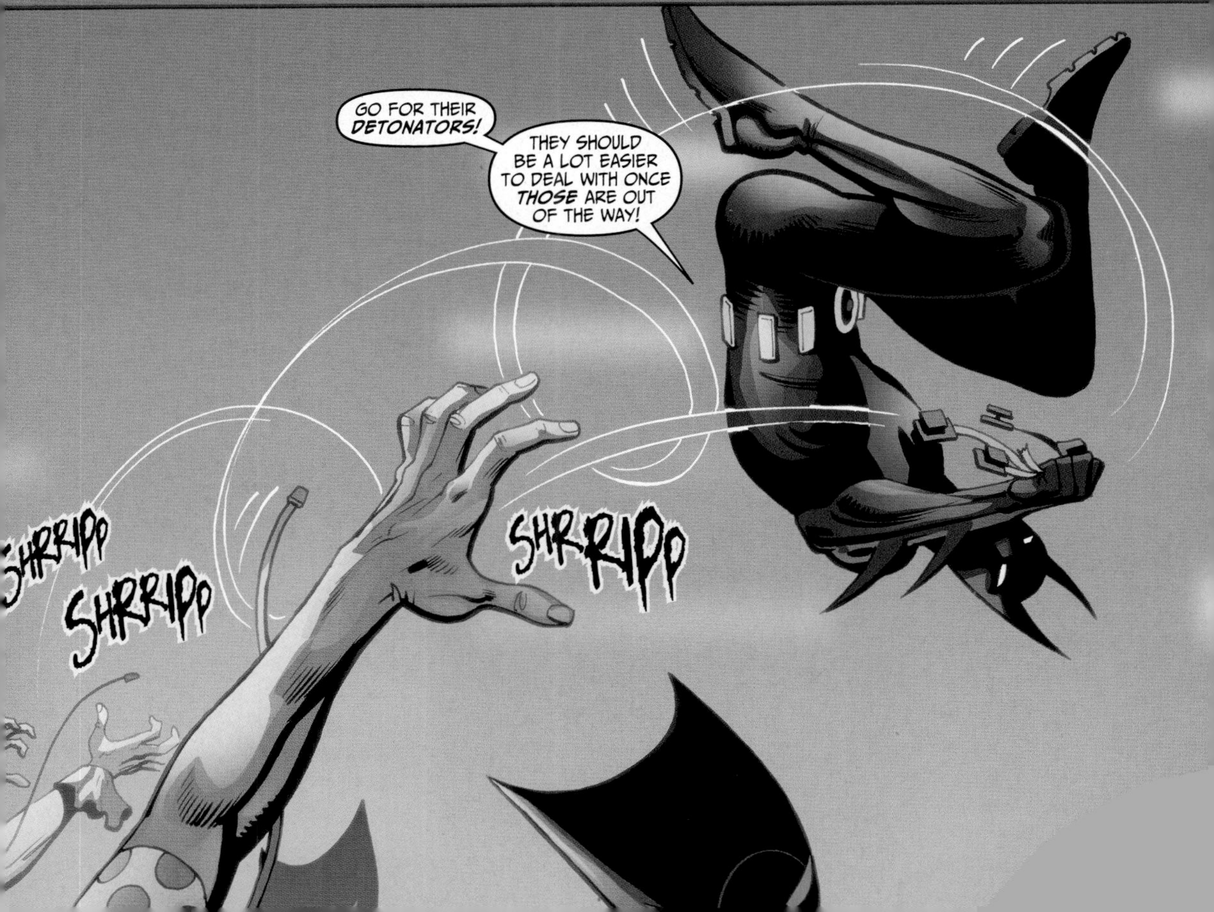
GO FOR THEIR DETONATORS!
THEY SHOULD BE A LOT EASIER TO DEAL WITH ONCE THOSE ARE OUT OF THE WAY!
SHRRIPP
SHRRIPP
SHRRIPP

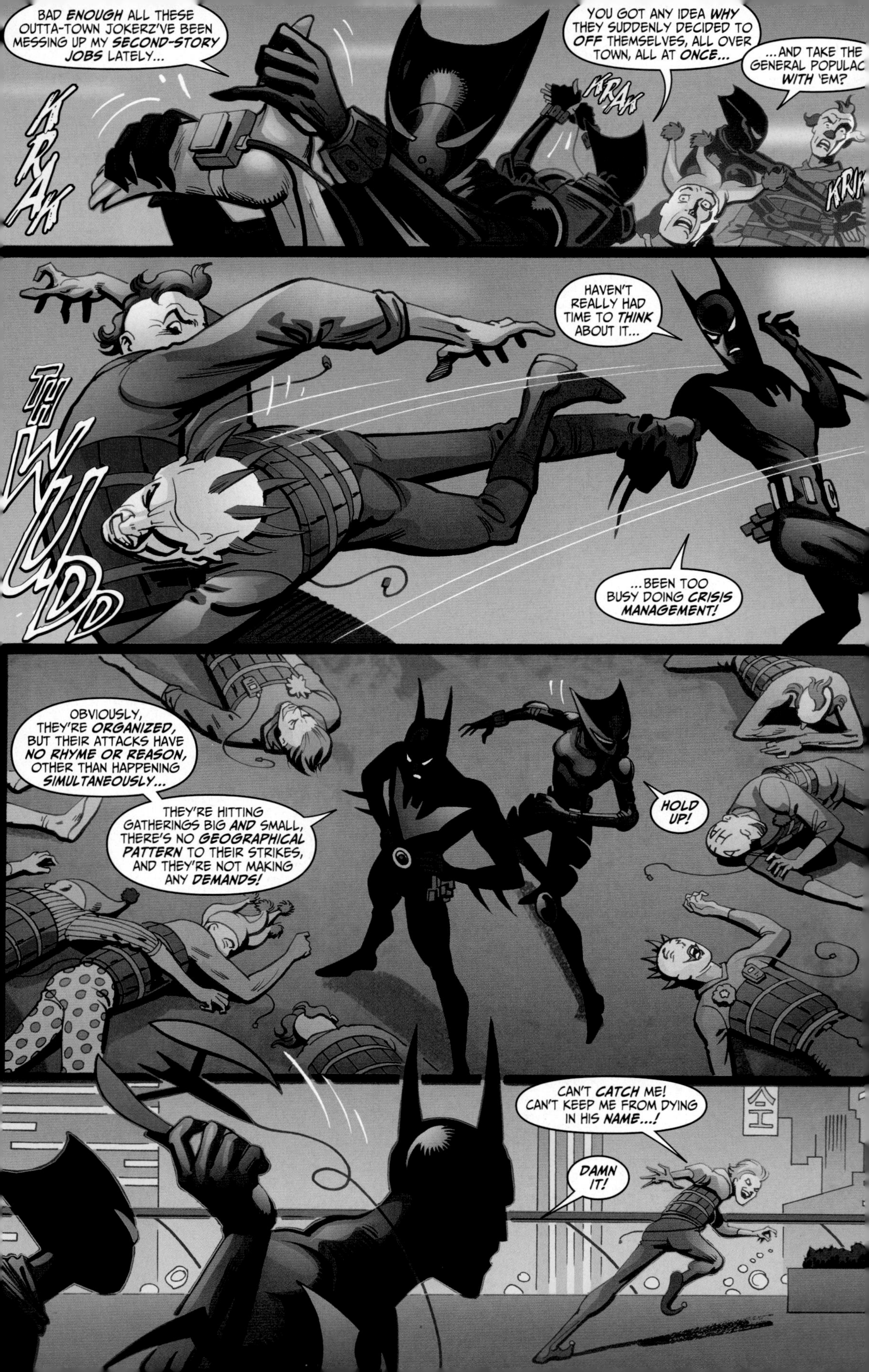
BAD ENOUGH ALL THESE OUTTA-TOWN JOKERZ'VE BEEN MESSING UP MY SECOND-STORY JOBS LATELY...
KRAK
YOU GOT ANY IDEA WHY THEY SUDDENLY DECIDED TO OFF THEMSELVES, ALL OVER TOWN, ALL AT ONCE...
KRAK
...AND TAKE THE GENERAL POPULAC WITH 'EM?
KRIK
HAVEN'T REALLY HAD TIME TO THINK ABOUT IT...
THWUDD
...BEEN TOO BUSY DOING CRISIS MANAGEMENT!
OBVIOUSLY, THEY'RE ORGANIZED, BUT THEIR ATTACKS HAVE NO RHYME OR REASON, OTHER THAN HAPPENING SIMULTANEOUSLY...
THEY'RE HITTING GATHERINGS BIG AND SMALL, THERE'S NO GEOGRAPHICAL PATTERN TO THEIR STRIKES, AND THEY'RE NOT MAKING ANY DEMANDS!
HOLD UP!
CAN'T CATCH ME! CAN'T KEEP ME FROM DYING IN HIS NAME...!
DAMN IT!

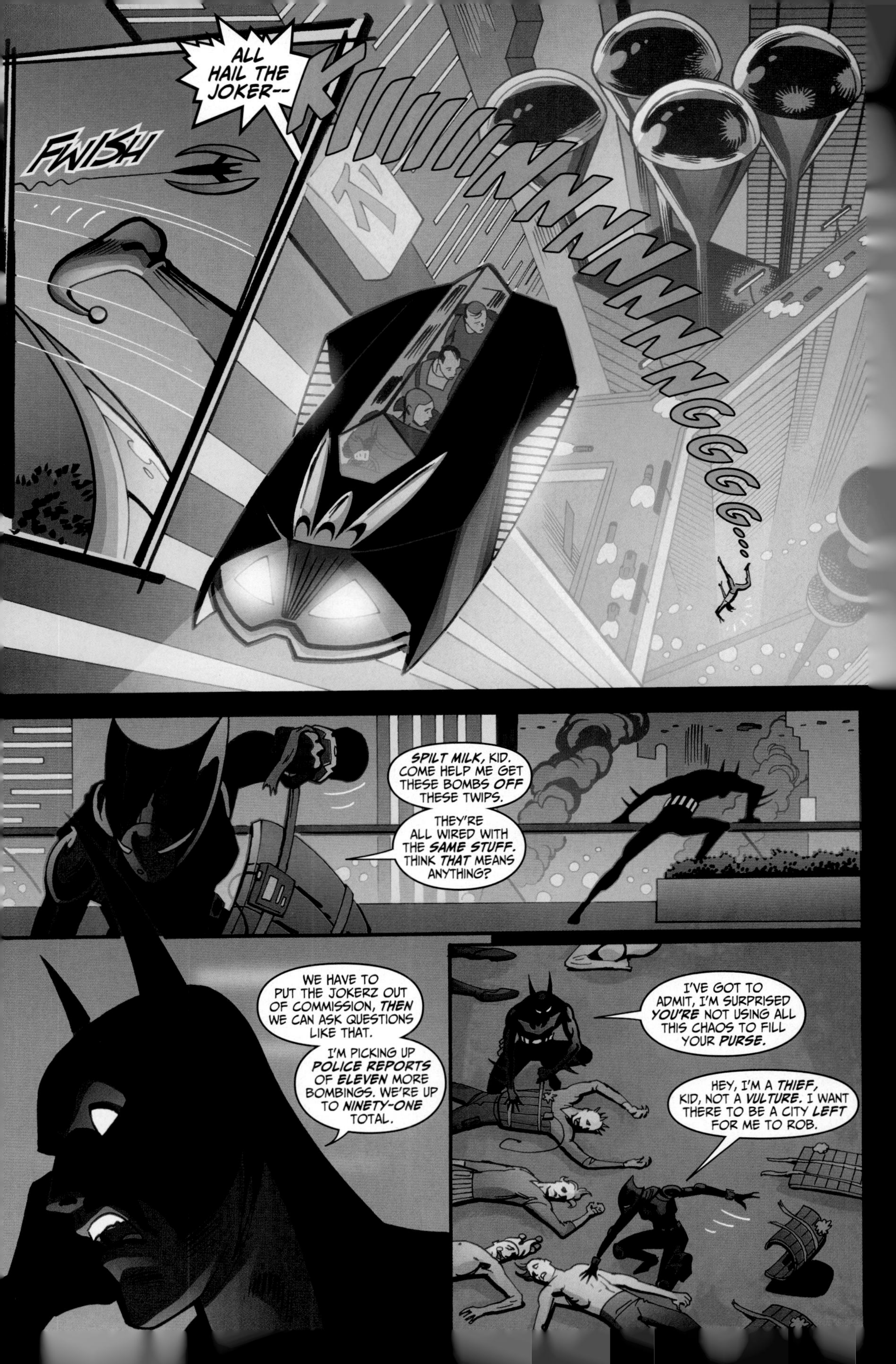
ALL HAIL THE JOKER--
KIIIIIINNNNNNNNNGGGGGooo
FWISH
SPILT MILK, KID. COME HELP ME GET THESE BOMBS OFF THESE TWIPS.
THEY'RE ALL WIRED WITH THE SAME STUFF. THINK THAT MEANS ANYTHING?
WE HAVE TO PUT THE JOKERZ OUT OF COMMISSION, THEN WE CAN ASK QUESTIONS LIKE THAT.
I'M PICKING UP POLICE REPORTS OF ELEVEN MORE BOMBINGS. WE'RE UP TO NINETY-ONE TOTAL.
I'VE GOT TO ADMIT, I'M SURPRISED YOU'RE NOT USING ALL THIS CHAOS TO FILL YOUR PURSE.
HEY, I'M A THIEF, KID, NOT A VULTURE. I WANT THERE TO BE A CITY LEFT FOR ME TO ROB.

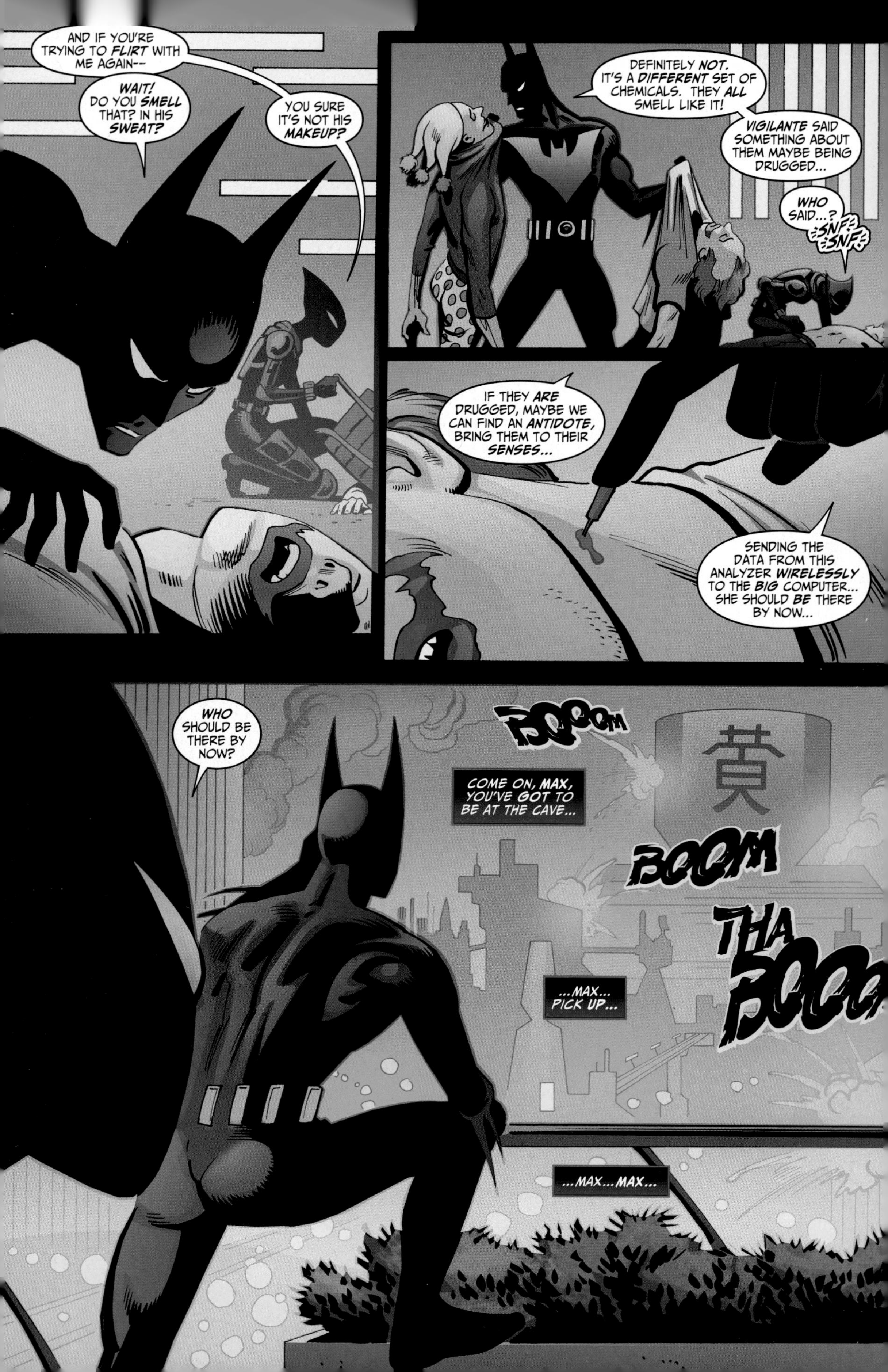
AND IF YOU'RE TRYING TO FLIRT WITH ME AGAIN--
WAIT! DO YOU SMELL THAT? IN HIS SWEAT?
YOU SURE IT'S NOT HIS MAKEUP?
DEFINITELY NOT. IT'S A DIFFERENT SET OF CHEMICALS. THEY ALL SMELL LIKE IT!
VIGILANTE SAID SOMETHING ABOUT THEM MAYBE BEING DRUGGED...
WHO SAID...?
SNF SNF
IF THEY ARE DRUGGED, MAYBE WE CAN FIND AN ANTIDOTE, BRING THEM TO THEIR SENSES...
SENDING THE DATA FROM THIS ANALYZER WIRELESSLY TO THE BIG COMPUTER... SHE SHOULD BE THERE BY NOW...
WHO SHOULD BE THERE BY NOW?
BOOOOM
COME ON, MAX, YOU'VE GOT TO BE AT THE CAVE...
BOOM
THA
...MAX... PICK UP...
...MAX...MAX...

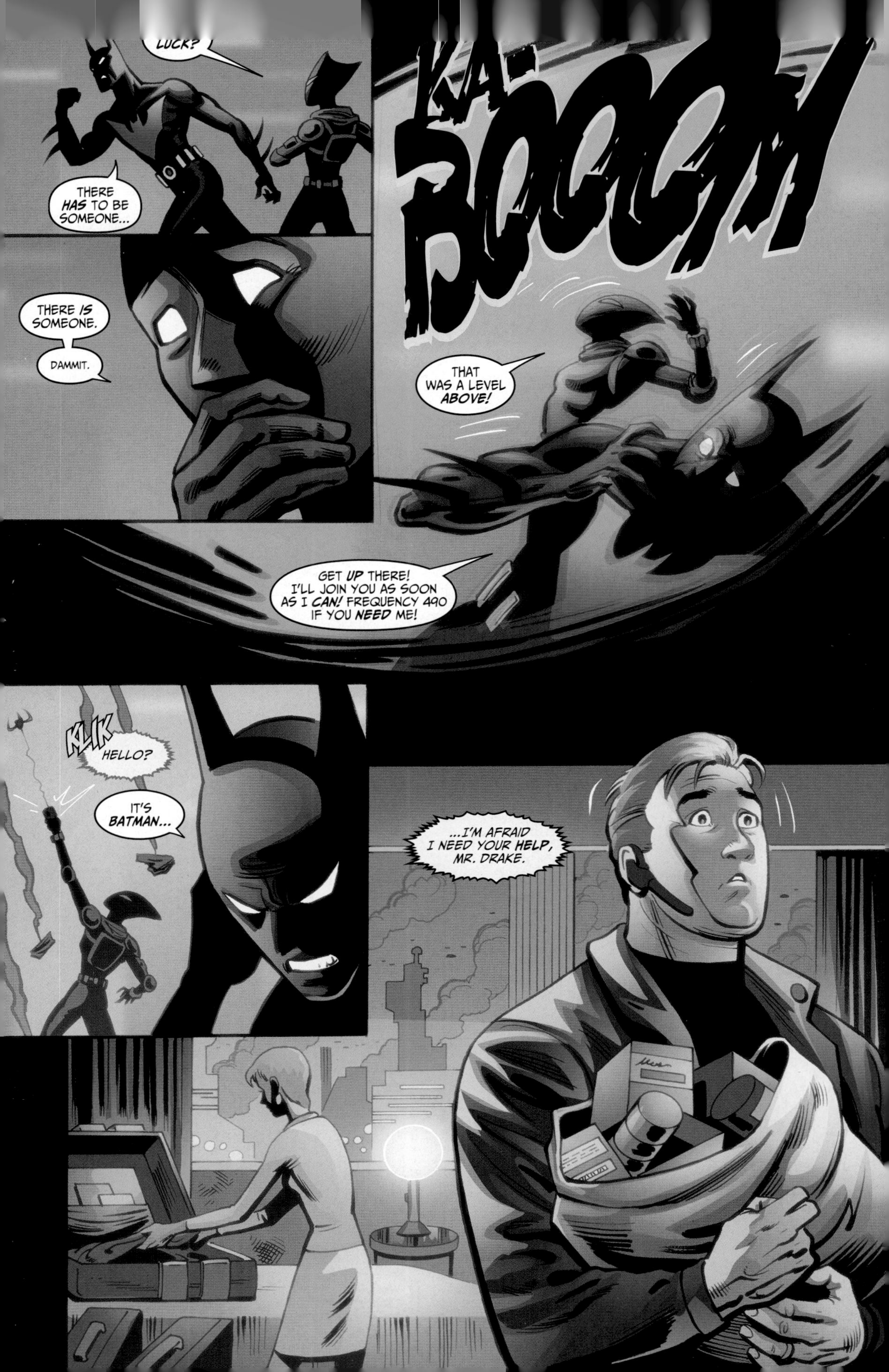
LUCK?
THERE HAS TO BE SOMEONE...
THERE IS SOMEONE.
DAMMIT.
KA-BOOOM
THAT WAS A LEVEL ABOVE!
GET UP THERE! I'LL JOIN YOU AS SOON AS I CAN! FREQUENCY 490 IF YOU NEED ME!
KLIK
HELLO?
IT'S BATMAN...
...I'M AFRAID I NEED YOUR HELP, MR. DRAKE.

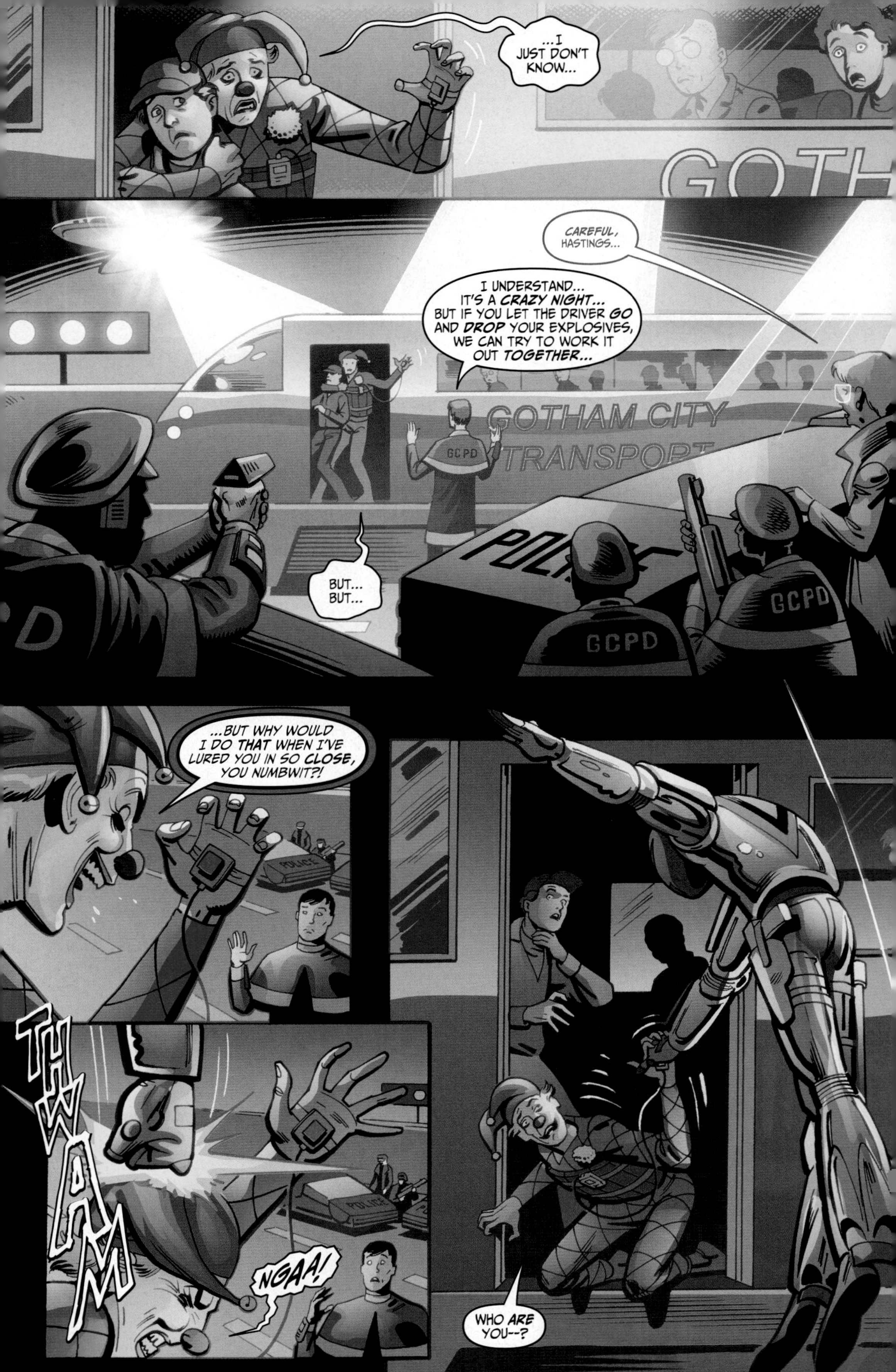

...I JUST DON'T KNOW...
GOTH
CAREFUL, HASTINGS...
I UNDERSTAND... IT'S A CRAZY NIGHT... BUT IF YOU LET THE DRIVER GO AND DROP YOUR EXPLOSIVES, WE CAN TRY TO WORK IT OUT TOGETHER...
GOTHAM CITY TRANSPORT
GCPD
BUT... BUT...
GCPD
GCPD
...BUT WHY WOULD I DO THAT WHEN I'VE LURED YOU IN SO CLOSE, YOU NUMBWIT?!
THWOMM
NGAA!
WHO ARE YOU--?

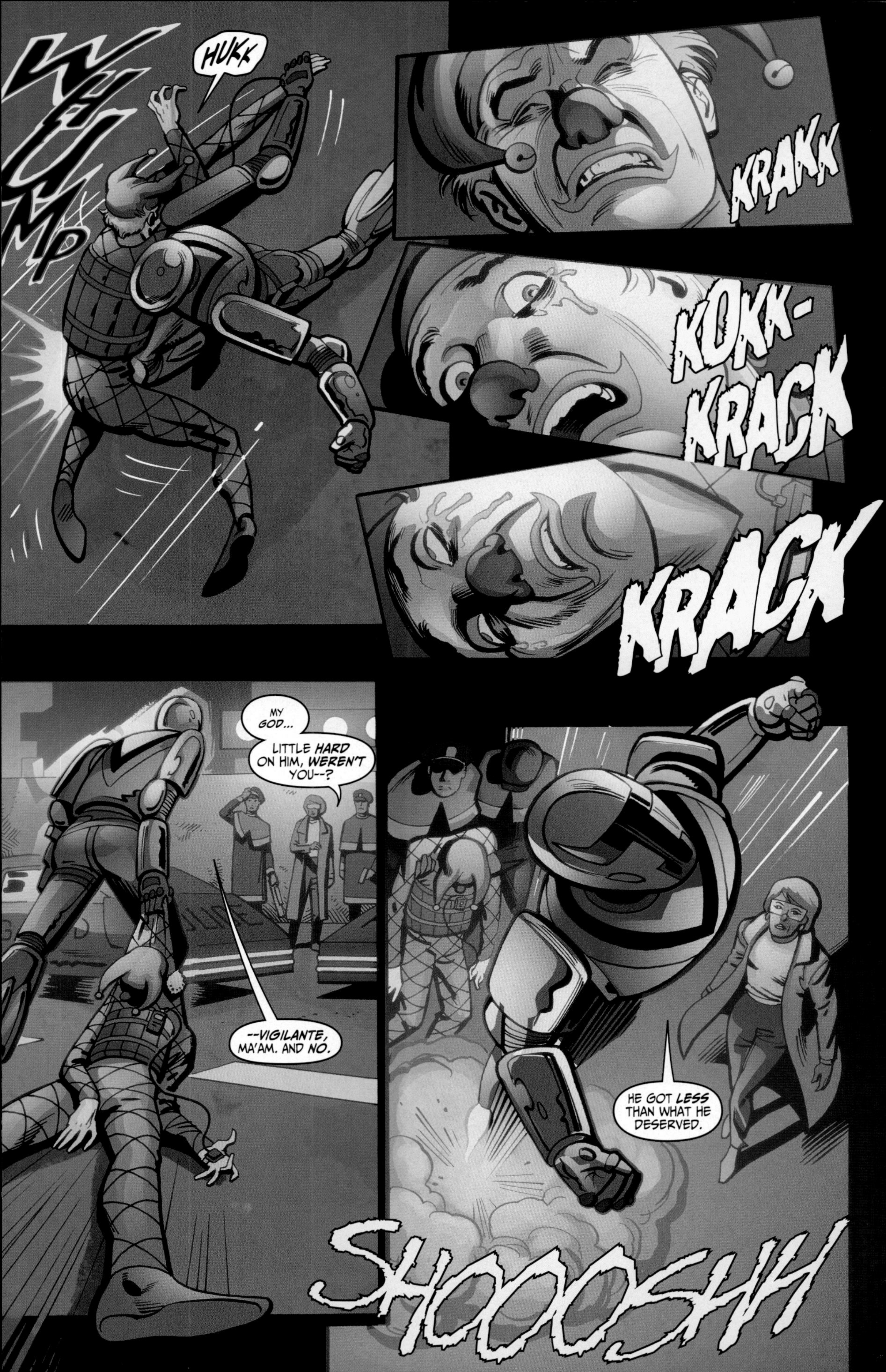
WHUMP
HUKK
KRAKK
KOKK-KRACK
KRACK
MY GOD...
LITTLE HARD ON HIM, WEREN'T YOU--?
--VIGILANTE, MA'AM. AND NO.
HE GOT LESS THAN WHAT HE DESERVED.
SHOOOSHH

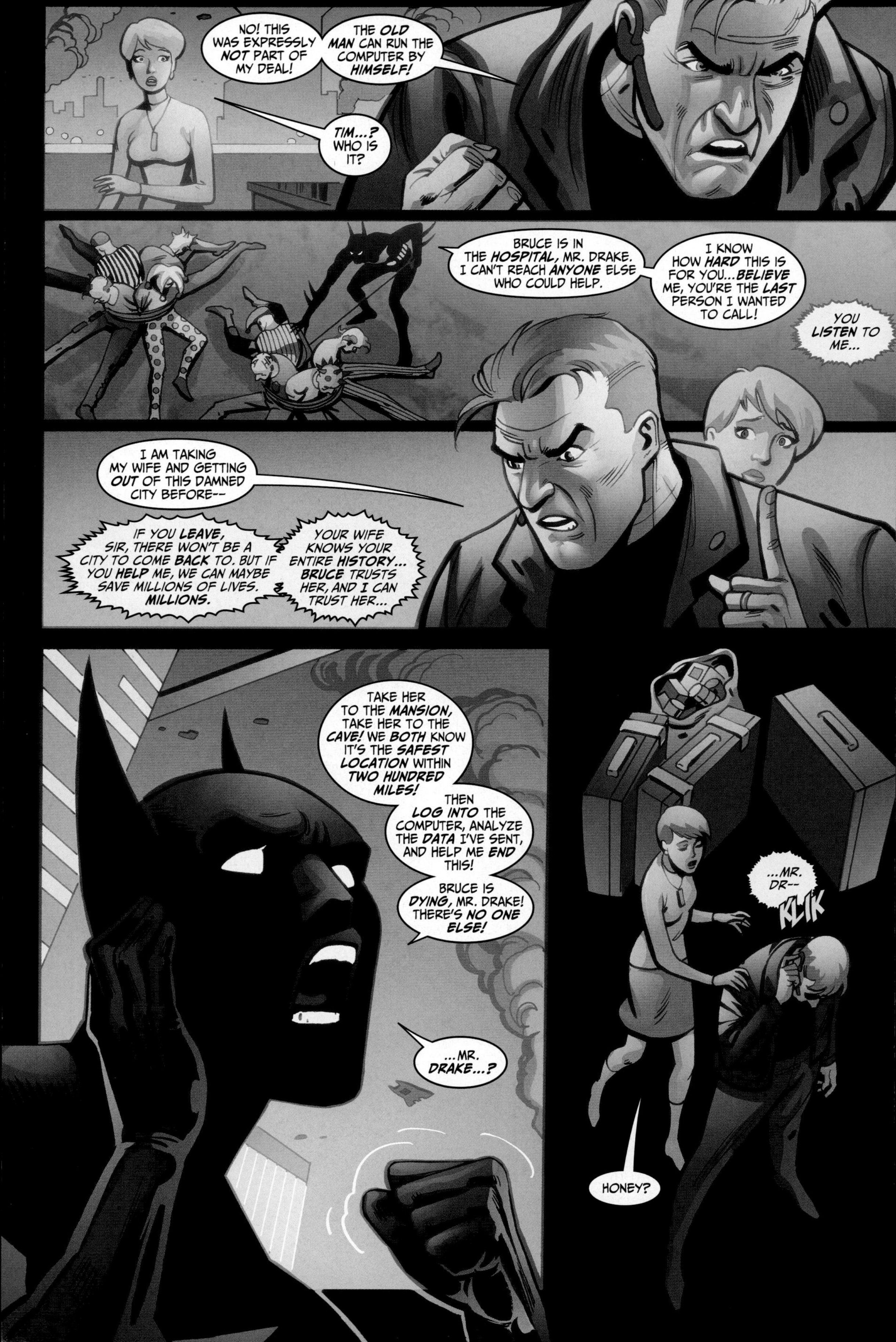

NO! THIS WAS EXPRESSLY NOT PART OF MY DEAL!
THE OLD MAN CAN RUN THE COMPUTER BY HIMSELF!
TIM...? WHO IS IT?
BRUCE IS IN THE HOSPITAL, MR. DRAKE. I CAN'T REACH ANYONE ELSE WHO COULD HELP.
I KNOW HOW HARD THIS IS FOR YOU...BELIEVE ME, YOU'RE THE LAST PERSON I WANTED TO CALL!
YOU LISTEN TO ME...
I AM TAKING MY WIFE AND GETTING OUT OF THIS DAMNED CITY BEFORE--
IF YOU LEAVE, SIR, THERE WON'T BE A CITY TO COME BACK TO. BUT IF YOU HELP ME, WE CAN MAYBE SAVE MILLIONS OF LIVES. MILLIONS.
YOUR WIFE KNOWS YOUR ENTIRE HISTORY... BRUCE TRUSTS HER, AND I CAN TRUST HER...
TAKE HER TO THE MANSION, TAKE HER TO THE CAVE! WE BOTH KNOW IT'S THE SAFEST LOCATION WITHIN TWO HUNDRED MILES!
THEN LOG INTO THE COMPUTER, ANALYZE THE DATA I'VE SENT, AND HELP ME END THIS!
BRUCE IS DYING, MR. DRAKE! THERE'S NO ONE ELSE!
...MR. DR--
KLIK
...MR. DRAKE...?
HONEY?

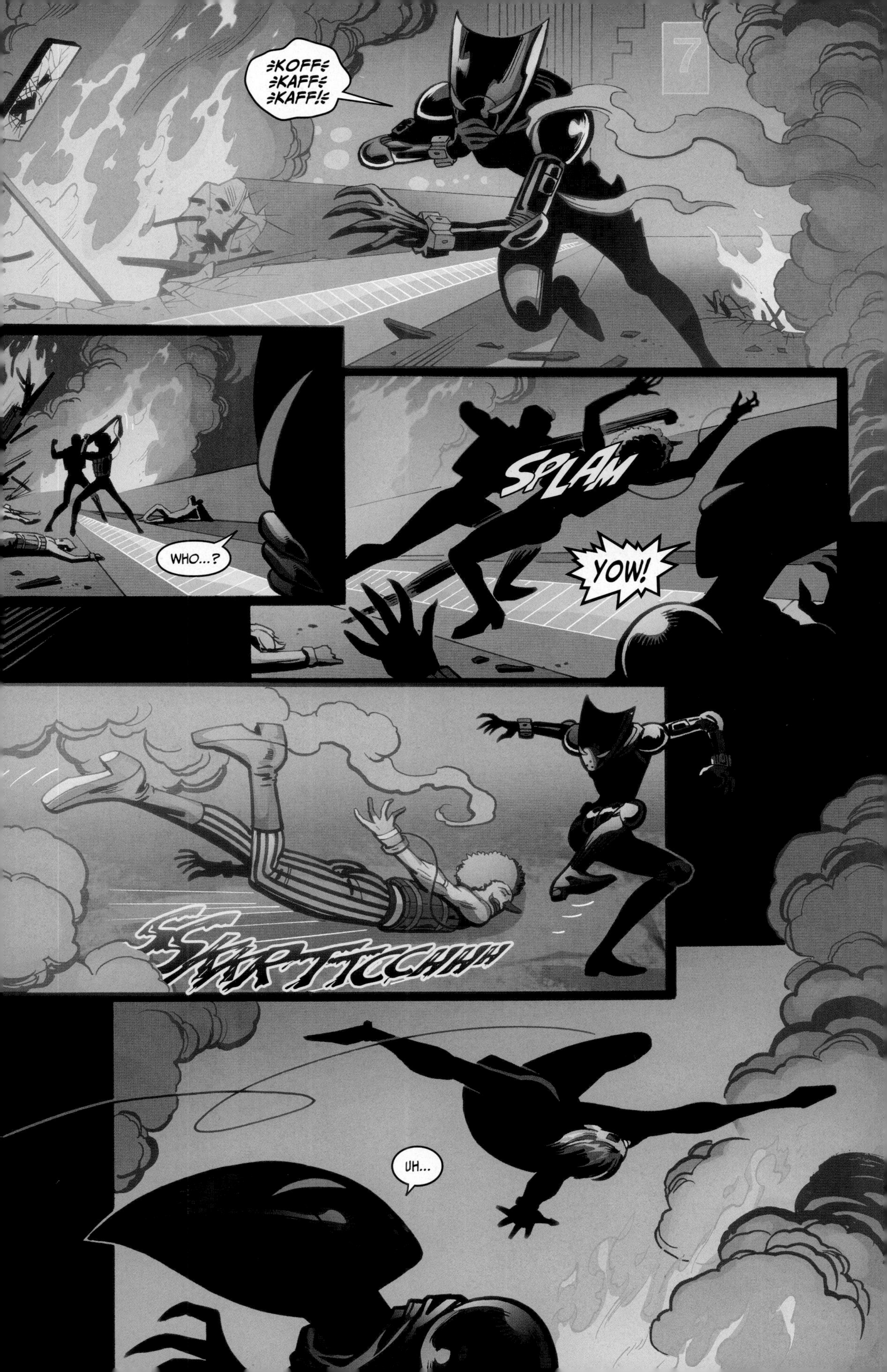
7
KOFF KAFF KAFF!
WHO...?
SPLAM
YOW!
SKRTTCCHHH
UH...

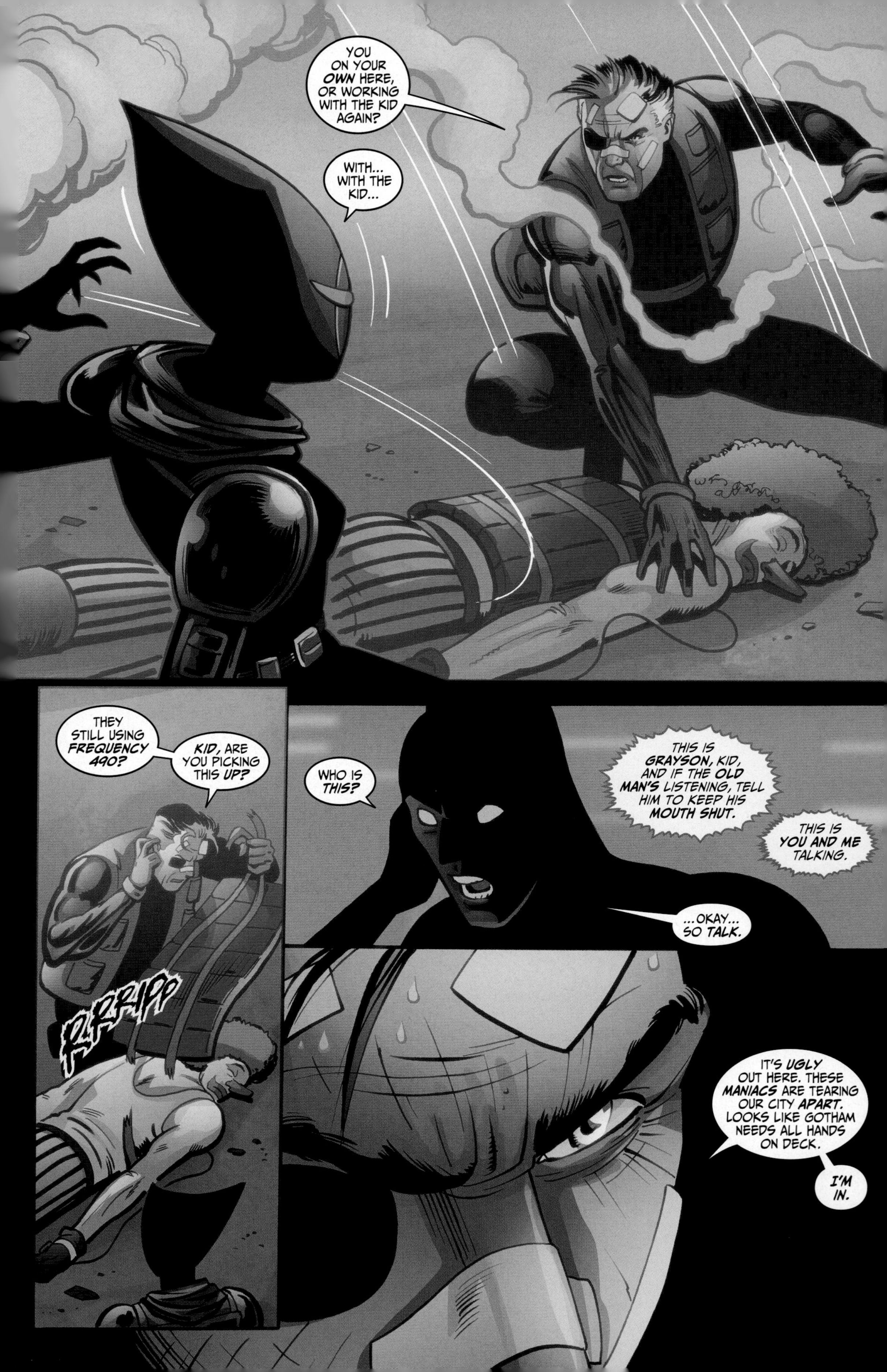
YOU ON YOUR OWN HERE, OR WORKING WITH THE KID AGAIN?
WITH... WITH THE KID...
THEY STILL USING FREQUENCY 490?
KID, ARE YOU PICKING THIS UP?
RRRIPP
WHO IS THIS?
THIS IS GRAYSON, KID, AND IF THE OLD MAN'S LISTENING, TELL HIM TO KEEP HIS MOUTH SHUT.
THIS IS YOU AND ME TALKING.
...OKAY... SO TALK.
IT'S UGLY OUT HERE. THESE MANIACS ARE TEARING OUR CITY APART. LOOKS LIKE GOTHAM NEEDS ALL HANDS ON DECK.
I'M IN.

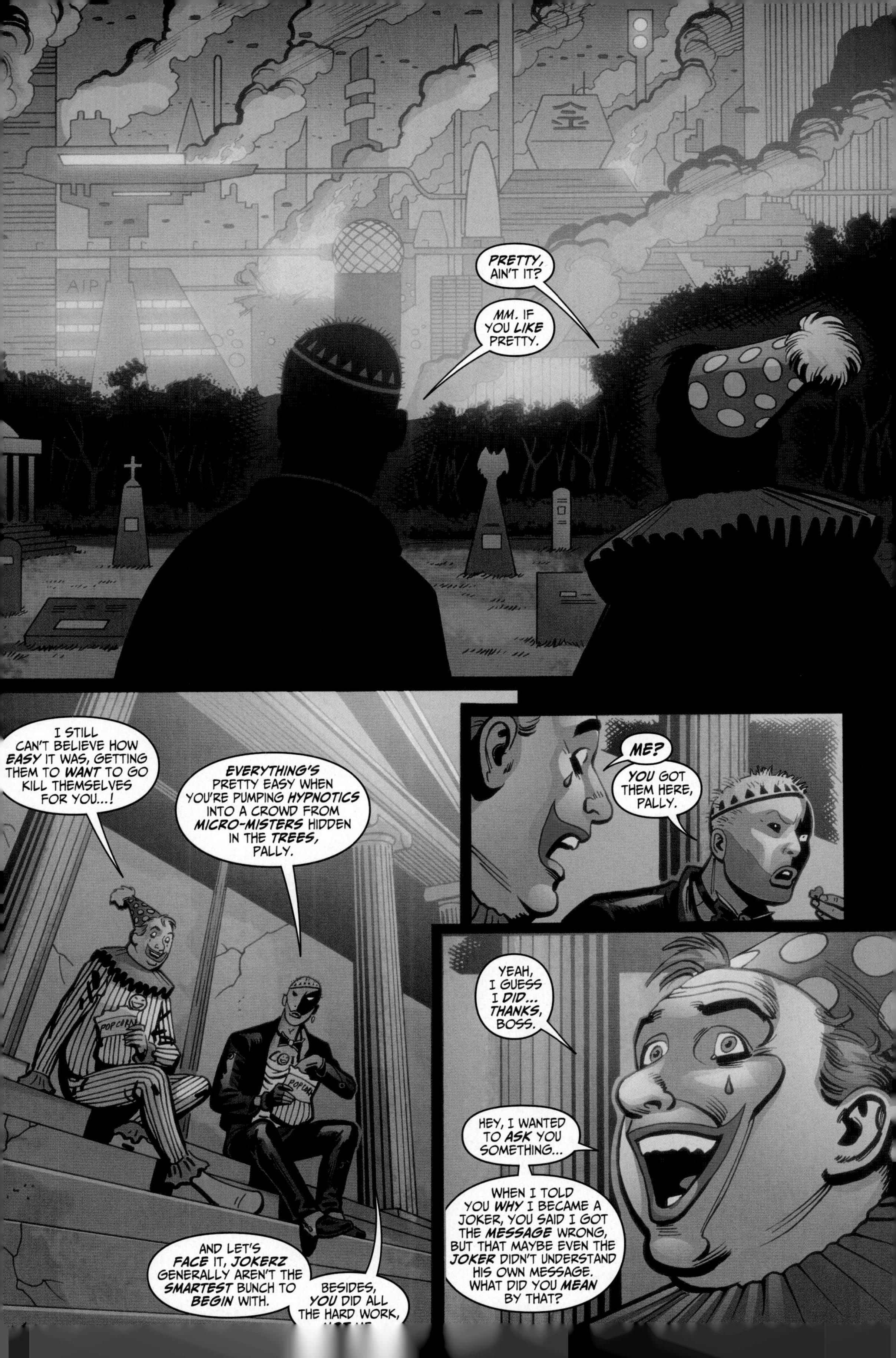

PRETTY, AIN'T IT?
MM. IF YOU LIKE PRETTY.
I STILL CAN'T BELIEVE HOW EASY IT WAS, GETTING THEM TO WANT TO GO KILL THEMSELVES FOR YOU...!
EVERYTHING'S PRETTY EASY WHEN YOU'RE PUMPING HYPNOTICS INTO A CROWD FROM MICRO-MISTERS HIDDEN IN THE TREES, PALLY.
AND LET'S FACE IT, JOKERZ GENERALLY AREN'T THE SMARTEST BUNCH TO BEGIN WITH.
BESIDES, YOU DID ALL THE HARD WORK,
ME?
YOU GOT THEM HERE, PALLY.
YEAH, I GUESS I DID... THANKS, BOSS.
HEY, I WANTED TO ASK YOU SOMETHING...
WHEN I TOLD YOU WHY I BECAME A JOKER, YOU SAID I GOT THE MESSAGE WRONG, BUT THAT MAYBE EVEN THE JOKER DIDN'T UNDERSTAND HIS OWN MESSAGE. WHAT DID YOU MEAN BY THAT?

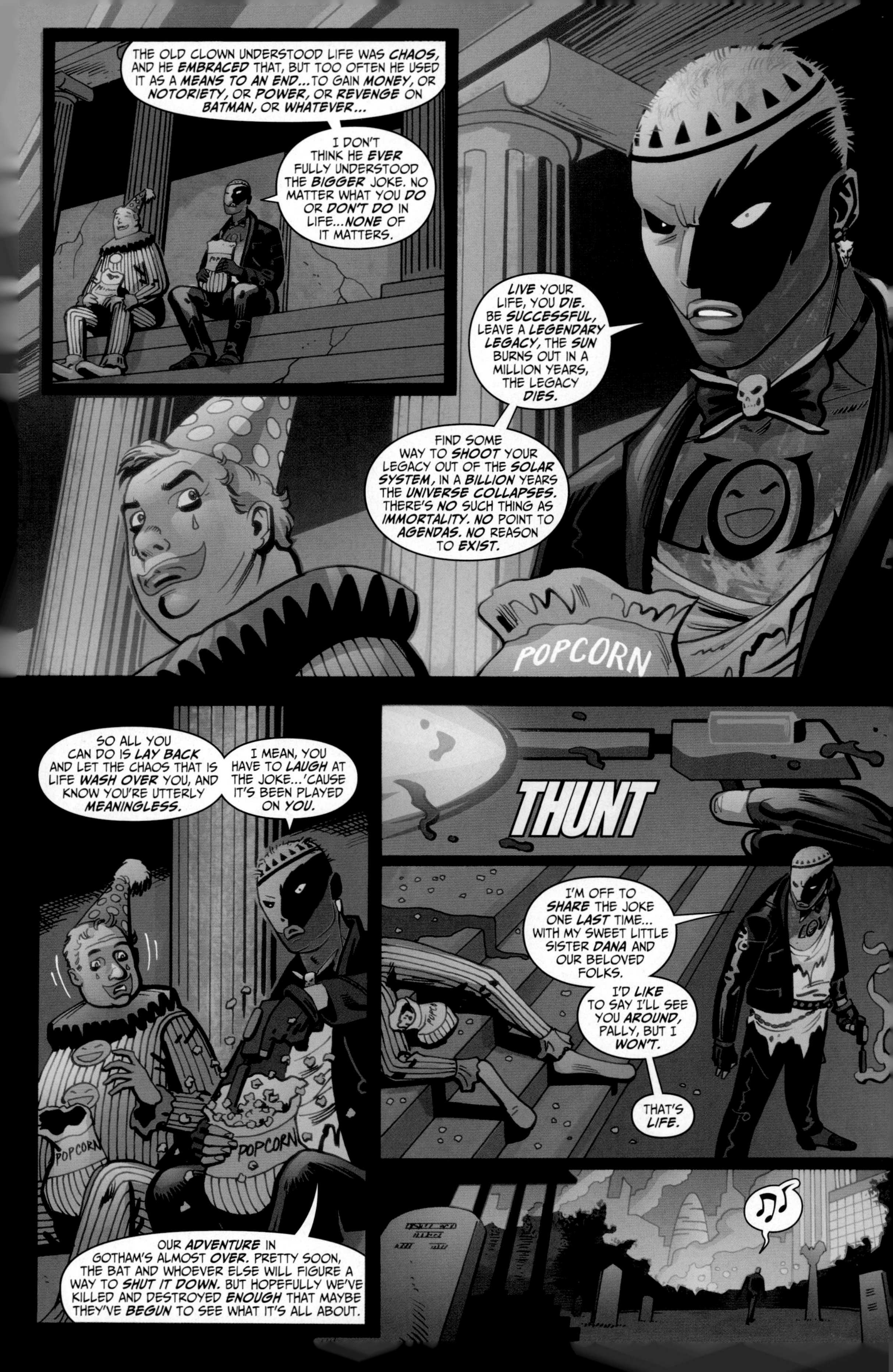
THE OLD CLOWN UNDERSTOOD LIFE WAS CHAOS, AND HE EMBRACED THAT, BUT TOO OFTEN HE USED IT AS A MEANS TO AN END...TO GAIN MONEY, OR NOTORIETY, OR POWER, OR REVENGE ON BATMAN, OR WHATEVER...
I DON'T THINK HE EVER FULLY UNDERSTOOD THE BIGGER JOKE. NO MATTER WHAT YOU DO OR DON'T DO IN LIFE...NONE OF IT MATTERS.
LIVE YOUR LIFE, YOU DIE. BE SUCCESSFUL, LEAVE A LEGENDARY LEGACY, THE SUN BURNS OUT IN A MILLION YEARS, THE LEGACY DIES.
FIND SOME WAY TO SHOOT YOUR LEGACY OUT OF THE SOLAR SYSTEM, IN A BILLION YEARS THE UNIVERSE COLLAPSES. THERE'S NO SUCH THING AS IMMORTALITY. NO POINT TO AGENDAS. NO REASON TO EXIST.
POPCORN
SO ALL YOU CAN DO IS LAY BACK AND LET THE CHAOS THAT IS LIFE WASH OVER YOU, AND KNOW YOU'RE UTTERLY MEANINGLESS.
I MEAN, YOU HAVE TO LAUGH AT THE JOKE...'CAUSE IT'S BEEN PLAYED ON YOU.
POPCORN
POPCORN
OUR ADVENTURE IN GOTHAM'S ALMOST OVER. PRETTY SOON, THE BAT AND WHOEVER ELSE WILL FIGURE A WAY TO SHUT IT DOWN. BUT HOPEFULLY WE'VE KILLED AND DESTROYED ENOUGH THAT MAYBE THEY'VE BEGUN TO SEE WHAT IT'S ALL ABOUT.
THUNT
I'M OFF TO SHARE THE JOKE ONE LAST TIME... WITH MY SWEET LITTLE SISTER DANA AND OUR BELOVED FOLKS.
I'D LIKE TO SAY I'LL SEE YOU AROUND, PALLY, BUT I WON'T.
THAT'S LIFE.

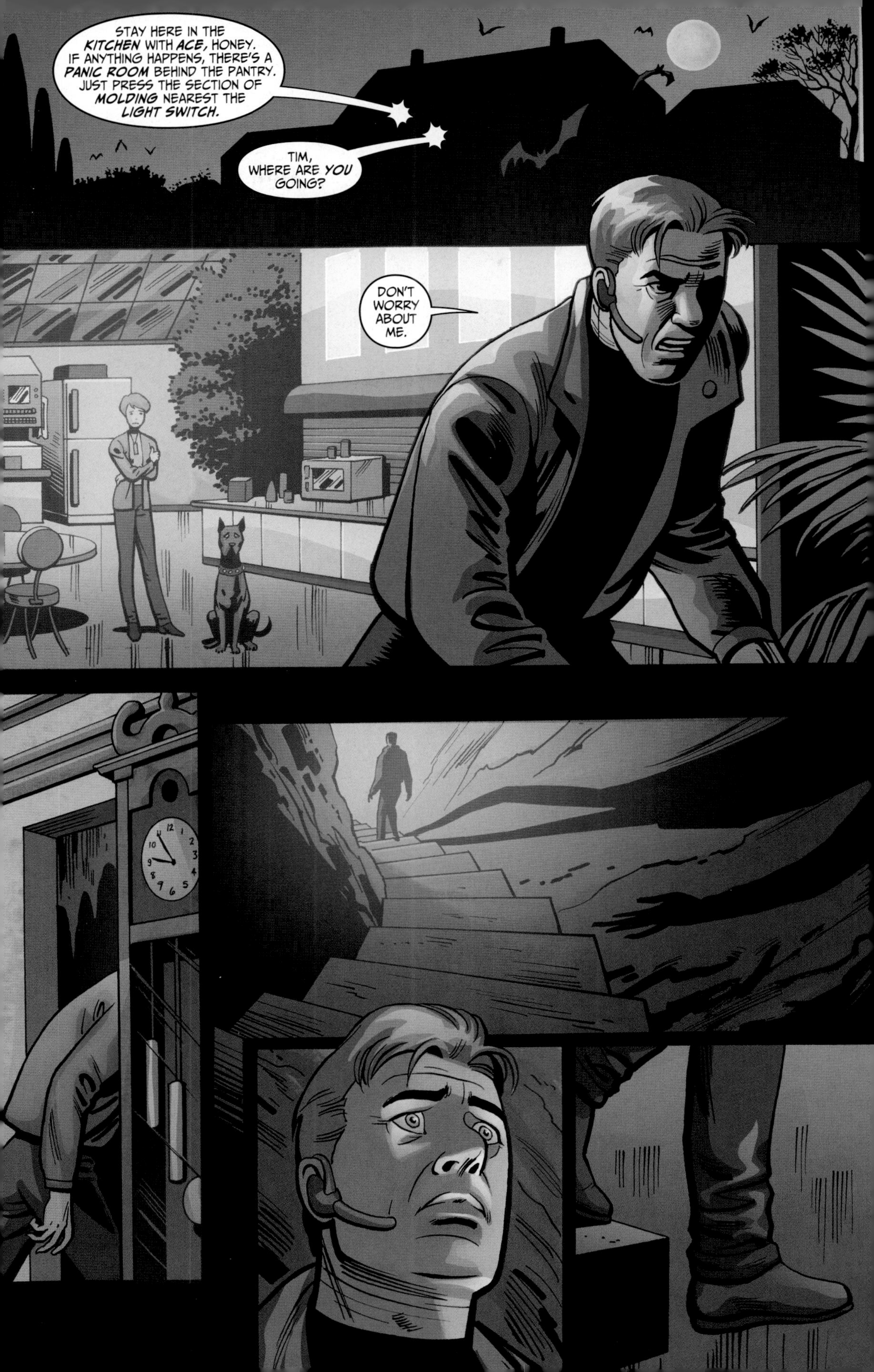

STAY HERE IN THE KITCHEN WITH ACE, HONEY. IF ANYTHING HAPPENS, THERE'S A PANIC ROOM BEHIND THE PANTRY. JUST PRESS THE SECTION OF MOLDING NEAREST THE LIGHT SWITCH.
TIM, WHERE ARE YOU GOING?
DON'T WORRY ABOUT ME.

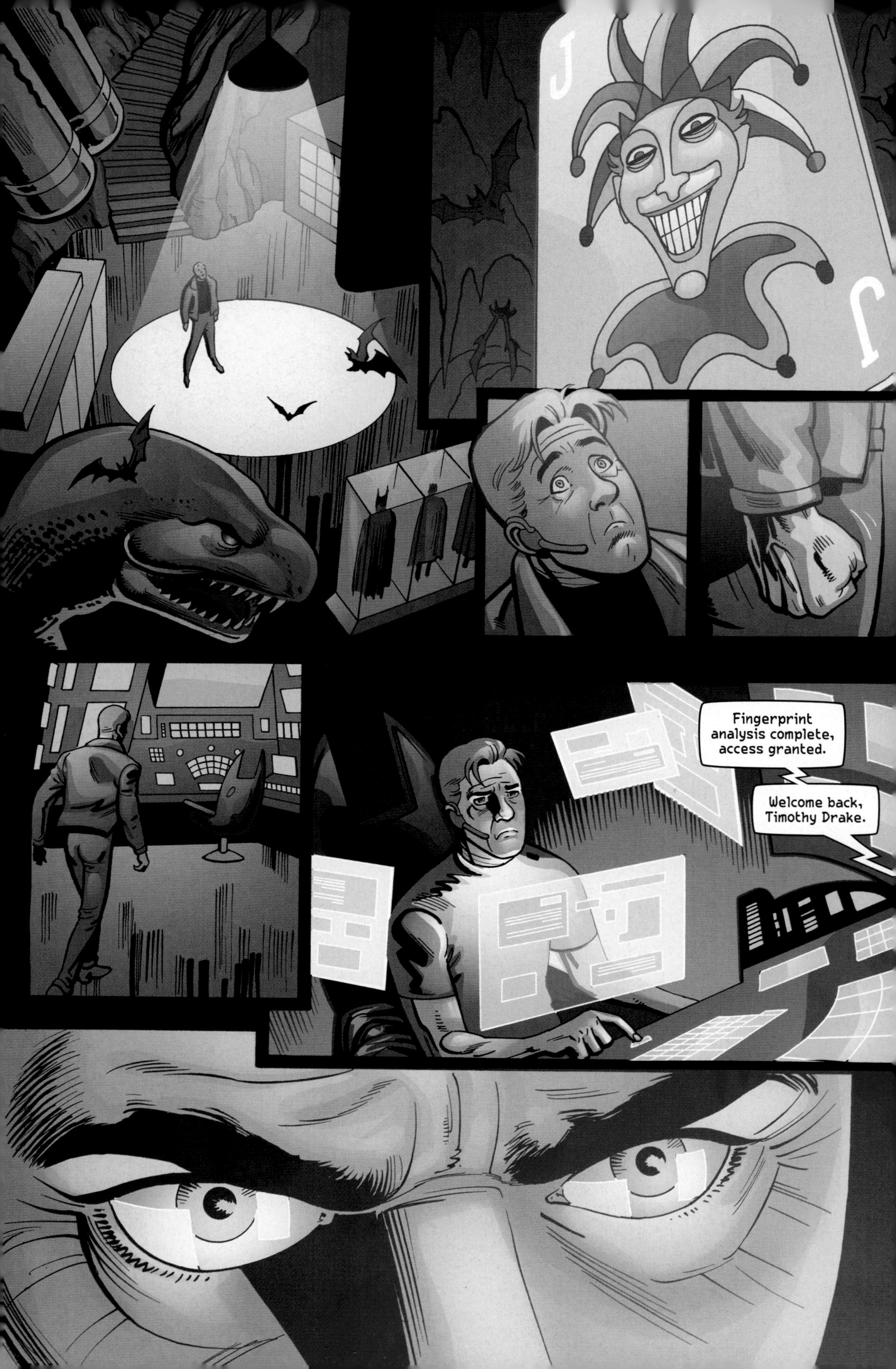
Fingerprint analysis complete, access granted.
Welcome back, Timothy Drake.

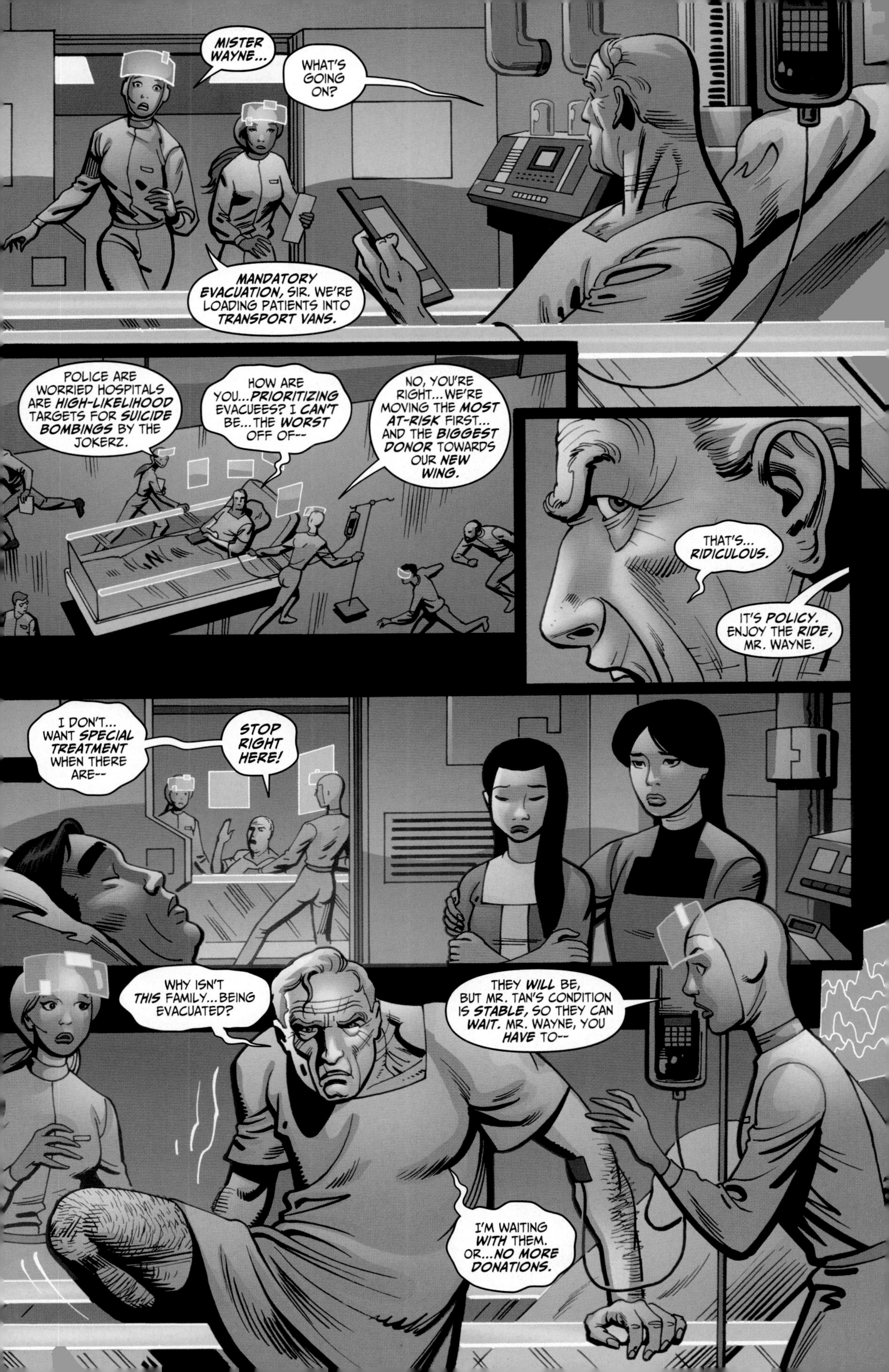
MISTER WAYNE...
WHAT'S GOING ON?
MANDATORY EVACUATION, SIR. WE'RE LOADING PATIENTS INTO TRANSPORT VANS.
POLICE ARE WORRIED HOSPITALS ARE HIGH-LIKELIHOOD TARGETS FOR SUICIDE BOMBINGS BY THE JOKERZ.
HOW ARE YOU...PRIORITIZING EVACUEES? I CAN'T BE...THE WORST OFF OF--
NO, YOU'RE RIGHT...WE'RE MOVING THE MOST AT-RISK FIRST... AND THE BIGGEST DONOR TOWARDS OUR NEW WING.
THAT'S... RIDICULOUS.
IT'S POLICY. ENJOY THE RIDE, MR. WAYNE.
I DON'T... WANT SPECIAL TREATMENT WHEN THERE ARE--
STOP RIGHT HERE!
WHY ISN'T THIS FAMILY...BEING EVACUATED?
THEY WILL BE, BUT MR. TAN'S CONDITION IS STABLE, SO THEY CAN WAIT. MR. WAYNE, YOU HAVE TO--
I'M WAITING WITH THEM. OR...NO MORE DONATIONS.

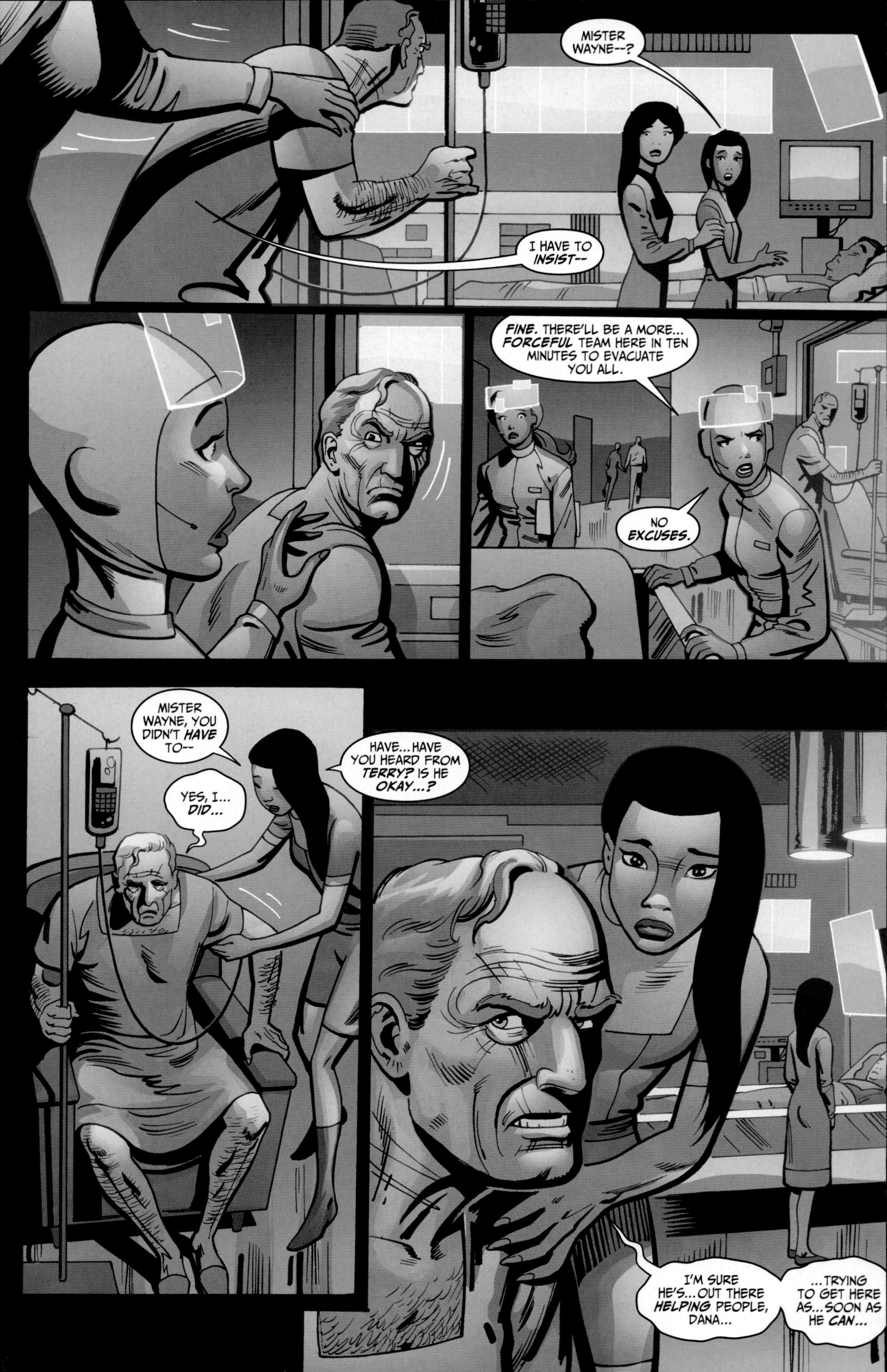
MISTER WAYNE--?
I HAVE TO INSIST--
FINE. THERE'LL BE A MORE... FORCEFUL TEAM HERE IN TEN MINUTES TO EVACUATE YOU ALL.
NO EXCUSES.
MISTER WAYNE, YOU DIDN'T HAVE TO--
YES, I... DID...
HAVE... HAVE YOU HEARD FROM TERRY? IS HE OKAY...?
I'M SURE HE'S... OUT THERE HELPING PEOPLE, DANA...
...TRYING TO GET HERE AS... SOON AS HE CAN...

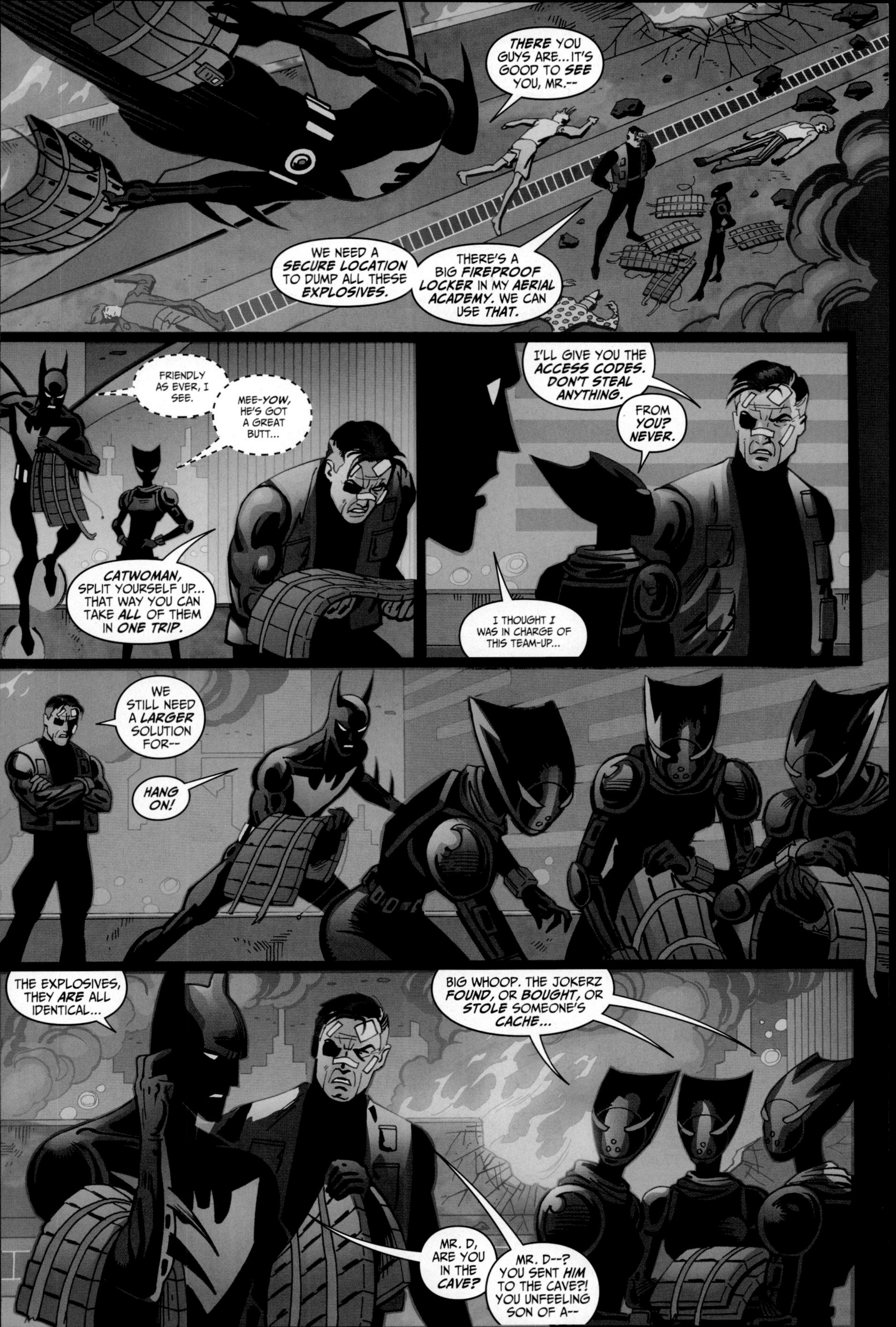
THERE YOU GUYS ARE...IT'S GOOD TO SEE YOU, MR.--
WE NEED A SECURE LOCATION TO DUMP ALL THESE EXPLOSIVES.
THERE'S A BIG FIREPROOF LOCKER IN MY AERIAL ACADEMY. WE CAN USE THAT.
FRIENDLY AS EVER, I SEE.
MEE-YOW, HE'S GOT A GREAT BUTT...
CATWOMAN, SPLIT YOURSELF UP... THAT WAY YOU CAN TAKE ALL OF THEM IN ONE TRIP.
I'LL GIVE YOU THE ACCESS CODES. DON'T STEAL ANYTHING.
FROM YOU? NEVER.
I THOUGHT I WAS IN CHARGE OF THIS TEAM-UP...
WE STILL NEED A LARGER SOLUTION FOR--
HANG ON!
THE EXPLOSIVES, THEY ARE ALL IDENTICAL...
BIG WHOOP. THE JOKERZ FOUND, OR BOUGHT, OR STOLE SOMEONE'S CACHE...
MR. D, ARE YOU IN THE CAVE?
MR. D--? YOU SENT HIM TO THE CAVE?! YOU UNFEELING SON OF A--

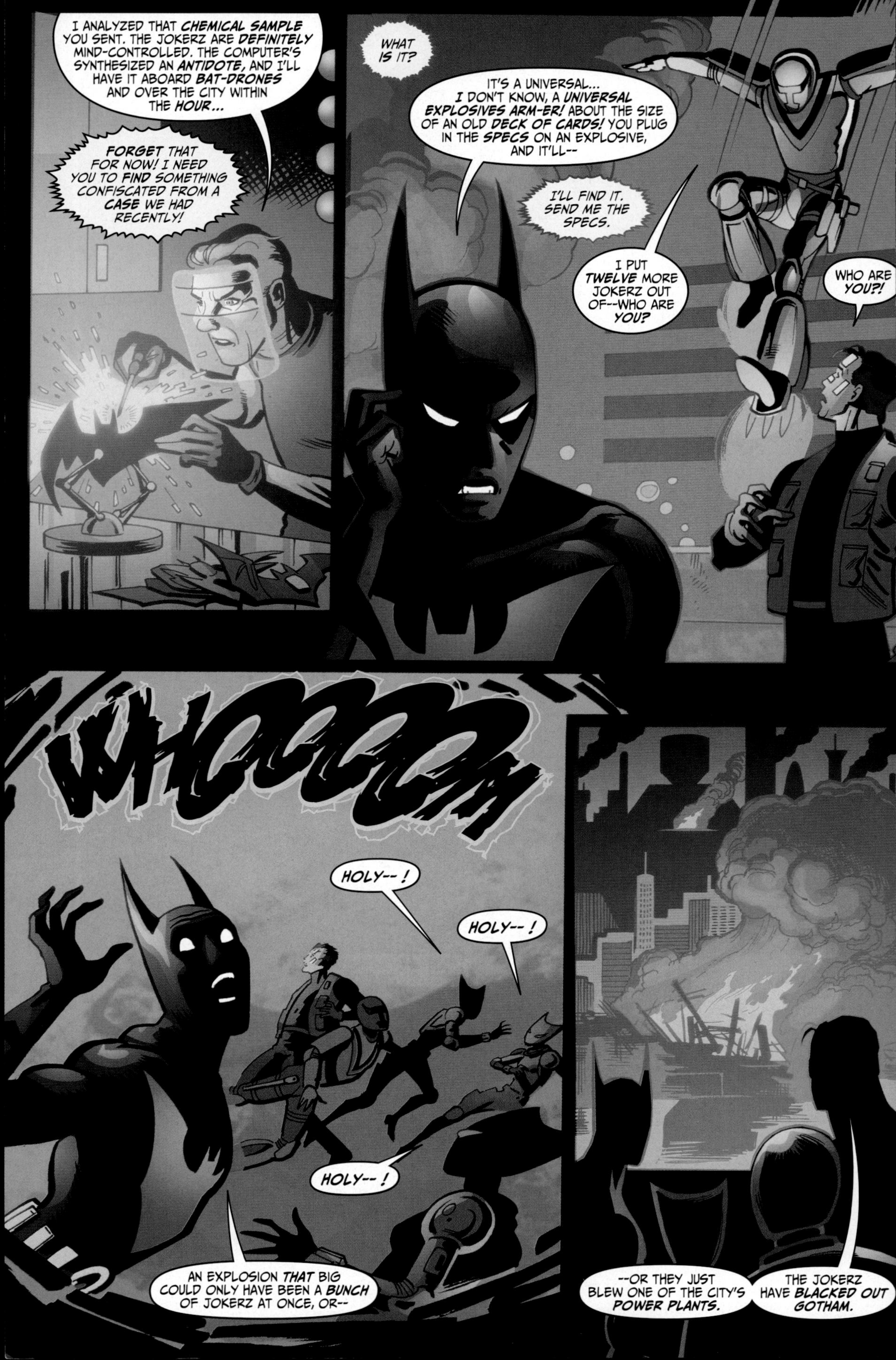
I ANALYZED THAT CHEMICAL SAMPLE YOU SENT. THE JOKERZ ARE DEFINITELY MIND-CONTROLLED. THE COMPUTER'S SYNTHESIZED AN ANTIDOTE, AND I'LL HAVE IT ABOARD BAT-DRONES AND OVER THE CITY WITHIN THE HOUR...
FORGET THAT FOR NOW! I NEED YOU TO FIND SOMETHING CONFISCATED FROM A CASE WE HAD RECENTLY!
WHAT IS IT?
IT'S A UNIVERSAL... I DON'T KNOW, A UNIVERSAL EXPLOSIVES ARM-ER! ABOUT THE SIZE OF AN OLD DECK OF CARDS! YOU PLUG IN THE SPECS ON AN EXPLOSIVE, AND IT'LL--
I'LL FIND IT. SEND ME THE SPECS.
I PUT TWELVE MORE JOKERZ OUT OF--WHO ARE YOU?
WHO ARE YOU?!
WHOOOOM
HOLY-- !
HOLY-- !
HOLY-- !
AN EXPLOSION THAT BIG COULD ONLY HAVE BEEN A BUNCH OF JOKERZ AT ONCE, OR--
--OR THEY JUST BLEW ONE OF THE CITY'S POWER PLANTS.
THE JOKERZ HAVE BLACKED OUT GOTHAM.

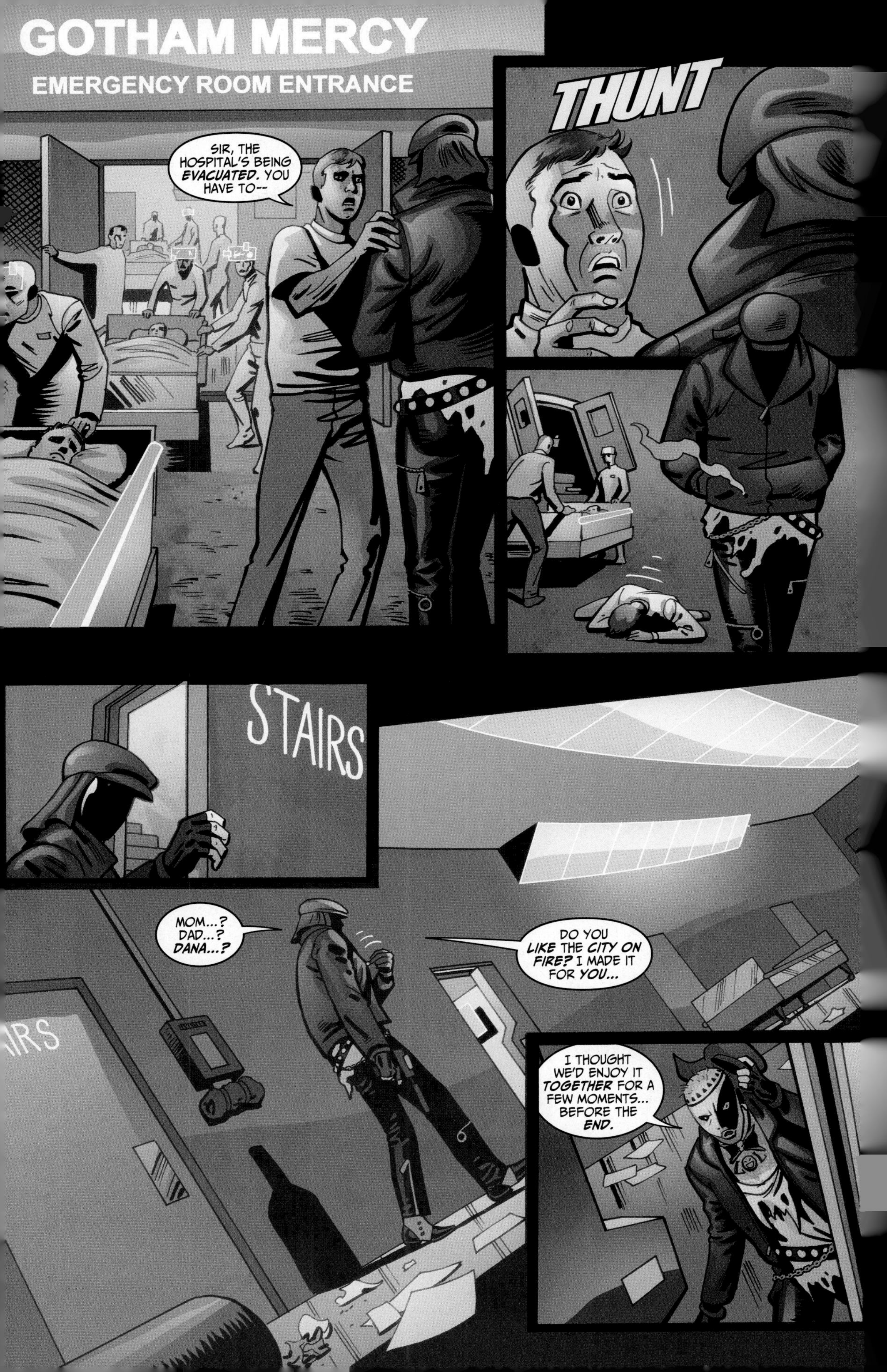
GOTHAM MERCY
EMERGENCY ROOM ENTRANCE
SIR, THE HOSPITAL'S BEING EVACUATED. YOU HAVE TO--
THUNT
STAIRS
MOM...? DAD...? DANA...?
DO YOU LIKE THE CITY ON FIRE? I MADE IT FOR YOU...
I THOUGHT WE'D ENJOY IT TOGETHER FOR A FEW MOMENTS... BEFORE THE END.

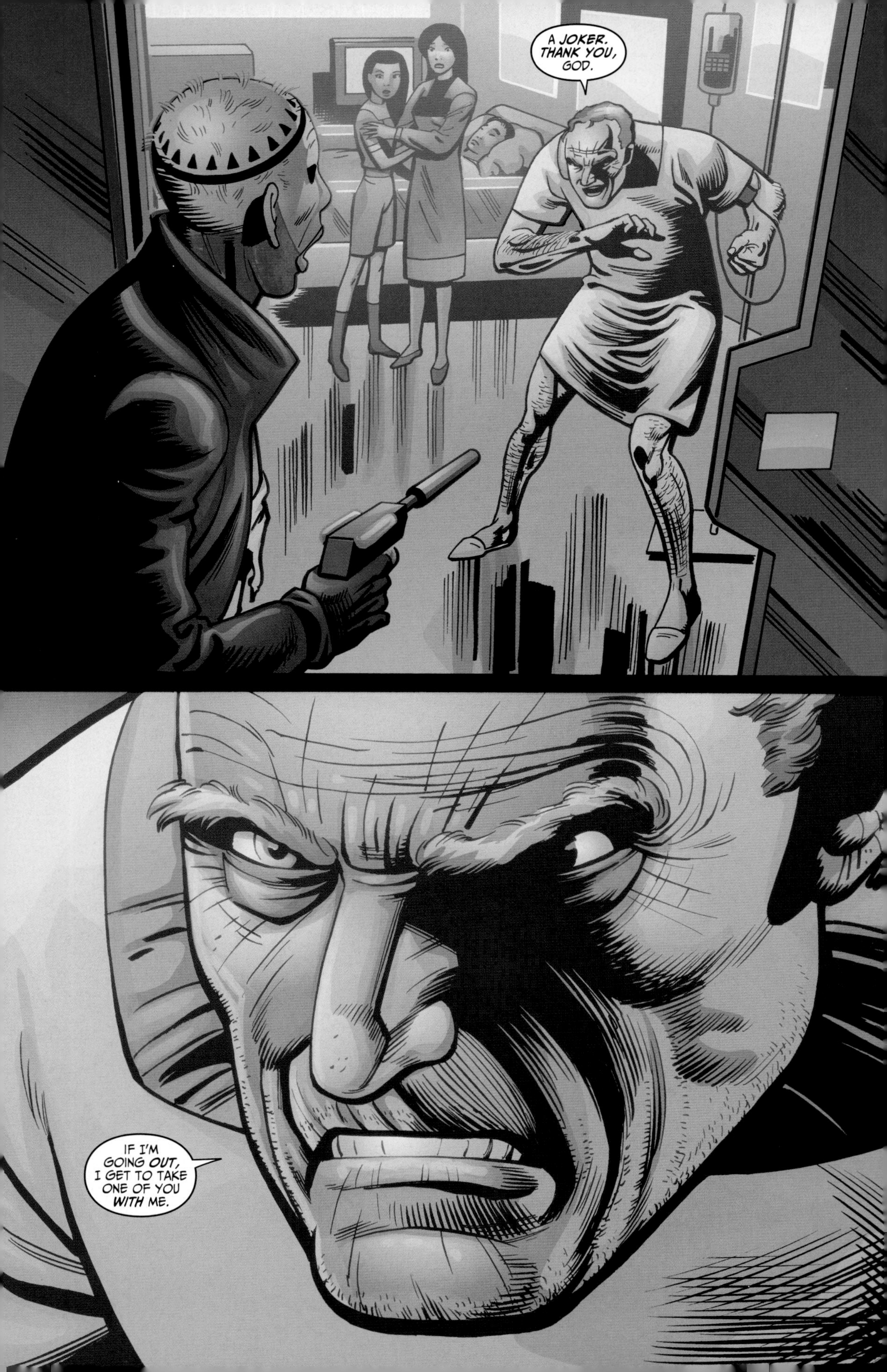
A JOKER. THANK YOU, GOD.
IF I'M GOING OUT, I GET TO TAKE ONE OF YOU WITH ME.

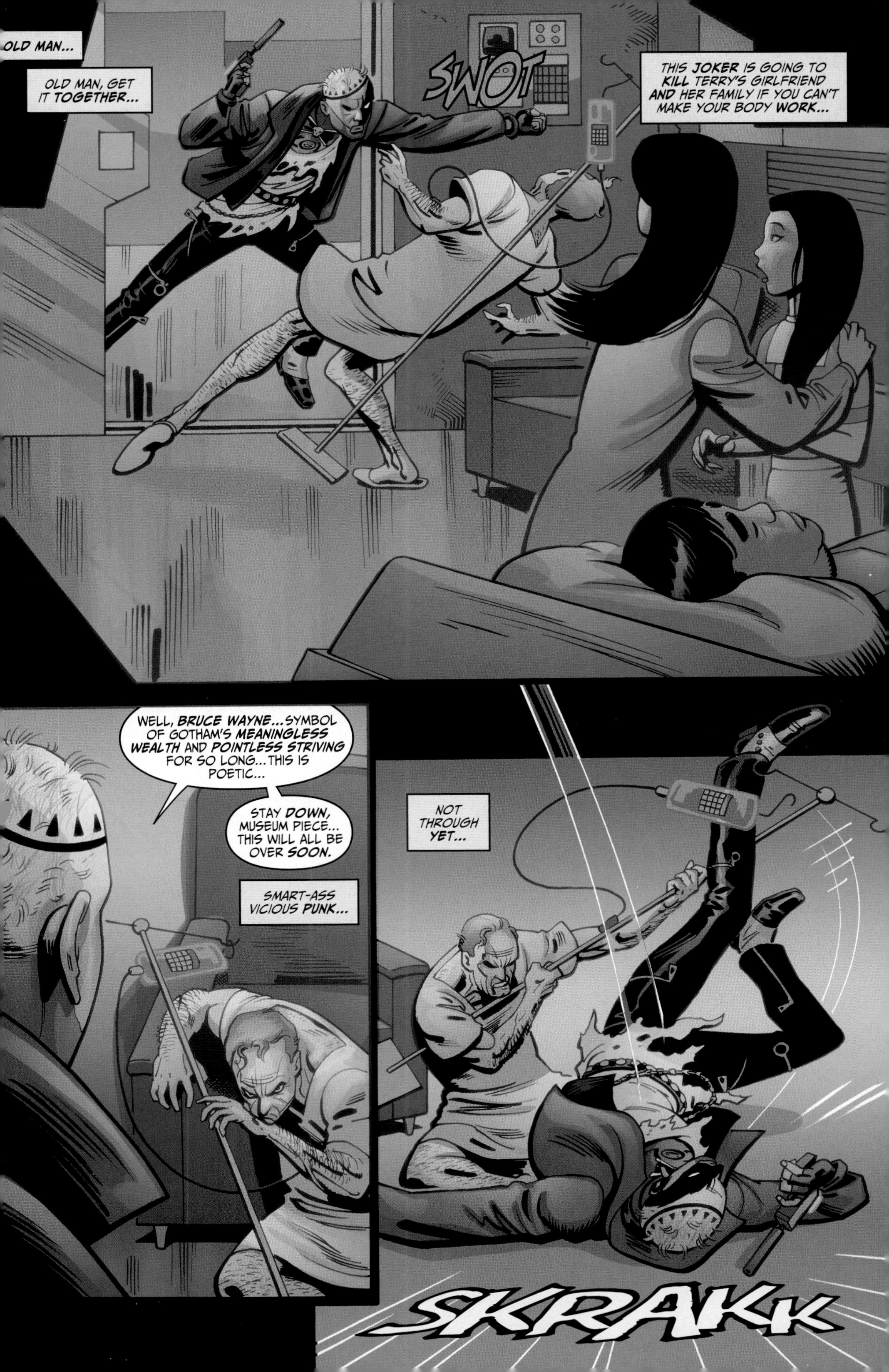
OLD MAN...
OLD MAN, GET IT TOGETHER...
SWOT
THIS JOKER IS GOING TO KILL TERRY'S GIRLFRIEND AND HER FAMILY IF YOU CAN'T MAKE YOUR BODY WORK...
WELL, BRUCE WAYNE...SYMBOL OF GOTHAM'S MEANINGLESS WEALTH AND POINTLESS STRIVING FOR SO LONG...THIS IS POETIC...
STAY DOWN, MUSEUM PIECE... THIS WILL ALL BE OVER SOON.
SMART-ASS VICIOUS PUNK...
NOT THROUGH YET...
SKRAKK

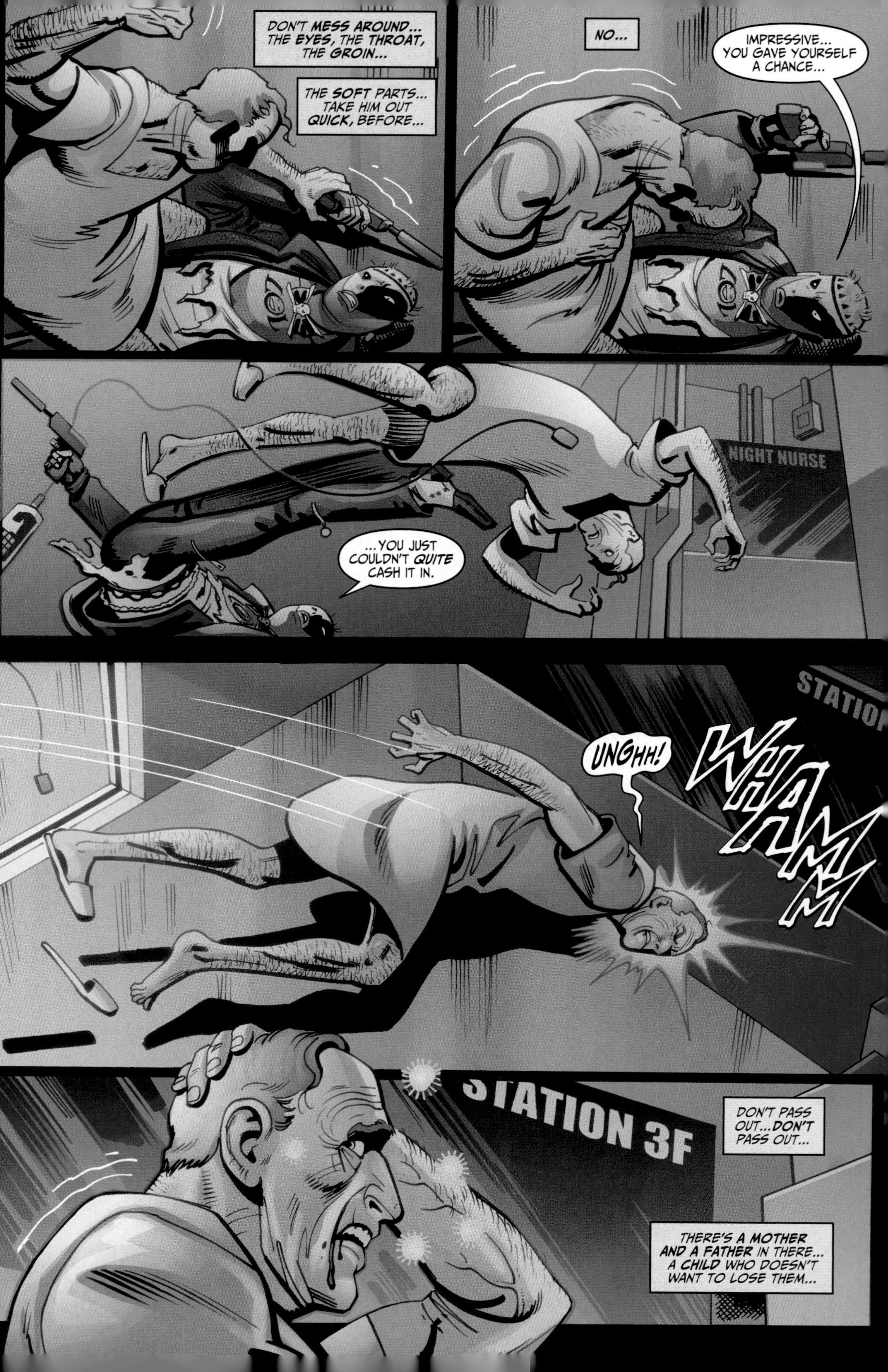
DON'T MESS AROUND... THE EYES, THE THROAT, THE GROIN...
THE SOFT PARTS... TAKE HIM OUT QUICK, BEFORE...
NO...
IMPRESSIVE... YOU GAVE YOURSELF A CHANCE...
NIGHT NURSE
...YOU JUST COULDN'T QUITE CASH IT IN.
STATIO
UNGHH!
WHAMM
STATION 3F
DON'T PASS OUT...DON'T PASS OUT...
THERE'S A MOTHER AND A FATHER IN THERE... A CHILD WHO DOESN'T WANT TO LOSE THEM...

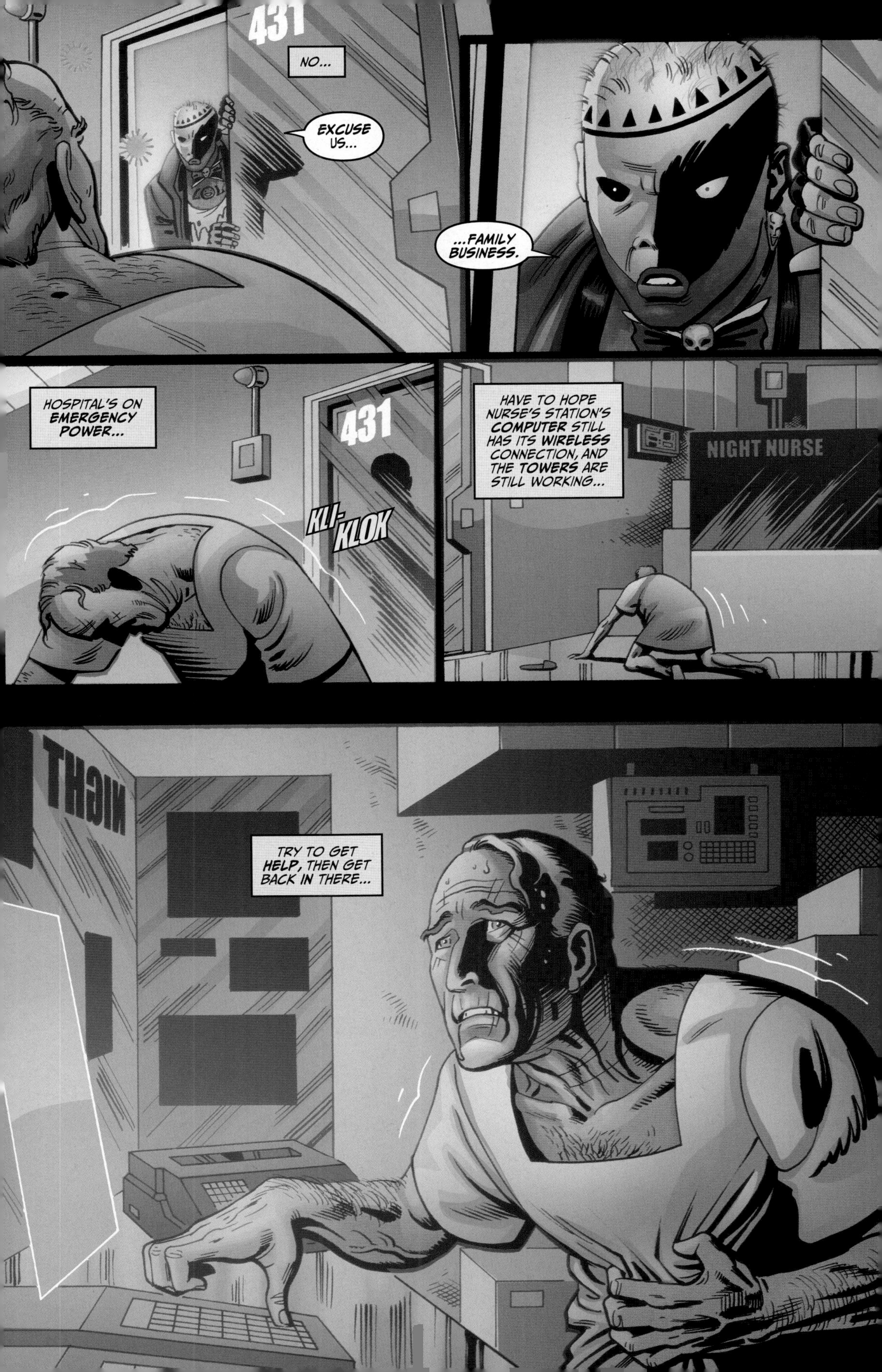
431
NO...
EXCUSE US...
...FAMILY BUSINESS.
HOSPITAL'S ON EMERGENCY POWER...
431
KLI-KLOK
HAVE TO HOPE NURSE'S STATION'S COMPUTER STILL HAS ITS WIRELESS CONNECTION, AND THE TOWERS ARE STILL WORKING...
NIGHT NURSE
TRY TO GET HELP, THEN GET BACK IN THERE...

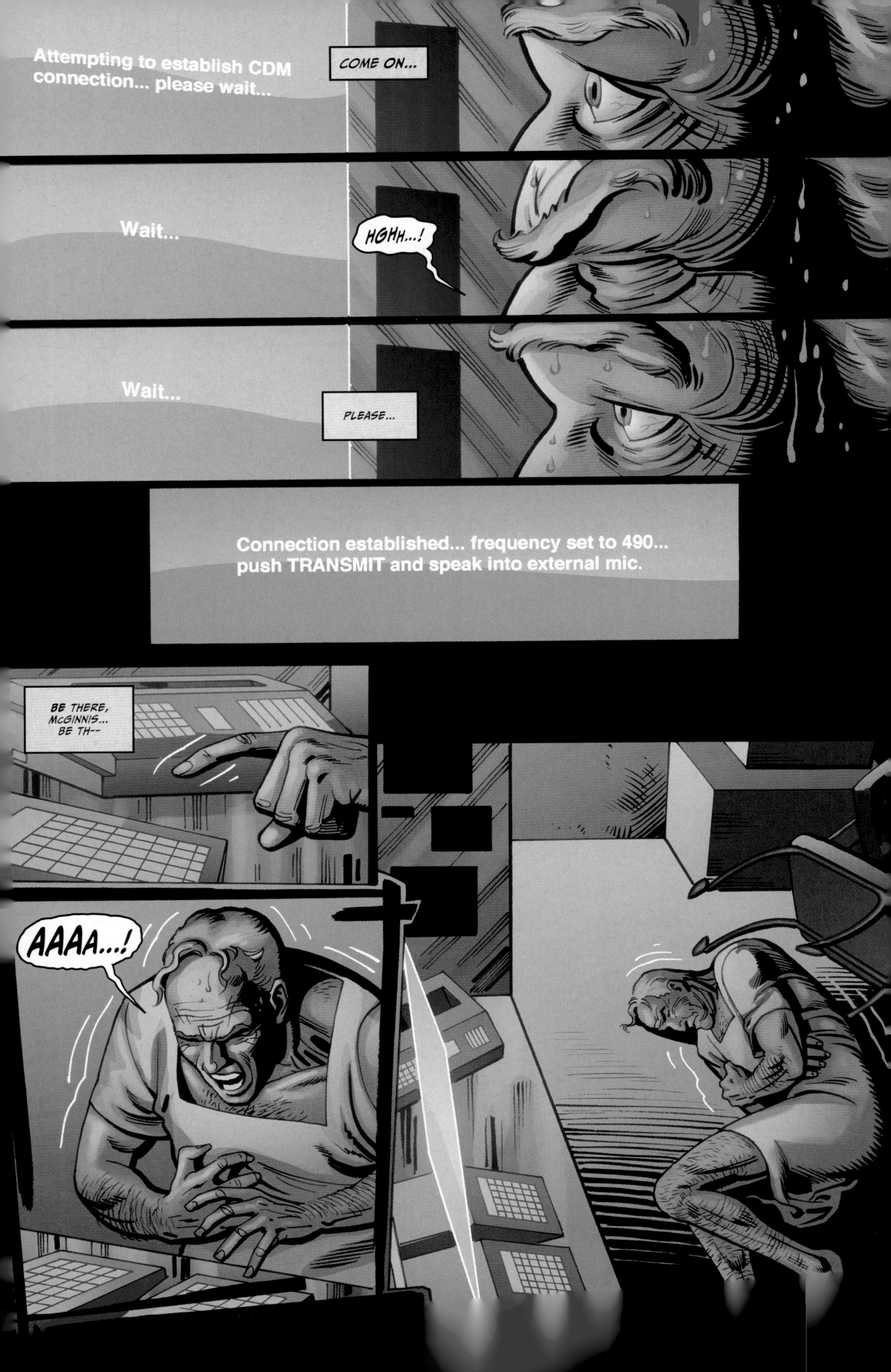
Attempting to establish CDM connection... please wait...
COME ON...
Wait...
HGHH...!
Wait...
PLEASE...
Connection established... frequency set to 490... push TRANSMIT and speak into external mic.
BE THERE, McGINNIS... BE TH--
AAAA...!

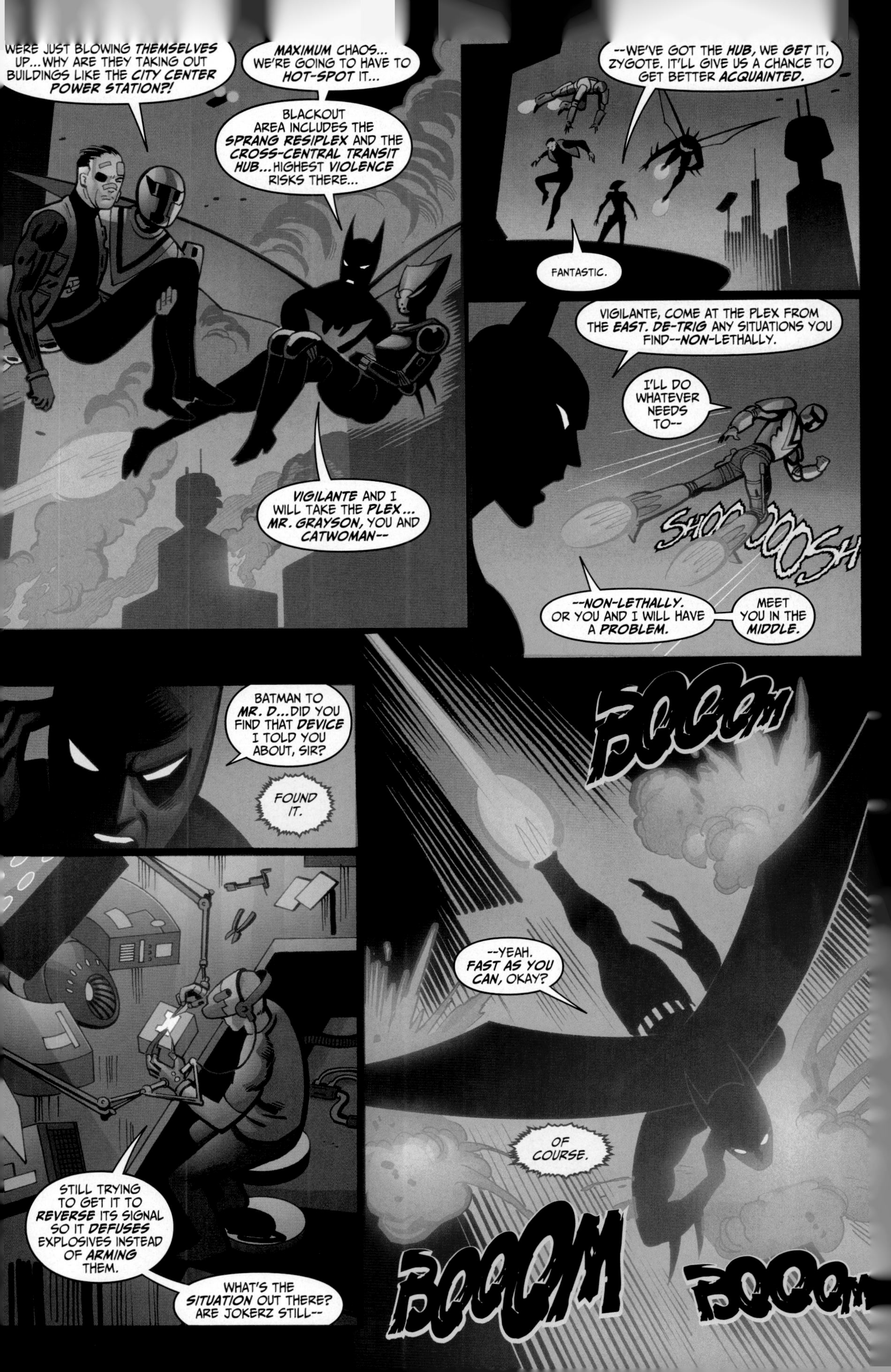

WERE JUST BLOWING THEMSELVES UP...WHY ARE THEY TAKING OUT BUILDINGS LIKE THE CITY CENTER POWER STATION?!
MAXIMUM CHAOS... WE'RE GOING TO HAVE TO HOT-SPOT IT...
BLACKOUT AREA INCLUDES THE SPRANG RESIPLEX AND THE CROSS-CENTRAL TRANSIT HUB...HIGHEST VIOLENCE RISKS THERE...
VIGILANTE AND I WILL TAKE THE PLEX... MR. GRAYSON, YOU AND CATWOMAN--
--WE'VE GOT THE HUB, WE GET IT, ZYGOTE. IT'LL GIVE US A CHANCE TO GET BETTER ACQUAINTED.
FANTASTIC.
VIGILANTE, COME AT THE PLEX FROM THE EAST. DE-TRIG ANY SITUATIONS YOU FIND--NON-LETHALLY.
I'LL DO WHATEVER NEEDS TO--
SHOOOOOOSH
--NON-LETHALLY. OR YOU AND I WILL HAVE A PROBLEM.
MEET YOU IN THE MIDDLE.
BATMAN TO MR. D...DID YOU FIND THAT DEVICE I TOLD YOU ABOUT, SIR?
FOUND IT.
STILL TRYING TO GET IT TO REVERSE ITS SIGNAL SO IT DEFUSES EXPLOSIVES INSTEAD OF ARMING THEM.
WHAT'S THE SITUATION OUT THERE? ARE JOKERZ STILL--
BOOOM
--YEAH. FAST AS YOU CAN, OKAY?
OF COURSE.
BOOOM
BOOOM

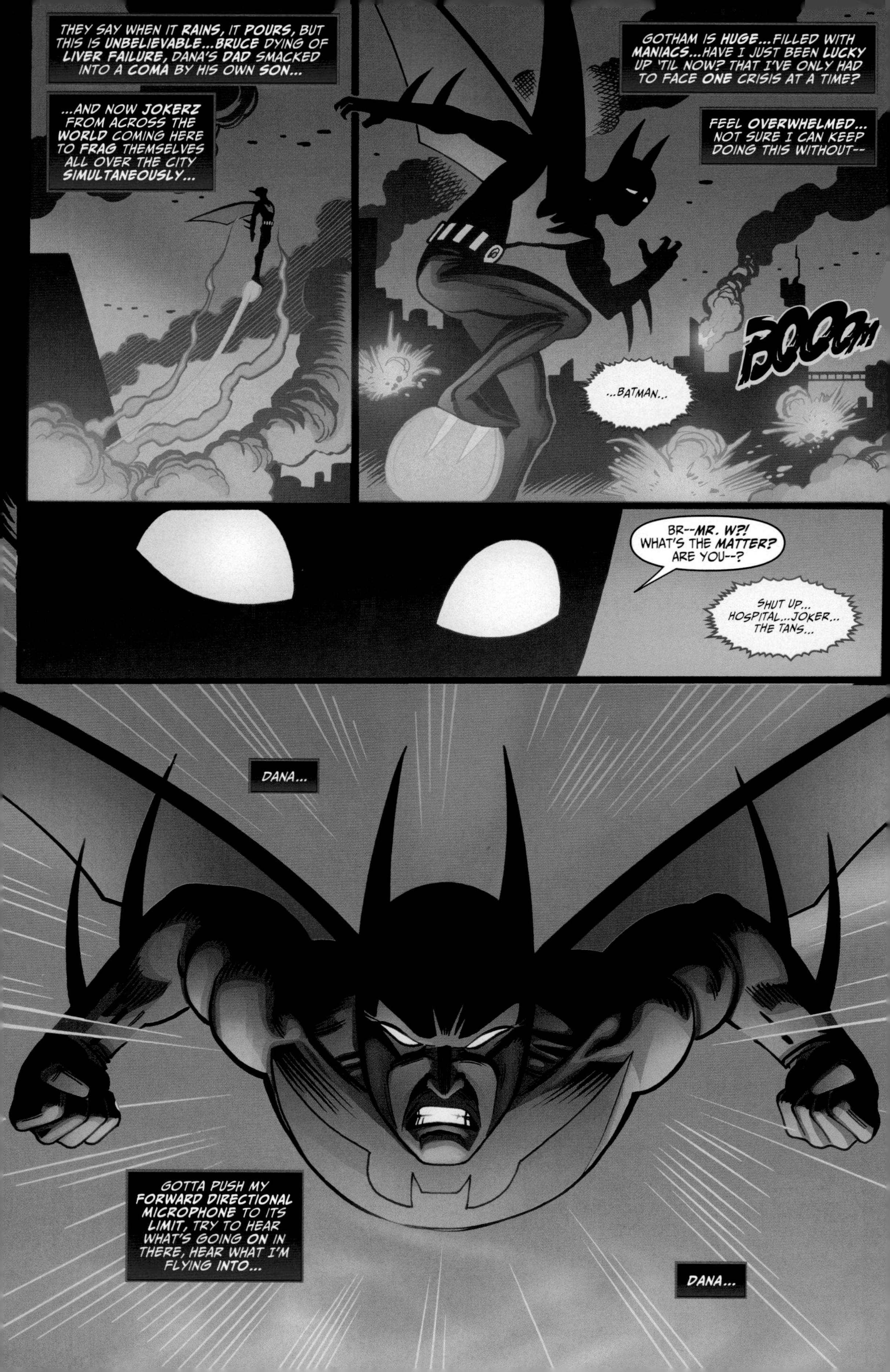
THEY SAY WHEN IT RAINS, IT POURS, BUT THIS IS UNBELIEVABLE...BRUCE DYING OF LIVER FAILURE, DANA'S DAD SMACKED INTO A COMA BY HIS OWN SON...
...AND NOW JOKERZ FROM ACROSS THE WORLD COMING HERE TO FRAG THEMSELVES ALL OVER THE CITY SIMULTANEOUSLY...
GOTHAM IS HUGE...FILLED WITH MANIACS...HAVE I JUST BEEN LUCKY UP 'TIL NOW? THAT I'VE ONLY HAD TO FACE ONE CRISIS AT A TIME?
FEEL OVERWHELMED... NOT SURE I CAN KEEP DOING THIS WITHOUT--
...BATMAN...
BOOOM
BR--MR. W?! WHAT'S THE MATTER? ARE YOU--?
SHUT UP... HOSPITAL...JOKER... THE TANS...
DANA...
GOTTA PUSH MY FORWARD DIRECTIONAL MICROPHONE TO ITS LIMIT, TRY TO HEAR WHAT'S GOING ON IN THERE, HEAR WHAT I'M FLYING INTO...
DANA...

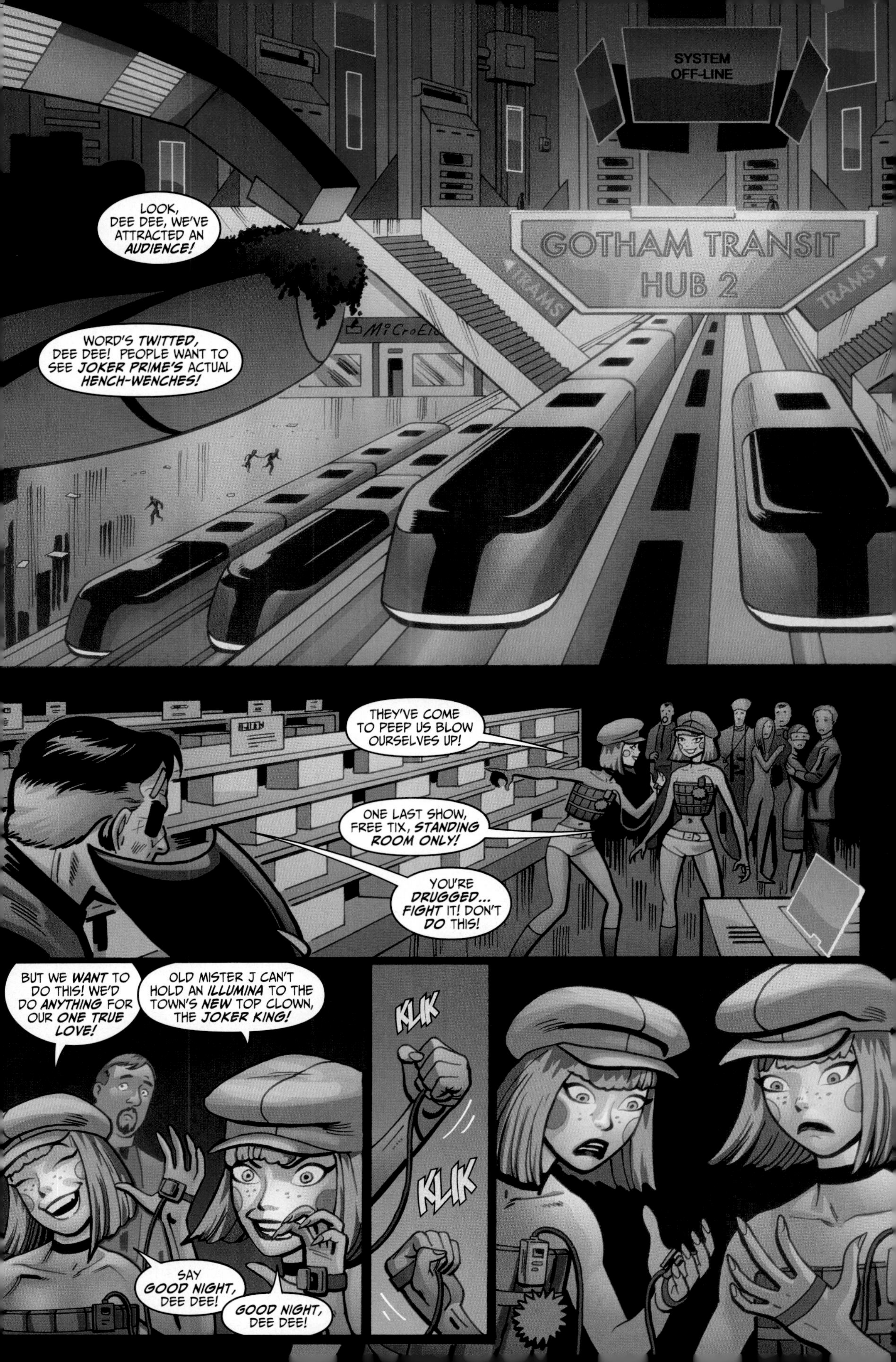
SYSTEM OFF-LINE
GOTHAM TRANSIT HUB 2
TRAMS
TRAMS
LOOK, DEE DEE, WE'VE ATTRACTED AN *AUDIENCE!*
WORD'S *TWITTED,* DEE DEE! PEOPLE WANT TO SEE *JOKER PRIME'S* ACTUAL *HENCH-WENCHES!*
THEY'VE COME TO PEEP US BLOW OURSELVES UP!
ONE LAST SHOW, FREE TIX, *STANDING ROOM ONLY!*
YOU'RE *DRUGGED...* *FIGHT* IT! DON'T *DO* THIS!
BUT WE *WANT* TO DO THIS! WE'D DO *ANYTHING* FOR OUR *ONE TRUE LOVE!*
OLD MISTER J CAN'T HOLD AN *ILLUMINA* TO THE TOWN'S *NEW* TOP CLOWN, THE *JOKER KING!*
SAY *GOOD NIGHT,* DEE DEE!
GOOD NIGHT, DEE DEE!
KLIK
KLIK

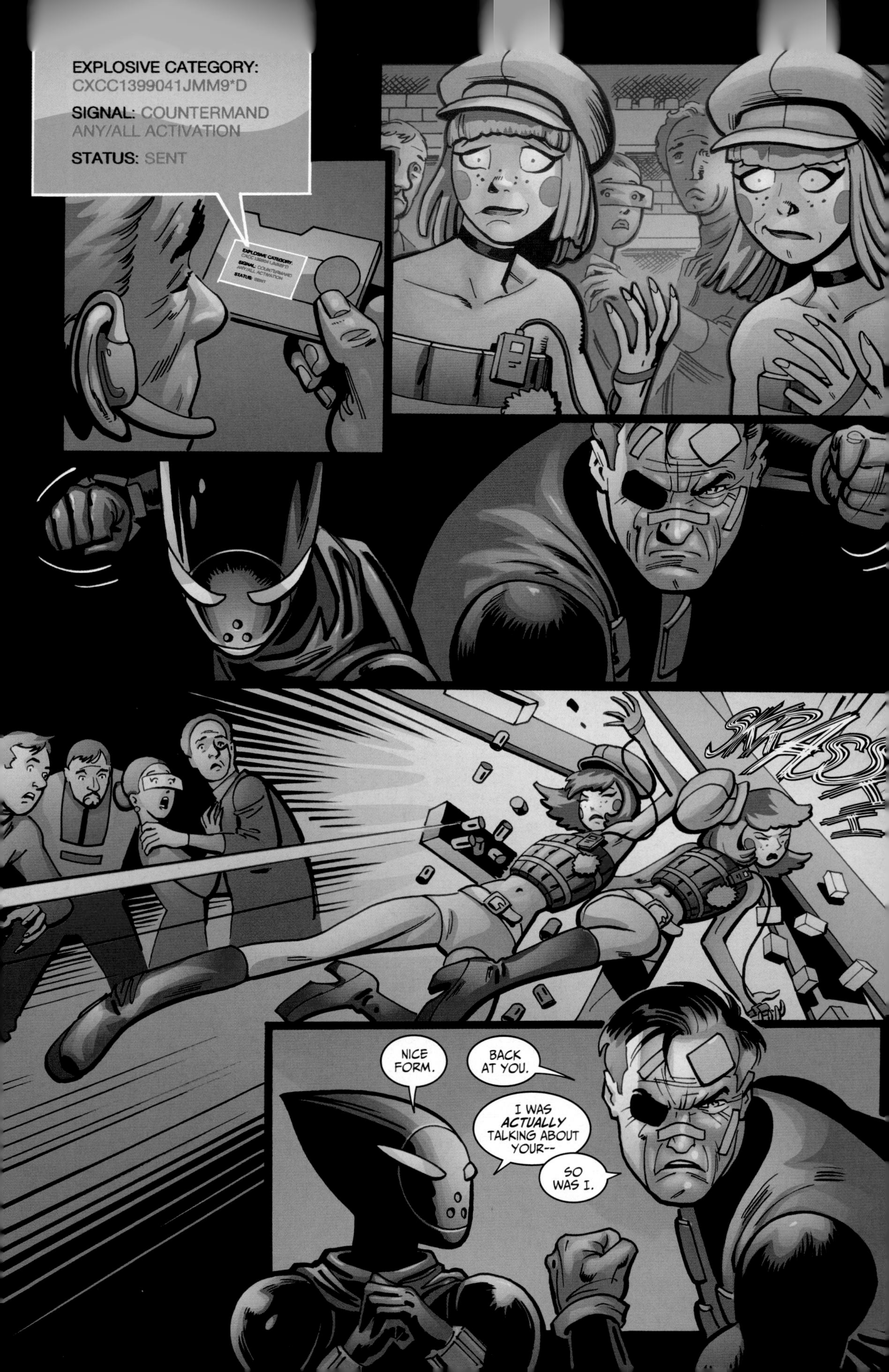
EXPLOSIVE CATEGORY:
CXCC1399041JMM9*D
SIGNAL: COUNTERMAND
ANY/ALL ACTIVATION
STATUS: SENT
SKRASSHH
NICE FORM.
BACK AT YOU.
I WAS ACTUALLY TALKING ABOUT YOUR--
SO WAS I.

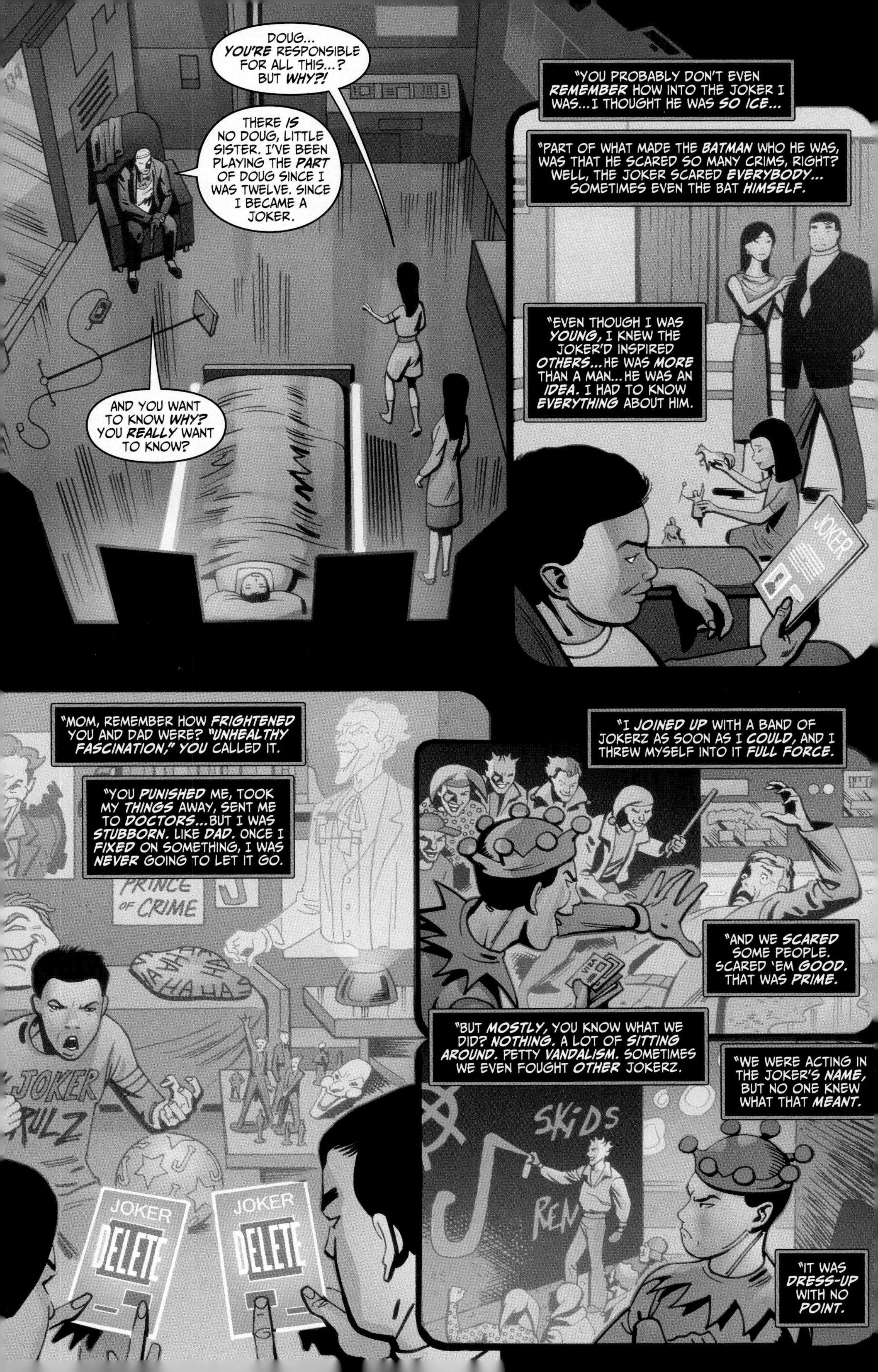

DOUG... YOU'RE RESPONSIBLE FOR ALL THIS...? BUT WHY?!
THERE IS NO DOUG, LITTLE SISTER. I'VE BEEN PLAYING THE PART OF DOUG SINCE I WAS TWELVE. SINCE I BECAME A JOKER.
AND YOU WANT TO KNOW WHY? YOU REALLY WANT TO KNOW?
"YOU PROBABLY DON'T EVEN REMEMBER HOW INTO THE JOKER I WAS...I THOUGHT HE WAS SO ICE...
"PART OF WHAT MADE THE BATMAN WHO HE WAS, WAS THAT HE SCARED SO MANY CRIMS, RIGHT? WELL, THE JOKER SCARED EVERYBODY... SOMETIMES EVEN THE BAT HIMSELF.
"EVEN THOUGH I WAS YOUNG, I KNEW THE JOKER'D INSPIRED OTHERS...HE WAS MORE THAN A MAN...HE WAS AN IDEA. I HAD TO KNOW EVERYTHING ABOUT HIM.
JOKER
"MOM, REMEMBER HOW FRIGHTENED YOU AND DAD WERE? "UNHEALTHY FASCINATION," YOU CALLED IT.
"YOU PUNISHED ME, TOOK MY THINGS AWAY, SENT ME TO DOCTORS...BUT I WAS STUBBORN. LIKE DAD. ONCE I FIXED ON SOMETHING, I WAS NEVER GOING TO LET IT GO.
PRINCE OF CRIME
JOKER RULZ
JOKER DELETE
JOKER DELETE
"I JOINED UP WITH A BAND OF JOKERZ AS SOON AS I COULD, AND I THREW MYSELF INTO IT FULL FORCE.
"AND WE SCARED SOME PEOPLE. SCARED 'EM GOOD. THAT WAS PRIME.
"BUT MOSTLY, YOU KNOW WHAT WE DID? NOTHING. A LOT OF SITTING AROUND. PETTY VANDALISM. SOMETIMES WE EVEN FOUGHT OTHER JOKERZ.
"WE WERE ACTING IN THE JOKER'S NAME, BUT NO ONE KNEW WHAT THAT MEANT.
SKIDS
"IT WAS DRESS-UP WITH NO POINT.

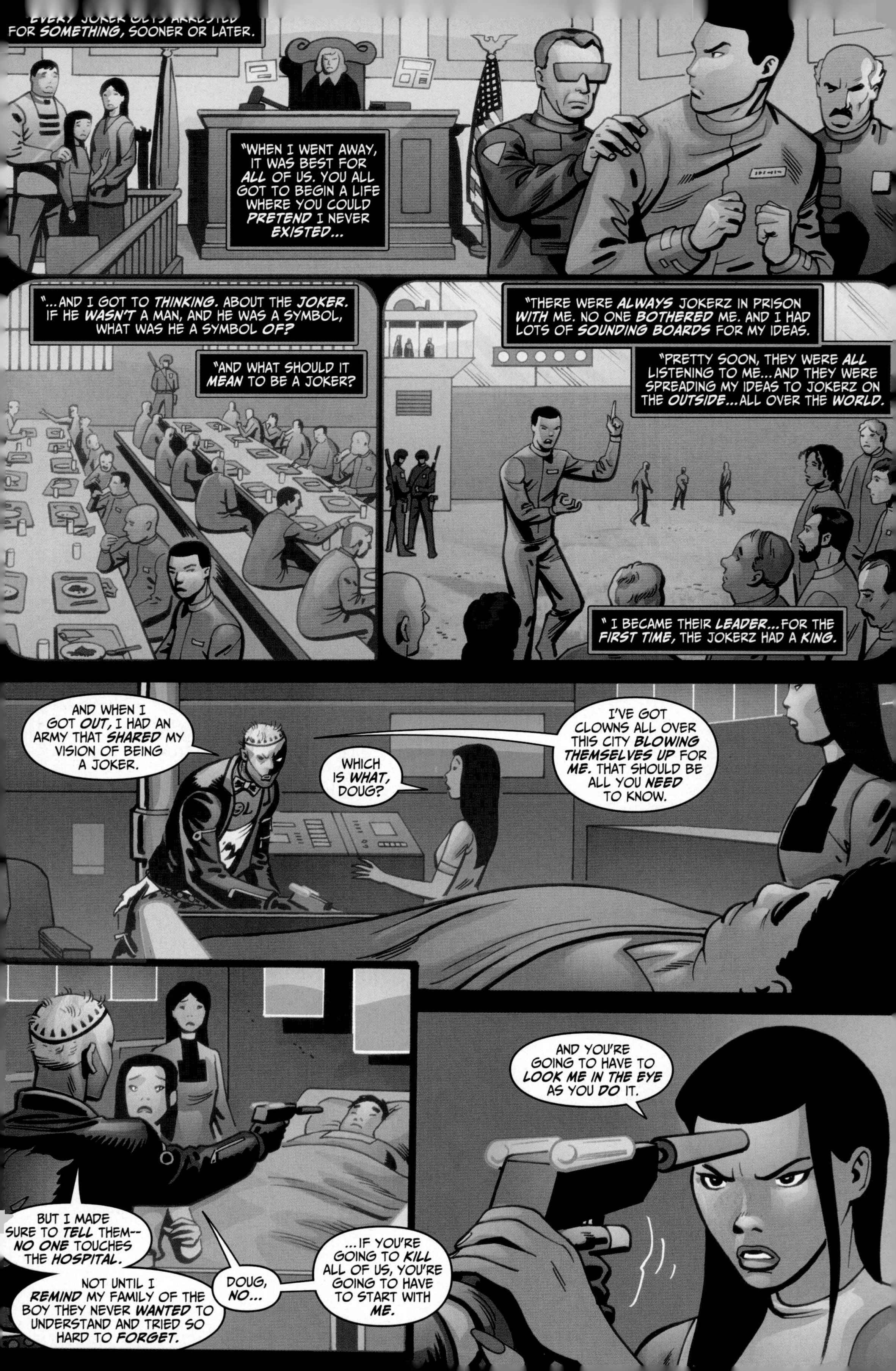
FOR SOMETHING, SOONER OR LATER.
"WHEN I WENT AWAY, IT WAS BEST FOR ALL OF US. YOU ALL GOT TO BEGIN A LIFE WHERE YOU COULD PRETEND I NEVER EXISTED...
"...AND I GOT TO THINKING. ABOUT THE JOKER. IF HE WASN'T A MAN, AND HE WAS A SYMBOL, WHAT WAS HE A SYMBOL OF?
"AND WHAT SHOULD IT MEAN TO BE A JOKER?
"THERE WERE ALWAYS JOKERZ IN PRISON WITH ME. NO ONE BOTHERED ME. AND I HAD LOTS OF SOUNDING BOARDS FOR MY IDEAS.
"PRETTY SOON, THEY WERE ALL LISTENING TO ME...AND THEY WERE SPREADING MY IDEAS TO JOKERZ ON THE OUTSIDE...ALL OVER THE WORLD.
" I BECAME THEIR LEADER...FOR THE FIRST TIME, THE JOKERZ HAD A KING.
AND WHEN I GOT OUT, I HAD AN ARMY THAT SHARED MY VISION OF BEING A JOKER.
WHICH IS WHAT, DOUG?
I'VE GOT CLOWNS ALL OVER THIS CITY BLOWING THEMSELVES UP FOR ME. THAT SHOULD BE ALL YOU NEED TO KNOW.
BUT I MADE SURE TO TELL THEM-- NO ONE TOUCHES THE HOSPITAL.
NOT UNTIL I REMIND MY FAMILY OF THE BOY THEY NEVER WANTED TO UNDERSTAND AND TRIED SO HARD TO FORGET.
DOUG, NO...
...IF YOU'RE GOING TO KILL ALL OF US, YOU'RE GOING TO HAVE TO START WITH ME.
AND YOU'RE GOING TO HAVE TO LOOK ME IN THE EYE AS YOU DO IT.

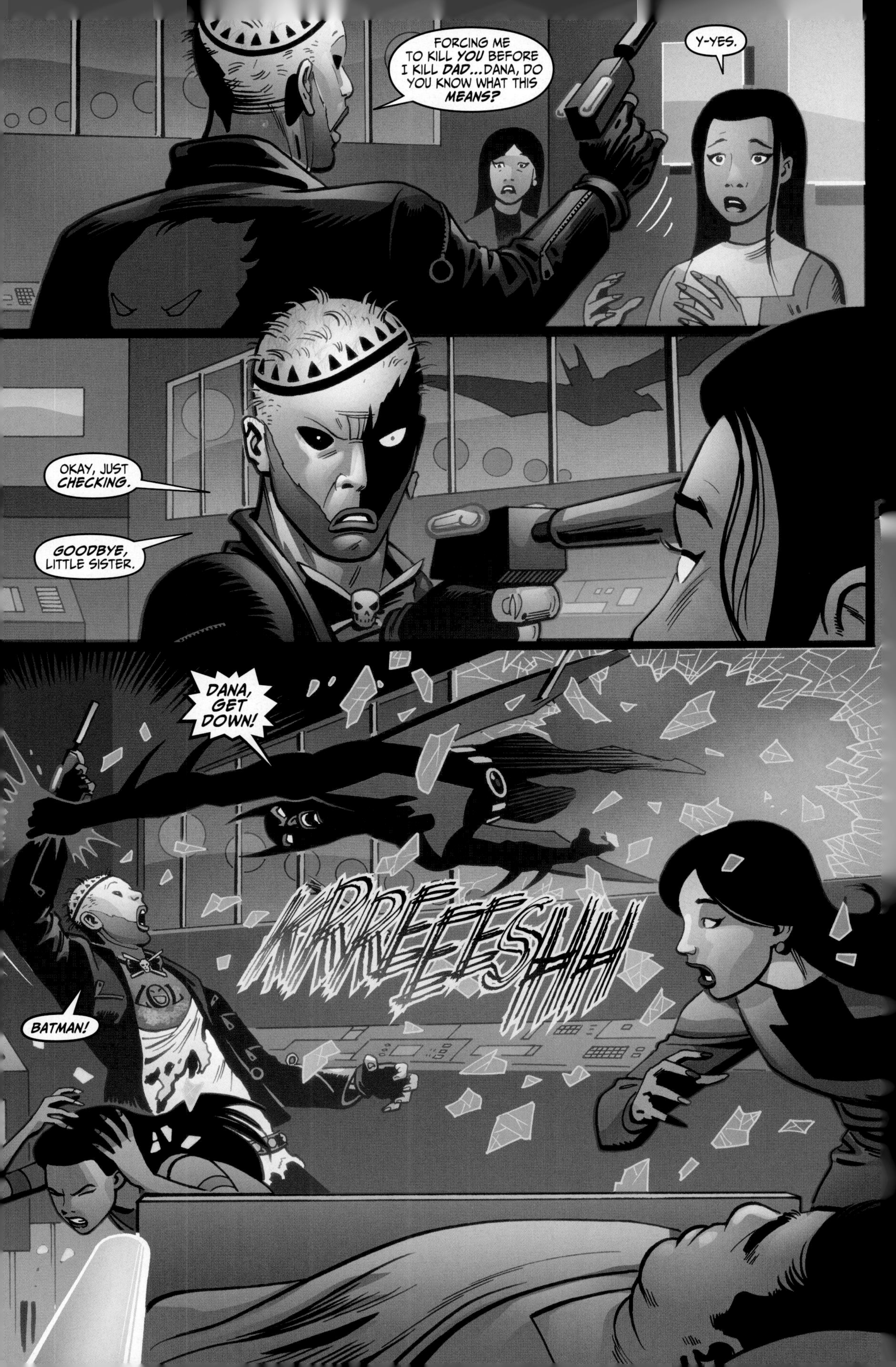
FORCING ME TO KILL YOU BEFORE I KILL DAD...DANA, DO YOU KNOW WHAT THIS MEANS?
Y-YES.
OKAY, JUST CHECKING.
GOODBYE, LITTLE SISTER.
DANA, GET DOWN!
KRRREEESHH
BATMAN!

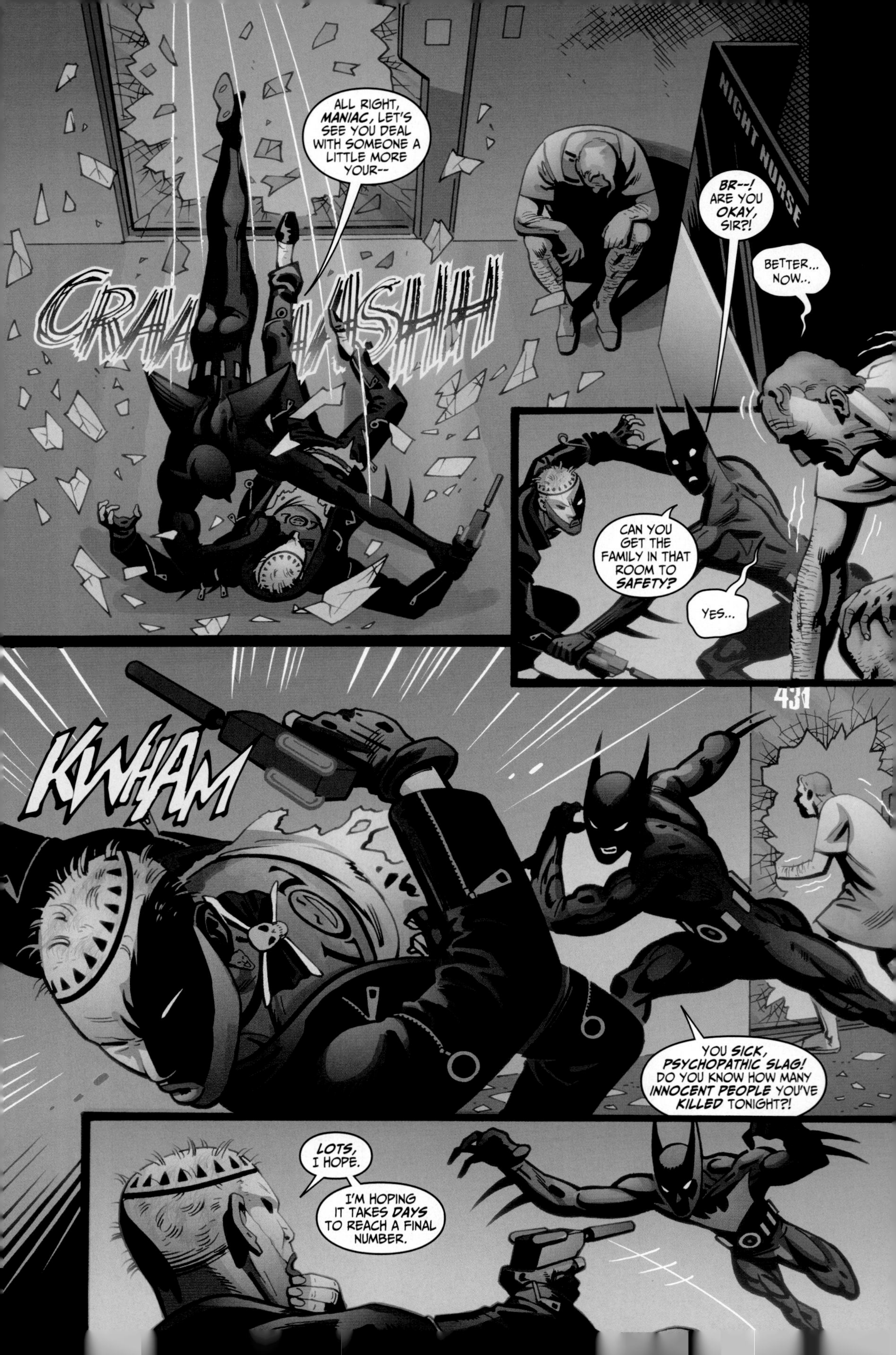
ALL RIGHT, MANIAC, LET'S SEE YOU DEAL WITH SOMEONE A LITTLE MORE YOUR--
CRAAASHH
BR--! ARE YOU OKAY, SIR?!
BETTER... NOW...
CAN YOU GET THE FAMILY IN THAT ROOM TO SAFETY?
YES...
431
KWHAM
YOU SICK, PSYCHOPATHIC SLAG! DO YOU KNOW HOW MANY INNOCENT PEOPLE YOU'VE KILLED TONIGHT?!
LOTS, I HOPE.
I'M HOPING IT TAKES DAYS TO REACH A FINAL NUMBER.

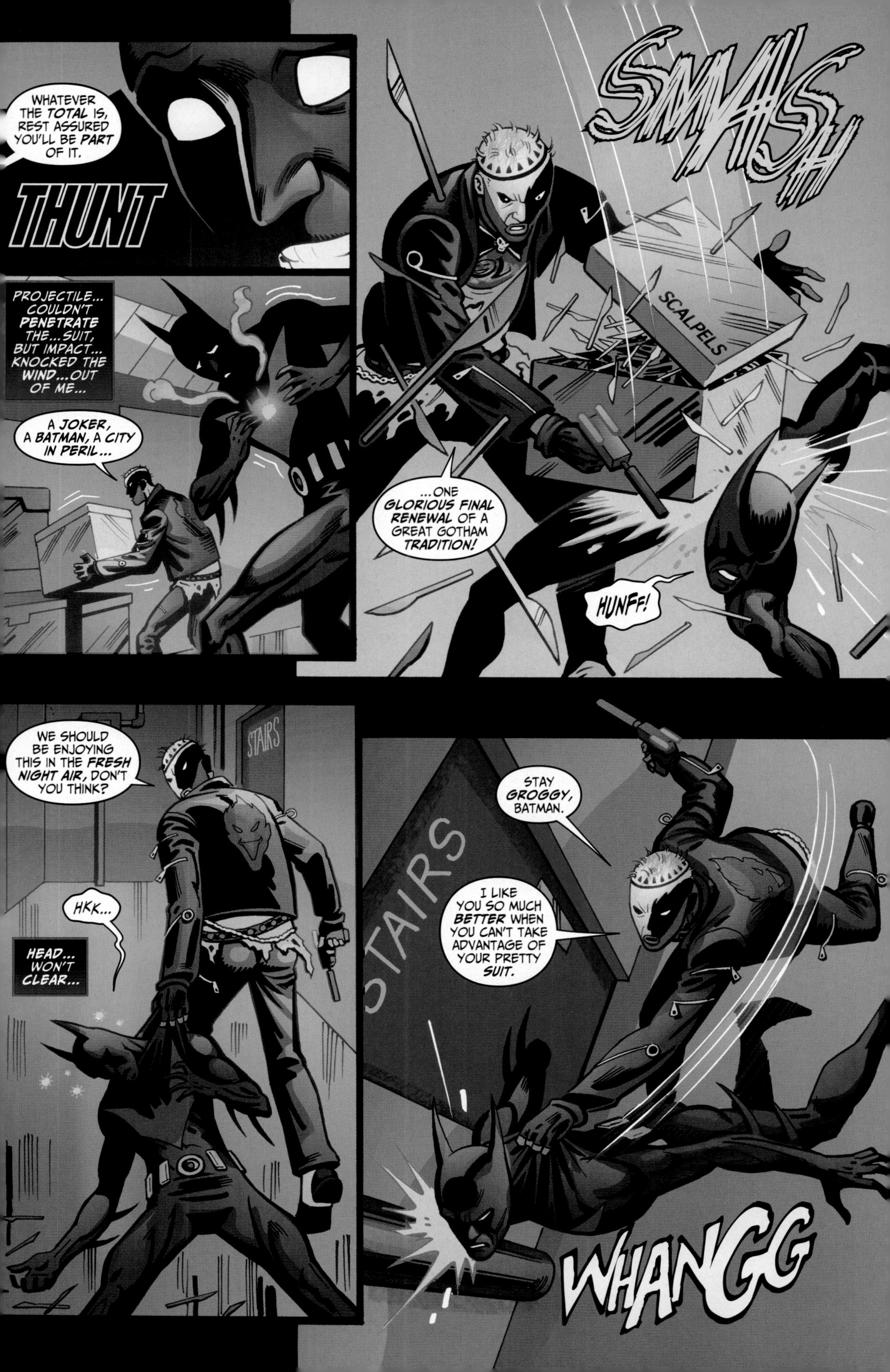
WHATEVER THE TOTAL IS, REST ASSURED YOU'LL BE PART OF IT.
THUNT
SMASH
PROJECTILE... COULDN'T PENETRATE THE...SUIT, BUT IMPACT... KNOCKED THE WIND...OUT OF ME...
A JOKER, A BATMAN, A CITY IN PERIL...
...ONE GLORIOUS FINAL RENEWAL OF A GREAT GOTHAM TRADITION!
SCALPELS
HUNFF!
STAIRS
WE SHOULD BE ENJOYING THIS IN THE FRESH NIGHT AIR, DON'T YOU THINK?
HKK...
HEAD... WON'T CLEAR...
STAIRS
STAY GROGGY, BATMAN.
I LIKE YOU SO MUCH BETTER WHEN YOU CAN'T TAKE ADVANTAGE OF YOUR PRETTY SUIT.
WHANGG

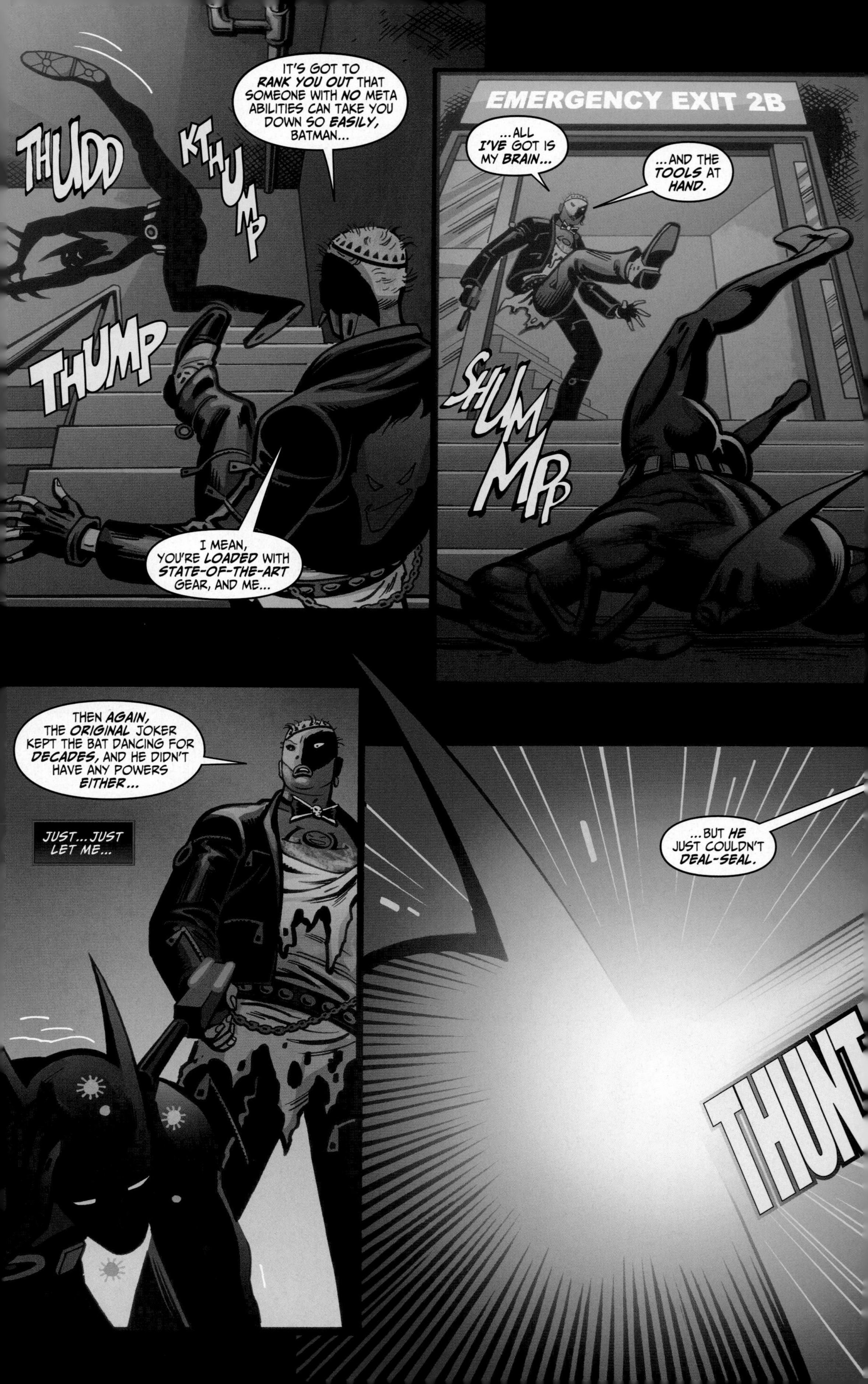
THUDD
KTHUMP
IT'S GOT TO RANK YOU OUT THAT SOMEONE WITH NO META ABILITIES CAN TAKE YOU DOWN SO EASILY, BATMAN...
THUMP
I MEAN, YOU'RE LOADED WITH STATE-OF-THE-ART GEAR, AND ME...
EMERGENCY EXIT 2B
...ALL I'VE GOT IS MY BRAIN...
...AND THE TOOLS AT HAND.
SHUMMPP
THEN AGAIN, THE ORIGINAL JOKER KEPT THE BAT DANCING FOR DECADES, AND HE DIDN'T HAVE ANY POWERS EITHER...
JUST... JUST LET ME...
...BUT HE JUST COULDN'T DEAL-SEAL.
THUNT

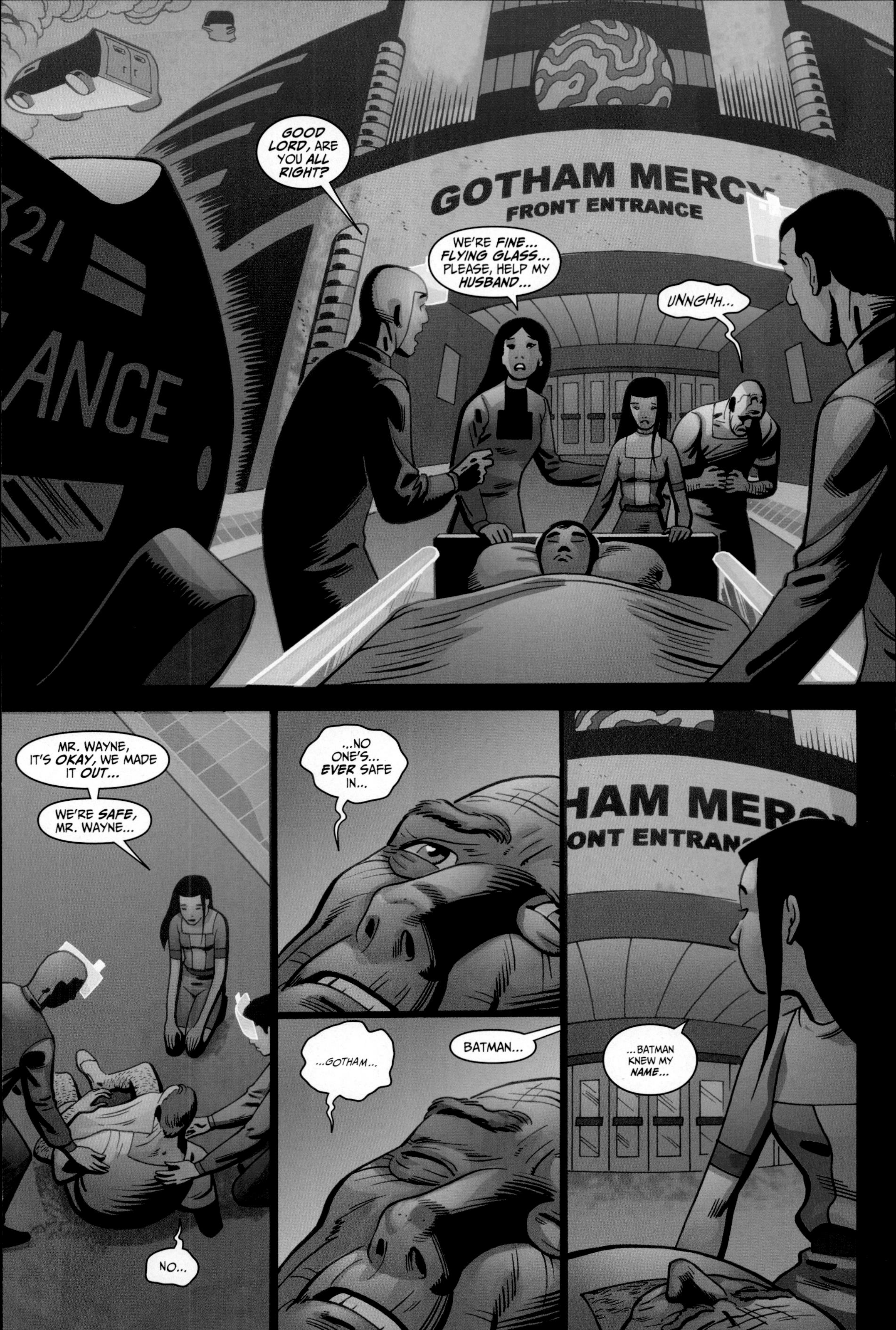

GOTHAM MERCY
FRONT ENTRANCE
GOOD LORD, ARE YOU ALL RIGHT?
WE'RE FINE... FLYING GLASS... PLEASE, HELP MY HUSBAND...
UNNGHH...
MR. WAYNE, IT'S OKAY, WE MADE IT OUT...
WE'RE SAFE, MR. WAYNE...
NO...
...NO ONE'S... EVER SAFE IN...
...GOTHAM...
BATMAN...
...BATMAN KNEW MY NAME...

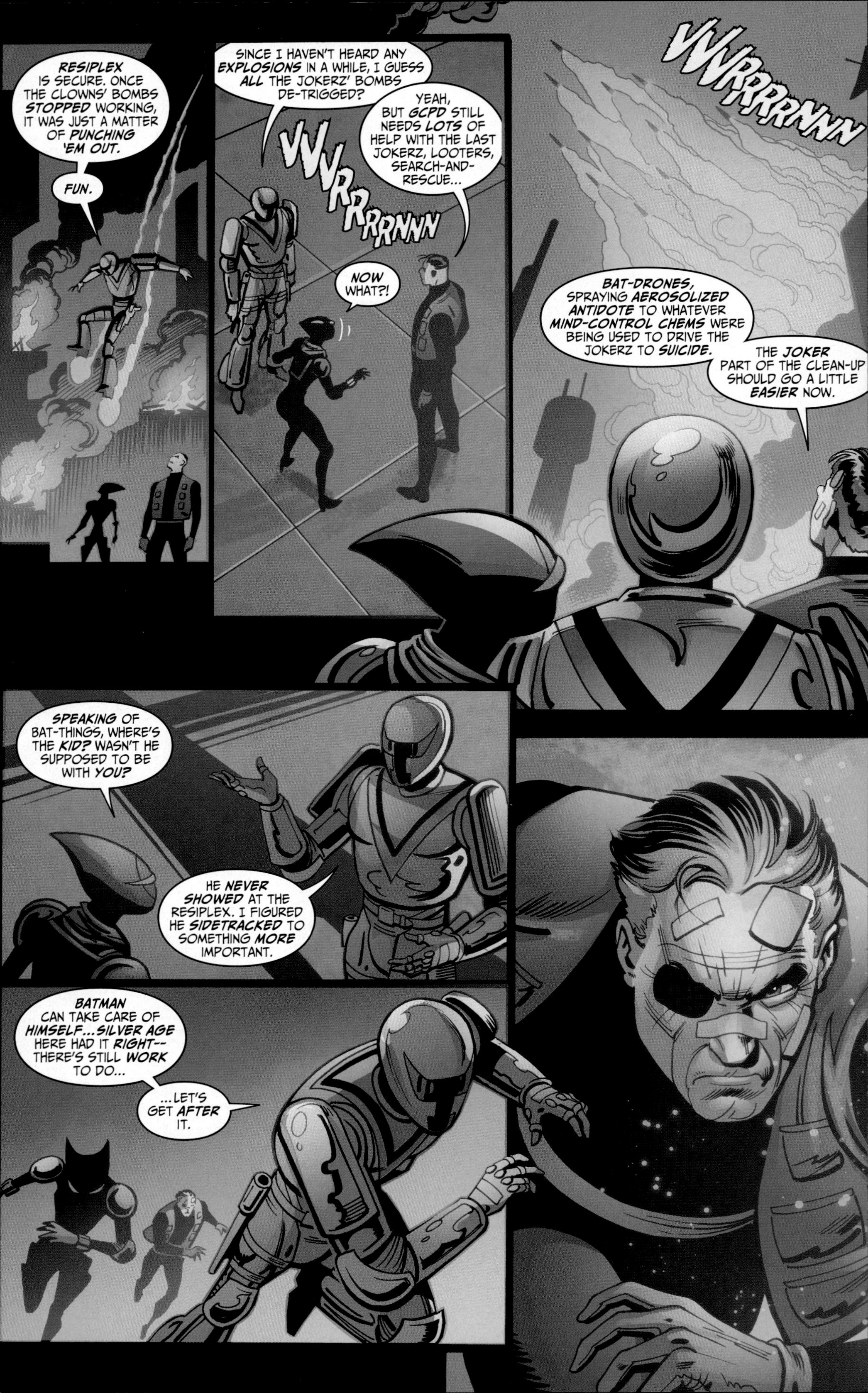

RESIPLEX IS SECURE. ONCE THE CLOWNS' BOMBS STOPPED WORKING, IT WAS JUST A MATTER OF PUNCHING 'EM OUT.
FUN.
SINCE I HAVEN'T HEARD ANY EXPLOSIONS IN A WHILE, I GUESS ALL THE JOKERZ' BOMBS DE-TRIGGED?
YEAH, BUT GCPD STILL NEEDS LOTS OF HELP WITH THE LAST JOKERZ, LOOTERS, SEARCH-AND-RESCUE...
VVVRRRRNNN
NOW WHAT?!
VVVRRRRRNNN
BAT-DRONES, SPRAYING AEROSOLIZED ANTIDOTE TO WHATEVER MIND-CONTROL CHEMS WERE BEING USED TO DRIVE THE JOKERZ TO SUICIDE.
THE JOKER PART OF THE CLEAN-UP SHOULD GO A LITTLE EASIER NOW.
SPEAKING OF BAT-THINGS, WHERE'S THE KID? WASN'T HE SUPPOSED TO BE WITH YOU?
HE NEVER SHOWED AT THE RESIPLEX. I FIGURED HE SIDETRACKED TO SOMETHING MORE IMPORTANT.
BATMAN CAN TAKE CARE OF HIMSELF...SILVER AGE HERE HAD IT RIGHT-- THERE'S STILL WORK TO DO...
...LET'S GET AFTER IT.

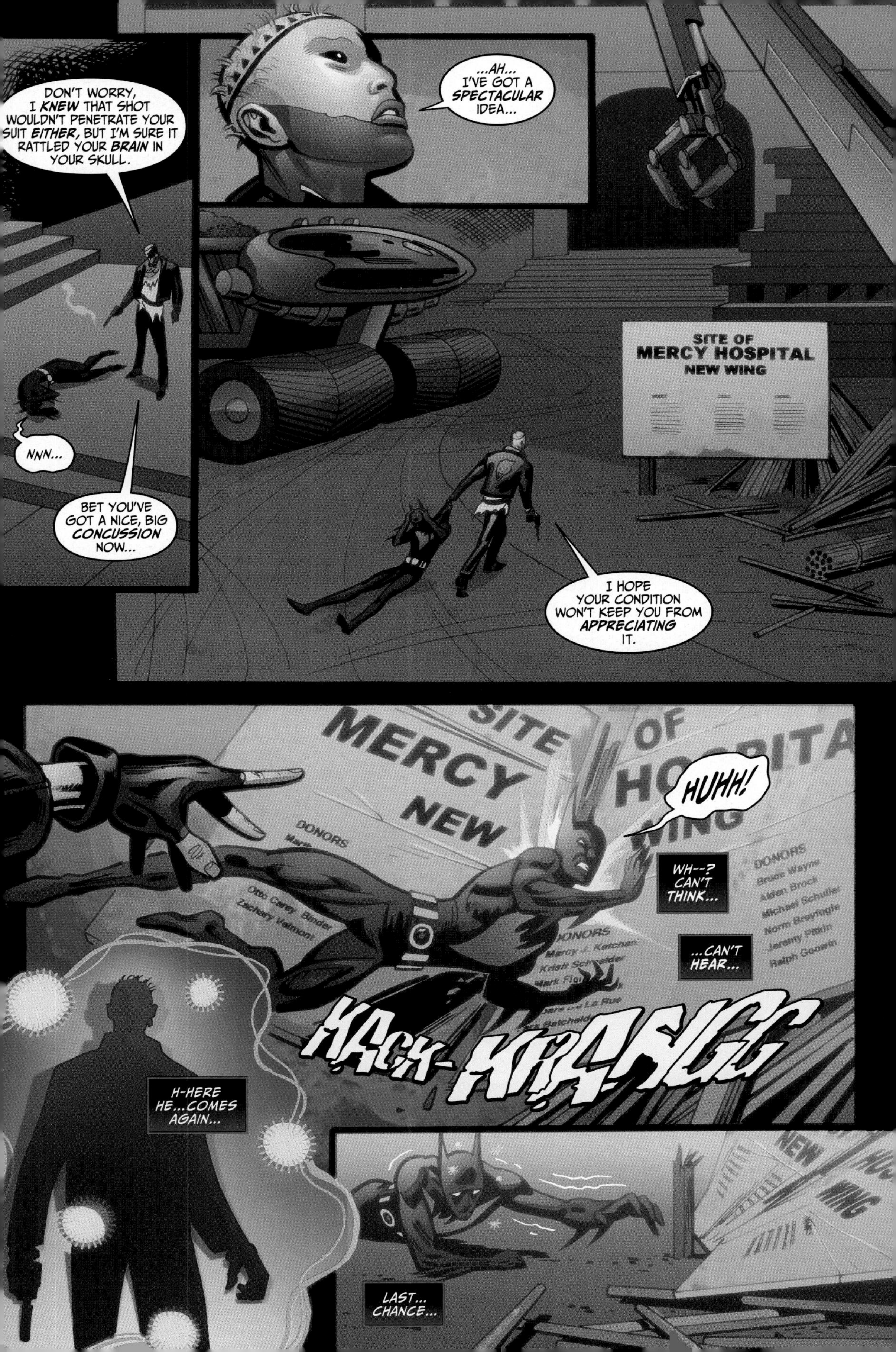

DON'T WORRY, I **KNEW** THAT SHOT WOULDN'T PENETRATE YOUR SUIT **EITHER**, BUT I'M SURE IT RATTLED YOUR **BRAIN** IN YOUR SKULL.
NNN...
BET YOU'VE GOT A NICE, BIG **CONCUSSION** NOW...
...AH... I'VE GOT A **SPECTACULAR** IDEA...
SITE OF MERCY HOSPITAL NEW WING
I HOPE YOUR CONDITION WON'T KEEP YOU FROM **APPRECIATING** IT.
SITE OF MERCY HOSPITA NEW WING
DONORS
Otto Carey Binder
Zachary Valmont
HUHH!
WH--? CAN'T THINK...
DONORS
Bruce Wayne
Alden Brock
Michael Schuller
Norm Breyfogle
Jeremy Pittkin
Ralph Goowin
...CAN'T HEAR...
KACK-KRANG
H-HERE HE...COMES AGAIN...
LAST... CHANCE...

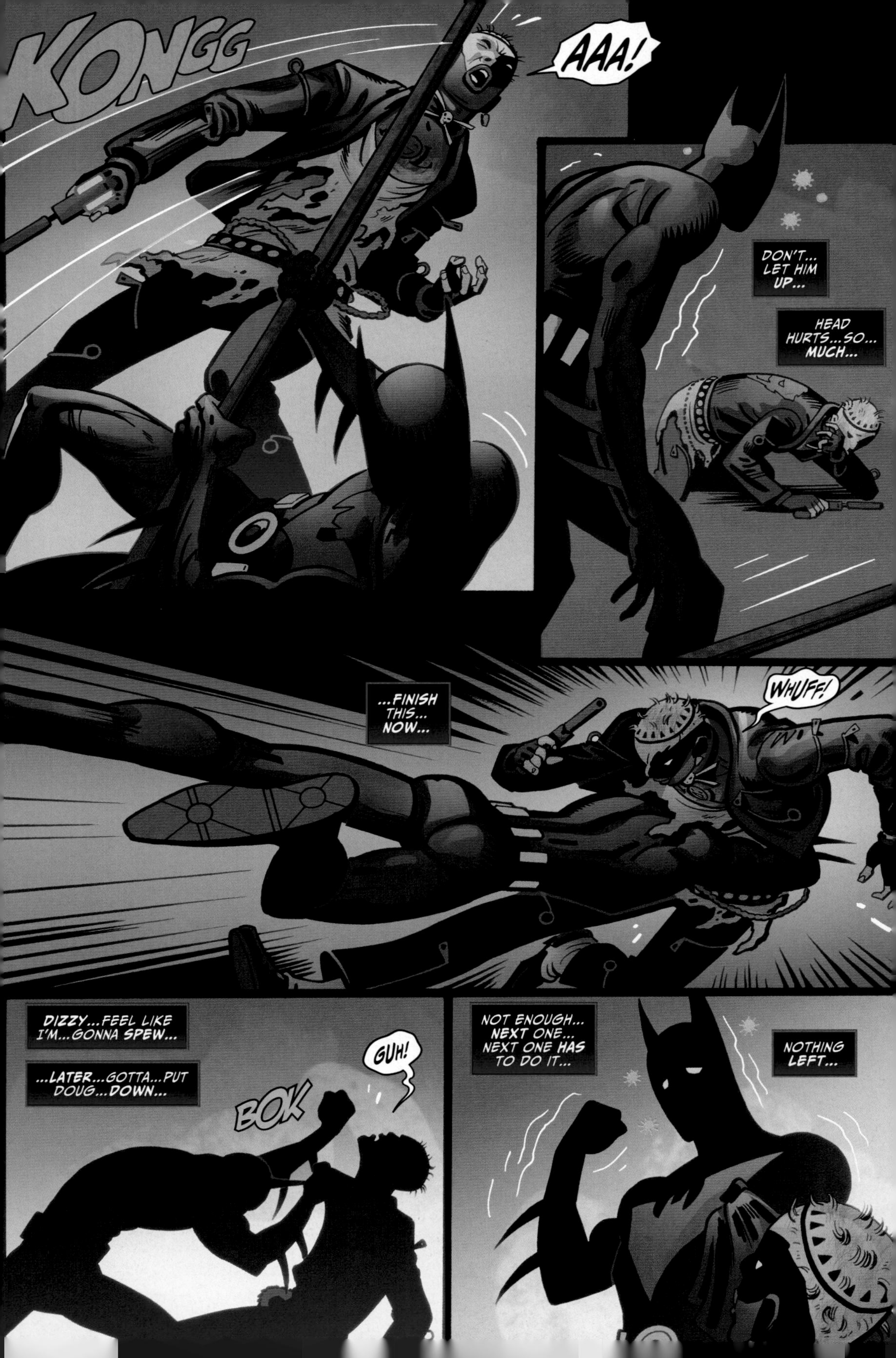
KONGG
AAA!
DON'T... LET HIM UP...
HEAD HURTS...SO... MUCH...
...FINISH THIS... NOW...
WHUFF!
DIZZY...FEEL LIKE I'M...GONNA SPEW...
...LATER...GOTTA...PUT DOUG...DOWN...
BOK
GUH!
NOT ENOUGH... NEXT ONE... NEXT ONE HAS TO DO IT...
NOTHING LEFT...

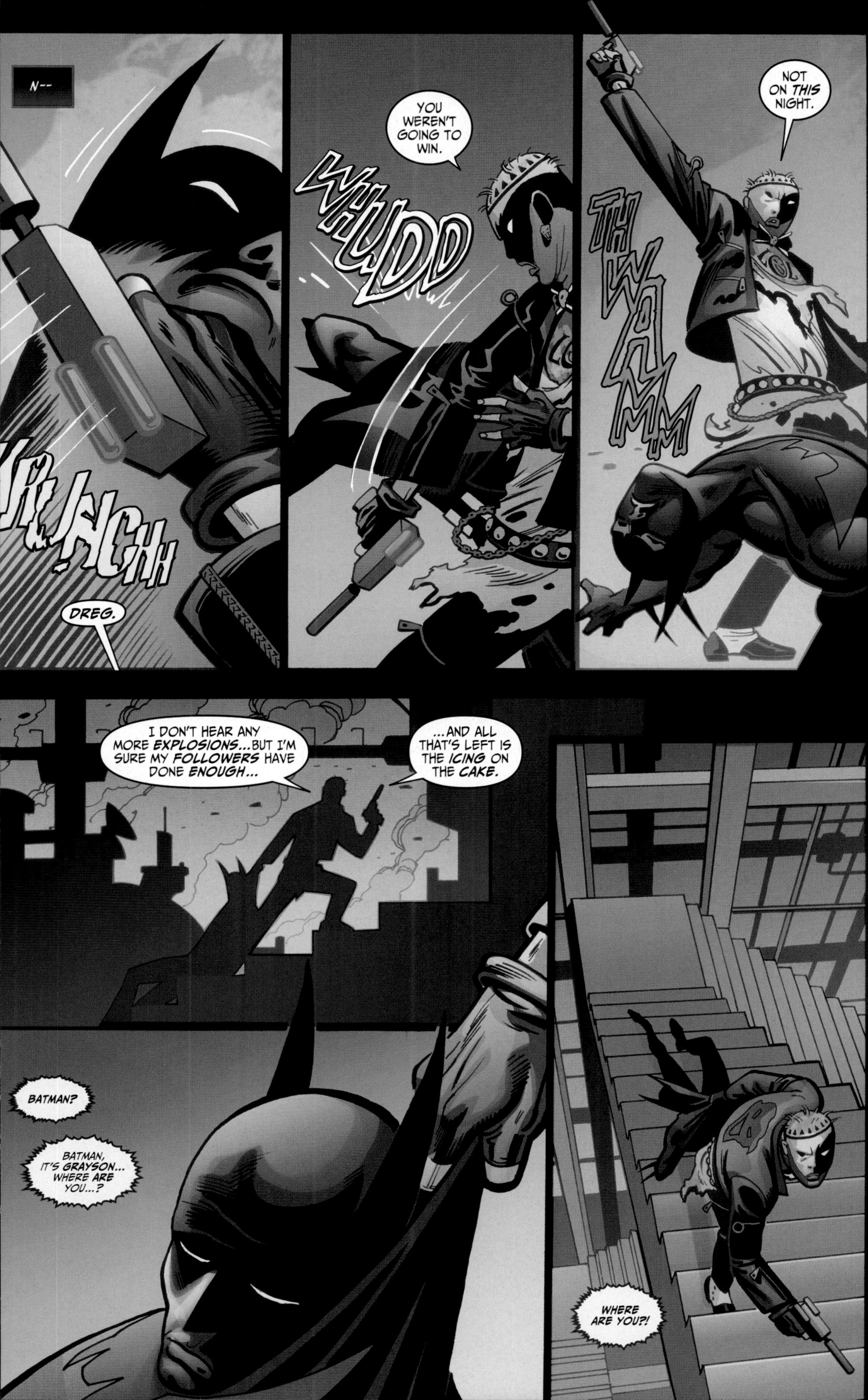
N--
KRUNCHH
DREG.
YOU WEREN'T GOING TO WIN.
WHUDD
NOT ON THIS NIGHT.
THWAMM
I DON'T HEAR ANY MORE EXPLOSIONS...BUT I'M SURE MY FOLLOWERS HAVE DONE ENOUGH...
...AND ALL THAT'S LEFT IS THE ICING ON THE CAKE.
BATMAN?
BATMAN, IT'S GRAYSON... WHERE ARE YOU...?
WHERE ARE YOU?!

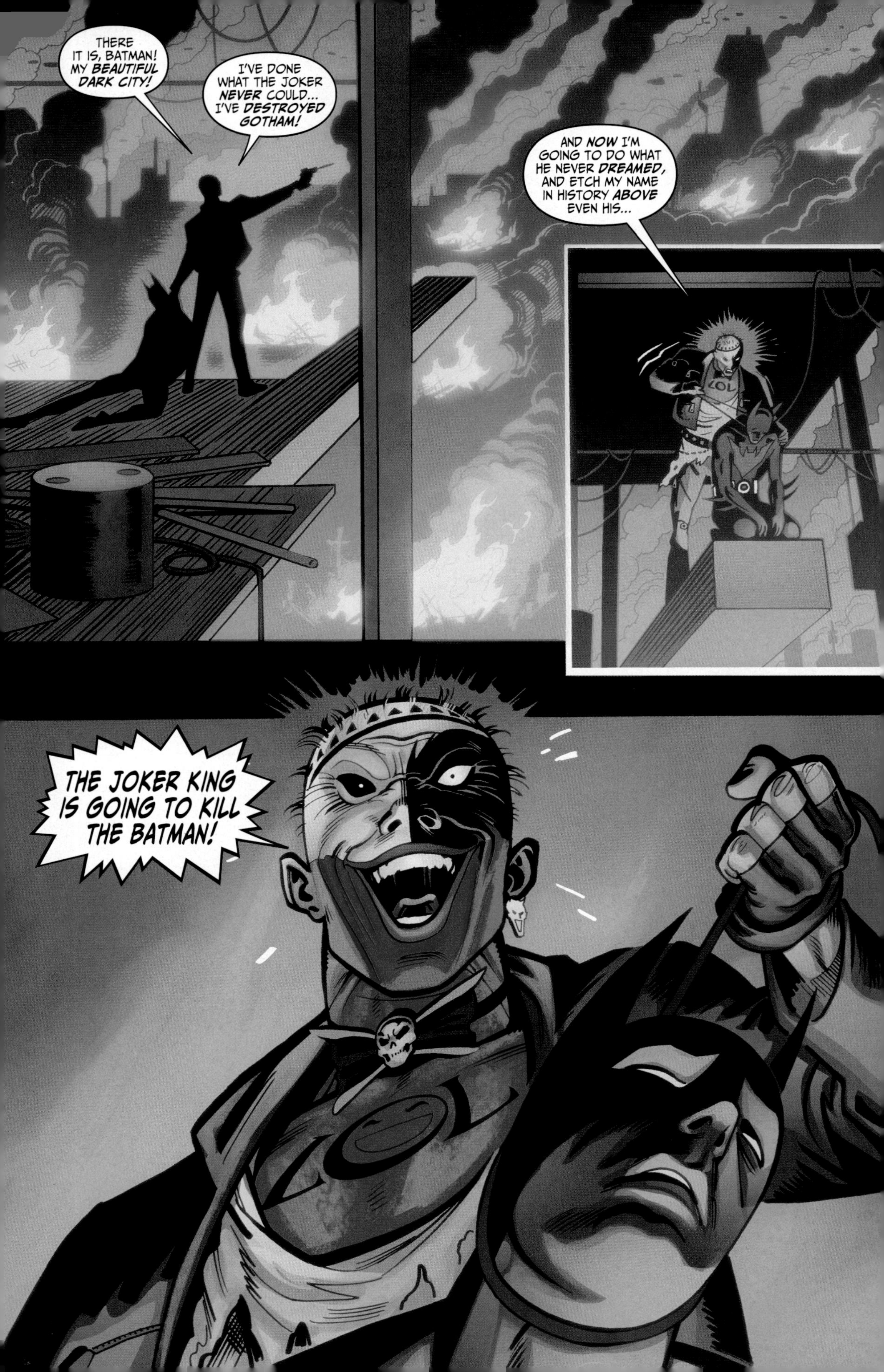
THERE IT IS, BATMAN! MY BEAUTIFUL DARK CITY!
I'VE DONE WHAT THE JOKER NEVER COULD... I'VE DESTROYED GOTHAM!
AND NOW I'M GOING TO DO WHAT HE NEVER DREAMED, AND ETCH MY NAME IN HISTORY ABOVE EVEN HIS...
LOL
THE JOKER KING IS GOING TO KILL THE BATMAN!

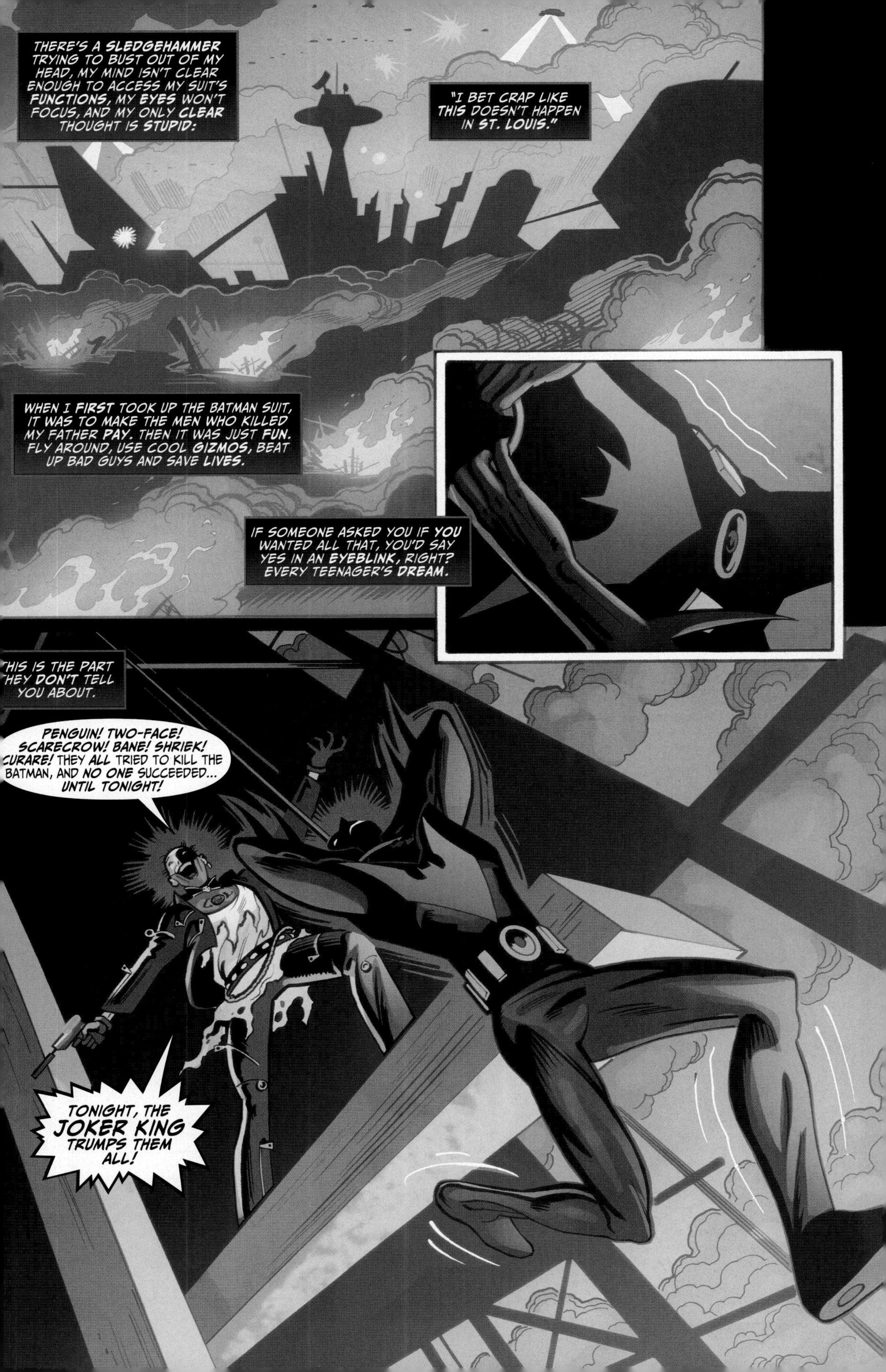
THERE'S A SLEDGEHAMMER TRYING TO BUST OUT OF MY HEAD, MY MIND ISN'T CLEAR ENOUGH TO ACCESS MY SUIT'S FUNCTIONS, MY EYES WON'T FOCUS, AND MY ONLY CLEAR THOUGHT IS STUPID:
"I BET CRAP LIKE THIS DOESN'T HAPPEN IN ST. LOUIS."
WHEN I FIRST TOOK UP THE BATMAN SUIT, IT WAS TO MAKE THE MEN WHO KILLED MY FATHER PAY. THEN IT WAS JUST FUN. FLY AROUND, USE COOL GIZMOS, BEAT UP BAD GUYS AND SAVE LIVES.
IF SOMEONE ASKED YOU IF YOU WANTED ALL THAT, YOU'D SAY YES IN AN EYEBLINK, RIGHT? EVERY TEENAGER'S DREAM.
THIS IS THE PART THEY DON'T TELL YOU ABOUT.
PENGUIN! TWO-FACE! SCARECROW! BANE! SHRIEK! CURARE! THEY ALL TRIED TO KILL THE BATMAN, AND NO ONE SUCCEEDED... UNTIL TONIGHT!
TONIGHT, THE JOKER KING TRUMPS THEM ALL!

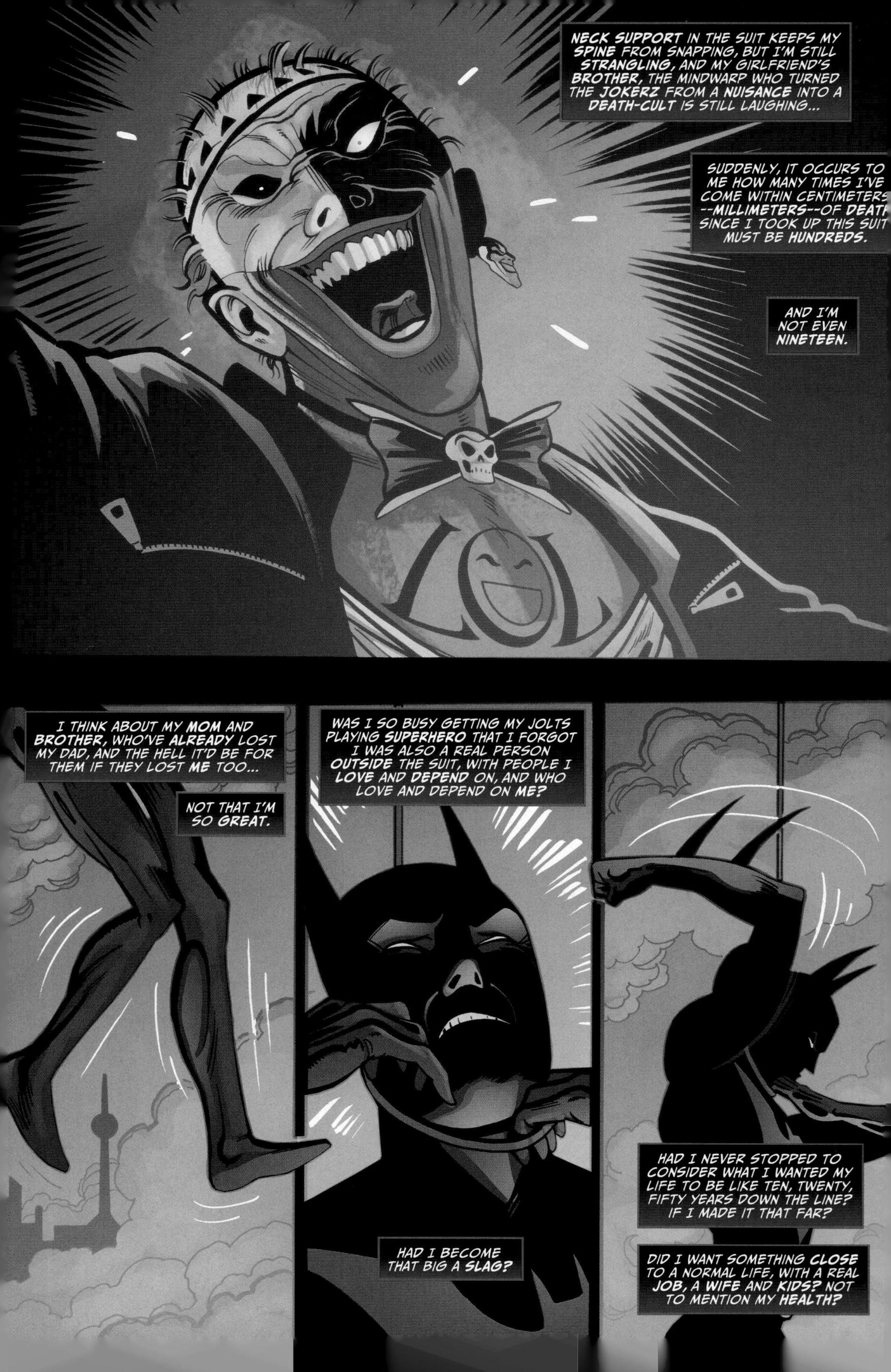

NECK SUPPORT IN THE SUIT KEEPS MY SPINE FROM SNAPPING, BUT I'M STILL STRANGLING, AND MY GIRLFRIEND'S BROTHER, THE MINDWARP WHO TURNED THE JOKERZ FROM A NUISANCE INTO A DEATH-CULT IS STILL LAUGHING...
SUDDENLY, IT OCCURS TO ME HOW MANY TIMES I'VE COME WITHIN CENTIMETERS --MILLIMETERS--OF DEATH SINCE I TOOK UP THIS SUIT. MUST BE HUNDREDS.
AND I'M NOT EVEN NINETEEN.
I THINK ABOUT MY MOM AND BROTHER, WHO'VE ALREADY LOST MY DAD, AND THE HELL IT'D BE FOR THEM IF THEY LOST ME TOO...
NOT THAT I'M SO GREAT.
WAS I SO BUSY GETTING MY JOLTS PLAYING SUPERHERO THAT I FORGOT I WAS ALSO A REAL PERSON OUTSIDE THE SUIT, WITH PEOPLE I LOVE AND DEPEND ON, AND WHO LOVE AND DEPEND ON ME?
HAD I BECOME THAT BIG A SLAG?
HAD I NEVER STOPPED TO CONSIDER WHAT I WANTED MY LIFE TO BE LIKE TEN, TWENTY, FIFTY YEARS DOWN THE LINE? IF I MADE IT THAT FAR?
DID I WANT SOMETHING CLOSE TO A NORMAL LIFE, WITH A REAL JOB, A WIFE AND KIDS? NOT TO MENTION MY HEALTH?

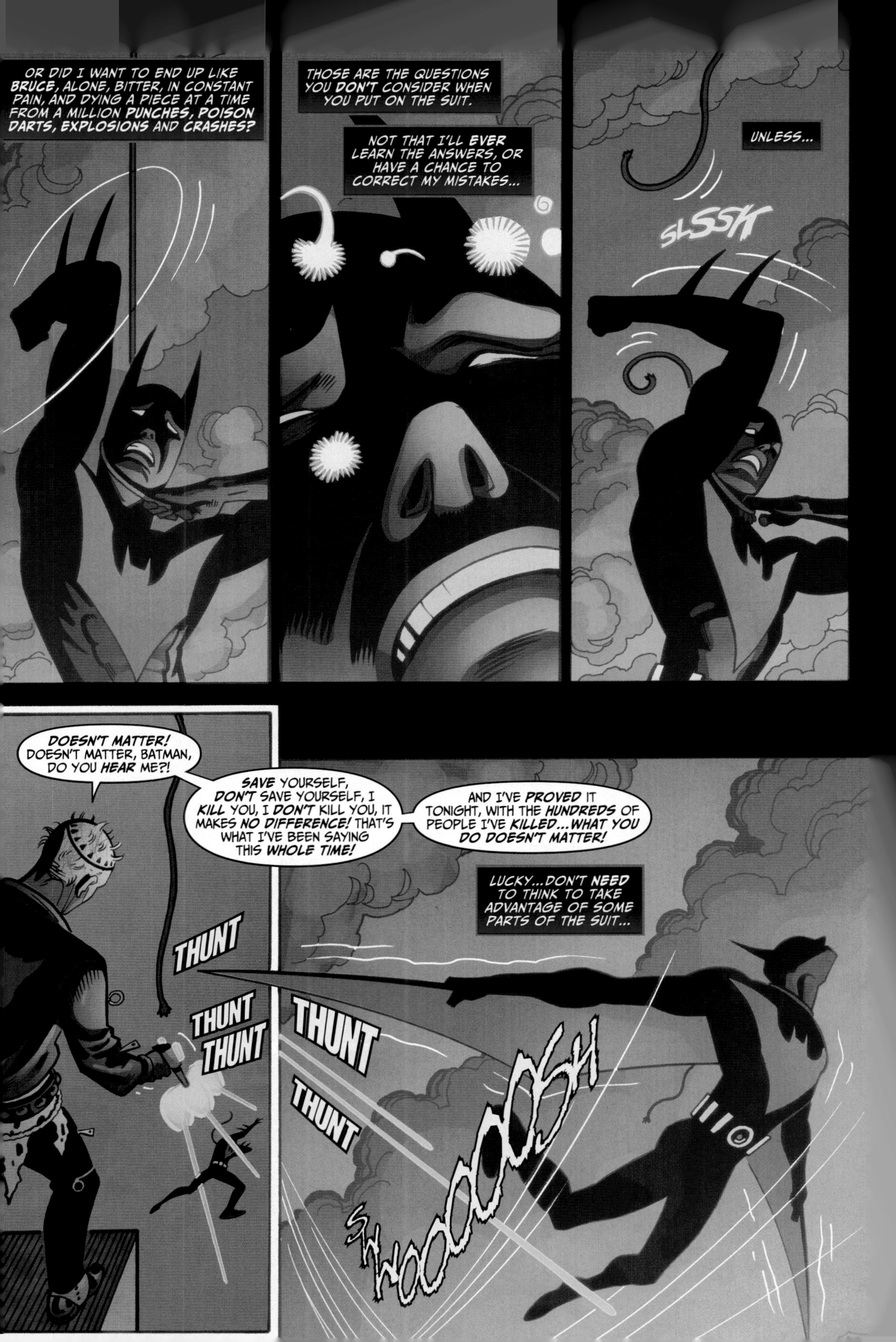
OR DID I WANT TO END UP LIKE BRUCE, ALONE, BITTER, IN CONSTANT PAIN, AND DYING A PIECE AT A TIME FROM A MILLION PUNCHES, POISON DARTS, EXPLOSIONS AND CRASHES?
THOSE ARE THE QUESTIONS YOU DON'T CONSIDER WHEN YOU PUT ON THE SUIT.
NOT THAT I'LL EVER LEARN THE ANSWERS, OR HAVE A CHANCE TO CORRECT MY MISTAKES...
UNLESS...
SLSSK
DOESN'T MATTER! DOESN'T MATTER, BATMAN, DO YOU HEAR ME?!
SAVE YOURSELF, DON'T SAVE YOURSELF, I KILL YOU, I DON'T KILL YOU, IT MAKES NO DIFFERENCE! THAT'S WHAT I'VE BEEN SAYING THIS WHOLE TIME!
AND I'VE PROVED IT TONIGHT, WITH THE HUNDREDS OF PEOPLE I'VE KILLED...WHAT YOU DO DOESN'T MATTER!
LUCKY...DON'T NEED TO THINK TO TAKE ADVANTAGE OF SOME PARTS OF THE SUIT...
THUNT
THUNT
THUNT
THUNT
THUNT
SHWOOOOOOSH

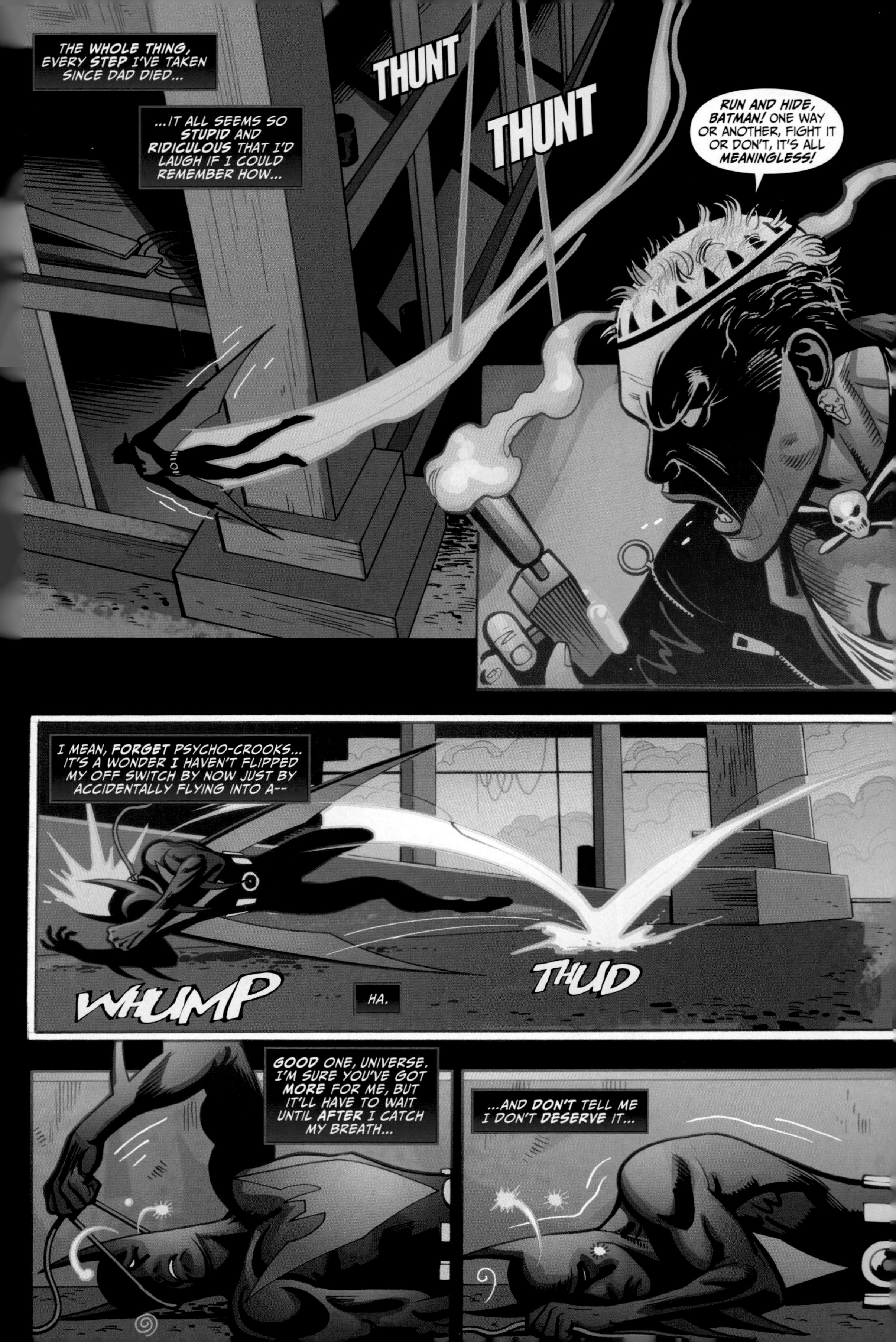
THE WHOLE THING, EVERY STEP I'VE TAKEN SINCE DAD DIED...
...IT ALL SEEMS SO STUPID AND RIDICULOUS THAT I'D LAUGH IF I COULD REMEMBER HOW...
THUNT
THUNT
RUN AND HIDE, BATMAN! ONE WAY OR ANOTHER, FIGHT IT OR DON'T, IT'S ALL MEANINGLESS!
I MEAN, FORGET PSYCHO-CROOKS... IT'S A WONDER I HAVEN'T FLIPPED MY OFF SWITCH BY NOW JUST BY ACCIDENTALLY FLYING INTO A--
WHUMP
HA.
THUD
GOOD ONE, UNIVERSE. I'M SURE YOU'VE GOT MORE FOR ME, BUT IT'LL HAVE TO WAIT UNTIL AFTER I CATCH MY BREATH...
...AND DON'T TELL ME I DON'T DESERVE IT...

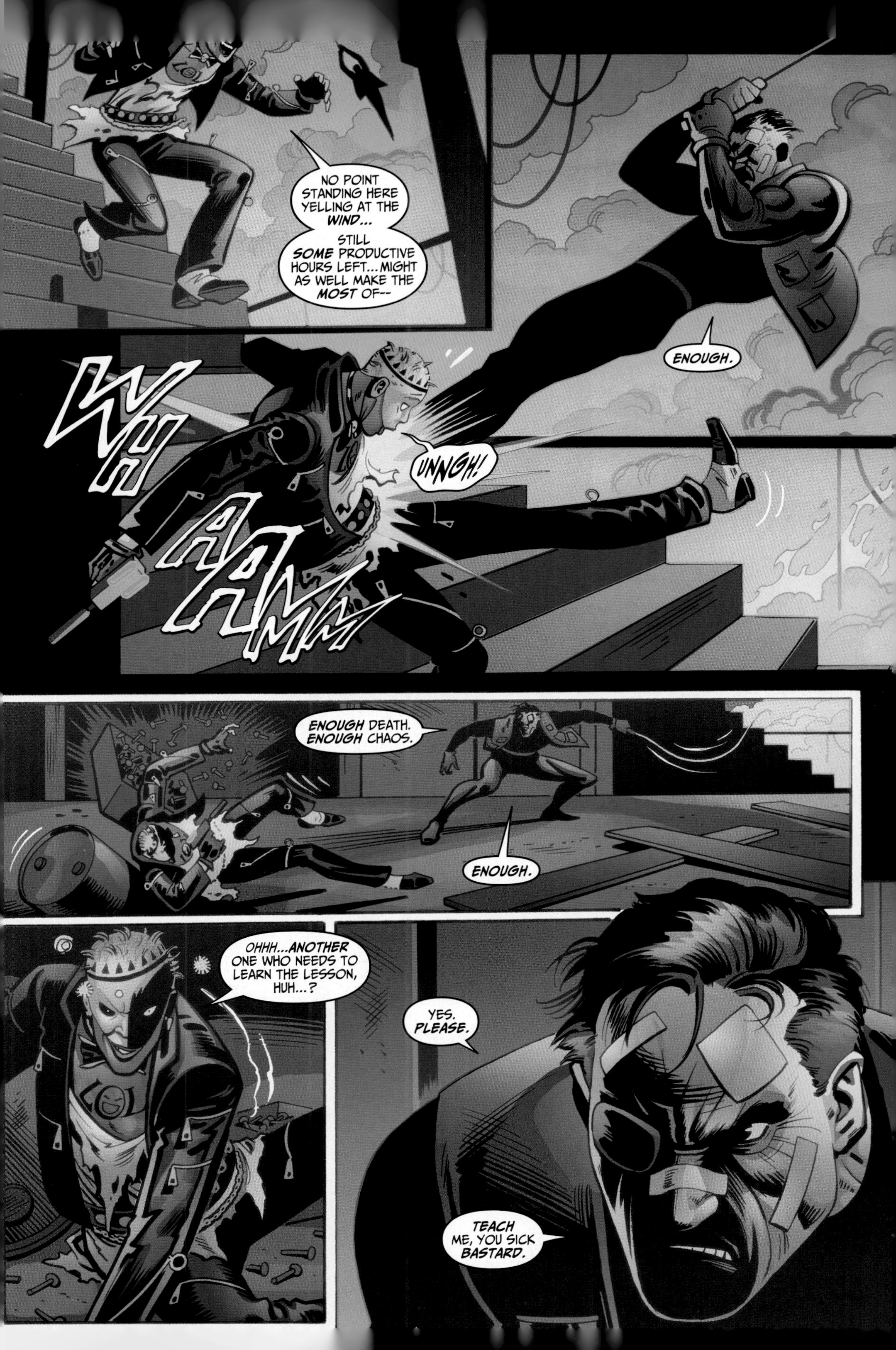
NO POINT STANDING HERE YELLING AT THE WIND...
STILL SOME PRODUCTIVE HOURS LEFT... MIGHT AS WELL MAKE THE MOST OF--
ENOUGH.
WHAMMM
UNNGH!
ENOUGH DEATH. ENOUGH CHAOS.
ENOUGH.
OHHH...ANOTHER ONE WHO NEEDS TO LEARN THE LESSON, HUH...?
YES. PLEASE.
TEACH ME, YOU SICK BASTARD.

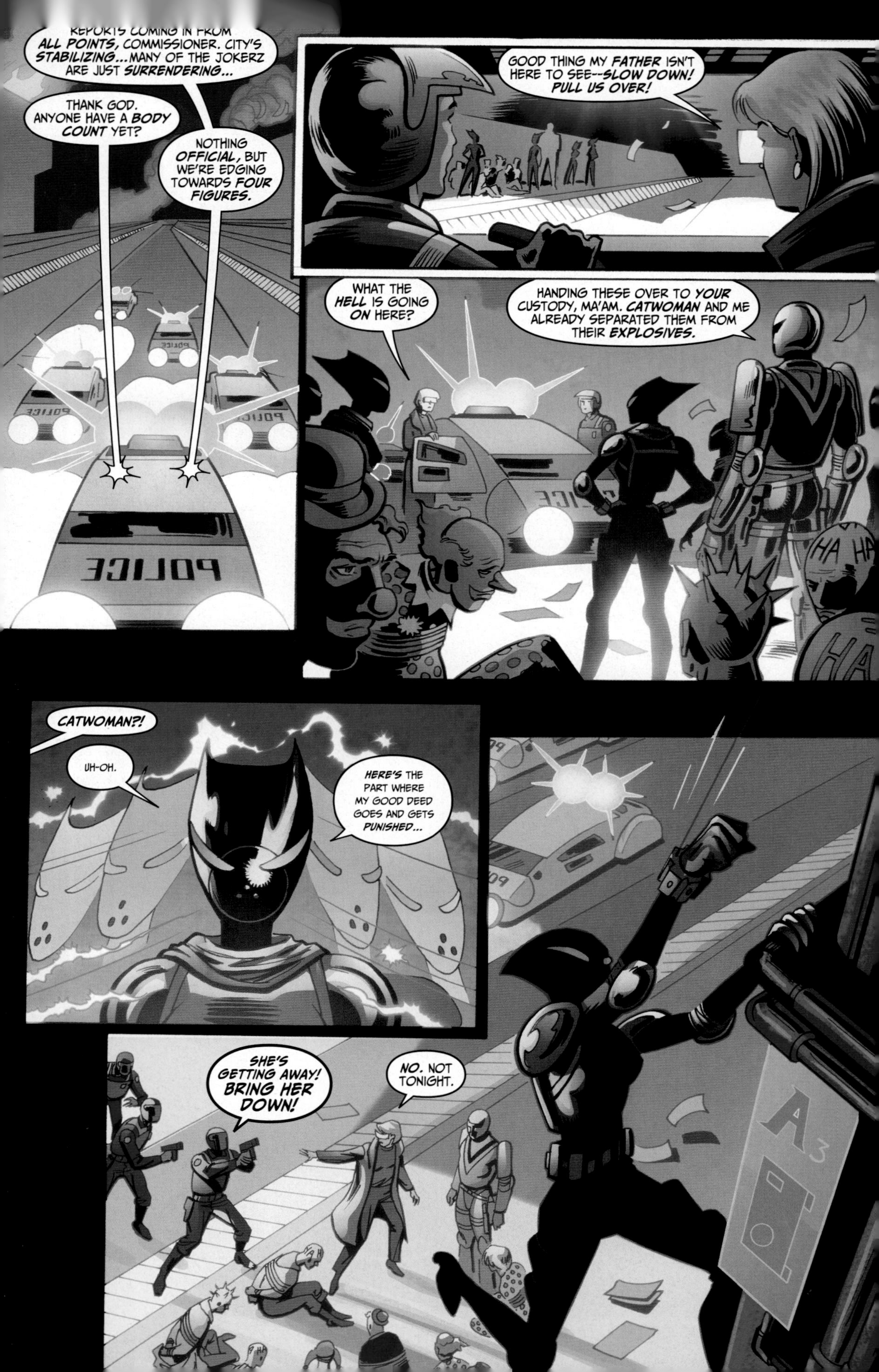
REPORTS COMING IN FROM ALL POINTS, COMMISSIONER. CITY'S STABILIZING... MANY OF THE JOKERZ ARE JUST SURRENDERING...
THANK GOD. ANYONE HAVE A BODY COUNT YET?
NOTHING OFFICIAL, BUT WE'RE EDGING TOWARDS FOUR FIGURES.
POLICE
POLICE
GOOD THING MY FATHER ISN'T HERE TO SEE--SLOW DOWN! PULL US OVER!
WHAT THE HELL IS GOING ON HERE?
HANDING THESE OVER TO YOUR CUSTODY, MA'AM. CATWOMAN AND ME ALREADY SEPARATED THEM FROM THEIR EXPLOSIVES.
HA HA
CATWOMAN?!
UH-OH.
HERE'S THE PART WHERE MY GOOD DEED GOES AND GETS PUNISHED...
SHE'S GETTING AWAY! BRING HER DOWN!
NO. NOT TONIGHT.

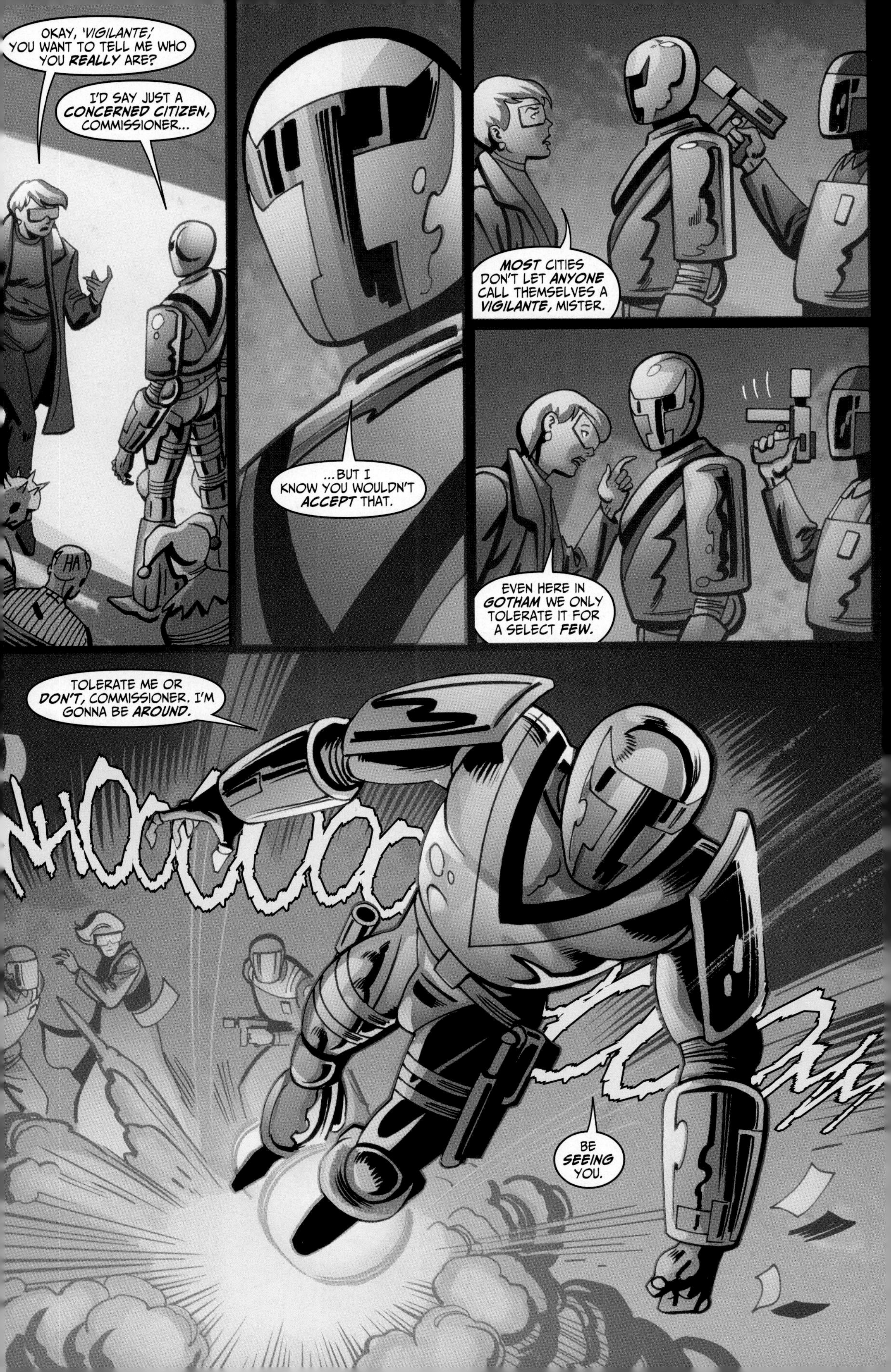

OKAY, 'VIGILANTE,' YOU WANT TO TELL ME WHO YOU *REALLY* ARE?
I'D SAY JUST A *CONCERNED CITIZEN,* COMMISSIONER...
...BUT I KNOW YOU WOULDN'T *ACCEPT* THAT.
MOST CITIES DON'T LET *ANYONE* CALL THEMSELVES A *VIGILANTE,* MISTER.
EVEN HERE IN *GOTHAM* WE ONLY TOLERATE IT FOR A SELECT *FEW.*
TOLERATE ME OR *DON'T,* COMMISSIONER. I'M GONNA BE *AROUND.*
WHOOOOOO
BE *SEEING* YOU.

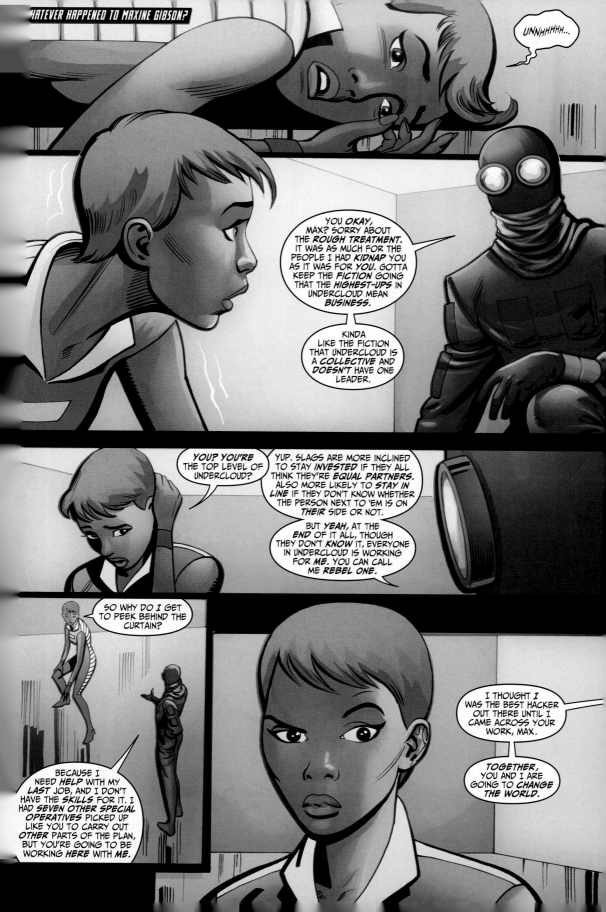

UNNHHHHH...

YOU *OKAY*, *MAX?* SORRY ABOUT THE *ROUGH* TREATMENT. IT WAS AS MUCH FOR THE PEOPLE I HAD *KIDNAP* YOU AS IT WAS FOR *YOU.* GOTTA KEEP THE *FICTION* GOING THAT THE *HIGHEST-UPS* IN UNDERCLOUD MEAN *BUSINESS.*

KINDA LIKE THE FICTION THAT UNDERCLOUD IS A *COLLECTIVE* AND *DOESN'T* HAVE ONE LEADER.

YOU? YOU'RE THE TOP LEVEL OF UNDERCLOUD?

YUP. SLAGS ARE MORE INCLINED TO STAY *INVESTED* IF THEY ALL THINK THEY'RE *EQUAL PARTNERS.* ALSO MORE LIKELY TO STAY *IN LINE* IF THEY DON'T KNOW WHETHER THE PERSON NEXT TO 'EM IS ON *THEIR* SIDE OR NOT.

BUT *YEAH*, AT THE *END* OF IT ALL, THOUGH THEY DON'T *KNOW* IT, EVERYONE IN UNDERCLOUD IS WORKING FOR *ME.* YOU CAN CALL ME *REBEL ONE.*

SO WHY DO I GET TO PEEK BEHIND THE CURTAIN?

I THOUGHT *I* WAS THE BEST HACKER OUT THERE UNTIL I CAME ACROSS YOUR WORK, MAX.

TOGETHER, YOU AND I ARE GOING TO *CHANGE* THE WORLD.

BECAUSE I NEED *HELP* WITH MY *LAST* JOB, AND I DON'T HAVE THE *SKILLS* FOR IT. I HAD *SEVEN OTHER SPECIAL OPERATIVES* PICKED UP LIKE YOU TO CARRY OUT *OTHER* PARTS OF THE PLAN, BUT YOU'RE GOING TO BE WORKING *HERE* WITH ME.

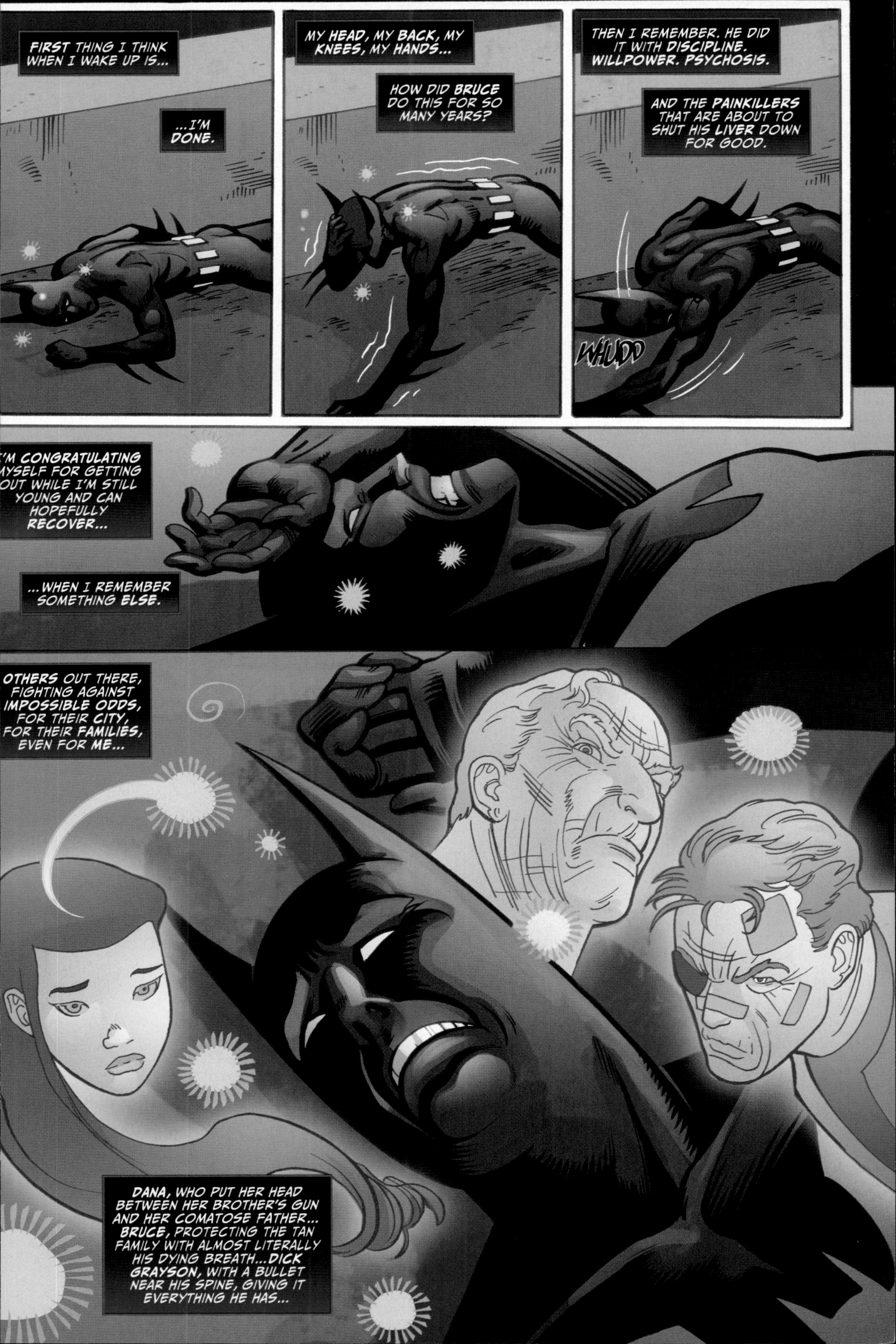
FIRST THING I THINK WHEN I WAKE UP IS...
...I'M DONE.
MY HEAD, MY BACK, MY KNEES, MY HANDS...
HOW DID BRUCE DO THIS FOR SO MANY YEARS?
THEN I REMEMBER. HE DID IT WITH DISCIPLINE. WILLPOWER. PSYCHOSIS.
AND THE PAINKILLERS THAT ARE ABOUT TO SHUT HIS LIVER DOWN FOR GOOD.
WHUDD
I'M CONGRATULATING MYSELF FOR GETTING OUT WHILE I'M STILL YOUNG AND CAN HOPEFULLY RECOVER...
...WHEN I REMEMBER SOMETHING ELSE.
OTHERS OUT THERE, FIGHTING AGAINST IMPOSSIBLE ODDS, FOR THEIR CITY, FOR THEIR FAMILIES, EVEN FOR ME...
DANA, WHO PUT HER HEAD BETWEEN HER BROTHER'S GUN AND HER COMATOSE FATHER... BRUCE, PROTECTING THE TAN FAMILY WITH ALMOST LITERALLY HIS DYING BREATH...DICK GRAYSON, WITH A BULLET NEAR HIS SPINE, GIVING IT EVERYTHING HE HAS...

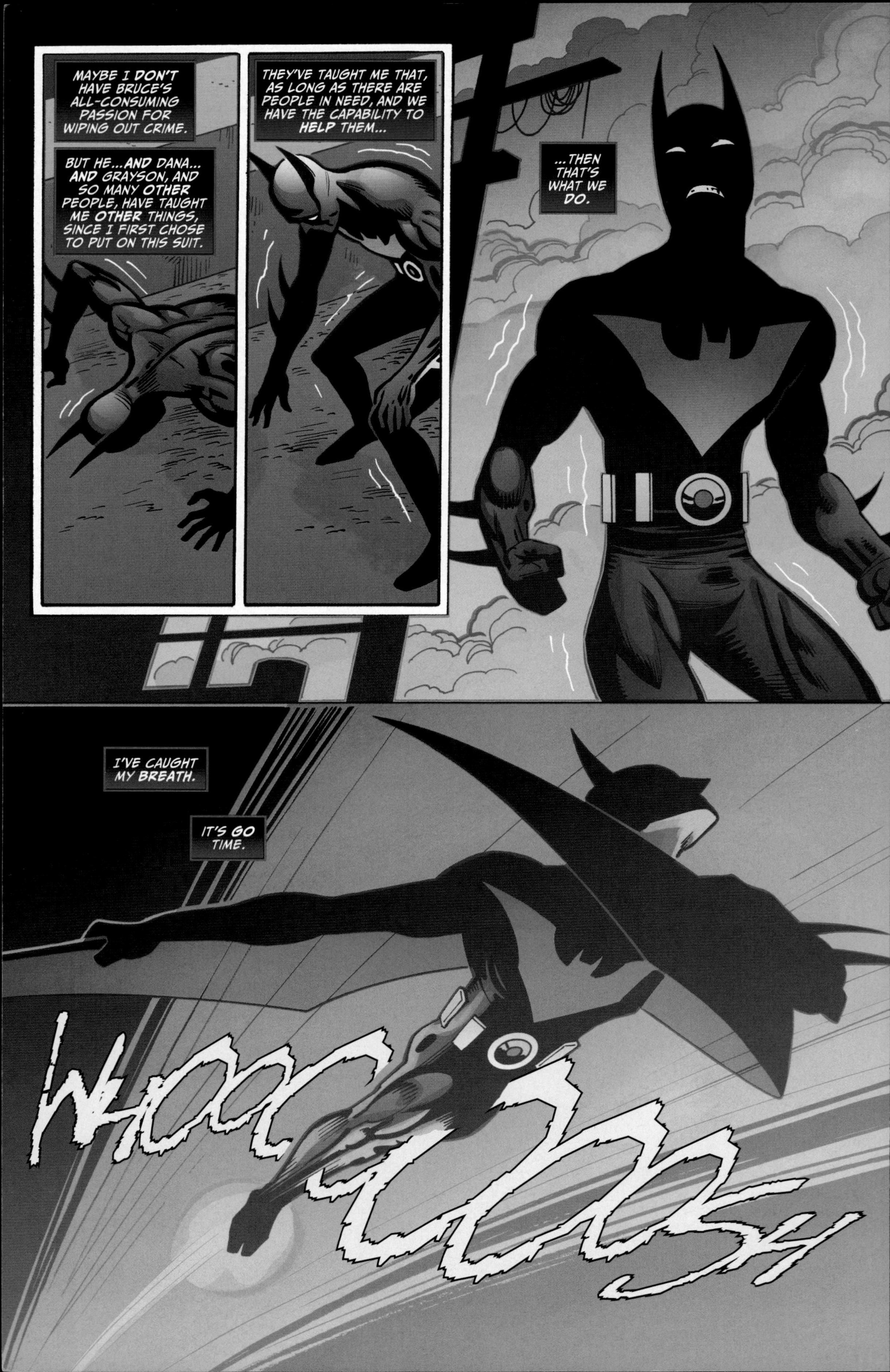
MAYBE I DON'T HAVE BRUCE'S ALL-CONSUMING PASSION FOR WIPING OUT CRIME.
BUT HE...AND DANA... AND GRAYSON, AND SO MANY OTHER PEOPLE, HAVE TAUGHT ME OTHER THINGS, SINCE I FIRST CHOSE TO PUT ON THIS SUIT.
THEY'VE TAUGHT ME THAT, AS LONG AS THERE ARE PEOPLE IN NEED, AND WE HAVE THE CAPABILITY TO HELP THEM...
...THEN THAT'S WHAT WE DO.
I'VE CAUGHT MY BREATH.
IT'S GO TIME.
WHOOOOOOSH

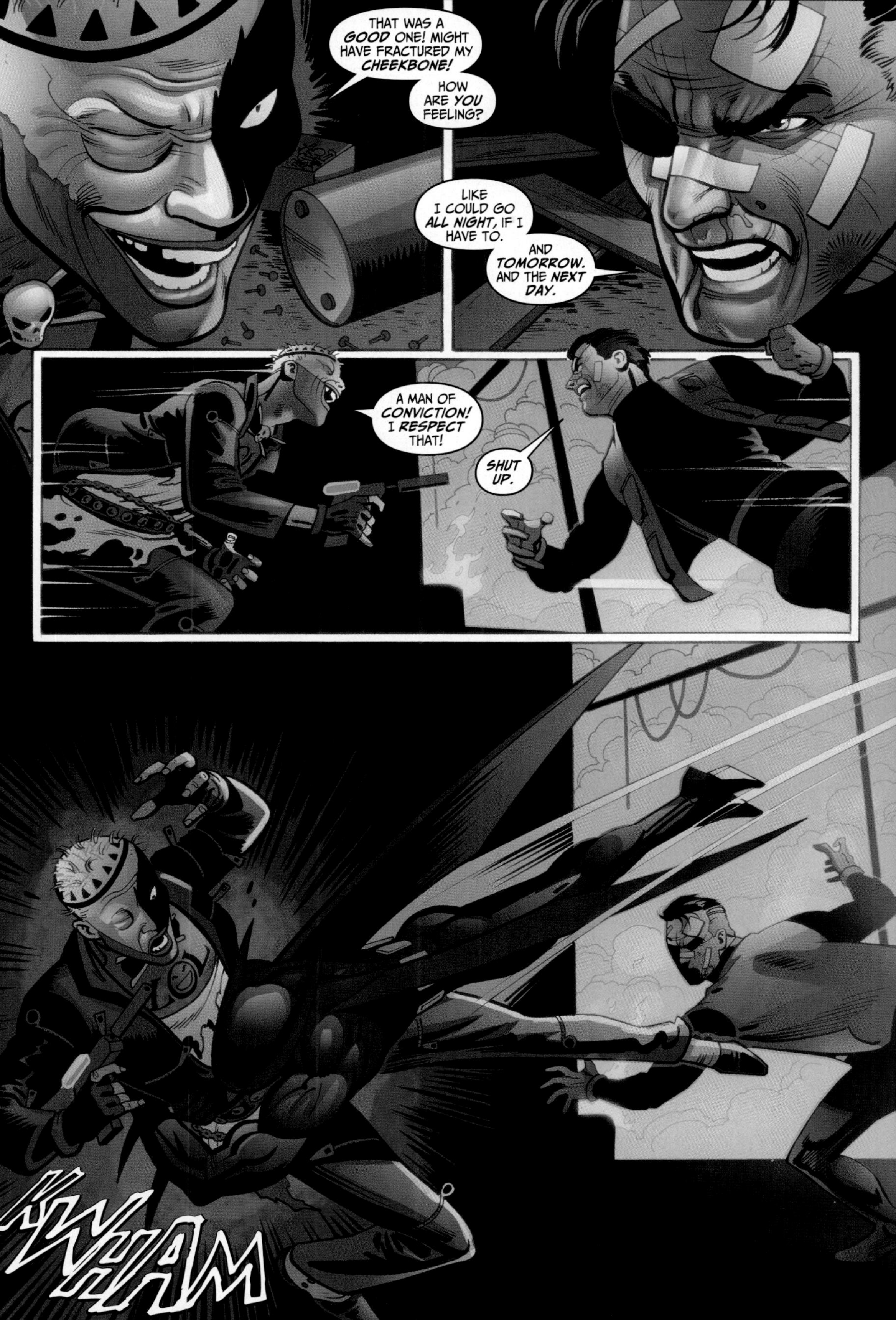
THAT WAS A GOOD ONE! MIGHT HAVE FRACTURED MY CHEEKBONE!
HOW ARE YOU FEELING?
LIKE I COULD GO ALL NIGHT, IF I HAVE TO.
AND TOMORROW. AND THE NEXT DAY.
A MAN OF CONVICTION! I RESPECT THAT!
SHUT UP.
KWHAM

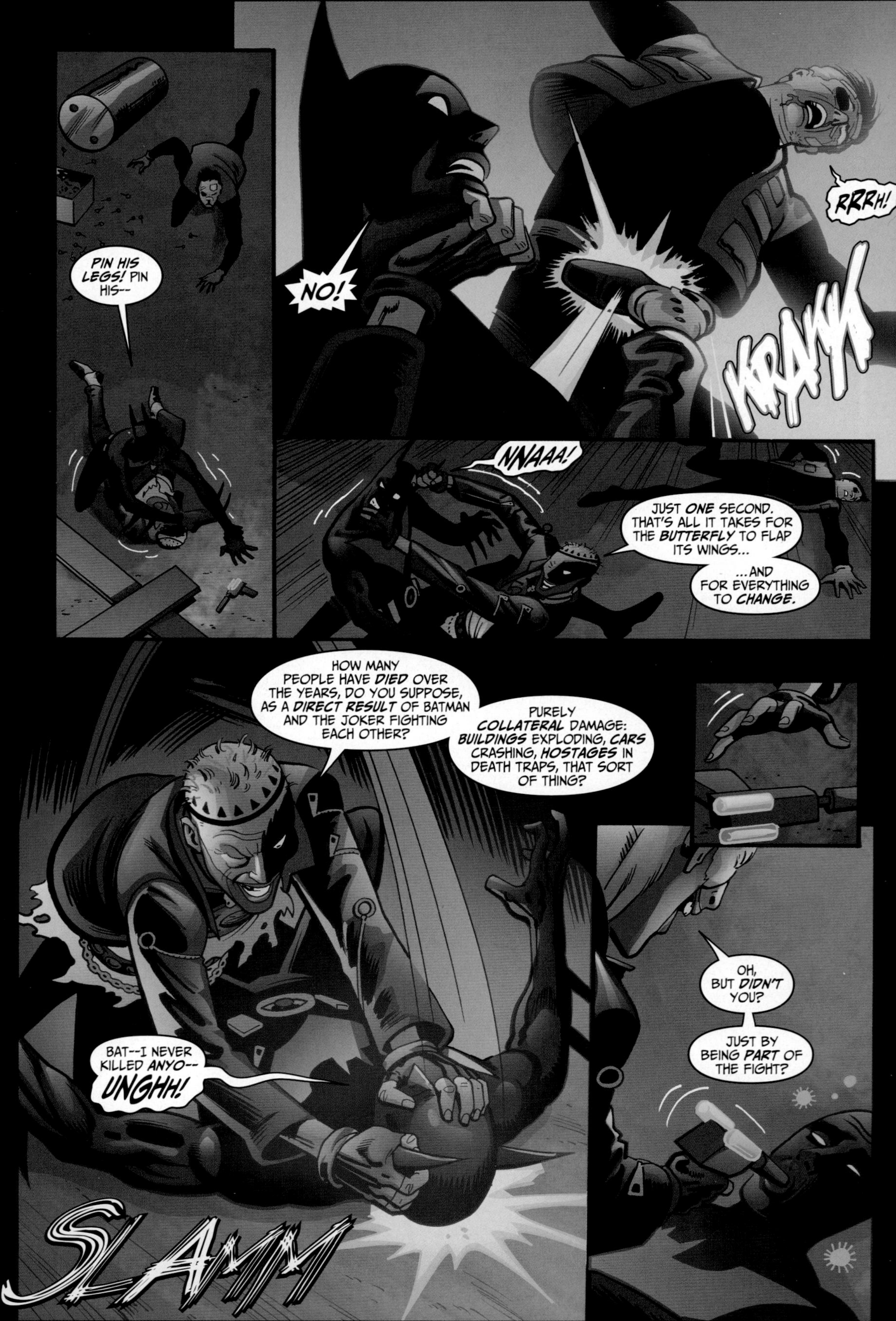
PIN HIS LEGS! PIN HIS--
NO!
RRRH!
KRAKK
NNAAA!
JUST ONE SECOND. THAT'S ALL IT TAKES FOR THE BUTTERFLY TO FLAP ITS WINGS...
...AND FOR EVERYTHING TO CHANGE.
HOW MANY PEOPLE HAVE DIED OVER THE YEARS, DO YOU SUPPOSE, AS A DIRECT RESULT OF BATMAN AND THE JOKER FIGHTING EACH OTHER?
PURELY COLLATERAL DAMAGE: BUILDINGS EXPLODING, CARS CRASHING, HOSTAGES IN DEATH TRAPS, THAT SORT OF THING?
BAT--I NEVER KILLED ANYO-- UNGHH!
SLAMM
OH, BUT DIDN'T YOU?
JUST BY BEING PART OF THE FIGHT?

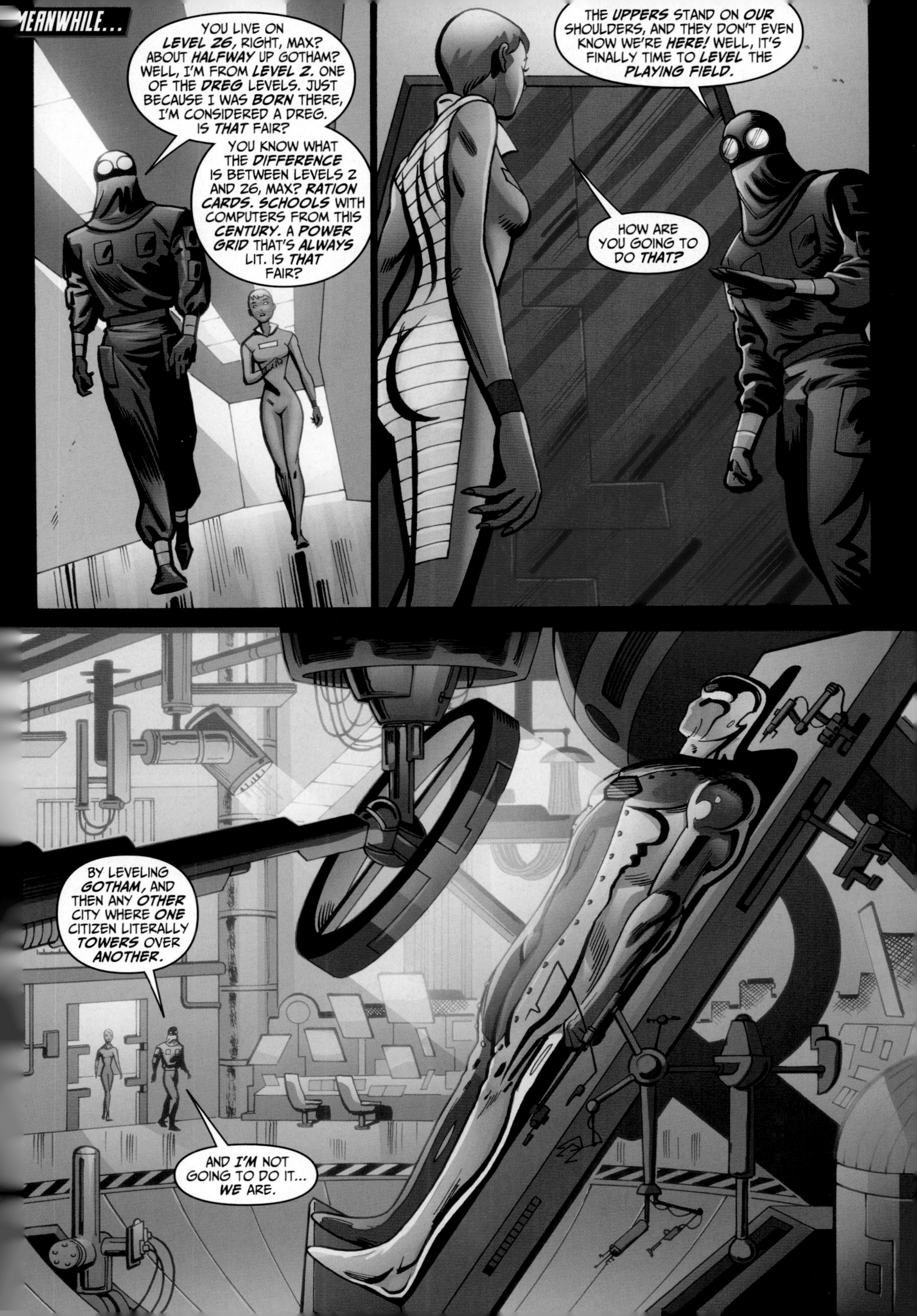
MEANWHILE...
YOU LIVE ON LEVEL 26, RIGHT, MAX? ABOUT HALFWAY UP GOTHAM? WELL, I'M FROM LEVEL 2. ONE OF THE DREG LEVELS. JUST BECAUSE I WAS BORN THERE, I'M CONSIDERED A DREG. IS THAT FAIR?
YOU KNOW WHAT THE DIFFERENCE IS BETWEEN LEVELS 2 AND 26, MAX? RATION CARDS. SCHOOLS WITH COMPUTERS FROM THIS CENTURY. A POWER GRID THAT'S ALWAYS LIT. IS THAT FAIR?
THE UPPERS STAND ON OUR SHOULDERS, AND THEY DON'T EVEN KNOW WE'RE HERE! WELL, IT'S FINALLY TIME TO LEVEL THE PLAYING FIELD.
HOW ARE YOU GOING TO DO THAT?
BY LEVELING GOTHAM, AND THEN ANY OTHER CITY WHERE ONE CITIZEN LITERALLY TOWERS OVER ANOTHER.
AND I'M NOT GOING TO DO IT... WE ARE.

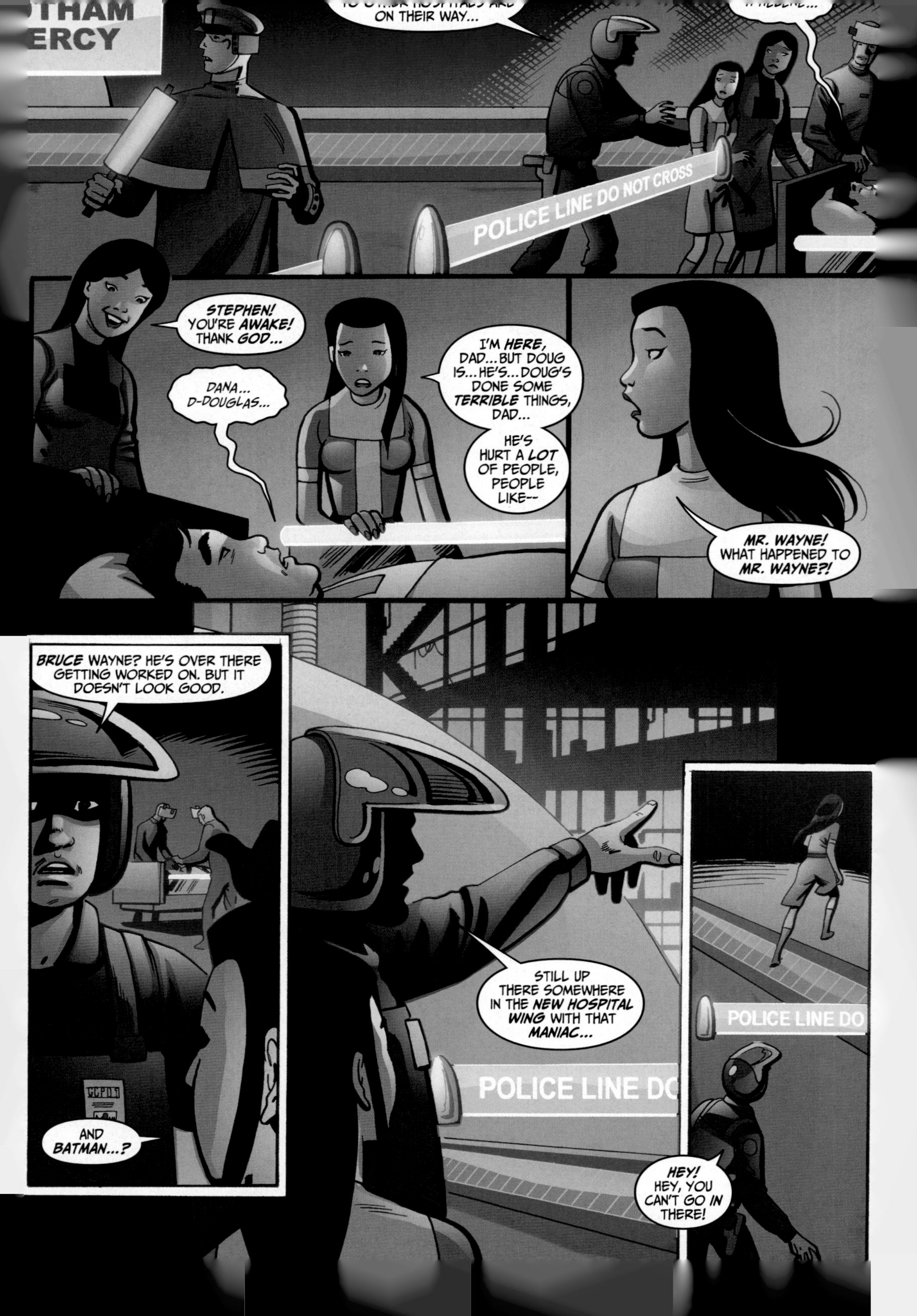

ON THEIR WAY...
POLICE LINE DO NOT CROSS
STEPHEN! YOU'RE AWAKE! THANK GOD...
DANA... D-DOUGLAS...
I'M HERE, DAD...BUT DOUG IS...HE'S...DOUG'S DONE SOME TERRIBLE THINGS, DAD...
HE'S HURT A LOT OF PEOPLE, PEOPLE LIKE--
MR. WAYNE! WHAT HAPPENED TO MR. WAYNE?!
BRUCE WAYNE? HE'S OVER THERE GETTING WORKED ON. BUT IT DOESN'T LOOK GOOD.
AND BATMAN...?
STILL UP THERE SOMEWHERE IN THE NEW HOSPITAL WING WITH THAT MANIAC...
POLICE LINE DO
POLICE LINE DO
HEY! HEY, YOU CAN'T GO IN THERE!

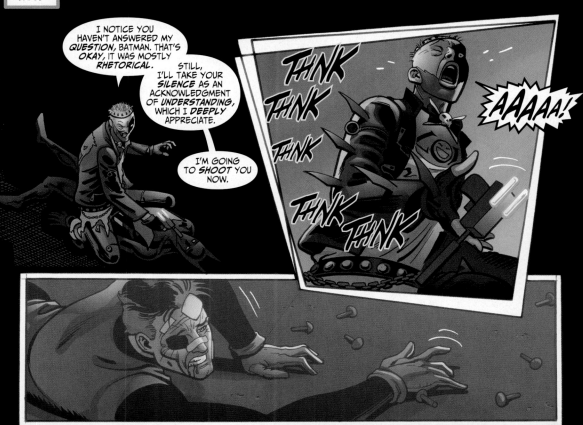

"IT'S NOT SAFE!"

I NOTICE YOU HAVEN'T ANSWERED MY *QUESTION*, BATMAN. THAT'S *OKAY*, IT WAS MOSTLY *RHETORICAL.*

STILL, I'LL TAKE YOUR *SILENCE* AS AN ACKNOWLEDGMENT OF *UNDERSTANDING*, WHICH I *DEEPLY* APPRECIATE.

I'M GOING TO *SHOOT* YOU NOW.

THINK THINK THINK THINK THINK

AAAAA!

HA...HAHA... A *ONE-EYED MAN* WITH *PERFECT AIM*...THAT'S PRETTY FUNNY...

THAT'S IT, MAN...

...YOU'RE *DONE.* OUT OF WEAPONS...

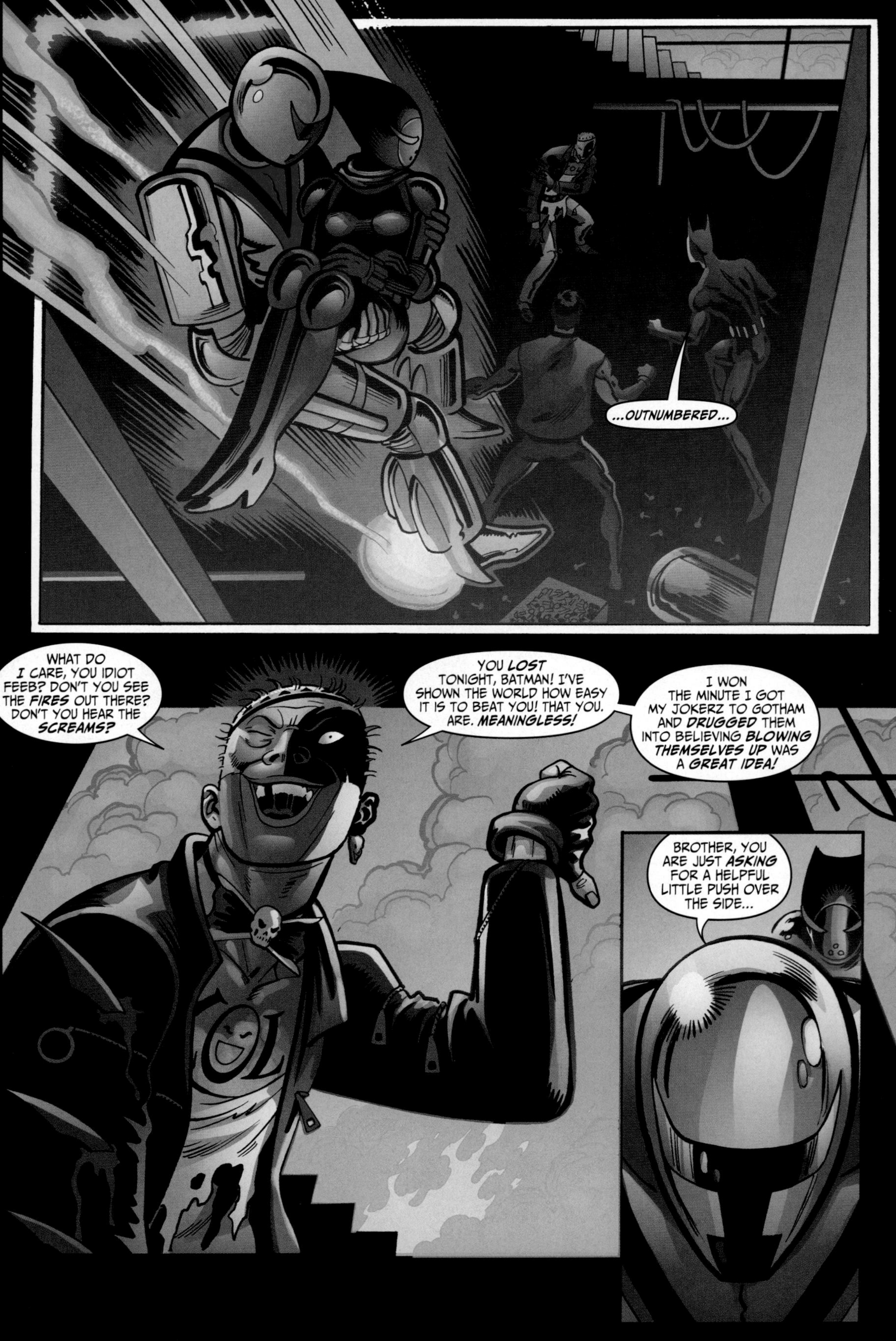
...OUTNUMBERED...
WHAT DO I CARE, YOU IDIOT FEEB? DON'T YOU SEE THE FIRES OUT THERE? DON'T YOU HEAR THE SCREAMS?
YOU LOST TONIGHT, BATMAN! I'VE SHOWN THE WORLD HOW EASY IT IS TO BEAT YOU! THAT YOU. ARE. MEANINGLESS!
I WON THE MINUTE I GOT MY JOKERZ TO GOTHAM AND DRUGGED THEM INTO BELIEVING BLOWING THEMSELVES UP WAS A GREAT IDEA!
BROTHER, YOU ARE JUST ASKING FOR A HELPFUL LITTLE PUSH OVER THE SIDE...

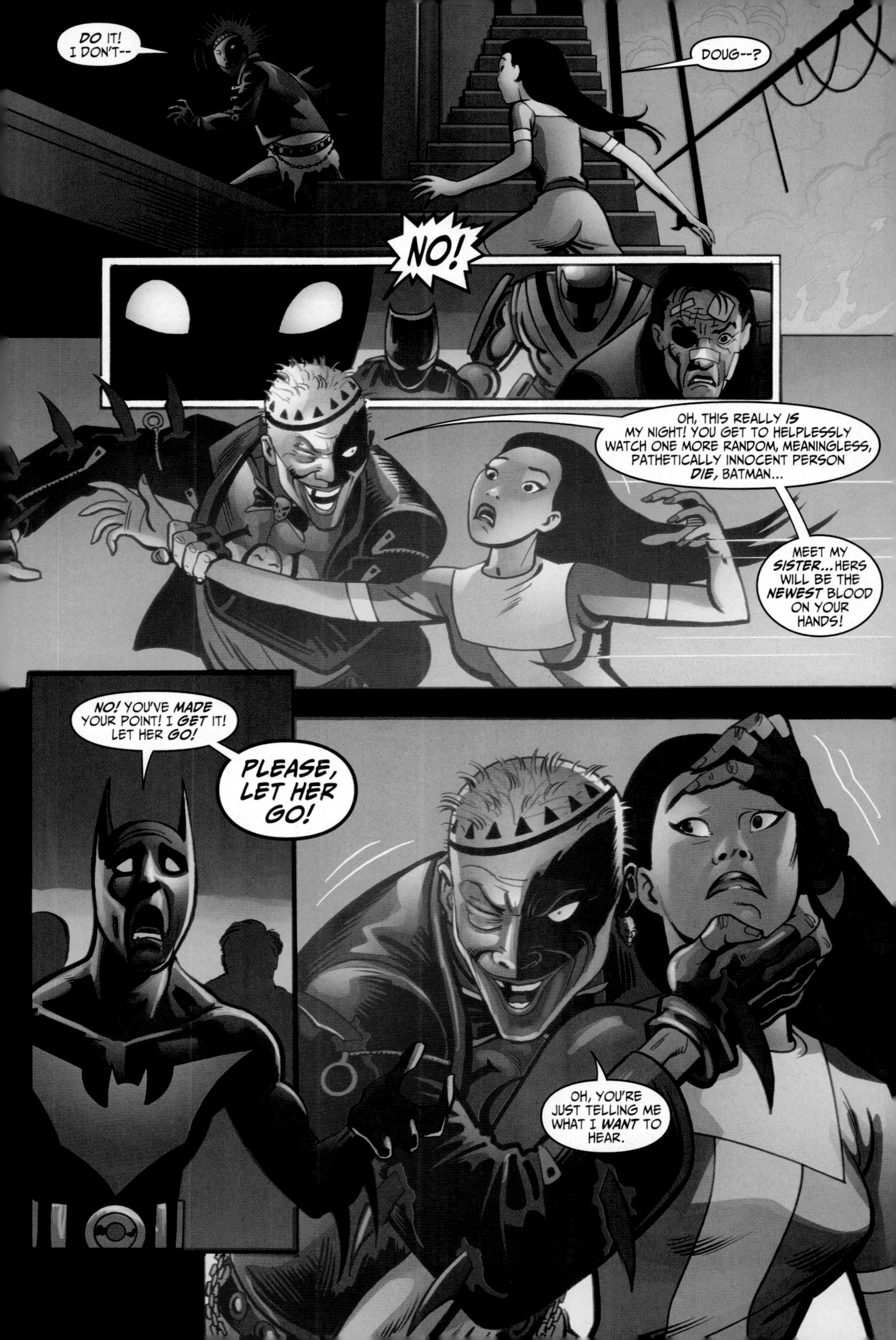
DO IT! I DON'T--
DOUG--?
NO!
OH, THIS REALLY IS MY NIGHT! YOU GET TO HELPLESSLY WATCH ONE MORE RANDOM, MEANINGLESS, PATHETICALLY INNOCENT PERSON DIE, BATMAN...
MEET MY SISTER...HERS WILL BE THE NEWEST BLOOD ON YOUR HANDS!
NO! YOU'VE MADE YOUR POINT! I GET IT! LET HER GO!
PLEASE, LET HER GO!
OH, YOU'RE JUST TELLING ME WHAT I WANT TO HEAR.

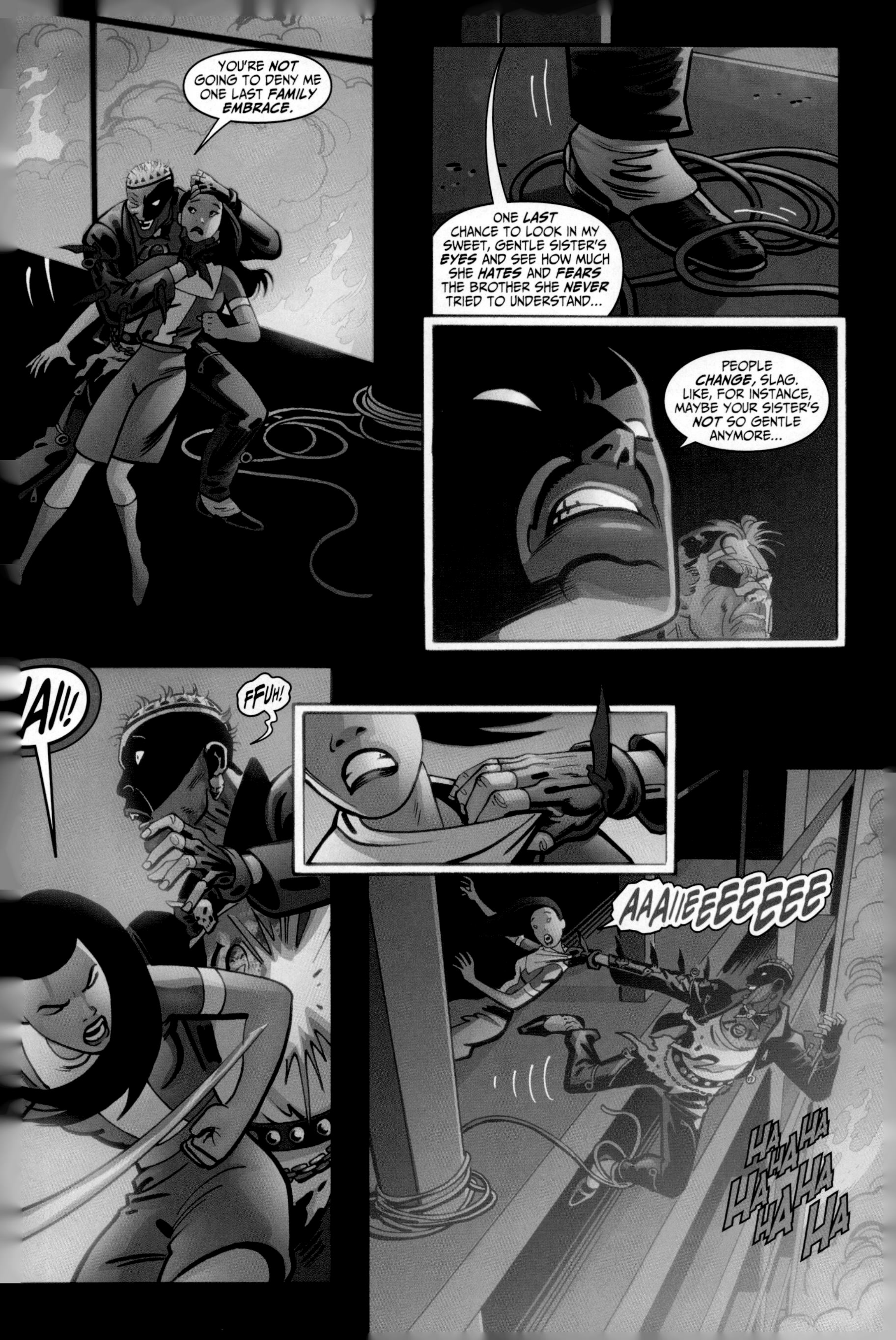
YOU'RE NOT GOING TO DENY ME ONE LAST FAMILY EMBRACE.
ONE LAST CHANCE TO LOOK IN MY SWEET, GENTLE SISTER'S EYES AND SEE HOW MUCH SHE HATES AND FEARS THE BROTHER SHE NEVER TRIED TO UNDERSTAND...
PEOPLE CHANGE, SLAG. LIKE, FOR INSTANCE, MAYBE YOUR SISTER'S NOT SO GENTLE ANYMORE...
AI!!
FFUH!
AAAIIIEEEEEEE
HA HA HA HA HA HA HA HA

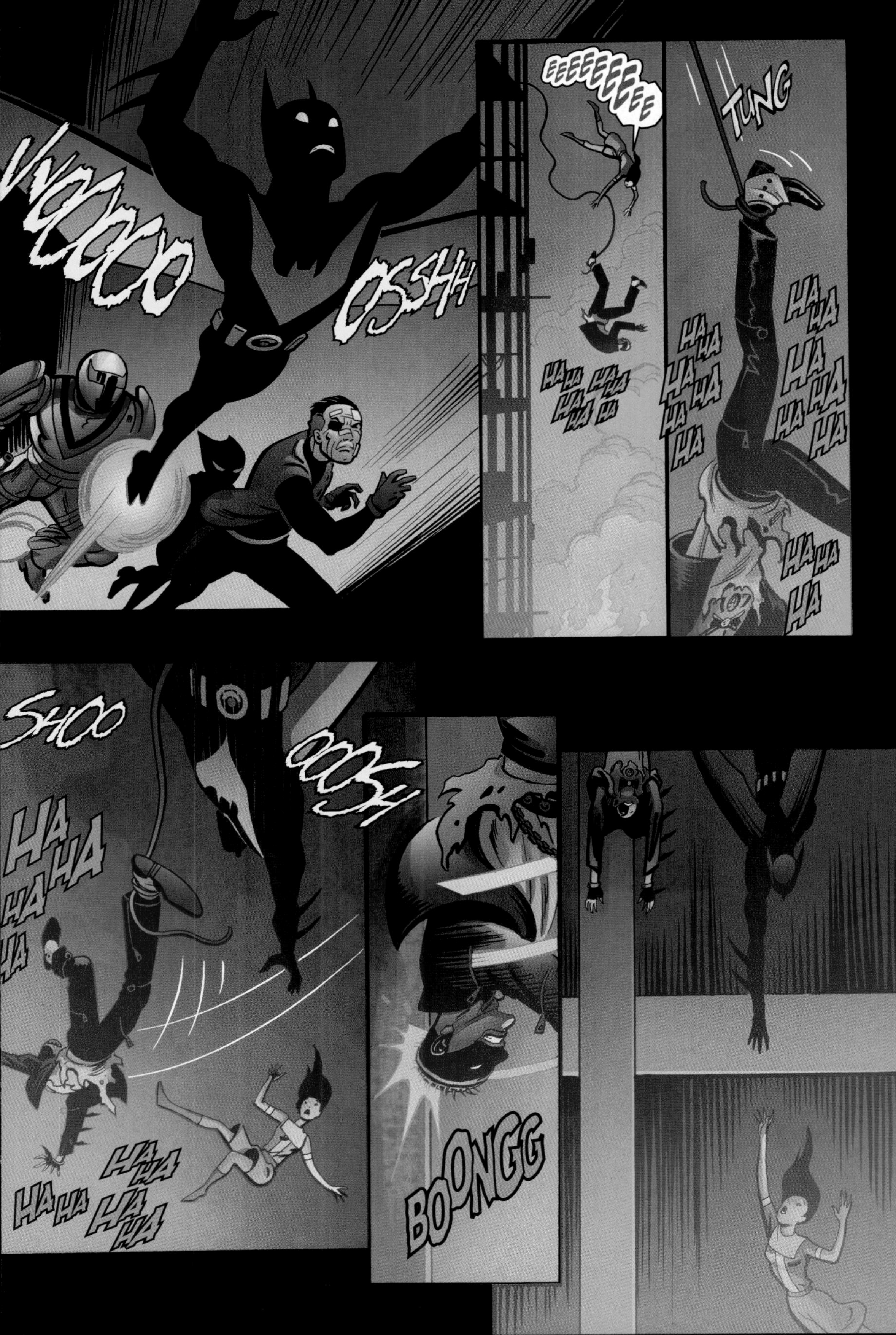
VVOOOOOO
OSSHH
EEEEEEEEEEEE
HA HA HA HA HA HA HA HA
TUNG
HA HA HA HA HA HA HA
HA HA HA HA HA HA HA
HA HA HA
SHOO
OOOSH
HA HA HA HA HA HA
HA HA HA HA HA HA HA
BOONGG

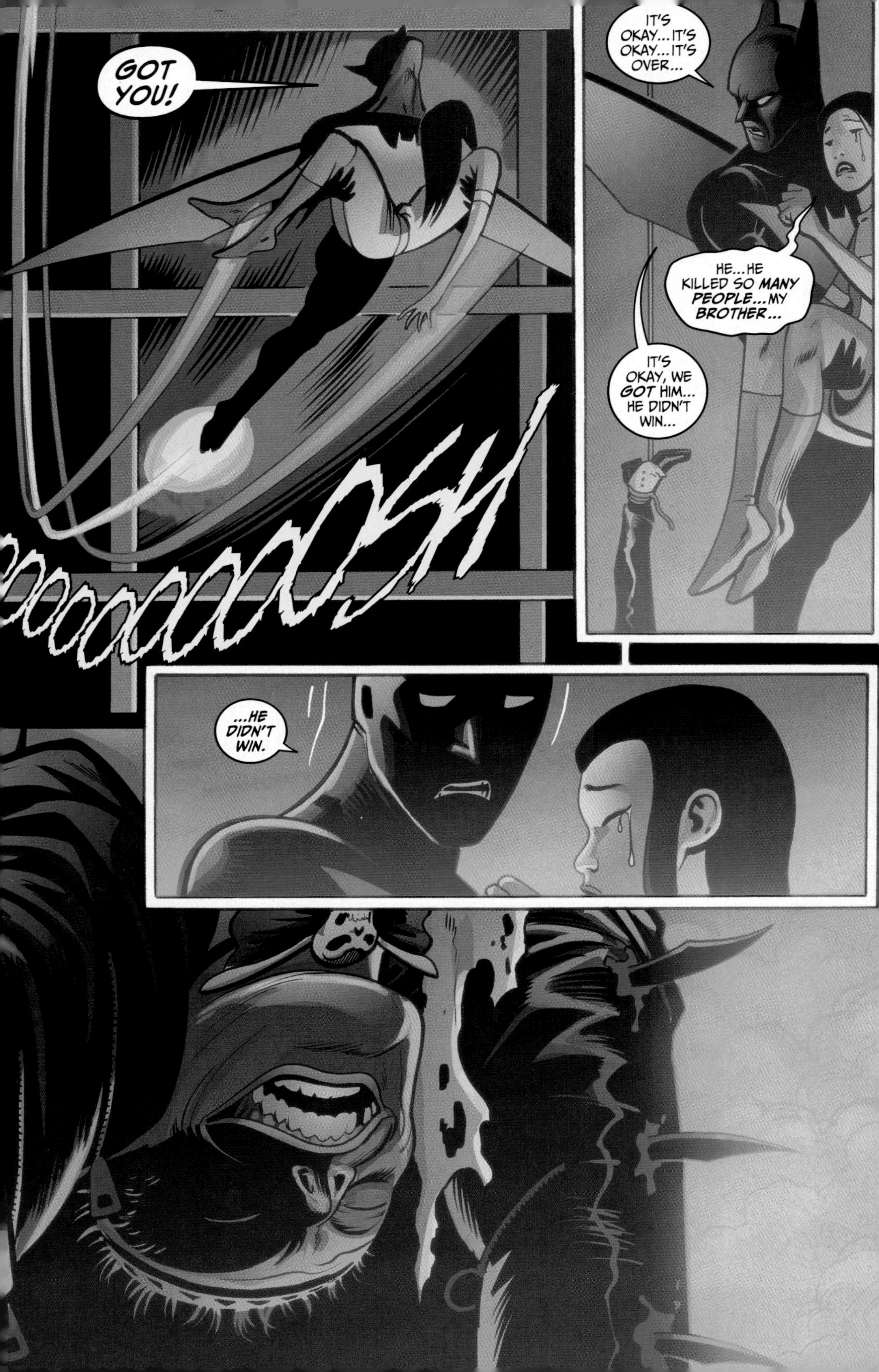
GOT YOU!
SSSSSSSSSSSSHHH
IT'S OKAY...IT'S OKAY...IT'S OVER...
HE...HE KILLED SO MANY PEOPLE...MY BROTHER...
IT'S OKAY, WE GOT HIM... HE DIDN'T WIN...
...HE DIDN'T WIN.

BATMAN BEYOND #5
Cover by Dustin Nguyen

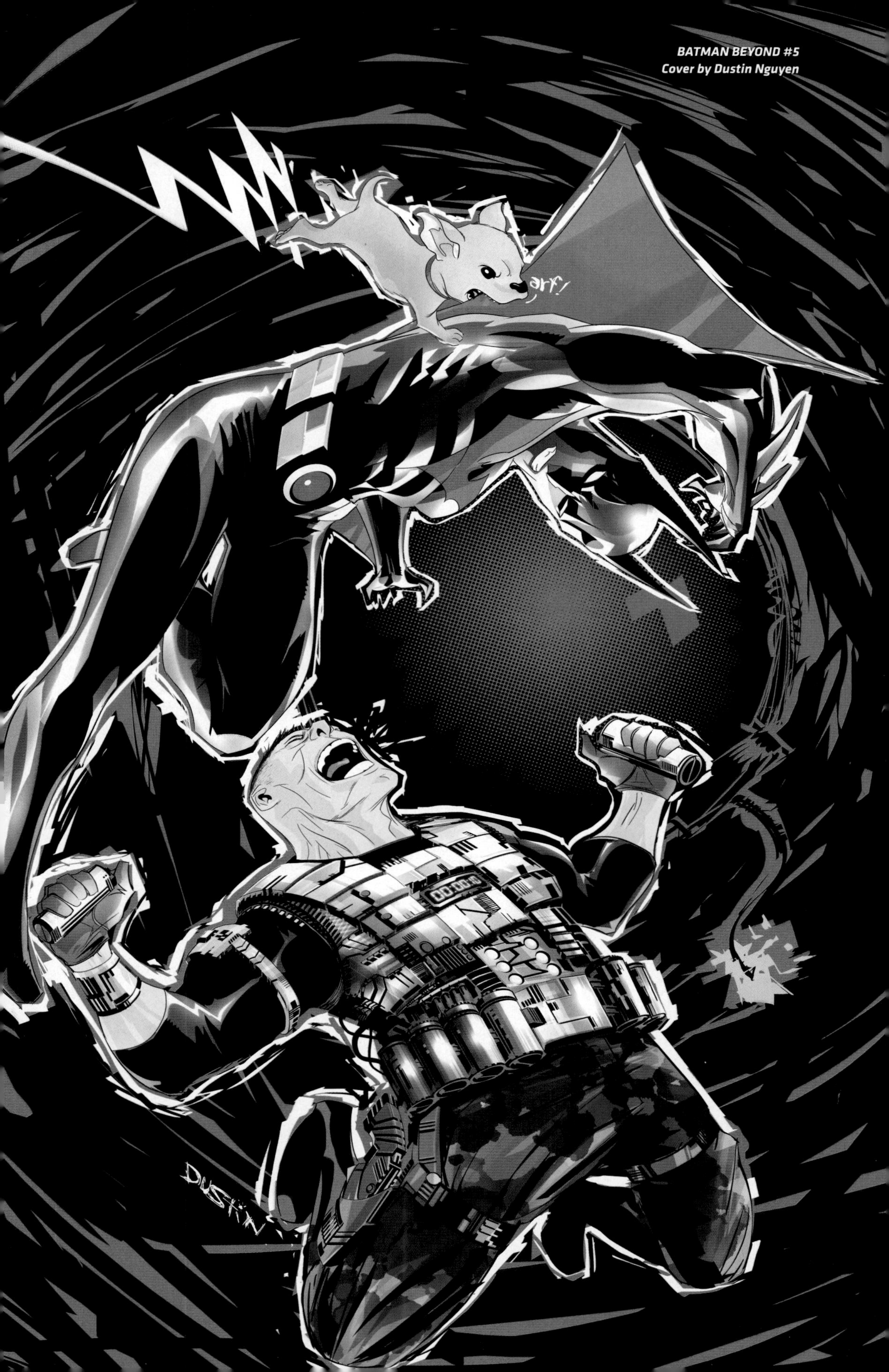
arf!
DUSTIN

BATMAN BEYOND #11
Cover by Dustin Nguyen

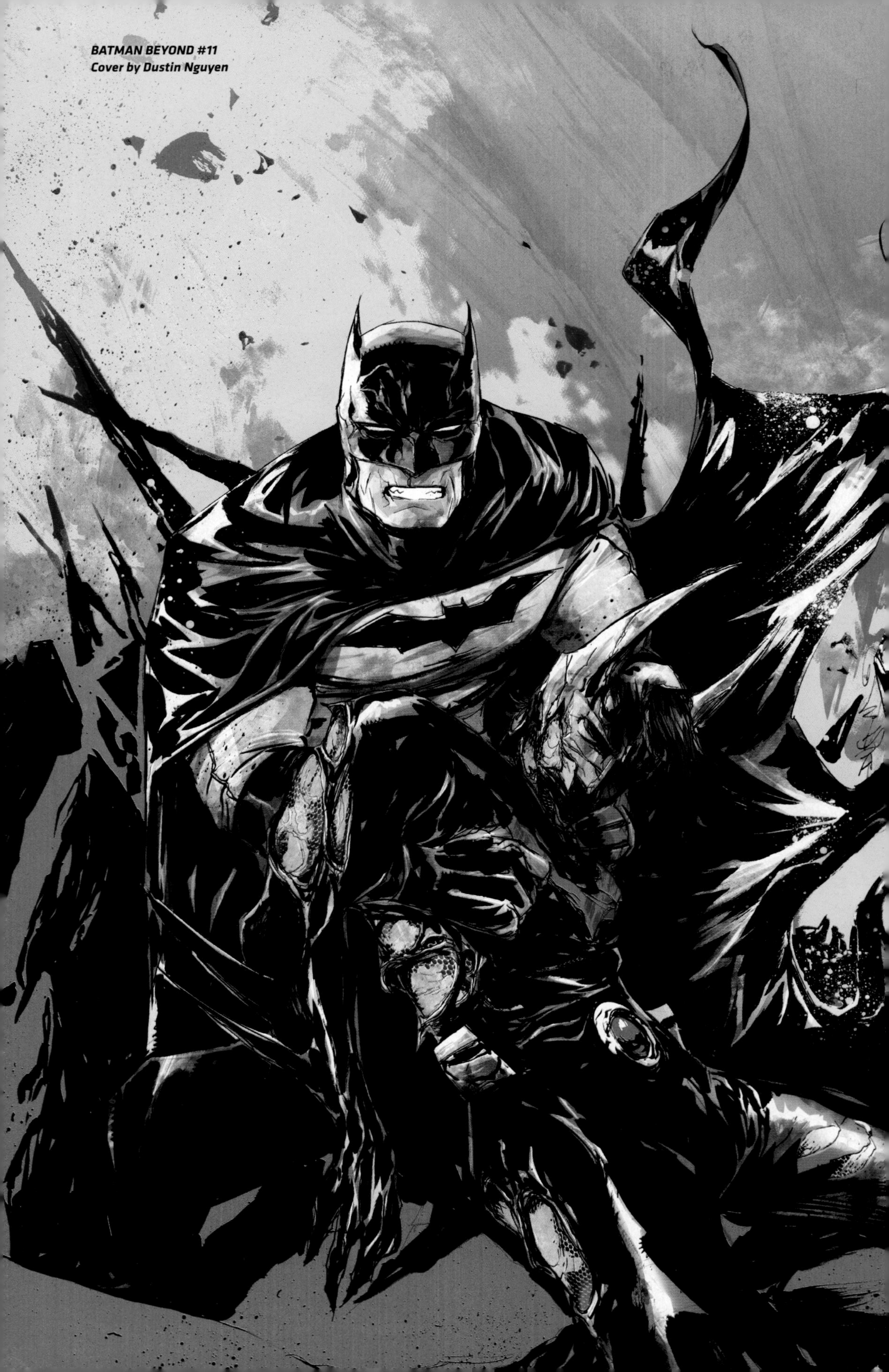

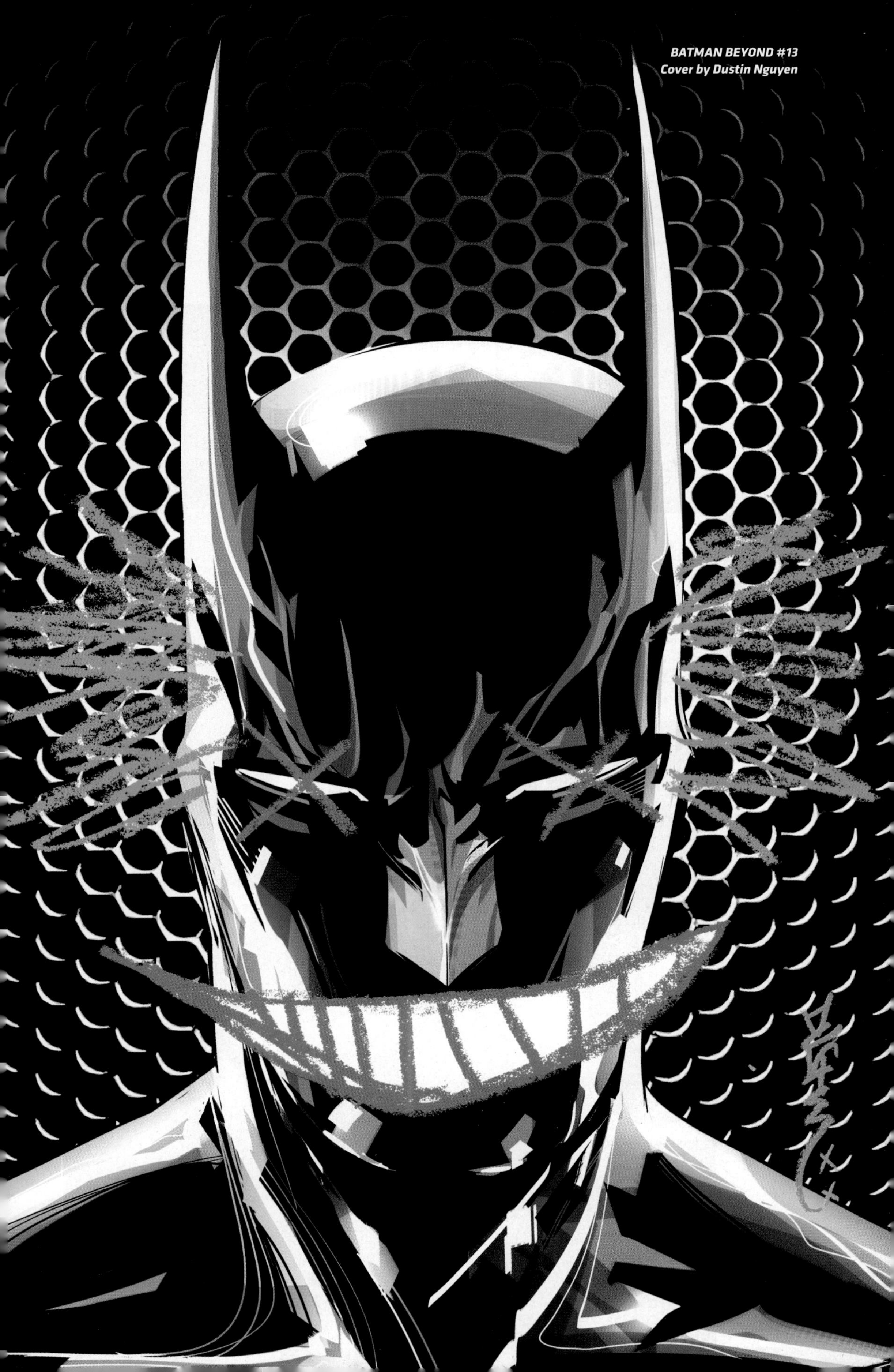

BATMAN BEYOND #13
Cover by Dustin Nguyen

BATMAN BEYOND #15
Cover by Dustin Nguyen

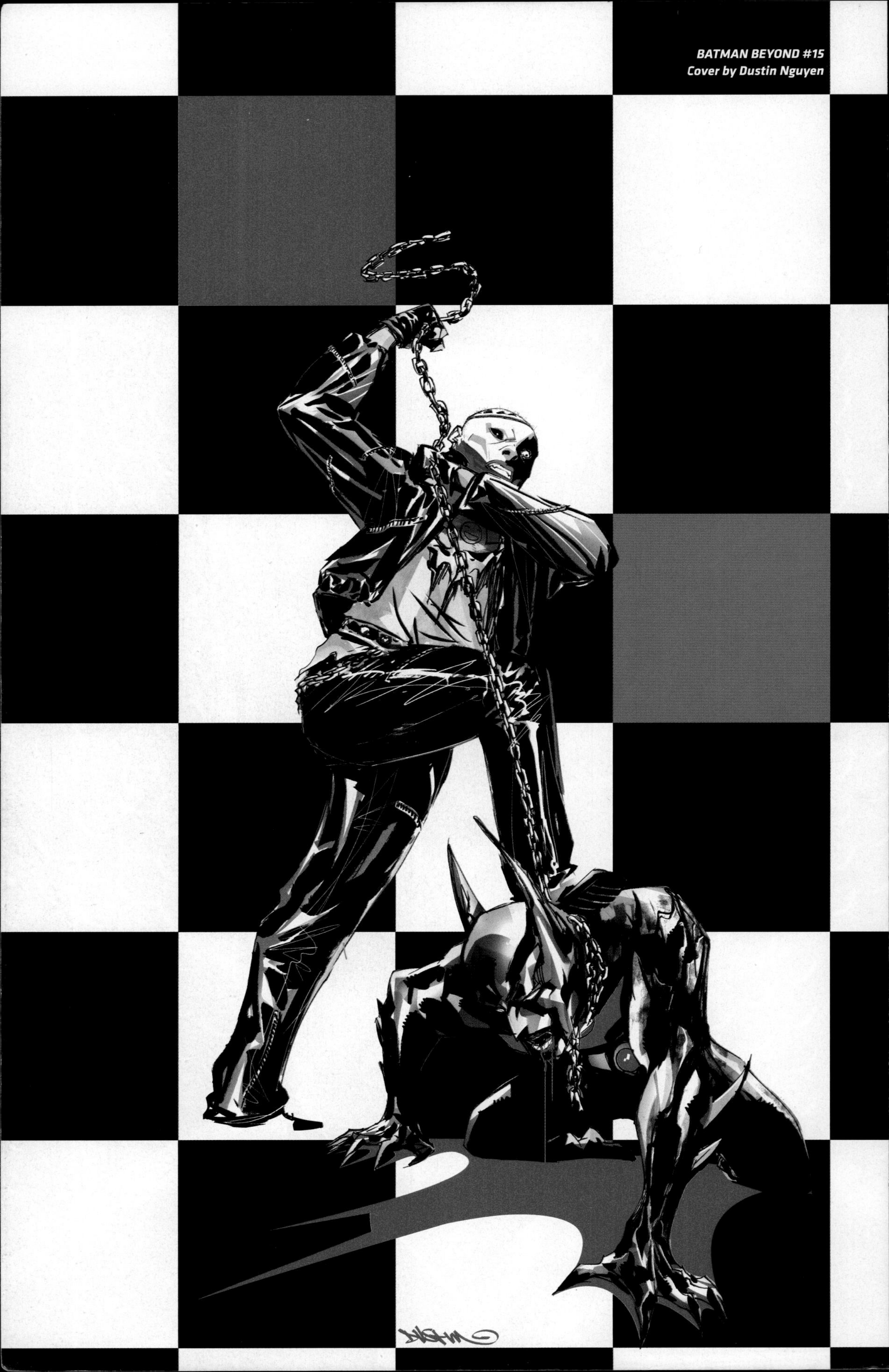

BATMAN BEYOND #17
Cover by Ryan Benjamin

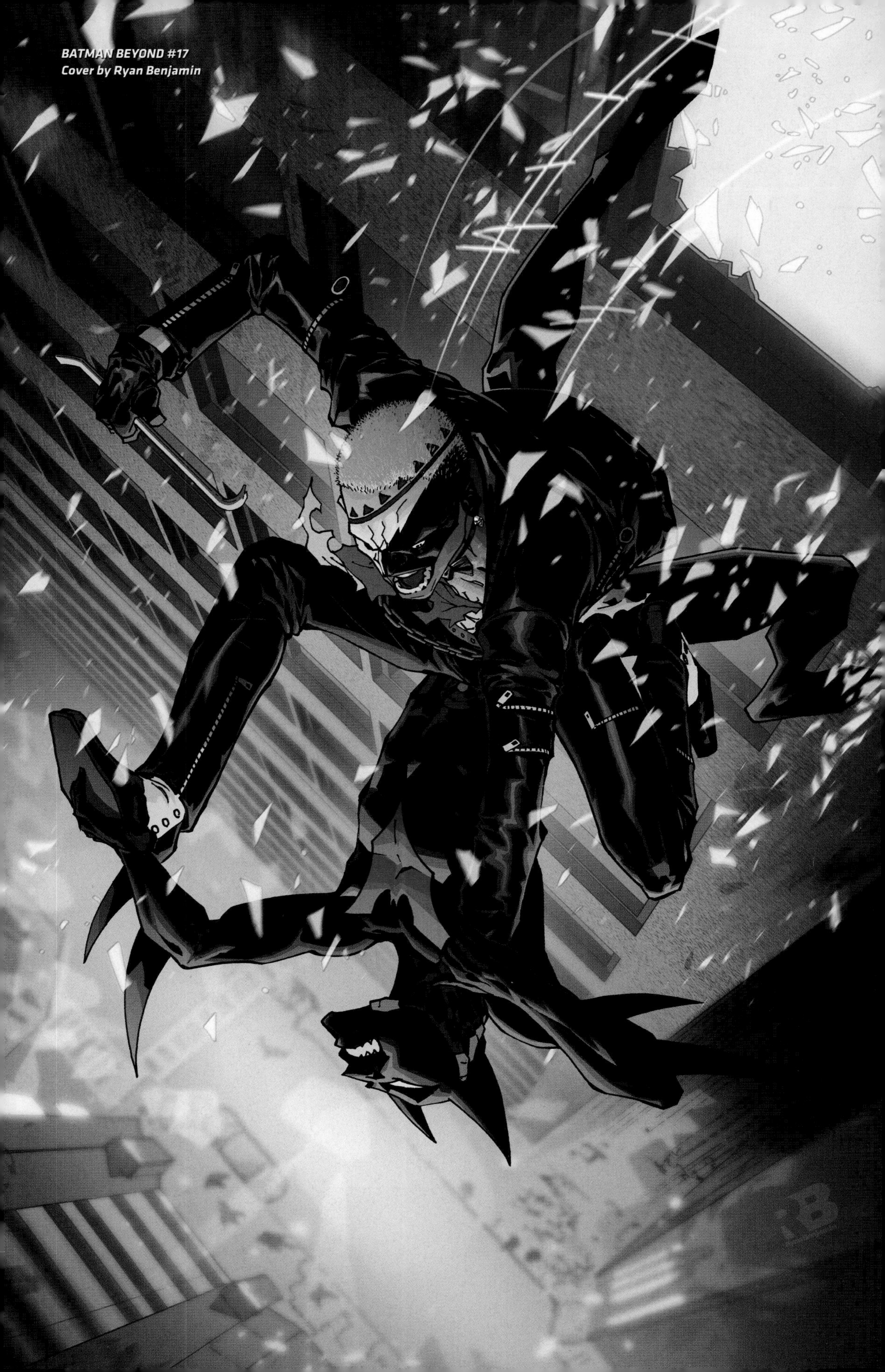

JOKER KING character designs by Norm Breyfogle

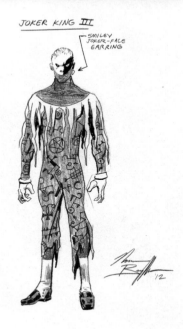

JOKER KING III
SMILEY JOKER-FACE EARRING
W PURPLE BODY SUIT + NO BOW TIE + WHITE GLOVES
JOKER KING V
SMILEY JOKER-FACE EARRING
BACK VIEW OF HEAD
EITHER CONTACT LENSES OR NANOTECH TO ALTER EYES
W TUXEDO + CARNATION ON LAPEL + CUMBERBUND
JOKER KING 6
(WITH ALTERNATE HEADS)
CROWN TATTOO
SMILEY JOKER FACE EARRING
CROWN TATTOO
"LAUGH OUT LOUD" TATTOO?
TEAR TATTOO OR MAKEUP
CROWN EARRING
JOKER KING 6
(WITH ALTERNATE HEADS)
COLOR INDICATIONS
CROWN TATTOO
SMILEY JOKER FACE EARRING
CROWN TATTOO
"LAUGH OUT LOUD" TATTOO?
BLACK, FINGERLESS GLOVES
W BLACK, TORN LEATHER PANTS
TEAR TATTOO OR MAKEUP
CROWN EARRING
'12

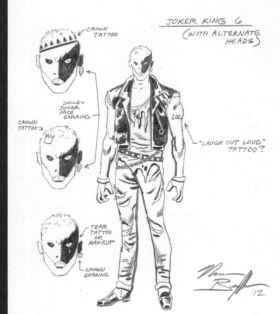

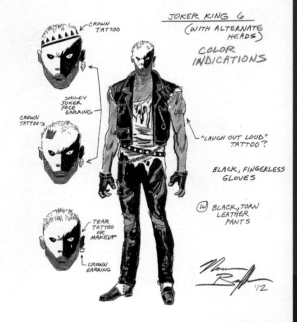

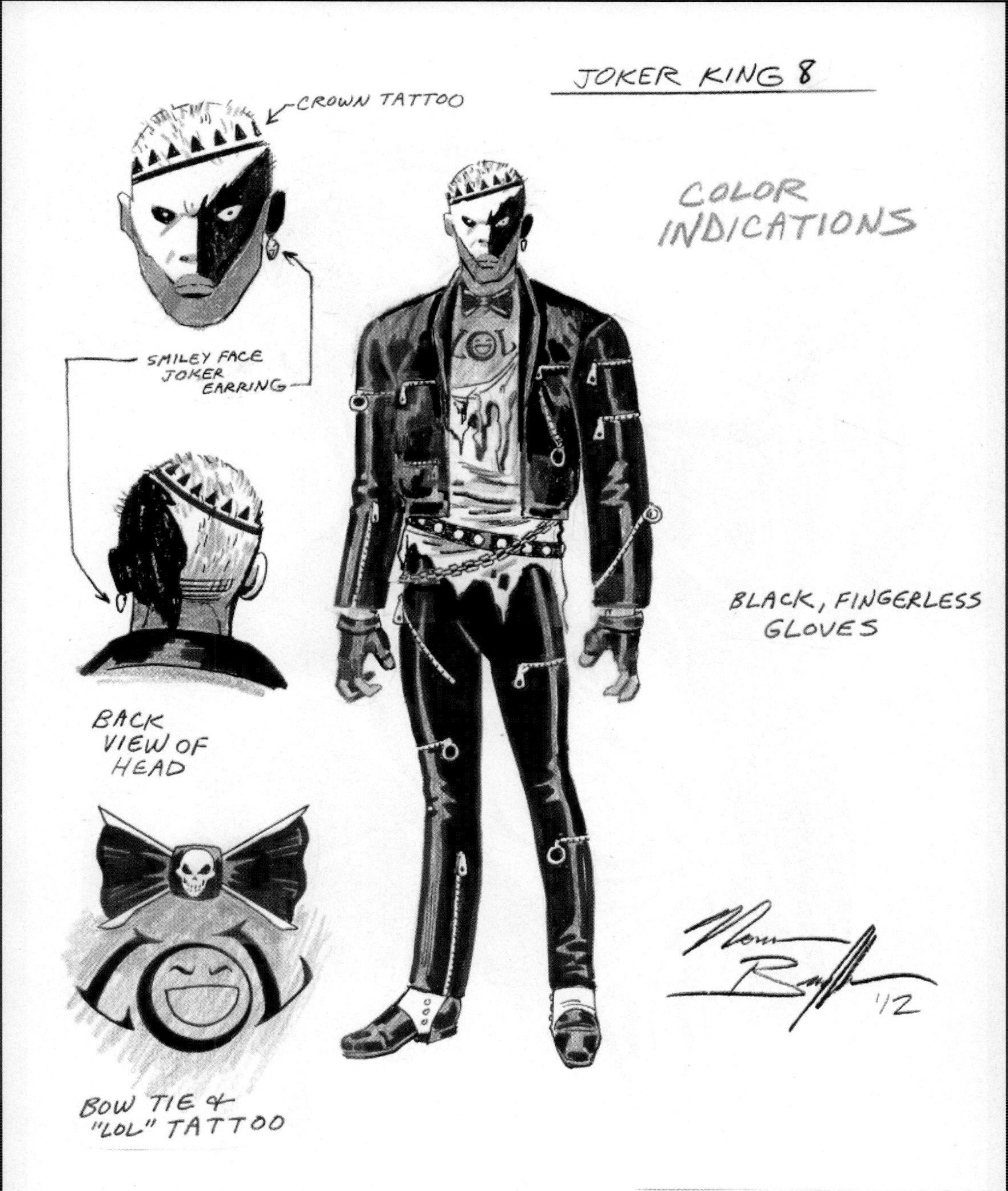
JOKER KING 8
CROWN TATTOO
COLOR INDICATIONS
SMILEY FACE JOKER EARRING
BACK VIEW OF HEAD
BLACK, FINGERLESS GLOVES
BOW TIE & "LOL" TATTOO
'12

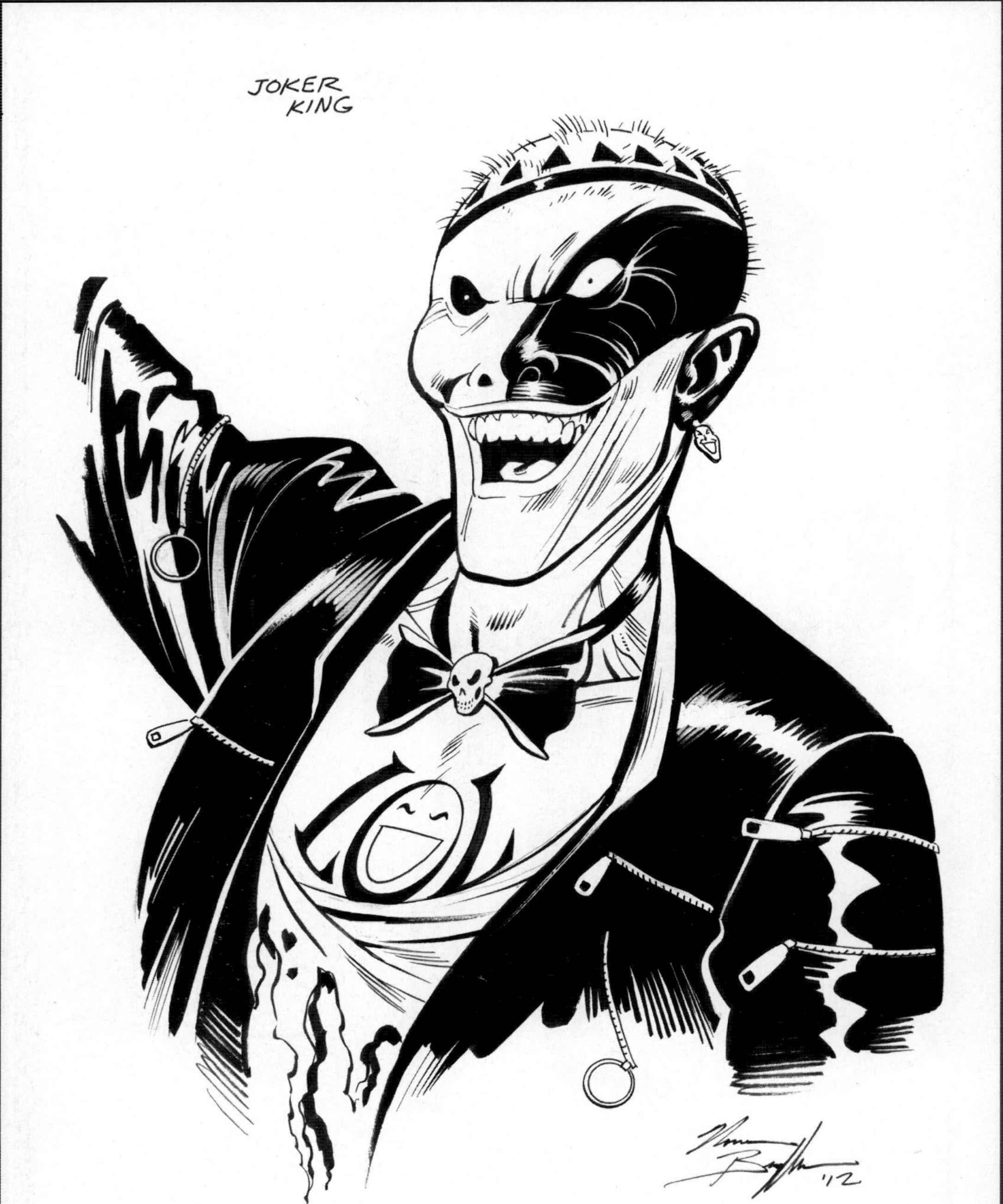
JOKER
KING
'12